Melba

If you wish to understand me at all you must understand first and foremost that I am an Australian.

Nellie Melba in her autobiography, *Melodies and Memories*

Melba

The Voice of Australia

Thérèse Radic

MMB MUSIC, INC.

Copyright © 1986 Thérèse Radic

First published 1986 by
THE MACMILLAN COMPANY OF AUSTRALIA PTY LTD
107 Moray Street, South Melbourne 3205
6 Clarke Street, Crows Nest 2065

Published in the United States by
Magnamusic-Baton Inc.
10370 Page Industrial Boulevard
Saint Louis
Missouri 63132

Library of Congress cataloging-in-publication data:
  Radic, Thérèse.
    Melba, the Voice of Australia.
    Discography: P.
    Bibliography: P.
    Includes index.
    1. Melba, Nellie, Dame, 1861-1931.   2. Singers—biography. I. Title.
  ML420. M35R3 1986   782.1'092'4(B)   86-10495
  ISBN 0-918812-45-3

Typeset in New Zealand by Computype Services, Wellington
Printed in Hong Kong.

CONTENTS

ACKNOWLEDGEMENTS

At the *Age*: Ray Blackbourn and the staff of the pictorial library; Richard Aitken; Peter Arnold; Chris Cunneen and Geoff Serle at the *Australian Dictionary of Biography*; Noel Carrick of the Australian Embassy in Brussels; Margaret Green of the Music Faculty library within the Baillieu Library; Georgina Binns; Ann Carr-Boyd; the staff of the Caulfield Library; Manning Clark; Mimi Colligan; Jim Davidson; Dawn Fletcher; Francesca Franci; Cathryn Game; Helen Gifford; Rosemary Graham; at the Grainger Museum: Kay Dreyfus, Rosemary Florrimell and Sheena Weaver; at the *Herald*: Les Carlyon, Christine Cooze, Susan Motherwell and the pictorial staff; Geoffrey Hutton; Farley Kelly; Marilyn Lake; at the La Trobe Library: Christine Downer and the pictorial library staff, Tony Marshall, Joan Maslen and Dianne Reilly; Nance Leigh; Harold Love; the staff of the Mitchell Library; Kerry Murphy; at the National Library of Australia: Silvia Carr, Melodie Johnston, Prue Neidorf, Barbara Perry, Pamela Ray and Bill Tully; at the National Sound and Film Archives: Peter Burgis, Marilyn Dooley and Bruce Skilton; Fay Patton; at the Performing Arts Museum, Melbourne: Frank van Straten and Charmian Watt; Len Radic; Celia Read; Bill Reed; Maria Rich; Harold Rosenthal; David Ross; Stanley Sadie; Glen Tomasetti; Mary Wilson; Elizabeth Wright.

I am particularly indebted to the director of the Melba Memorial Conservatorium, Joan Arnold, to her assistant Maggie Linigen, and to Alfred Ruskin of the board, for access to that institution's archive, opened for research for the first time.

To those who wished to remain anonymous, my thanks for research selflessly undertaken in the archives of Covent Garden, the Metropolitan, the New York Public Library, the state operas of Vienna and Leningrad, the Paris Opera, the Monnaie, at Monte Carlo, and in Washington, Chicago and Windsor.

PREFACE

Melba the diva was regretted in her passing as the last and greatest exponent of a dying art. Time has proved the art of bel canto to be far from dead, and opera itself is booming. But what *is* a diva and what is her significance? Does it matter now that Melba ever existed? Was she just a brilliant entertainer, a champion vocal aerialist in the same league as Olympic gold-medal athletes, admired for doing something we can all do but doing it superlatively well? What *was* the skill she possessed? Did it die with her or have we received it as a cultural heritage? If we have, what is its value? And the art that she served, what of it? Is it largely the melodramatic product of male sexual fantasy, as it appears to be? Was Melba really some some kind of geisha in the service of the composers, a vertical and vocal *grande horizontale* of the creative mind, if not the flesh, or was she simply a first-rate professional in an industry undergoing a period of distortion? Was she a lackey of Empire and class as was said, or a nationalist leading her countrymen to true self-consciousness? These are some of the questions I look at in this biography. Melba was and still is a legendary figure, but what does that mean? How did this legend come into being?

The answers lie partly in the earlier biographies, partly in the way Melba herself built up her own image and partly in the special conditions of the social and musical life of the times. Legends are created and transmitted through the voices of many people – there is never a single source, nor a single version of the legend. I give you here some of those many voices as well as my own, but you will create your own legend by remembering what catches your imagination, rejecting what does not – that is as it should be. But here, too, are facts not exposed before – the Australian musical background, that rich, fecund vocal culture from which she came; the Royal Affair; the arduous nature of the singer's life; the nature of her commitment to teaching her skills.

Helen Porter Armstrong, née Mitchell, was variously called a vexatious daughter, a runaway wife, a bad mother and a loose woman; she was a divorcee, and mistress of the pretender to the French throne. She was a fat soprano, vain, vulgar, imperious and a snob. She had a taste for second-class music and she swore, but she was not a drunkard as rumour had it. She was racist and, men said, sexist. She was also a shrewd, self-made woman whose miraculous voice helped her amass a fortune and win her international acclaim; Australians worshipped at the shrine of her success.

What did they worship? Possibly her voice. More likely her ability to take a gift of nature and turn it into diamonds, furs, cars, houses, travel, parties and investments made on the advice of Alfred de Rothschild that enabled her to lead what can only be called the grand life. It was the kind of envious admiration only accorded by women to other women who strike it lucky and become glamorously rich: great beauties who marry royalty or Greek shipping magnates, actresses, prima ballerinas – and opera singers. They are performers of special female rites of fantastic passage and as such go with every woman's blessing.

As the finest of vessels that pour the wine matured in male minds (women opera composers were once as rare as hen's teeth), the diva delivers the ultimate in service. The actress has a wide spectrum of parts but the prima donna is limited by the small available repertoire. Because of this she has little choice but to accept the dictates of managements and agree to give life to male projections of transsexual dreams, rape fantasies, incest taboos, moral fears and political theory, exalted by transformation into a high art form designed to appeal to a ruling class, whether aristocratic or bourgeois, for whom she acts as high priestess (see *The Ring*, *Fidelio*, *Norma*, *Lucia di Lammermoor*, *Lurline*, *Lucrezia*, *Figaro*, *La Bohème*, *Tosca* and *Aida* to begin with). Her reward is to be considered not bound by the conventions of women's lives, provided decorum is observed. As George Eliot's prima donna in *Armgart* says: 'Let it excuse me that my kind is rare; Commonness is its own security'.

Melba was born on 19 May 1861 in Richmond, Melbourne. She died on 23 February 1931 in Sydney. She was buried like a hero. But apart from the modest little monument that marks the spot in Lilydale cemetery no real memorial was erected to her memory. Yet she is the most famous woman Australia has produced. She was a world figure, no mere local heroine. She remains one of the few names that spring to mind when the national myth is discussed; she ranks with Ned Kelly, Don Bradman and Phar Lap in the popular imagination. She made it possible for Australians to be proud of their cultural origins and aware of the quality of what they could produce. With Melba we realised it was possible to stop cringing to the English and to get up off our knees.

For all that, she was a conservative force, sharing the common belief of contemporary musicians and music-lovers that 'good music', as defined by an educated middle class, was of moral benefit. But she failed to understand the implications of willingly selling her services and, because of her status, the country's cultural development, in order to foster the political aims of those with a vested interest in the continuance of faith in a failing Empire. In propagating the notion of ennoblement through a narrowly defined art form, she underlined the continuing worthiness of the conservative structures which sustained it, reassuring the faithful through acts of continuing tradition. In a society ostensibly built on the ideal of equality she advocated literal worship of an art form in the service of an ascendant middle class, its structures, its religion and its wars. In this she was astonishingly successful. An independent Australia was beyond Melba's ken.

As Dame Nellie, Melba was the fulfilment and the symbol of the Australian dream. In two generations her family moved from poverty and artisan status to wealth and the highest artistic success. Melba was financially and personally independent, dictating the terms of her own life, brooking no opposition, refusing to be cowed by anyone, and rising to unsurpassed heights in a chosen profession. She was the friend of royalty and of the powerful; she was honoured by the English, who, as a rule, despised their colonial offspring – she marked their coming-of-age. Instead of casting off the Australian stigma and trying to pass herself off as, say, a Scot, she flaunted her origins with great pride and, in the end, went home to give her teaching gift to a new generation. She remained as proud of her country as her countrymen were of her, for all they said behind her back. No wonder, then, that carved into the steps before her gravestone are Mimi's words: *Addio senza rancore* – 'Farewell without bitterness'.

Chapter 1

ADDIO SENZA RANCORE

On 23 February 1931, in a white room at St Vincent's Hospital, Sydney, the corpse of an old woman lay embalmed under a white tulle veil, white roses on her pillow, frangipani on her breast. In the next room her packed bags waited to be removed.

A press banner-heading, two days before, read: 'Some unknown curse of Egypt killed desire to live in Melba. What was strange Cairo infection that may still world's noblest voice? Instinct that brought great Australian singer home – to die?'

And shortly afterwards, striking an operatic pose, one journalist wrote:

> Egypt, the old midden of the world, has laid its curse on the singing spark that was Nellie Melba, in whom life throbbed and shouted, whose magic could touch dumb stones to beauty, whose mere passing was like a breath of warm and glorious existence – Melba, who loved the taste of living, who suffered and pleasured without stint and sang while she was doing it – is dead.[1]

For a month the diva had lain semi-conscious. Two weeks before her death she suddenly struggled up in the arms of her nurses and sang, falteringly, what was termed her last song – snatches of Gounod's 'Ave Maria'. Sometimes, when delirious, there were attempts at scales, trills, the voice weak but clear, already tugging loose, steadying to be gone. John Lemmone, a flautist and a friend, came, tried to speak and, gathering up an armful of flowers from the hundreds sent, went out weeping uncontrollably. Two days before, the patient asked for Canon Lear of St Mark's, Darling Point, who told her what she wanted to hear, heard what she wanted to say, and left her to her son, George. Towards evening she died.

In London it was reported that the

> Health Authorities were sceptical of the assertation that Dame Nellie Melba died from a disease caused by eating watercress in England. They pointed out that practically all the watercress in England was grown in properly supervised beds.[2]

In Brussels, where she made her operatic début, a street was named after her for her efforts to raise funds for the Belgian Red Cross some fifteen years before.

THE ORIGIN OF THE DIVA

The Christian church excluded women singers from ecclesiastical music for centuries, possibly in response to the fact that the best female musicians in Europe, from Greek times on, were almost all from the courtesan class. As late as the 15th century daughters of the nobility were taught a little music as part of a minimal education but they made music only with women of their own class. Gentlemen made music with other gentlemen, not with ladies, since this was considered effeminate. The public entertainment of men involved the courtesanry and because this lowered the social tone of the event the best composers were wary of jeopardising their court positions by providing music for distractions not approved of by the church or by wives of the peerage.

However, in the first half of the 16th century female members of powerful and influential noble families, among them such figures as Isabella d'Este, Marchioness of Mantua (1474–1539), used their position to acquire genuine education and to distinguish themselves as committed musicians and patrons of the arts. The madrigal repertory developed as a direct response to the call for music for female voices. At Ferrara, under the patronage of Alfonso d'Este II the famous 'concerto delle dame' was developed and although this at first involved women of the courtesanry Alfonso replaced them with skilled singers brought from other cities, marrying them to members of his court and generally promoting the women musicians in rank and prestige. The fashion for female vocal music became widespread. At the time of the Counter-Reformation, however, the Catholic church found it had no music to rival the attractions of the high female voices used for Protestant services. Rather than risk promiscuity in the organ loft the church introduced the castrato as a substitute voice, ignoring the moral difficulties this brought with it.

The first soprano divas appeared late in the 16th century; these were women credited with possessing a feminine mystique that deeply affected audiences – Lucrezia Bendidio, Laura Peverara, Tarquinia Molza at the court of Ferrara, and Vittoria Archilei, who sang the title role in Peri's *Euridice* (Florence 1600). The diva and the development of opera are synonymous. With the baroque period came a development of brilliant vocal display – a duelling between sopranos and castrati, culminating in the pyrotechnics of the chamber cantata where all pretence at dramatic presentation could be arrested for up to twenty minutes to cater for the exhibitionism of the singer.

In the 18th century the

In Melbourne, where she was born and whose name she had made her own, it was suggested a carillon of bells be raised in the Alexandra Gardens as a memorial. Hadn't Melba once suggested bells as a war memorial before the Shrine was built? But no bells were raised.

A photograph of Melba as the dead Juliette appeared in newspapers world-wide. She had had it taken years before for release at just this moment. She lies, an aged bride, roses at feet and breast, embedded in velvet. The original, before cropping, shows two tables with a clutter of metal legs showing below the drapes. As a two-page spread in the *New York Times* of 1 March 1931 the effect was eerie.

Over a year before, a Parisian winter clutching at her bones, she had sought warmth in Egypt. Intermittent fever took hold. Distrusting Egyptian doctors she left for Badenfel and the reassurance meted out by a reputedly great German doctor.

The press claimed that 'Some instinct drew her out to Australia'. Whatever it was drove her to return home to Melbourne in the *Cathay*, where she broke out in boils, lost hope and submitted, for a time, to the regimen of a private hospital run by a matron Melba nicknamed 'The Great White Hawk'. Why Sydney? A restless search for health, a doctor recommended by her daughter-in-law, the curse of Egypt? Perhaps her granddaughter's friend, Maie Casey, was nearer the mark when she wrote in 1975:

In 1930 she became ill of a fever that for a while was not identified. Finally it was diagnosed as para-typhoid by Evie's brother Dr William Doyle of Sydney. Nowadays it would probably have yielded to knowledge and treatment.[3]

But legends do not yield to any amount of cold water being poured from whatever heights and by 1931 Melba was already a formidable legend. It was all very well for her to scold a sycophantic friend assuring her of immortality – 'Don't tell me lies. I'm dying and you know it' – but the public, *her* public, wanted myths, not truth.

The truth? Melba had undergone surgery to have her face lifted while she was in Europe, but an infection had developed. By the time her homeward voyage had progresssed as far as the Red Sea she had erysipelas and was seriously ill. She was put into a private room, no. 5 on the ground floor of the hospital, and the whole matter was kept strictly confidential. Her attendants found her in great pain in both sides of the face. There was also a heart condition to cope with.

Melba had been transferred to the care of the Sisters of Charity at St Vincent's Private Hospital in Darlinghurst for treatment by a relative. She requested that after her death she was to be embalmed and that a beautician should make up her face before anyone was permitted to see her. The bed coverlet was to be strewn with frangipani. All of this was done.[4]

They put her in a coffin made of English woods, and twenty-four hours after her death it was put on board the Melbourne express. She was going home in true Melba style, the flag-draped coffin clearly visible behind a specially installed plate-glass window. Red roses lay on the casket lid, the gift of one of her 'girl' students, Marie Bremner. At every station along the way people were waiting silently to see her pass slowly.

By nightfall she lay in state in Scots Church in Collins Street. It was, in every sense, her father's house; he had built the church in the 1870s and she had worshipped in its Victorian Gothic gloom as a child. Great masses of white, yellow and delicate pink flowers were heaped against walls, screens, pews and the laurel-wreathed pillars as the crowd passed through in homage. There are photographs of the queues in the street waiting for her grand final performance, only this time it was her public that had taken centre-stage, determined, for all their Anglo-Saxon heritage, to make a Celtic wake of it. What happened was uncharacteristic and all the more memorable because of that.

It was given to the Moderator of the Presbyterian Assembly, the Right Reverend Dr W. Borland, to deliver the panegyric. In honour of her money-raising efforts in the First World War he dubbed Melba 'queen of hearts as well as queen of song', and then, rising well above the occasion, added that 'from her matchless music there spoke to all human hearts of the mass and of the multitude of all the world, essential womanhood, essential motherhood'.

Through suburban Kew, Deepdene, Balwyn and as far as Box Hill, the hearse and its half-mile of entourage drove between silent ranks of mourners. In the country beyond they stood on the hilltops that commanded a view of the procession. They grouped at sudden turns in the road. School children were shepherded out to watch. Workers left farms in a body to turn out for the grand old lady, a legend in her lifetime. Everywhere houses and shops were deserted.

In Melbourne politicians crowded the steps of Parliament House. Outside the Albert Street conservatorium everyone she had ever taught seemed to be assembled. At her old school, the Presbyterian Ladies College, the procession halted. Flowers were passed down to the half-dozen open cars already trailing the hearse. At Blackburn State School the fife and drum band played 'Onward Christian soldiers' and added yet more flowers. At the Ringwood borough hall a mayoral wreath was added. At Lilydale, shops cleared windows to display Melba photographs, and a guard of honour from Cave Hill Estate, consisting of returned soldiers from the district who felt they owed her a debt of gratitude, the Lilydale Fire Brigade, and the Boy Scouts from Camberwell who were known as Melba's Own, lined the final stages of the route. It was a homespun, spontaneous send-off.

By the time the cortège reached the graveyard what had been a

most prized attribute of a soprano was technical precision, not the ability to take C in alt. Dr Burney wrote that 'such cork-cutting notes. . .are unworthy of a great singer'. Top-ranking performers were given the title 'prima donna', a rank that gave them the right to sing more arias than other members of the cast and to be assigned the more difficult music of the opera.

The specialist soprano, distinguished by technical facility, range, timbre and character, came into existence late in the century when the castrati were in decline. One of these soprano types was the coloratura, a singer capable of the complex ornamentation of the vocal line who was able to 'colour' it, in effect. It was for this voice that Bellini, Rossini and Donizetti wrote in the first part of the 19th century, and though the voices required were not expected to have great volume they needed to be centrally pitched, that is, to be without waver and to be capable of passing smoothly from one register to another. This was the art of 'bel canto' and its greatest exponents were Giuditta Pasta (1797–1865), Wilhelmine Schroder-Devrient (1804–60), Henriette Sontag (1806–54) and Giulia Grisi (1811–69).

In the years just before Melba's birth the building of larger concert-halls and opera-houses necessitated bigger orchestras and, as a corollary, bigger voices to be heard through the pit sound. To fill the new spaces violins and violas were fitted with metal top strings sounded with heavy-haired Tourte bows, creating more problems, for the sopranos in particular. As Wagnerian music, with its enlarged orchestral demands, grew in popularity and spread into spaces not designed to keep the orchestral sound hooded as at Bayreuth, voices of even greater power were employed. Even Verdi was affected by this cult of the big voice, creating roles that required exceptional tone control rather than the agility of an earlier era.

The castrati finally fell out of favour early in the 19th century. As their star faded that of the sopranos blazed. Adulation of the diva reached extraordinary heights. At the same time her status was boosted by the demand for her services as the jewel in the crown of European culture transposed in the newly rich colonies and in America. The new steamships and trains made it possible for circuits to be established and time, audiences and profits maximised. The opera-house became a symbol of civic progress but it could survive only with the right international stars. Jenny Lind, Adelina Patti and Melba were such stars. Without them the opera-houses faced financial disaster. Melba's early flirtation with Wagnerian roles had its origin in this desire to be able to command the house. Hers was a carrying voice but it lacked the dramatic weight of a Kundry or an Austral. Her fear was that what were already regarded as operas of another era would pass out of favour altogether and leave her stranded. It did not happen of course. The 20th century has seen a rekindling of interest in performing works of earlier times as authentically as possible. As Joan Sutherland

bright afternoon had become a greying evening. The coffin was transferred to a gun carriage. An escort from the 22nd Battery of the Australian Field Artillery stepped smartly in to replace the amateur townsmen for a professional finish. There were already hundreds of mourners round the patch of ground kept clear by police. The wind began to whip up the red ensign used to shield the clerics gathered on the carpet of fresh-cut cypress by the flower-walled grave. Across a hedge nearby a tall pillared marble tomb housed the Mitchell parents and three of Melba's siblings.

The pallbearers were: Professor (later Sir) Bernard Heinze, the Ormond Professor of Music; Fritz Hart (composer, friend, colleague and the putative father of a child Melba was rumoured to have had at the age of 56); George Chirnside (wealth and pelph, and family friend and neighbour); Garret Marnane; E. Leslie Newbigin; and William Stawell. The family – Armstrongs, Mitchells and Pattersons – tried valiantly to control themselves as the Royal Victorian Liedertafel all-male choir sang Sullivan's 'The long day closes'. Birds rose suddenly in flight from neighbouring trees and broke the tension. But as Trumpeter-Sgt. K. P. Holt and G. Barber of the 8th Brigade Australian Field Artillery sounded the 'Last Post', drops of rain began to fall. A reporter saw 'the setting sun issue from a nimbus sheath and glint on the brass of the trumpets'. Nellie was home and there was not a dry eye in the house.

Later in the press it was reported that

Never in the history of Melbourne – not even in the emotional stress of the war years – have the streets witnessed such scenes as marked Melba's funeral procession. For more than three hours it flowed slowly between two banks of mourning men, women and children. Few of them could restrain entirely the spontaneous expression of their sense of loss. Probably scores of thousands of people were at the roadside between Scots Church and the cypress-walled cemetery at Lilydale, where Melba was laid to rest simply and sadly in a grave of flowers.[5]

But who, or perhaps it should be what, was Melba? Her American–Czech biographer, Joseph Wechsberg, called her 'the perfect prima donna' whose reputation has now been confirmed by the judgement of history:

Melba had everything – commanding presence and beautiful voice, talent and technique, wealth and power. The moment she came on the stage, even before she sang a tone, she could cast a spell. There would be that subtle quickening of her audience's pulse. She was worshipped even by people who had never heard her. She lived at a time that adored its prima donnas, and she was the symbol of that time; the best known woman in the world, the most applauded and the most highly paid.[6]

In her autobiography, ghost-written by Beverley Nichols, Melba reveals that a fortune-teller she met as a child predicted that 'You will visit almost every country in the world ... I see you everywhere in great halls, crowded with people. And you are always the centre of attention – the one at whom all eyes are directed'.[7] Was she a superstitious exhibitionist?

Was she the grotesque, overweight, over-dressed, over-aged opera star, Irela, of Nichol's novel *Evensong*? Or is it mere coincidence that a man who knew her so well should write:

'This must be your *last* farewell, Irela.'

Irela looked at him indignantly, 'What do you mean?'

'You know very well what I mean.'

'I've never given a farewell before,' she said. 'I'm not like' – (and here she named a woman who is still annually saying goodbye to the concert platforms of the world, in ever shriller accents). 'I'm not like *her*, I hope! She's been saying farewell, for the last time, every season since the war. And her voice said farewell to *her* long before the war was ever heard of. I hope you're not accusing me of that?'

'You have said farewell before.' His voice was smooth as ever. 'Not to *opera*,' she replied sharply.

'No. Not to opera. But your name has been placarded on huge posters all over London, all over New York, all over the provinces, with the word Farewell on it, in very large type, on more than one occasion.'

'But with the words "prior to world tour" underneath,' she retorted.

To which he added: 'Yes, in very *small* type.'[8]

No. Of course it couldn't be Melba. Still, there *is* an old ocker saying – 'More farewells than Nellie Melba'.

Was it true that Melba was a drunkard, a miser, a drug addict, that she had no roof to her mouth, that she swallowed three raw eggs with Worcestershire sauce before each act of *La Bohème*, that she showed off in church by singing the hymns an octave higher than the congregation, that she never signed a contract, that she insisted on being paid in gold coins before the curtain went up on any perform- ance, that she held seances, was a whore, a neglectful mother, a runaway wife, a vexatious daughter, a snob, the victim of a tragic love affair with the pretender to the French throne, a millionairess who made it by 'singing 'em muck', or that she regularly ate mice until she was ill? Was the fatal facelift the result of vanity or a gesture of rebellion, a refusal to face reality or a courageous act of defiance?

Like many famous women, Melba became surrounded with apo-

has proved, the bel canto voice is still a drawcard and modern composers are less interested in power than in purity of tone. After all, volume can be supplied electronically these days.

The modern diva can still command great respect and enthrall a special following, but there are none who can rival the veneration accorded the Victorian Patti or the Edwardian Melba. The periods that produced them are gone and with them the cast of mind that could think of the diva as high priestess of a sacred cult, the divine woman, acting out the secret dreams of the ruling classes in public ritual. The modern diva is now, like the English queen, an ordinary mortal in paid, if special, service, a professional, not a demigoddess.

THEY SAY

The following quotations were taken from an ABC documentary on the life of Dame Nellie Melba which was broadcast on 23 February 1971 and produced by Brian Adams and collected by Wilfrid Thomas.

Dame Sybil Thorndike said (of Melba's voice): '. . . the sort of purity you find in a choirboy, yet with all the warmth belonging to a woman. It was the purest sound I ever heard. . . . She used to throw ripe loquats into Mary Tempest's bed. Mary Tempest was a lady, but Melba was a rowdy. I just loved her'.

Beverley Nichols, writer and once her private secretary: 'One of the things that makes me most angry about the Melba legend is the persistent rumour that she drank. This is astonishingly stupid. She had a voice of exceptional delicacy that was affected even if she took too much salt in an omelette, and it is inconceivable that she could have sung with such clarity into her sixties if she had indulged in any form of excess'.

Dame Mabel Brookes, who was at Melba's first return concert (1902) at the Melbourne Town Hall: 'Few people in Australia had heard her. It was an incredible concert, everyone was transfixed. Nobody realised she could be as good as she was . . . She liked success. Even if she was giving a party and it went extra well, she would trip down the hall and sing at the top of her voice, "We've had a beautiful party". She was childish about her desire for success'.

Gertrude Johnson, Melba's protégé and former principal coloratura at Covent Garden, found her difficult to work with: 'We used to clash and I, as the younger woman, naturally deferred to her. But it wasn't easy'.

Ivor Newton, also her accompanist in her last years: 'She was more feared than loved by her fellow sopranos'.

cryphal tales designed to discredit her, not professionally, but personally. In Victorian times, and even now, the way to do that was by sexual innuendo or by revelations of some kind of uncontrollable passion. In the collection of anecdotes for this biography one of the country's leading historians and an archivist both told me stories of Melba's promiscuity. Both informants were male, both got pleasure from the telling and from my reaction. Both admitted they had no evidence to support the notion of Melba as a promiscuous woman. When I asked people I met along the research path what Melba died from, the majority said, without hesitation, syphilis.

A legend is a compound of a little truth and a great deal of nonsense, but one thing is certain, as Melba herself said, 'If you wish to understand me at all you must understand first and foremost that I am an Australian'.[9]

Chapter 2

HELEN PORTER MITCHELL

Helen Porter Mitchell was born at Doonside, Richmond, a suburb of Melbourne, on 19 May 1861, the third of Isabella and David Mitchell's ten children and the first to survive infancy. On 25 March William Saurin Lyster, the wild Irish opera entrepreneur, launched his company's first Australian season with *Lucia di Lammermoor*, the opera in which Melba made her Covent Garden début twenty-seven years later. Two of the most important figures in the history of Australian opera had arrived together.

David Mitchell was a shareholder in Lyster's Prince of Wales Opera House, an investment which was probably prompted more from an interest in the profitability of bricks and mortar than the vagaries of operatic life, since Mitchell was a builder. In middle age Melba conceded: 'Throughout my life there has been one man who meant more than all others, one man for whose praise I thirsted, whose character I have tried to copy – my father'.[1]

Mitchell was a Scot, born in Forfarshire on 16 February 1829, the son of a tenant farmer, William Mitchell, and his wife Anne. At seventeen he was apprenticed to a master mason at Kirriemuir. His indenture completed, he rejected the narrow future ahead of him at home and shipped out of Liverpool on 6 April 1852 in the three-masted sailing ship *Anna* with seventy-two other steerage passengers all headed for Australia.

He left Scotland with a purse containing 200 sovereigns, the gift of his widowed mother. By day he carried it with him. At night he slept on it. A dawn mutiny led by the crew forced a fight with Mitchell and other passengers that went on for some hours; at the end of it the purse was missing. David Mitchell stepped ashore at Melbourne on 24 July at the height of the gold-rush with a single gold piece in his pocket. When he died at eighty-seven he left nearly half a million pounds. As his daughter put it, 'the history of his endeavour is a romance before which I feel that my own history is commonplace'.[2] An exaggeration if ever there was one.

Mitchell was simply a taciturn Scot with a nose for business and the skills a newly rich society needed. For a while he worked as a stonemason in Melbourne, saving enough to set up a shanty on the site in Richmond where he was to spend most of his life. In 1853 he

MELBOURNE'S OPERA BEFORE MELBA

Fully-fledged opera performances came to Melbourne only in 1853. The first was the opera that seems to haunt the Melba story, Donizetti's *Lucia di Lammermoor*, with Madame Marie Carandini as Lucia. Carandini (1826–94) was the English-born daughter of a coachman but came to Australia at the age of seven. She married a travelling musician, the counter-tenor Jerome, tenth Marquis di Carandini of Sanzano, who was exiled from Italy in 1835 for revolutionary activities. In Sydney Marie studied with the *émigré* Jewish composer Isaac Nathan and with Madame Wallace Bushelle, sister of the English composer, Vincent Wallace. She became the country's leading soprano, forming her own travelling opera company which toured Australia, India, America and New Zealand. All five of her daughters became singers who worked intermittently with the Carandini company. Since Marie's farewell was given in the Melbourne Town Hall on 3 February 1892, and her best-known daughter, Rosina Palmer, was the mainstay of the Melbourne Philharmonic Society oratorio performances after her marriage in 1860 and the soprano soloist of Scots Church after 1880, there can be little doubt that the family was known to Melba at least by reputation. The Carandini enterprise and the female independence it fostered, stemming as it did from financial necessity, could not have been lost on the equally resolute and independent Mitchell girl.

The *Lucia* of 1853 was a

was contracted to put up a building in Bendigo, but the contractor went bankrupt just before the work was completed and Mitchell was forced to try his luck on the Castlemaine gold-fields. He panned with some success, but when his health began to fail he returned to Melbourne to set up as a building contractor, using the Burnley Street site in industrial, river-side Richmond as the centre of his business operations.

In 1857 he married Isabella Ann Dow, a girl four years his junior, one of the four daughters of James Dow, an engineer at Langland Iron Foundry. (Dow emigrated from Forfarshire in 1842 and Mitchell met the family soon after he landed from the *Anna*.) That year a large brick and stucco house, Doonside, began to rise in place of the shanty Mitchell built Menzies' Hotel in William Street; and he won the tender for the masonry work to repair St Patrick's Cathedral. Two years later it was decided to demolish the old cathedral, just as Mitchell was completing the first stage of his work. Not daunted, he set up a factory for steam-made and pressed bricks on the land next to Doonside.

By the time Nellie, his eldest daughter, was 13 he held shares in the Melbourne Builders' Lime and Cement Company, formed to break the monopoly of the Geelong limeburners. When she was 17 he bought Cave Hill Farm at Lilydale, where he worked the limestone and handled its distribution. His operations scarred the hills and stained the sky over a superb landscape. Melba described it as 'Mess, muck and money'.

In 1871 Mitchell built the huge warehouse of Paterson, Laing and Bruce in Flinders Lane. A year later he began work on Scots Church in Collins Street. He attended services there and sang in its choir for years. In death Melba lay there in state. In 1874 he built the Presbyterian Ladies College where his daughter became one of the first pupils. He was later to build the Prell's Building (1887), the Masonic Hall in Collins Street (1888), the Equitable Insurance Building (1893), the National Bank, and the New Zealand Loan Company's wool and grain warehouses at Kensington. In 1880 he employed 400 men for his biggest venture, the Royal Exhibition Buildings. The Melbourne International Exhibition opened there on 1 October with an 800-voice choir singing Leon Caron's cantata, 'Victoria'. The orchestra of 100 was drawn from the resources of the local Philharmonic societies and the Liedertafels, whose numbers included many ex-members of the leading English choral bodies. Possibly the 19-year-old Melba attended with her father, but probably not with her mother, who was by then fatally ill.

Caron's cantata ends:

> O Thou whose arm hath for our fathers fought
> Whose guiding hand their sons hath hither brought

Lead onward till Australia's land shall rise
A greater Britain, neath these Southern skies[3]

It was the prevailing view of the colonists at the time and Melba unquestionably shared it.

At the time of Nellie Mitchell's birth her parents had already been through the agony of losing two babies, a girl and a boy; consequently, Nellie's infancy was a time of anxiety. In all Isabella bore ten live children, seven of whom reached maturity: of these three were boys (Frank, Charles and Ernest) and four were girls (Helen, i.e. Nellie; Anne, known as Annie and later Mrs H. Box; Dora, later Mrs C. Lempriere; and Isabel, later Mrs T. Patterson). The youngest girl, Vere, died when Nellie was 20.

Melba's earliest memories were not of the Richmond house, the brickworks next door, the polluted river beyond, nor the dusty streets faced by workmen's timber cottages that surrounded Doonside itself; they were of an old farmhouse 45 miles away, shaded by huge gums and set on a steep hill. Because of its river frontage it was called Steel's Flats. When Melba came to build a permanent home just before the First World War she chose a site near this property of her father's in order to be

almost within sight and sound of the same trees and vineyards in which I played as a child, under the same brilliant sunshine, facing the same sudden storms that sweep in like giants from the hills.[4]

In her fifties she wanted to return to a childhood landscape remembered as full of quiet and eternal things, bright parrots winging, the yellow of the wattle in winter, magpies carolling outside her window at dawn, distant blue mountains and the kind of rich but sedate greenness found only in southern Australia.

In season, the Mitchell children, their nurses and their carpet bags were bundled unceremoniously into a rickety stage-coach and four outside the Burnley Street house at 8 a.m. in order to make Lilydale, 25 miles out, by midday. There they would lunch unhurriedly, covering the last 13 miles in the family wagonette, riding sideways to the wind, an uncomfortable way of travelling which Melba detested.

Nellie always insisted on sitting beside the driver, partly because she felt it was more exciting, partly to be the first to sight her beloved blue hills, and partly to enjoy the driver's problems as they jolted through the hazards of corrugated dirt roads, watching out for the occasional black snake which lay in wait in the shimmering heat and frightened the horses. Drovers herded cattle past slowly in a dust cloud that engulfed children, horses, wagon and driver as they converged, the men cracking stockwhips to impress their audience. Beyond the road merinos grazed in sunburned paddocks.

But at Steel's Flats the mountains closed in, the air was fresh again,

two-performance affair, a mere testing of the waters. The first real season only got under way in October 1855 at the Theatre Royal, which had opened on 16 July under John Black's management. In the next three months Carandini appeared with the soprano Catherine Hayes and contralto Sara Flower in a series of operas which included *La Sonnambula* (Bellini), *Lucia di Lammermoor* (Donizetti), *Norma* (Bellini), *The Bohemian Girl* (Balfe), *The Beggar's Opera* (John Gay), *Lucrezia Borgia* (Donizetti), and *Linda di Chamounix* (Donizetti).

In the years before Melba's birth there was a swarm of small opera companies buzzing in and out of the city, little contingents of core performers which hovered round some queen bee on the Empire circuit, intent on making an elusive fortune from following the mining boom. They came for a year or two, picked up with local pit players and choruses culled from the better harmonic societies, occasionally leaving behind them their financially embarrassed members to become teachers of a new generation of aspiring opera singers.

In 1856 George Coppin took over the Theatre Royal to present Madame Anna Bishop for a six-month season with Carandini, Theodoria Guerin, Monsieur Laglaise, Frank Howson, Emile Coulon and Walter Sherwin. *Norma, Sonnambula, Lucrezia, The Bohemian Girl* were all repeated, with new works: *Martha* (Flotow), *Der Freischütz* (Weber), *L'Elisir d'Amore* (Donizetti), *The Daughter of the Regiment*

(Donizetti), *Maritana* (Wallace), and *Masaniello* (Auber).

In 1857 Anna Bishop's second three-month season at the Princess Theatre consisted of *Norma*, *La Sonnambula*, *Lucrezia Borgia*, *Linda di Chamounix* (Donizetti), *Robert le Diable* (Meyerbeer), *Ernani* (Verdi), *L'Elisir d'Amore* and *Lucia di Lammermoor*.

The following year at the Theatre Royal the only new operas in two short seasons were *Il Trovatore* (Verdi), *La Favorita* (Donizetti), *Fra Diavolo* (Auber) and *Don Pasquale* (Donzetti.)

In 1859 the only new work was *Luisa Miller* (Verdi), but in 1860 *Attila* (Verdi), *La Cenerentola* (Rossini), *Nabucco* (Verdi), *Macbeth* (Verdi) and *Rigoletto* (Verdi) were presented.

and the way was lined by tree-ferns – green, lush, curling and primeval. Nellie could barely wait for the wagonette to stop before she went hurtling down the hill through the bush, to sit by the water-wheel, letting the cool water drip round her to the detriment of dress, shoes and dust-lightened long hair.

In the dining-room of the house there was a mirror that faced a window. Nellie liked to sit facing it, her back to the mountains which were reflected hazily in the mirror's perished surface; she loved the faded wistfulness of it. In the parlour she sat silent and still under the grand piano, embraced by the resonating sound as her mother practised. There is a legend that the defeated and dispersed ships of the Spanish Armada fetched up in the remote coves of Scotland and Ireland and that the dark looks of some Celts is the result of a few passionate encounters between the Spanish crews and the local women. Melba's mother was said to have Spanish blood and certainly the photographs of her eldest daughter could be read that way, possibly because the girl played up to the romantic image through her hairstyle and ornaments. For all that the prosaic fact is that the Celts overran an older, darker race whose genes sometimes prevailed.

The freedom of life at Steel's Flats suited Nellie. She liked to tramp about, to fish and to ride with her father. It was Mitchell who taught her to handle a horse. She called him 'a good master', though he never found a word of praise for her efforts nor had a moment's patience if she fumbled with hat or harness, and would ride on regardless, taking no excuses for anything less than his own perfect command of a mount.

At the time this freedom of country living was an acceptable release for middle-class Australian girls who otherwise found themselves physically limited by social conventions. The trouble with Nellie was that she found it hard to give up her independence once she was back in Melbourne. However, unlike her brothers, she was prepared to settle for flickers of rebellion against authority rather than outright war. The boys managed to be thrown out of every school their father could get to accept them, then made the lives of the tutors he hired so unbearable that none would stay. Though her younger brothers could behave like barbarians and be thought merely spirited, the same behaviour in a girl would have brought down the wrath of God (i.e. that of her father), and Nellie was never prepared to go as far as that. She preferred to use her rebelliousness to win his attention and his admiration.

Nellie Mitchell's early education was directed by two maternal aunts, whose tolerance was worn so thin by their unruly pupil that the child was packed off as a boarder to Leigh House, a school in Bridge Road, Richmond. Melba described the regimen there, which included 6 a.m. cold showers, as Spartan. In defiance she made her morning ablutions under the protection of an open umbrella. When the flooded state of the bathroom and a dripping brolly betrayed her, she was obliged to shower under supervision.

The upstairs windows of the building faced towards the distant tower of Doonside. Nellie would stand pressed to the glass, staring out at it, screaming to be taken home. In a strange attempt to placate her, Mitchell arranged for her to watch out for him as he went to and from town on business in his buggy or on the open-top seats of the local bus, but his remote visitations only made matters worse. Nellie was taken home to a house full of quarrelsome younger siblings, servants and a mother whose frequent pregnancies were beginning to take their toll.

Isabella Mitchell and her sisters were considered, by the standards of the day, well-educated. Nellie's mother could also sing well enough and played the harp, organ and piano, and was able to subdue her eldest child long enough to teach her the rudiments of the keyboard. Aunt Lizzie Dow was later described by her niece as having a soprano voice of 'extraordinary beauty'. As for David Mitchell, it seems that the best that can be said of his musical talents was that he sang a little and that he was a self-taught violinist.

Nellie remembered that

> when I was quite a baby, it was my great joy to sit on my father's knee on Sunday afternoons when he used to amuse himself at the harmonium. He would blow the bellows and sing a bass accompaniment to the hymn which I picked out on the keyboard with one finger.[5]

Two of Nellie's siblings had voices of some quality but neither possessed the temperament to push for a career.

At the age of six she made her first public appearance as a singer at a school concert arranged by her aunts. She sang 'Shells of ocean', a far from simple ballad with music by J. W. Cherry and the words by J. W. Leke. The words take on an odd meaning when the singer is on record as saying she didn't play with the toys usually offered girls and that she disliked dolls; only a wooden rocking-horse given to her by her father's confidential manager, Mr Newbiggin, found any place in her affections.

> One Summer eve, with pensive thought,
> I wandered on the sea-beat shore,
> Where oft in heedless infant sport
> I gathered shells in days before;
> The plashing waves like music fell
> Responsive to my fancy wild;
> A dream came o'er me like a spell,
> I thought I was again a child . . .
> I stooped upon the pebbly strand,

To cull the toys that round me lay,
But as I took them in my hand,
I threw them one by one away,
Oh! Alas, I said, in every stage
By toys our fancy is beguiled,
We gather shells from youth to age,
And then we leave them like a child.[6]

This sombre piece was followed by 'Comin' through the rye' which she sang with a Scottish accent taught to her by her grandmother Dow.

Tales of Melba's childhood proliferated in embroidered forms even in her own day, mainly because she kept on repeating them for the purpose of publicity and because reporters were forever looking for something new to add. Today it is hard to distinguish fact from fancy, plain from pearl, but where it can be done, a comparison of the various versions, even the authorised ones, can be illuminating. Melba herself gave the details of this first concert to her first biographer, Agnes Murphy, some time before 1909, and to Beverley Nichols who ghosted her autobiography published in 1925. She told Murphy that she sang 'Shells of ocean' first and then 'Comin' through the rye', with the coached accent. To Nichols she reversed the order and 'Shells' became a song her grandmother taught her, sung at the Richmond Public Hall, not simply 'in Richmond', as Murphy has it. Possibly Melba meant the building that preceeded the Richmond Town Hall on the same site. The programme for the opening of the town hall on 6 December 1869 gives Miss Mitchell's name against 'Can't you dance the polka' in the first half and 'Barney O'Hea' in the second. The concert was to aid the building fund of the Richmond Presbyterian Church, so it seems that Melba herself was not very clear on the facts, let alone the dates of her own life.

Agnes Murphy wrote that the 6-year-old Nellie was so excited by the applause and encores that she could not sleep and next day sought out a 'best friend' who lived in the same street to share her excitement. The friend resolutely refused to bring up the subject. Nellie finally burst out: 'But the concert, the concert! I sang last night and I was encored!' The friend withered her with the socially damning remark: 'Yes; and Nellie Mitchell, I saw your garter'. In *Melodies and Memories*, her autobiography, Melba retells this as: 'Nellie Mitchell, I saw your drawers'. Between 1909 and 1925 she also remembered that she had sung from a high stool, not mentioned in Murphy – a necessary embellishment if the perspective of the friend was to include her underwear above garter level.

What all this amounts to is that even at six she showed talent. But it was as a pianist that she first made any real musical mark. Two years later she was said to have mastered the opening of Beethoven's

Moonlight Sonata and had woken the house with it late at night. Her father's response was to pick her up from the piano and carry her back to bed, his anger disarmed by the unusual sight of a docile Nellie trying to impress him with her diligence.

Her mother had less patience and would shout in desperation, 'For heaven's sake, child, stop that humming', when Nellie's *sotto voce* vocalising got the better of her. In self-defence Nellie learned to whistle and to ignore the ridicule when she was called a 'whistling hen', that is, to continue the rhyme aimed at curbing masculine behaviour in a girl, she was 'good for neither God nor men'.

At 12 she was taking organ lessons on Tuesdays and Fridays at St Peter's, presumably the East Melbourne church, since there was none of that name in Richmond. The organ was built by William Hill of London before 1855, but it was repaired and improved by George Fincham, the Australian organ builder, when Nellie was four. Nellie's teacher, Joseph S. Summers, was organist from 1868 to 1880, and at one time government inspector of music. He was organist of the Melbourne Philharmonic Society from 1869 to 1873, and from 1874 to 1876 was its conductor. In 1882 he accepted the post of organist to the Metropolitan Liedertafel for a brief period. The connection with the two largest and most socially active of Melbourne's choral societies cannot have been without its influence on the Mitchells, whose class and kind spent a good deal of their leisure attending the popular but highly respectable concerts of these groups.

Summers was a disciple of Mendelssohn, as were many of Melbourne's English-born musicians. He was described by his successor, George Peake, as having:

> a touch of genius of the Mendelssohn order. Under stress of excitement, he apparently failed to perceive the faults or blemishes of any performance of which he was the conductor. His imagination seemed to supply the missing qualities of perfection and probably saved him from much bitter disappointment. Under other conditions he could be a keen critic. Passing over this peculiarity, it must be admitted that his term of office was characterised by a fine spirit of enterprise, in which lofty musical ideas and a true conception of the influence of musical art predominated.[7]

In 1875 Nellie and her sister Anne were sent as day scholars to the Presbyterian Ladies College in East Melbourne, then housed in the new building for which David Mitchell was the contractor. The school opened in February but the Mitchell girls' names do not appear in class lists until late in the year; Nellie was No. 116 in the enrolment lists.

The first headmaster, Professor Charles H. Pearson, was an enlightened educationist who saw music studies as something other than ornamental drawing-room training:

I have spoken of music and drawing as branches of education, as I cannot regard them as mere accomplishments. The first trains the attention in a degree second only to mathematics; the second is an admirable adjunct or introduction to the physical sciences, by the demand it makes on the power of accurate observation. Hence when the question has come before me, as it occasionally does, whether a girl with a marked taste for music or drawing should not give up a portion of her College lessons for extra work at the piano or easel, I have always, I hope not unwisely, recommended that she should do so.[8]

Isabella Mitchell had 'used her brush effectively in the creation of pictures both on canvas and china' and Nellie was inclined the same way, according to J. P. Wilson, headmaster at PLC for part of the time the Mitchells were there. She took advantage of Pearson's views on arts training to steal time from general studies for keyboard lessons and for practice. Drawing lessons had to wait until after school.

In the meantime, Otto Vogt, the organist of St Mark's, Fitzroy from 1877 to 1884, had succeeded Summers as Nellie's organ teacher. It is Vogt who is credited with adding to the Melba legends the tale that 'promptly at the end of her organ lessons, Nellie would gallop down to the Yarra River, strip off and swim nude with the local boys'. Vogt described his madcap pupil to his family as 'terrifying'.

During the PLC years Nellie's piano teacher was Alice Charbonnet-Kellermann, and her first professionally trained singing teacher was Mary Ellen Christian. A contralto born in Quebec but educated in London, Madame Christian was a pupil of Manuel Garcia the younger at the Royal Academy of Music. Through her, the first connection between Melba and the great European traditions of singing was established.

Christian had a phenomenal range (from D in the bass to the soprano high B), easy production and a vocal style described by *The Times* as 'a dramatic talent which any artist in London might envy'.[9] She had won the Westmoreland Scholarship and been awarded the Cipriani Potter exhibition at the RAM. This was no faded governess stretching doubtful skills in order to make a living in the colonies, as had all too often been the case. Mary Christian had a brief but brilliant London-based career before a serious respiratory illness forced her to migrate to Australia in 1871 on medical advice.

One of the entrepreneurs who tried to secure Madame Christian's services in London was William Saurin Lyster. He managed to coax her into studying six of the operatic roles he needed for his Melbourne operation, but the singer decided that the life of a colonial opera company was not for her and she refused to sign the contract at the last moment. But though she was not to be a Lyster star, Madame Christian made her début in the colonies on 26 August 1871 at the

Melbourne Town Hall at the testimonial marking the entrepreneur's tenth year as an impresario in Australia.

Christian's first tours were made with the visiting French violinist Jennie Claus and the English pianist Arabella Goddard. She appeared frequently thereafter as a concert singer and forty-three times as soloist with the Melbourne Philharmonic, mostly in oratorio. In 1889 her name disappeared from sight after a final 'Elijah' with Charles Santley in Sydney and in 1894 she became Sister Mary Paul of the Cross, a Sister of Charity. In 1905 she founded the Garcia School of Music at Potts Point, Sydney, which became a mecca for young singers still under the spell of the Garcia name. Twenty years later she said of this Australian talent: 'The majority of students of high promise who passed through my hands either had no ambition for a public career, or having it, retired early on their marriage'.[10] Of Nellie at PLC she said:

> At that time her youthful voice boasted a sweetness in the lower register by which it resembled a violin tone of Kubelik in legato passages, a fact revealed to me years later while listening to a phonograph record. As 'Melba' she lost the timbre in question under the training necessary to acquire the top notes characteristic of the coloratura repertoire.[11]

She found Australian voices had a distinctive fullness of quality but they needed particularly careful training and were easily ruined by forcing either 'up' or 'down', or by being developed too rapidly.

Years later Melba managed to forget that she had early teachers of such quality in an excess of loyalty to Marchesi, but it seems that at the very least Madame Christian's dictums on teaching methods were known to and accepted by her; her own manual takes a similar tack, though she acknowledges Marchesi's influence, not Garcia's, in spite of the fact that both Christian and Marchesi were products of the same school.

Christian died at St Vincent's College on 31 May 1941 aged 93. She left no contribution to the legends of Nellie's school days, as Vogt did, but her discretion was not matched by others, least of all by Nellie herself. At one time the legend included expulsion from PLC. In November 1924 when Melba spoke to the Old Collegians' Association she accepted what was being said without comment. She made it a point never to refute rumours, but allowed them to play themselves out without help from her. This time she roused a champion in her defence. Dr Wilson wrote to the *Argus* on 4 November 1924:

> I have cross-examined many of her former teachers and fellow students. So fortified, I brand the whole legend as spitefully, impudently false, and deserving of all the penalties of a clergy discipline act. Miss Nellie Mitchell was, in fact, quite a normal schoolgirl;

no plaster saint, maybe; just a healthy, happy young person, over-flowing with life and energy and having, perhaps, a spice of mischievous fun in her composition. In her school classes she was a diligent, honourable and obedient pupil. True, her talents did not run to arithmetic and geometry, but she held high places in English and was the pet elocution pupil of the late Mr George Lupton. It was art, however, that claimed her highest devotion. Not music only. She was ready to stay on after school for extra tuition in drawing, for which she showed decided ability. In her lunch hours she used to rush off to Scots Church for a practice on the organ. I have no recollection of any vocal displays, but I did hear a rumour that in private life she was a splendid whistler. When in the ripeness of age she left the College, she departed in the full odour of scholastic sanctity, and took with her the goodwill of her teachers and the affection of her comrades. She has retained and reciprocated both their goodwill and their affection from that day to this. No! No! Dame Melba; you really must not let go by default the reputation of our dear young friend, Nellie Mitchell, so fine a specimen of the frank, spirited, lovable, Scoto-Australian maiden.[12]

That maiden was variously reported to have indulged in more than skinny-dipping with the local boys; to have used language unsuitable for ladies of her class in the hearing of her teachers; to have thrown milk, her breakfast and scissors at someone who offended her; to have attempted the seduction of her minister; and to have so offended her father at one stage that he took a strap kept for the purpose and laid into her when she was naked. All legend. There is no evidence to support any of it.

Melba herself had a hand in shaping the schoolgirl legends of the naughty-but-nice variety. Her Australianness was a selling point, especially in America. There the English rose image was useless. Instead Melba fed the press the image of a Mary Grant Bruce heroine, self-assertive, vigorous, frank, independent, but a character working within convention, not an outsider. The questionable conduct attributed to her at PLC seems to have gone no further than a tendency to whistle popular tunes in a cheeky manner at the backs of authority, and by entertaining her friends with making 'that funny noise' in her throat which was later interpreted as practising the natural trill she capitalised on later in her career. Nellie was no scholar either, even by her own account; her interest in the usual range of academic subjects was close to nil. In her memoirs she refused to comment: 'Of my school-days I do not wish to write at length. They were much as other girls' schooldays'.

But at the various country properties owned by her father over the years, she seems to have allowed herself liberties beyond those tolerated at PLC and even at home. On the coach back to Melbourne she had the habit of passing the time by shouting jokey comments to everyone they passed, to the amusement of other travellers, if not her family. She once mounted the momentarily vacant seat of the local horse bus and drove off, haphazard and far too fast, down one of the city's main streets, scattering pedestrians and generally getting out of control. She hated to be still and disliked seeing others quiet. At concerts her criticism was so loud and severe that her mother occasionally left her at home and took the younger children instead as a disciplinary measure. At one of the newer country properties she found there was no piano, only a 'dislocated harmonium and a concertina'. She taught herself the rudiments of the concertina but remained resentful at being deprived of proper keyboard practice. When the lay preacher came round one Sunday in the usual country cycle of services for the propertied families, their servants, station hands and, in season, the shearers, Nellie took the chance to protest in front of a sizeable audience. Her mother asked her to accompany the first hymn on the wheezy harmonium. To the horror of her parents she dashed out 'You should see me dance the polka' and was sent to bed for the rest of the day for her social and religious fall from grace.

Murphy gives most of the tales of Melba's childhood in quotes, as if Melba were being directly consulted which, considering Murphy's years of service as her secretary and Murphy's training as a journalist, was probably the case. The tone is bright and indulgent and the stories have no murky undercurrents, yet when Melba came to tell the same tales in the memoirs they take a rather different turn. In the harmonium story Murphy gives the correct title of the popular tune; the memoirs give 'Can't you dance the polka?' Murphy's lay preacher becomes 'a very old parson of great piety and excessive dullness' and Nellie's petulance at the lack of a piano becomes a protest against the 'gloom and solemnity' of strict Presbyterian Sundays which were 'so great a nightmare to me that one day I deliberately fell in the mud in order to avoid going to church'. She was 'seized bodily' from the harmonium and kept in disgrace for a week. Murphy gives the same story of falling in the mud, but with no mention of avoiding going to church, adding that Nellie picked herself up, bought a ticket to the nearby sea baths, threw herself in, clothes and all, dried out in the sun and then went home clean enough not to draw too much attention to herself in the streets. It was this portrait of the resourceful, determined girl that Melba played up in interviews before and after the publication of Murphy's book in 1909. Considering the faith Melba placed in her sometime secretary, sometime agent's judgement it may have been more Murphy than Melba whose voice was heard in the international publicity that created the Melba legend. When it came to Nichols, her ghost writer, Melba's confidence was misplaced. There is a subtle shift towards self-justification. The portrait is of a monstrously vain woman, patronising, self-satisfied, unctuous. This, too, became part of the legend, not because Nichols controlled Melba's publicity but because by the time *Melodies and Memories* was published anything about Melba got instant world-wide circulation. The fact that Nichols wrote the book while living at Coombe Cottage, Melba's house, a fact that he made very well known, gave the public the idea that what was said in the book came directly from Melba. It probably did, but by then she couldn't be bothered checking the work done in her name, and neither could Nichols. The memoirs are significant more for what they omit than for what they include in any case. Several of the well-worn Murphy episodes disappear: Nichols omits Nellie's impersonation of a begging nun who got a sovereign out of David Mitchell at his own front door, for example. More importantly he – or Melba – omits any reference to Nellie's efforts to entrepreneur her own concerts. Murphy records that when Nellie first decided to perform in proper style in the drawing room of Doonside, by then equipped with a built-in chamber organ, her father took it as a sign that she was contemplating a career as a professional musician. He contacted everyone she invited, reducing the size of the audience brave enough to defy him to two. Nellie met the challenge by going through the entire programme exactly as if the room were full.

Mitchell's opposition to his daughter becoming a paid entertainer is well documented. He seems to have shared the commonly held Victorian view of the *Sydney Gazette* (1827) that:

> No man of feeling will suffer his wife, sister, or daughter to become a public singer or performer of any description, who has any other means of providing for her. It is the hard weapon of necessity alone that will induce women of delicacy to appear before the public for hire.[13]

The sub-text of this attitude was that the life of such women was considered morally suspect because of the relative sexual freedom travelling artists were presumed to enjoy. Behind that again was a memory of centuries of religious sanctions against acting troupes who were distrusted everywhere because of their ability to inform fantasies, both social and political.

But if a lady could not put herself out for hire as a singer, she could perform in public for nothing. Which is why women joined the oratorio societies and why Melba's teacher, Madame Christian, could act as a soloist for an honorarium which was enough for cab fares and a pair of gloves for the night, but which could hardly be called a fee. In any case David Mitchell was torn in two directions. On the one hand a daughter forced to earn her own income would have made him appear too tight-fisted even for a Melburnian Scot and would have left him open to ridicule. On the other he admired his eldest child's enterprise, seeing something of himself reflected in her determination to go her own way.

Sometime after the vetoed house concert Nellie arranged an event at beach-side Sorrento. It was ostensibly to raise funds for a new fence for the cemetery, but it was probably simply a way out of summer holiday boredom. According to her testimony to Murphy, Nellie's money ran out before the bill-posting was done. She waited until after dark, then went out to paste up notices herself; by then it was too late for her father to object on financial or any other grounds. She won the day, singing 'The angel at the window' (Tours) and 'Sing sweet bird' (Ganz), raising £20 for the fence and getting a good review in the local press, right under David Mitchell's nose.

It should be added that the Royal Victorian Liedertafel records show that on 21 January 1885, when Nellie was 23 years old, the impresario, George Coppin, organised a concert in Sorrento, the proceeds of which were to go to the erection of railings round the graveyard. Mrs Armstrong, as Nellie was then known, sang the songs she purports to have sung years before – she was careful not to give exact dates – but there was a duet, 'Oh maetana', with a Mr Cadden as well. Melba's version of the story has survived as fact in the memories of another generation but the Coppin version at least points to another interpretation.

David Mitchell's meanness, however, is one part of the legend based on fact. Nellie took an odd attitude to her father's 'canniness'. She called him a stern master and herself a willing pupil, even when his treatment of her was harsh and close-fisted. He once promised her a gold watch if she could memorise twelve organ pieces. In twelve days she had earned the trophy and Mitchell honoured his word. But Nellie dropped her prize in a Melbourne gutter. It was returned, broken, by the police. She wrote:

I shall never forget the look of black disapproval on Daddy's face when he saw the ruins of the watch in my hand. 'You will never get another from me', he said. And I never did, but I keep the old watch to this day in one of the drawers reserved for happy memories.[14]

In October 1881, when Nellie was 20, her mother died after a long illness. For a time she acted as household manager in her mother's place, but her duties were soon taken over by her sister Annie. Three months later her youngest sibling, Vere, then aged four and a half, died suddenly.

In her last moments Isabella called her children to her and gave each a duty to perform after her death. For Nellie it was 'always be a mother to little Vere'. In response Nellie moved the child's cot into her own room. When Vere became ill during the night Nellie and the nursemaid did what they could but, unwilling to disturb her father at such an hour, Nellie decided not to ask for a doctor. She stoked the bedroom fire and prepared to sleep, but as she lay drowsing she realised her mother was beside her, dressed in the black dress in which she had last seen her. Isabella walked slowly across the room to the cot, pointed at the child, made a sweeping gesture with her arm and disappeared. Unnerved, Nellie went to her father as soon as she dared next morning and asked for a doctor to be brought at once. Mitchell told her not to be foolish, he would see how the child was when he got back from business that evening. At 4 p.m. Vere died. Melba wrote, 'These are the facts, bare and unadorned. I do not seek to explain them'. Nellie never once spoke a word against her father. This tale of guilt and remorse remains the only reproach she ever made in public.

Chapter_3

MRS ARMSTRONG

Nellie Mitchell left PLC at the end of 1880. She was 19 years old, the personable daughter of a moderately wealthy man, ripened for the marriage market and, by nature, ready for the plucking. She began, discreetly, to be socially visible. In the Melbourne of 1880 that meant something rather different from the equivalent English experience, though it was British custom that shaped the more robust social forms of colonial Victorian life.

Melba knew 'Marvellous Melbourne' at its zenith. The title was bestowed by George Augustus Sala, then England's best-known journalist, when on a writer's tour of the outposts of Empire. In 1885 he wrote of 'an astonishing city . . . teeming with wealth and humanity'. The combination of push and energy which Sala and many other itinerant authors regarded as uniquely Melburnian had transformed the industrial town of Nellie's childhood into a genuine metropolis in record time. Sala attributed the spectacular rise of this 'New York of the Southern Hemisphere' to the vigour of the men of the gold-rush, a residium of "real live men", as the Americans say, and those live men and their sons made Melbourne what she is, magnificent and marvellous'. According to historian Graeme Davison the Americans themselves, those 'champions of urban bluster', saw Melbourne as one of the 'marvels of the world' on a par with Chicago and San Francisco. Melbourne's population leapt from 288 169 to 486 620 in a single decade (1881–1891). In 1861, the year of Melba's birth, it was 139 916, while in the year David Mitchell set up business in Richmond it had been 76 565; shortly before his arrival it was a mere 23 143.

It was a boom town, sprawled out over a flat plain rimmed by distant blue hills, a city essentially on the make, its conduct governed by commercial values which, in the six years before Melba emigrated, were destined to increase its wealth at the expense of its integrity.

It was not a beautiful city but it was impressive. From its immense and sombre bluestone warehouses, its colonial Gothic churches and Italianate banks and mansions, to the ornateness of its parliament and the splendour of the viceregal palace-like Government House, Melbourne was, until the 1890s depression, one huge construction site, a

HOME SWEET HOME

'Home sweet home' has always been regarded by Australians as Melba's private property, but it was also used by Adelina Patti and by most of the great sopranos of that and the following generation in much the same way. It had been in the public repertoire in this country since 4 January 1834 when it appeared as an incidental song in a Hobart version of *Clari, the Maid of Milan*, then billed as a melodrama. In the same guise it turned up in Sydney on 31 October. A year later, in September 1835, *Clari*, as the opera by Sir Henry Bishop, made its first appearance in Sydney, again with 'Home sweet home' included.

The Australian Opera Library in Sydney holds lists of first performances which give 18 July 1842 in Hobart as the *Clari* Australian première. Professor Roger Covell, in *Australia's music: Themes of a new society*, gives *Clari* as the first opera performed in Sydney. There is a certain irony in the fact that Sir Henry Bishop's wife, Anna, a distinguished singer, ran away with a French harp virtuoso, forger and bigamist Nicolas Bochsa, in 1839, travelling the world with him before landing in 1855 in Sydney. Bochsa died shortly afterwards and was buried in Sydney's Camperdown cemetery. Anna was a daughter of the Rivière family of artists and great-great aunt of the Australian chronicler of the Lyster opera companies, Dr Harold Love. Thus 'Home sweet home', which Anna used so often to end her concerts, continues its influence in more ways than one.

city always only partly built. The canny Mitchell was able to amass his fortune at a time when 'surburbanism was becoming the opiate of the middle classes, a fact which may account for the choice of *Home Sweet Home* as Victoria's anthem at the [1880] International Exhibition'.[1]

The young Melburnian lady of the 1880s was the product of all that money could buy. She may have had more freedom than her English cousins, but it was a freedom curbed by the ambitions of her *nouveau-riche* parents; after all, the town was still trying to live down a recent past of gold-rush lawlessness and, more remotely, the memory of convicts labouring in the streets and on the wharves. Girls of the Mitchells' class were expected to keep up a carefully chaperoned social round which included a series of 15-minute morning and afternoon carriage calls which involved the leaving of cards; shopping in the right places; fittings by the right dressmaker; lunches with the daughters of the right people; excursions to exhibitions, art galleries and museums and places of 'improvement'; attendance at concerts given by visiting celebrities; inoffensive theatre, if the family was not too strict; active membership of a harmonic society if she sang; lessons in social graces – piano and dancing were usual; evening parties and balls at the right houses; and a little exercise in the form of walking, horse-riding, racquet games and sea bathing. On Sundays the church took over. Melba recalled it as the day on which 'no one might smile or hum a tune', though her own father's brand of Presbyterianism does not seem to have resulted in a total ban on music in the Mitchell household. But for all the pious appearances of Melburnian Sundays the Reverend Charles Strong could write tartly of colonial congregations: 'Their hearts are more in the price of shares, or so-and-so's new bonnet, than in the Kingdom of love and righteousness'.[2] Novelist Ada Cambridge, who was also a clergyman's wife, wrote of Melbourne's social life in the 1880s:

> It was never that I heard so much good music, saw so much good acting, met so many interesting travellers, enjoyed the greatest race meetings in the history of splendid Flemington, the hospitality of Government House in its best days, the most memorable entertainments of a time when nothing but the first-rate was tolerated.[3]

Henry Gyles Turner called it 'an era of extravagance in balls, garden fetes, dinner parties and private theatricals'.[4]

What Melba's own social life was like before her mother's death is not a matter she cared to include in the memoirs. Balls, theatre, subscription choral concerts, and exhibitions proliferated, yet she remains silent. What is more, Agnes Murphy names only one visiting celebrity concert artist Nellie heard – the pianist Arabella Goddard, wife of the *Times* critic, J. W. Davidson, and a pupil of Kalkbrenner Madame Goddard arrived in 1873, toured the eastern states of Australia, performed in India and returned briefly to Melbourne late in 1874, using Melba's teacher, Mary Ellen Christian, as her associate singer. At the time Nellie's interests were instrumental rather than vocal. (She did not discard hopes of a professional life as a pianist until a Government House concert she gave some time after her marriage. The Governor's wife, the Marchioness of Normanby, advised her to forget the piano when she heard her sing. Why this should have been taken as anything more than polite criticism remains a mystery, but Nellie dated her final resolve to become a singer from the time of the Marchioness' advice.)

Did Nellie hear Goddard at the charity concert she gave with the Melbourne Philharmonic Society for the Hospital Sunday Fund? If the family patronised the highly respectable Philharmonic's concerts, which is likely because of their social standing, did she also hear the not quite so respectable coloratura soprano Ilma di Murska in *The Creation* the following year? Or in the Mad Scene from *Lucia di Lammermoor* at the packed concerts at the town hall?

Di Murska, then 39 years old, created something of a sensation in Melbourne on 2 August 1875 when she was serenaded outside Menzies Hotel by 150 male choristers from the Metropolitan Liedertafel. With her Newfoundland dog at heel and her maid carrying her angora cat on a cushion, she descended at the conclusion of the pavement concert, which by then had attracted the entire clientele of the hotel and half the neighbourhood, kissed the conductor, Julius Herz, and invited all present to drink her health in the bar. The result was the biggest shout in the history of the Menzies. There was even more of a sensation when it was discovered the singer was a bigamist. She was hardly the kind of public figure to win David Mitchell's approval.

In spite of what the sterner moralists of the day may have thought of her conduct, di Murska was among the great voices of her time. She was the Senta in the first *Flying Dutchman* heard in England, and her interpretation of the Queen of the Night was considered one of the finest. In Melbourne in 1876 she appeared under Lyster's management in *Lucia di Lammermoor, La Sonnambula, Il Trovatore* and *Faust*. If Nellie heard her in *Lucia* and *Faust*, roles that were to make the Melba name, she would have heard a voice in its prime, one which closely resembled her own and for good reason – Mathilde Marchesi was di Murska's teacher and she was shortly to become Melba's. Henry Pleasants has identified the hallmarks of Marchesi's teaching methods by studying the extant recordings of her students. The qualities he lists – even scale, light and precise attack, effortless tone production, clean intonation and ease in the upper register – are the di Murska qualities described by the Australian critics in 1876 and those credited to Melba when she returned home in 1902.

But the Lyster company and its rivals and inheritors had more to offer than di Murska's brief appearances as far as Nellie was concerned.

Incidentally, Dame Joan Sutherland also uses the song to conclude concerts and seasons. In Melbourne the tune only appears in the public records in 1852 and then as a violin solo at a Mechanics' Institute concert. The soloist was a Mr Megson. *Clari* was not produced in her home town during Melba's formative years in spite of the long seasons of operas given under Lyster's management during that period.

OPERA IN MELBOURNE WHEN MELBA WAS A GIRL

With Lyster's advent as an entrepreneur in 1861 the twenty-year long golden age of opera in colonial Australia began. In its first seven years the Melbourne-based Lyster company toured Australia and New Zealand with a repertoire of forty-six operas giving a total of 1459 performances.

Lyster died in November 1880 in the middle of the excitement surrounding bushranger Ned Kelly's trial – he had been captured on the opening night of *HMS Pinafore* – and of the solemn festival of the International Exhibition. It is true that seasons of grand opera continued in Melbourne, if spasmodically, but no company thereafter did more than exploit the taste for opera that Lyster had cultivated. By the time J. C. Williamson took over the theatrical scene the impetus was lost, and in any case Williamson was no grand opera buff. For Lyster it was a passion; for Williamson it was a matter of profit and personal prestige. But for Melba, who shared Lyster's passion, the educational impact of the later seasons, and the musical and social climate they created, must have been considerable. What was more, the musically literate – and they were proportionally far more numerous than they are now – could buy the major arias at a nominal cost from Allan's, Glen's or Sutton's music warehouses in the city for private familiarisation, if nothing else.

In the decade leading to her departure in 1886 Melburnians were offered: *Ruy Blas* (Marchetti), *Linda di Chamounix* (Donizetti), *Il Trovatore* (Verdi), *The Barber of Seville* (Rossini), *Faust* (Gounod), *The Daughter of the Regiment* (Donizetti), *A Masked Ball* (Verdi), *La Sonnambula* (Bellini), *Lucrezia Borgia* (Donizetti), *Don Giovanni* (Mozart), *Lucia di Lammermoor* (Donizetti), *Norma* (Bellini), *Satanella* (Balfe), *Martha* (Flotow), *The Hermit's Bell* (Maillart), *Maritana* (Wallace), *The Bohemian Girl* (Balfe), *Roberto il Diavolo* (Meyerbeer), *Semiramide* (Rossini), *Lohengrin* (Wagner), *Aida* (Verdi), *Die Fledermaus* (J.Strauss), *The Merry Wives of Windsor* (Nicolai), *La Forza del Destino* (Verdi), *Don Pasquale* (Donizetti), *Der Freischütz* (Weber), *The Rose of Castille* (Balfe), *Mosè in Egitto* (Rossini), *The Lily of Killarney* (Benedict), *Carmen* (Bizet), *Les Huguenots* (Meyerbeer), *L'Africaine* (Meyerbeer), *Rigoletto* (Verdi), *Mignon* (Thomas), *L'Ombre* (Flotow), and *Fidelio* (Beethoven).

From this list alone it can be deduced that Melbourne was not the uncultured outpost the English thought it to be when they expressed astonishment that a musician such as Melba could have sprung from so remote a place. It was presumed, too, that Marchesi was her only real teacher. Melba spoke disparagingly of earlier teachers, but were they really so inept? Julius Buddee, Monsieur Guernett and Madame Charbonnet-Kellermann from PLC days were her later instrumental teachers; Pietro Cecchi was her singing teacher.

Buddee was an *émigré* German, blown off course by the 1848 revolutions, who washed up in Melbourne at the time of the goldrush. He remained to found the Liedertafel Harmonia, but at one stage in his early career he had been Jenny Lind's accompanist. Guernett was pianist to the Zerbini Quartet and accompanist to Mary Ellen Christian. Cecchi is the only one Melba publicly acknowledged, and then only to condemn him.

Pietro Cecchi was a tenor who arrived in Melbourne from California in 1872 with the American soprano Agatha States and her opera troupe. After a successful concert series at the town hall, Lyster organised thirteen opera performances for them in tandem with his English company. When States returned to America, Lyster took on the company's baritone, Carlo Orlandini, its bass, Augusto Susini, the conductor, Paolo Giorza, and the manager, Signor Biscaccanti, but not Cecchi, whose reviews had been lukewarm for his appearances in *Ernani*, *Il Trovatore*, *The Barber of Seville*, *Faust*, *Lucia di Lammermoor*, *A Masked Ball*, *La Traviata* and *The Sicilian Vespers*. He did not return to the stage, though he sang several times with the Metropolitan Liedertafel. Did his familiarity with at least this particular set of operas have an influence on Melba? Some sources say she spent as many as seven years as his pupil but only one as Marchesi's, a period not long enough to explain Melba's detailed knowledge of the roles she sang a short time after her European début.

Whatever social life Nellie had before the deaths of her mother and her youngest sister ceased abruptly as the house went into mourning and its duties fell to the two older girls. Nellie was 'shocked and bewildered'. Her spirits sank to such a low level that her father, no less affected, decided that drastic measures were in order. He prescribed a travel cure for himself, Annie and Nellie and booked a 1400-mile steamship cruise to Mackay in northern Queensland. Mitchell had no intention of taking anything so wasteful as a holiday, however. Mackay was the nearest port to Marion, a town 12 miles inland where he had contracted to run up a sugar mill. The real object of the exercise was to see what prospects for expansion the area had to offer the Mitchell building industry at a time when kanaka slave labour was making even the Mackay swamp lands profitable.

From the 1860s the Queensland central plantations had used Polynesian workers for cotton picking, but the cotton market collapsed at the end of the American Civil War. A sugar-cane crop, suited to the semitropics but hard to cut, was substituted and recruiters kidnapped the inhabitants of the nearer Pacific Islands in order to strengthen the cheap kanaka labour force. Known as black-birding, this trade continued until after 1901 when the new Commonwealth took on the burden of sugar produced by expensive, white unionised labour. The Mackay the Mitchells knew was built on a work system and an ethic similar to that of the American south.

At Marion Mitchell busied himself finding labour for the construction of the mill, while in Mackay his daughters occupied themselves with the limited social life the town had to offer. Nellie acted as a concert accompanist to a local singer, Julia Wheeler, then began to appear as an associate artist. On 15 September 1882 she wrote to Cecchi from Port Mackay:

My dear Signor Cecchi,
    I suppose you will be astonished to hear from me, but I want to tell you that although I am nearly 2,000 miles from Melbourne I am not forgetting my practising, for I manage to get a little every day. I am going to sing at two concerts, one on Monday and the other on Saturday. I hope I shall be successful.
    Will you please send me six or seven nice *English* songs up, as the people here do not understand Italian. I daresay you will be able to find some pretty ones; send them as soon as possible.
    I shall not be home for two or three months yet. I intend taking a long holiday, as I am enjoying myself so well. I go out either riding, driving or yachting every day. Will you kindly remember me to Mr Nobili, also Mr Bracchi, if he is in Town?
                    Believe me,
                        Your affectionate pupil,
                              Nellie Mitchell.[5]

Cecchi obliged. She wrote to thank him on 15 October 1882, ending with Italianate courtesy:

> I had *great success* at the two concerts I sang at, so much so that all the ladies up here are jealous of me. I was encored twice for each song, and they hurrahed me and threw me no end of bouquets. Everyone asks me who my master is, and when I say Signor Cecchi, they all say, 'When I go to Melbourne he shall be my master, too!'[6]

In Mackay Nellie met Charles Armstrong. She had written to Cecchi telling him she would be home in January 1883. However, she married Armstrong on 22 December 1882, and her son George, her only child, was born on 16 October 1883 at Marion Mill just over nine months later. The lessons with Cecchi had to wait.

Charles Nesbitt Frederick Armstrong was the youngest of the six sons of Sir Andrew Armstrong, first baronet of Gallen Priory, King's County, Ireland. In the memoirs Melba called him an Irishman, but his name was antique Scottish. The family was said to have moved to Ireland in the 17th century after an ancestor was hanged for his part in an English border raid. Intermarriage with the Anglo-Irish gentry meant that there was also English blood warring with the Celt in Kangaroo Charlie, as he was ironically known in Mackay. He was (according to Maie Casey)' a handsome man with sparkling eyes . . . full of vitality, humour, intolerance and charm'. He was also tall, lean, muscular and athletic, with a determined jaw squaring off a long face; just the sort of physically attractive male to take Nellie's fancy. She was then a dark-haired, oval-faced, slender girl, who had a faintly hooked nose, and was a little over average height. She was strong bodied and quick in her movements but had a dreaminess in her red-brown eyes when she was still. She had looks, if not beauty, and presence, if not grace.

Armstrong was only three years older than Nellie but he had seen a great deal more of the world. He had 'served as an apprentice before the mast' in his late teens for a few voyages, then swallowed the anchor to become a jackaroo in Queensland. For a time he drifted, taking work where he could find it, buying and selling horses, living rough with other drovers in moves across Queensland and New South Wales while gaining a reputation as a hard-drinking, hot-tempered young buck too ready with his fists who could ride anything from a brumby stallion to a race-horse. He was no intellectual, but then neither was Nellie. She was as restless and active as he was and as quick to reach boiling point. But Charlie's interest in music went no further than Gilbert and Sullivan and the popular tunes of the day, a fact that Nellie overlooked until too late.

David Mitchell opposed the match. He liked Armstrong but at 24 and without capital, what kind of husband would he make for a girl used to something close to luxury? For all that he gave the bride away t the ceremony conducted by the Reverend Charles Ogg in the minister's study in the manse of St Ann's Presbyterian Church, Brisbane, three days before the Christmas of 1882. It was a very simple affair. Annie Mitchell; the best man, Arthur Feez, later a Brisbane barrister; and Margaret Ogg, the minister's daughter, were the only other witnesses.

Feez disliked Nellie. In later years he said that the night before the wedding an agitated Armstrong came to him wanting to call the whole thing off. Some Melbourne friend had let him know that he wasn't the first man in Nellie's life. Feez talked him round, aware of what a social disgrace it would be for the girl if Armstrong jilted her at the last minute. What was to turn into a disastrous marriage went ahead more or less through his professional persuasiveness.

The newly married couple, the bridesmaid and the father of the bride then packed their trunks and shipped out together, heading south for Melbourne. During three months' honeymoon at Doonside, Charlie was off on business most of the time and Nellie resumed lessons with Cecchi. By April the Armstrongs were on the way north again. If David Mitchell had wanted Nellie near him and had consequently tried to settle Charlie into suitable work in Melbourne, he had failed. Armstrong seems to have left, briskly and alone, for Mackay. Nellie followed only to find that when the ship docked in Sydney there was a week to fill in before the connection to Mackay berthed. On 12 April 1883 she wrote to Cecchi from Mrs Bagge's at Rushcutter's Bay, Sydney:

I might have stayed a week or two longer in dear old Melbourne, for when I arrived here I found that my husband could not meet me for some time, and I have been quite miserable here, just thinking how many lessons I have missed.

I start for Port Mackay and I expect to arrive there on Monday week, so I shall soon be in the tropical regions again. I met a German gentleman here that you know. His name is Mr Ampt. He thought a great deal of my singing, as indeed everyone does, for they all call me the 'Australian Nightingale'. I have had four musical parties given me since I have been in Sydney. I was asked to sing at a Liedertafel concert, but of course I had no time; I have promised to sing for them next time I am here.

I hear Mrs Kemmis leaves Melbourne today [possibly the wife of Canon Kemmis, of the fashionable St Mark's, Darling Point]. She has not had much time for singing lessons; she is a regular grand. I am staying with Mrs Bagge, who has been most kind and nice to me. The Italian opera season commences here tonight. I hope they will have more success here than they had in Melbourne. I intend going to hear them on Monday night. I wish Alice Rees [wife of pianist-composer Max Vogrich, later both of New York] were going to sing, for I would like to hear her so much.[7]

In Mackay Nellie's ordeal began. It was the wet season, very humid and hot. The house at Marion was not ready when they arrived and they had to take makeshift quarters until the little oven of a building with its galvanised-iron roof and poor ventilation, was ready. It rained solidly for six weeks.

By then Nellie was over the morning sickness period of pregnancy and beginning to swell. At a time when a little parental cossetting would not have gone amiss in the form of money for a servant or an aunt or sister to help her through her confinement, she was left alone in what she was rapidly coming to regard as a hostile environment. On 11 May 1883 she wrote to Cecchi, hungry for news of home:

> I am once more in Mackay and 2,000 miles away from dear Melbourne and all my dear friends there. I arrived here last Tuesday week after a most dreadful trip, for I was seasick the whole way. It has been raining in torrents ever since I have been here. I have just come in nicely for the end of the wet season, and it is really most dreary and miserable. We are not in our own house yet. We do not expect to get into it for six weeks. The Montague–Turner company are expected to arrive here in a week or two. I sincerely hope they will do well, for they have been unfortunate lately.
>
> How is my sister getting along with her singing? I hope she goes regularly and practises well. Will you kindly send me up the low copy of a song called *Ehren on the Rhine?*
>
> I hope to be able to get down to Melbourne early next year, so it will not be so long before I see you all again. I shall now stop, as there is no news to tell you, except that my voice is in very good order, and I practise every day. My husband wishes to be kindly remembered to you.[8]

Over forty years later she wrote:

> A strange period ensued – a period which to most modern girls would sound something of a nightmare. My husband lived in the heart of the Bush, as the manager of a sugar plantation ... We had a little house with a galvanised iron roof, desolate and lonely, with no other company than that of the birds and especially of the reptiles.[9]

In short order her piano grew mildew, her clothes turned damp, the furniture fell apart and there was an invasion of ticks and spiders 'to say nothing of snakes, which had a habit of appearing underneath one's bed at the most inopportune moments'. Charlie had a horror of snakes. A green variety hung from the trees on Nellie's path to the river. Leeches at the water's edge clung painfully when she tried to go swimming. There was supposed to be a giant crocodile in residence a few yards upstream. When Charlie took her sailing with a friend off Port Mackay a squall capsized the little yacht. Young Mrs Armstrong almost drowned, but by then her life was so dull, she said, that any excitement was a welcome relief.

It could not have been quite as dull as Nellie made out. Soon after she arrived back in Mackay, she was acting as hostess and guide to the touring opera troupe run by Annis Montague and Charles Turner. She and Charlie drove them out to look at the sugar plantations. The Montague–Turner Grand Opera Company was known to Nellie in Melbourne. In 1882 and 1883 it appeared there in *The Bohemian Girl, Lucia, Maritana, Il Trovatore, Faust, The Rose of Castille, Mignon, Lucrezia Borgia, The Lily of Killarney, Martha* and *Norma*. In Lyster's day Montague and Turner had played leads in his lavish 1880 International Exhibition production of Genée's comic opera *The Royal Middy or the Chess Tournament*. They were still touring with their troupe ten years later.

Whatever the connection may have been, the reminder of Melbourne and of her life there made Nellie even more restless. She tried to distract herself with new friendships. Mr and Mrs Charlie Rawson are the only ones she names in her memoirs, but there were others – the sugar miller John Ewen Davidson and his wife Amy among them. Amy acted as Nellie's accompanist at private parties and the few concerts the town offered, but in spite of a later Mackay legend, Nellie did not sing Tosti's 'Goodbye' there for the first of thousands of times; that particular *morceau* was not composed until 1885, a year after she left Queensland.

On 4 July she wrote to Cecchi:

The Montague–Turner Company are up here just now. I called on Mrs Turner and like her very much indeed. This afternoon Mr Armstrong and I are going to take them for a drive and show them some of the sugar plantations. They are having very good houses, I am happy to say, and I think will do very good business. They charge six shillings for dress-circle seats, and it is well filled every night, so they ought to be satisfied.

I have quite recovered from my small illness, and feel very jolly and happy. My voice, I think, is better than ever, although I am afraid I do not practise as I ought.

Mackay is very gay just now. Any amount of dances and balls. I am glad to hear Annie is improving in her singing; it would please me so much if I thought she would ever be able to sing well. You never told me how Alice Rees got on in opera. There was a gentleman here from Melbourne the other day, and he said she was simply perfection – lost all her stiffness, and was altogether charming. Is that true? I hope we shall be able to get to Melbourne in January. Of course I shall go on with my singing when we come . . .[10]

As her pregnancy neared its end she began to feel that the only

MELBA'S PATRONS – THE LIEDERTAFELS OF MELBOURNE

In Melba's day Melbourne boasted two central city-based choral groups called Liedertafels. Every capital city and many country towns had similar all-male singing clubs but the biggest and best belonged to Melbourne. The 1880s were their heyday, though they were by no means the only choral societies. The Melbourne Philharmonic Society and its suburban and country imitators – with their annual subscription series of oratorios – were formidable rivals, but they could not compete with the social life that surrounded the musical activities of the Liedertafels.

The older club, the Melbourne Liedertafel, was founded in 1868 as a German-speaking club but it re-formed in 1879 with English as the official language of the meetings. The Metropolitan Liedertafel began life in 1870, was granted the patent Royal in 1871 and fused with the Melbourne Liedertafel in 1905 to become the present Royal Victorian Liedertafel. But though the formal foundation dates only go back to 1868 and 1879 German nationalist clubs, with music as an adjunct, had existed in Melbourne from the 1840s, and included the German Quartette founded by Julius Buddee in 1849, which was the probable origin of the Liedertafel Harmonia, and a German Glee Club, as well as several gymnastic clubs which also used music in their activities. Membership grew rapidly with the influx of Germans who emigrated in the wake of the revolutions of

way out for her was to get Charlie's consent to let her go south. The bright letters to Cecchi change tone. In the finish she was turning to him, desperate for help. If she could establish herself as a professional singer there was a hope that she could raise the money needed to bail not only herself but Charlie out of a situation she could no longer tolerate. Shortly after George's birth she wrote again:

I suppose you have heard from my sister that we have arrived safely in Mackay, after a rather tedious journey. My baby is very well, and stood the journey better than I expected. It is very hot up here, and I feel it very much.

Now to business. My husband is quite agreeable for me to adopt *music* as a profession. I do not mind telling you that times are very bad here, and we are as *poor* as it is possible for anyone to be. We have both come to the conclusion that it is no use letting my voice go to waste up here, for the pianos here are all so bad it is impossible to sing in tune to them. Not only that, the heat is so intense that I feel my voice is getting weaker every day. So you will understand that I am anxious to leave Queensland as soon as possible. *I must make some money*. Could you not form a small company and let us go touring through the Colonies, for of course I should like to study for the opera, but would have to be earning money at the same time. My husband will accompany me, and my baby will be quite big enough to leave in Melbourne with my sisters. Madame Emblad would join us, I am sure. Do you think we could make money? I shall wait anxiously for a letter from you, for I am very unhappy, here where there is no music, no nothing. We spoke of August next year; let it be much earlier than that if you can possibly arrange it, for I believe I shall be *dead* by then. I shall be advised by what you say in this. I hope what I say will be agreeable to you. I hope you will answer this letter as soon as you receive it, so as to let me know what ought to be done. Remember, whenever you are ready for me I can come at once, for there is nothing to detain me now that Mr Armstrong is agreeable. I want you to keep this quite a secret from my sisters and friends. Do not mention it to anyone until everything is settled.[11]

This letter, according to Hetherington, was sent from Charlie Rawson's sugar plantation at Mirani on the Pioneer River some miles upstream from the Armstrongs' house, but the letter as published by Waters gives only 'The Hollow, c/o Mrs Rawson, Port Mackay, N. Queensland'. The bickering between Nellie and Kangaroo Charlie had culminated in a series of genuine fights. The young wife, in self-defence, took her baby and shifted to more friendly territory, but she was already in flight. Cecchi sent a telegram telling her he would see to her interests and to come home at once. She took ship for Melbourne via Brisbane and Sydney on 19 January, taking George, but leaving

Charlie behind. Melba wrote tersely in her memoirs, 'I returned to my father's house. I never went back'.

Cecchi was as good as his word. On Saturday 17 May 1884 Mrs Armstrong made her professional début as a concert artist in the Melbourne Town Hall singing 'Ah! fors'è lui' from *La Traviata* (Verdi) in the first half and filling in for a missing soprano in a quartet in the second half. Mary Ellen Christian appeared on the same programme, a benefit for composer–conductor Gottlieb Elsasser given by the Metropolitan Liedertafel.

Four of Melba's teachers were associated as artists with the Metropolitan Liedertafel – Charbonnet, Lupton, Vogt and Christian. Vogt and Lupton were members – it was a society for men only and a very fashionable one at that. With its backing Melba had every chance of success; without it the pickings would have been very thin.

But in spite of Nellie's later claims for him, the Herr Elsasser of her first professional concert was never the conductor of either the Melbourne or Metropolitan Liedertafel. He was a member of both groups but was engaged only occasionally as a guest conductor. His official appointment as a conductor was with the Melbourne Philharmonic Society, and then only for a year in 1861. He was 'a typical German musician of the old school – genial, pleasant and scholarly', but not exactly another Mendelssohn.

John Lemmone's name also appears on the Elsasser programme, but not, as was to be the case for so many years afterwards, as her obbligatist. Between the time the concert was advertised and the night itself Mrs Cutter, one of the vocal soloists, was taken ill. A Miss Vanderpeer replaced her, singing 'Robert, a cher adore' with Lemmone as her flautist. Like Melba and Miss Vanderpeer, he was making his début. In 1946 Lemmone recalled that on 17 May 1884:

> Nellie Melba and I made our debut together in Melbourne. I remember she sang *The Bird That Came in Spring* by Julius Benedict, a song now known as *The Wren*, and I played two of my own compositions – *The Aria* and *Fantasy*. It was the beginning of a long association and a life-long friendship that lasted until the final curtain on 23 February 1931, when I was at the great Diva's bedside at St Vincent's Hospital, Sydney, when she died.[12]

In 1941, in a broadcast from 2FC Sydney, he said: 'We made our début together and our farewell to the public from the same platform – which in itself is, I think, unique'. Lemmone was presumed by many to be Melba's lover. In the memoirs she refers to him simply as her manager.

On the day of the concert Mrs Armstrong woke to find she had a sore throat, a psychosomatic symptom that was to reappear before performances for the rest of her life. By five she had already completed the long Victorian ritual of dressing and sat in her 'simple gown of

1848; in the gold-rush of the 1850s the migration of the Adelaide community across country fed membership, though there was a trickle of direct migrants as well.

In the 1870s and 1880s English, Irish and Scottish migration fuelled the societies, notably with ex-members of the English choral clubs. The political origins of the Liedertafels were quickly lost but they remained all-male gatherings assembled to drink, smoke and sing in an informal atmosphere. They became a useful way of making business contacts and, in the case of the Melbourne Liedertafel, an ally of the Masonic movement. David Mitchell's name appears in the minutes as a nominee proposed by the conductor Julius Siede on 10 July 1883.

Sir Charles Hallé was quoted during his 1890 Australian tour as saying of the Sydney and Melbourne Liedertafels he visited, 'they have taken me quite by surprise. Their singing is excellent; and, given the same number of voices, I don't think they can be beaten anywhere'.

Hamilton Clarke, the stiff-necked Englishman who succeeded Sir Frederick Cowen as conductor of what became the Victorian Orchestra after the 1888 Exhibition Orchestra ceased to operate under that title, and conductor of the Melbourne Liedertafel in 1891, spoke of: 'These choirs, composed of male voices, number[ing] each from a hundred to a hundred and twenty performing members' of whom he believed 'there can be no doubt whatever that no great and valuable musical undertaking could be brought to an established success in this extraordinary city unless the prevailing and quite overbearing amateur element should be more or less subdued, still it is only common justice to say, that for what it is worth this wealth of private and unprofessional attainment is both remarkable and to be admired. And there is no point to which attention can be directed which shines out with such thrilling lustre as the quality of voice prevailing in this colony'.[1]

Henry Keily, critic of the *Argus*, took a different view: 'These societies have started from small beginnings, and in the course of years have grown to such large proportions as to be in a fair – (or evil) – way to monopolise the attention paid by the well-to-do classes to music outside the social circle ... their studies are directed to the performance of the spirited part-songs written for the male quartet, and mostly of the German school ... The Liedertafel, or songtable, is, as its name implies, a society for the sociable practice among men of music, of a not too severe character. Sympathetic musical feeling and community of taste bring about most delightful meetings for practice; and periodical concerts, given when a programme has been sufficiently well rehearsed, are open to the families and friends of singers, who are quite numerous enough to crowd the Town Hall to excess ... they perform always before a well dressed, polite and very friendly audience, and the audience in turn are delighted with the doings of their fathers, brothers and friends

golden satin' beside her father, trying to keep calm. Her major worr was that she was about to make a fool of herself in front of her famil and friends and the fashionable society of her home town. At a quarte to eight she put on her cloak, stepped, trembling, into her father' buggy with him and set off for the town hall. She spoke of the nigh afterwards as 'two hours of wonderful triumph', though her perform ance was only one of a large number of items. But who could ask fo more than to be described as 'like one picked out of ten thousand' as the *Australasian* did? She had this highly flavoured critique reprinte in the memoirs, but there were others, not quite so high-sounding Still, she wrote:

It was this concert that made me realise that there must b something in my voice. You must remember that I had never hear a great singer in my life, that I had never been to an opera, that had no possible means of comparing my own voice with the voice of singers who had already made their reputation. But still, I fel the people of Melbourne could not be after all so very differer from the people of Europe, and if I could have this success befor them, surely I could at least command a hearing in other place: And from now onwards to go to England was my ruling ambition.

Was it true that she had heard no great singer, been to no oper heard no one with whom to compare herself? The environment i which she lived could certainly have supplied them. She was not th sort of young woman to ignore opportunities because of her father anyone or anything else. She had money and contacts. Why, then, di she insist Melbourne was something other than it was? Part of th reason seems to lie in the Cecchi story which now comes into focus

Cecchi is usually credited with getting the Elsasser engagement fo Nellie, but considering her father's association with both Liedertafe it is possible David Mitchell had a hand in the matter. Certainly h had the influence to block her if he chose, but Melba says she sat b him the day of her début and travelled with him in his buggy to th concert. Whichever way it went the Liedertafel exposure had its effec George Musgrove, the young entrepreneur who was to form part c the triumvirate of J. C. Williamson's in later years – he was, inciden tally, Lyster's nephew and actress Nellie Stewart's de facto – offere her £20 a week for a season with the Johann Kruse concert party. (I 1902 Melba returned to give nine recitals for Musgrove for £21 000 She wrote to Cecchi from the Metropolitan Hotel in Sydney on 7 Jul 1885 during this tour:

Although I have had great success as regards public taste, m critique in the *Sydney Morning Herald*, although not bad, was no good. Mrs Fisher writes for that paper, and as she is a great frien of Alice Rees, I can understand why she is afraid to praise me to much. In one of the evening papers, it said that I was the best singer that had ever visited Sydney. We have all been run down, even Kruse, in two papers yesterday, and we all wish we were back again in Melbourne. I cannot think what the people want here. I feel too disgusted to write any more. I shall send you the papers. With love to Miss Dawson, Believe me, Your affect. pupil, Nellie Armstrong.[14]

A month later she was writing from Doonside to a friend:

I would give ten years of my life to be able to get to Europe to have a trial, I feel certain I would have some success for I am so anxious to get on, I work like a trojan now, so what would I do if I had a proper trial. I do not want to boast, dear, but since I have been singing with Kruse I have made a great name for myself. All the papers say that I am the *first concert* singer in Australia and the *Argus* the other day likened me to *De [sic] Murska*. Kruse thought a great deal of me, he says he never met anyone more musical than I am. He says I ought to have been Home four years ago. The more I think of it the more desperate I get, I am twenty three years old now and I feel every day I stay here is another day wasted, there is no one that can teach me anything here, Cecchi is very good for Italian music, but after that he is no good – But enough about myself, all I can say is that I would give my head to get Home, I cannot understand my Father being so pig-headed, especially as I have had such great success in Melbourne. Oh God if I only had a few hundred pounds, but I suppose it is not to be . . . I am suffering from a sore throat and hoarseness, it is very unfortunate as I have a good many engagements. I get twenty five guineas for singing at the next Philharmonic. I sing at Ballarat on Thursday and Friday.[15]

Johann Kruse, the celebrity of the tour, was born in Melbourne in 1859. His German family lived in Richmond and Nellie attended musical gatherings there, though by 1875 Johann had left for Berlin and studies under Joachim at the Hochschule für Musik. Kruse was to head that institution, become part of the world-famous Joachim Quartet, leader of the Bremen Philharmonic Orchestra and a noted touring virtuoso. As an old friend of the family Kruse was acceptable as far as Mitchell was concerned and neither then nor later in Melbourne did he put insuperable barriers in the way of Nellie's music. Agnes Murphy seems to think he was glad to see his eldest daughter married because it would put a stop to her ambitions as a singer, yet when she was not touring she lived at Doonside with her infant son, both of them cared for by her family. As Charlie was still struggling to make a go of it up north, Nellie's bills must have been met by her father since she was not earning enough to do more than pay for

on the platform; a social meeting on a grand scale has been successfully brought about', a meeting, Keily added, only too content with the 'musical bon-bons' offered by the choirs.

But, he went on, 'the Liedertafels do not rely upon their own unassisted attractions – they engage from time to time the leading musical celebrities who may be present in the city and generally retain the services of one or two of the most accomplished of local players and singers, and an occasional orchestra is also engaged. But it is questionable if these societies, in stepping out of the circle of their own social practice of the art to become promoters of grand concert undertakings, are doing good either to art or artists.

Between them they give about two concerts per month, of very pretty if not of the grandest music, and with subscribers numbering over a thousand persons and representing probably five thousand persons, (in a city, I might add of around a million), the time of a vast audience is pretty well taken up with Liedertafelism. No local artist, however, who has been resident here for any time, has a chance of giving a concert on his own account with any chance of profit to himself. The profit and the fame remain with the two societies who are content with their limited culture of the art, and their subscribers are content with their extremely cheap and sociable entertainments, while there remains a wider and nobler sphere of music into which they have apparently no ambition to enter. We do not say the Liedertafels should be blamed for cultivating the success which is to be found in their pleasant paths, but we are compelled to take notice, in contrasting their position with that of the chief society in Melbourne [the Philharmonic] of the obvious want of musical taste displayed by the public in which all three exist. In the cultivation of the art of part singing amongst men the Liedertafels have undeniably done a great amount of good, and this is the extent of their function'.[2]

Keily's disapproval made no impact. The balls and picnics, moonlight bay trips and interstate excursions gave the Liedertafels a social attractiveness for marriageable girls and their mothers. In their safe activities where a man's reputation was easily checked and where chaperonage could be achieved unobtrusively, the marriage market could function alongside the stock market tipstering of the smoke-night rehearsals. Music took second place. Melba would have had no chance of launching herself as a professional singer in Melbourne without the aid of the societies and the audiences brought in by something other than music. Pietro Cecchi's and her father's influence with the Liedertafels was crucial.

1. *Argus*, Melbourne, 17 March 1894. Reprinted from a lecture entitled 'Two years music in Australia – a personal narrative by one of the survivors' delivered by Hamilton Clarke before the Royal College of Organists, London.
2. *Victorian Review*, 1 March 1880.

her stage clothes, and she had to borrow from a friend to pay for Cecchi's lessons.

During those months there were a number of concert engagements though hardly enough to do more than give Nellie a taste of professional life. On 21 July she appeared with the Metropolitan Liedertafel at the Melbourne Town Hall in the aftermath of *Oedipus at Colonus*. A month later she sang 'Regnava nel silenzio' from *Lucia* at a soirée at Allan's to advertise a new piano. Four days after that she took part in a benefit at the Athenaeum with Kruse for a pupil of Max Vogrich 13-year-old Ernest Hutcheson, who went on to a distinguished career as a pianist in America and to become president of the Juilliard School in 1937.

In August Nellie was ill with fever, fretting to get to Sydney for concerts in September with Kowalski, and anxious not to waste time. She wrote to Arthur Hilliger, a friend in Sydney: 'if I could only practise mentally, get a *mass* and study it in bed; but he [the doctor] won't let me . . . I sing every Sunday in the Roman Catholic Church'.[16] Ten days later she was making plans for a Tasmanian tour with M. Valmency, but felt it might not pay. She wrote again to Hilliger, asking if one or two concerts in Sydney would pay any better 'We are going quite on our own account so I do not wish to risk more than is necessary'. By then she was feeling better and though still weak was going to a dance at the Assembly as 'they are always very enjoyable, the floor being the best in Melbourne.'[17]

Both of these letters seem to have been meant to be passed to Mr Moore. The first warned Hilliger to tell her sister, should she ask that he had not written. The second asked him to visit her and should he bring Mr Moore she would not mind. On 21 September 1885 she wrote again:

I have not heard anything of my husband for such a long time. am rather glad for when he writes it is only to insult me . . . I am awfully unhappy. If I could see you I would tell you my trouble but I dare not put it in black and white.[18]

Nellie sang 'I heard a voice' and 'The pilgrim' at the Metropolitan Liedertafel's farewell to Julius Buddee on 13 December. George Coppin gave the Sorrento concert on 21 January 1885 in aid of the church, as has been discussed previously. On 13 April Mrs Armstrong sang 'The shadow song' from *Dinorah* (Meyerbeer) and 'When the heart is young' by Dudley Buck for a Melbourne Liedertafel concert The Metropolitan Liedertafel upgraded her to female soloist for its 4 August Kruse concert when she sang 'Lo, the orb of day' (Schubert) with their choir, *Beatrice di Tenda* (Bellini) and the duet 'Sulla tomba from *Lucia* with Armes Beaumont. On 17 October she sang with the Melbourne Liedertafel at Ernest Hutcheson's farewell and two days later performed with the Met. an orchestral version of 'The erl king

Schubert), 'Lo, the orb of day', 'Qui la voce' from *I Puritani* (Bellini) and, with Beaumont, the duet, 'O that we two were Maying' by Alice May Smith. At Christmas she sang in the annual *Messiah* of the Sydney Philharmonic Society. During that year there were engagements not only in Sydney but in Victoria's provincial centres, including Ballarat, Bendigo and Hamilton.

None of it was particularly lucrative. Melba was paid a mere £10 to Armes Beaumont's £21 for the same concert in 1885, but Beaumont was a long-time favourite with audiences and Melba a mere beginner. Even the receipts of the last concert tour of January 1886, when she was better known, failed to cover the rent of the halls.

In the last weeks of 1885 Nellie accepted the paid position of soprano soloist at St Francis' Roman Catholic Church in Lonsdale Street, Melbourne. Its director, the composer–conductor Alfred Plumpton, and his wife, the church organist Madame Carlotta Tasca, had connections with the Liedertafels, Plumpton as a composer and both as performers, which may account for their knowing of Nellie's need for a position at the time.

Annie once wrote to Arthur Hilliger that her sister was frowned at by a senior male choir member for talking to her neighbour during mass. The man lent over and asked in a fierce whisper whether she would like to be reprimanded from the altar. 'Very much', Nellie replied coolly.[19]

The fact that the daughter of a strict Presbyterian household should be allowed to sing in a Catholic church seems odd, but St Francis' was noted for its high standard of performance and fees that attracted even visiting celebrities. It was not unusual to find the soloists and chorus of the Lyster opera company supplementing the St Francis choir for a Mozart or Haydn mass, with an orchestra culled from the theatre pits and directed by one of the Liedertafel conductors. It would have been unreasonable of David Mitchell to try to curtail Nellie's involvement with St Francis' since religion was hardly at issue and the contacts she made there were necessary to her career. What he did was to escort her in the family carriage to St Francis' on Sundays and set her down in full view of the crowd with Margaret Littis, one of several Catholic servants from Doonside, saying loudly, 'Shame on you Nellie! You ought to be singing at your own kirk'. He'd then order Dan the coachman to drive the rest of the family on to Scots Church. When Nellie did sing at Scots many years later and finally had the courage to ask her silent father what he thought of her performance as he was carving the Sunday roast, Mitchell went on wielding the knife for a time, then said, 'I dinna like your hat'.

The first of all Melba's farewells was arranged by Alfred Plumpton and Madame Tasca at St Francis' Church. On 22 February 1886 Mrs Armstrong appeared there as soloist in Haydn's *Imperial Mass*, ending the concert with the Gounod 'Ave Maria', which she was also to sing

MRS ARMSTRONG'S CONCERTS

This list, though incomplete, gives some indication of the type of engagements the young Melba was able to command.

21 July 1884 After *Oedipus at Colonus* at the 93rd concert of the Metropolitan Liedertafel, Melbourne Town Hall, she sang 'Variations de concert sur le carneval de Venice' (Benedict) with orchestral accompaniment.

21 August 1884 Concert at Allan's music warehouse, Collins Street, to advertise a new piano. She sang 'Regnava nel silenzio'.

25 August 1884 Athenaeum Hall, Collins Street. Benefit concert for child prodigy pianist, Ernest Hutcheson. She sang an extract from *Mireille* (Gounod) and a duet with Armes Beaumont.

13 December 1884 Farewell concert for Julius Buddee given by the Metropolitan Liedertafel. She sang 'I heard a voice' and 'The pilgrim'.

In late 1884 Associate artist with violinist Johann Kruse for his Australian tour.

21 January 1885 Coppin's Sorrento concert to raise money for railings for the graveyard. She sang 'Sing, sweet bird' and 'The angel at the window', with Mr Cadden.

13 April 1885 The Melbourne Liedertafel production of Brahm's *Rinaldo* was followed by solos. She sang 'The shadow song' (*Dinorah*) by Meyerbeer and 'When the heart is young', by Dudley Buck.

4 August 1885 101st concert

of the Metropolitan Liedertafel at the Melbourne Town Hall. She sang 'Lo, the orb of day' by Schubert, with the Liedertafel choir; Recit. and cantata from Bellini's *Beatrice di Tenda*; and the duet from *Lucia di Lammermoor*, 'Sulla tomba', with the ex-Lyster star, Armes Beaumont. Kruse appeared in the same programme.

17 October 1885 Farewell concert for Ernest Hutcheson by the Metropolitan Liedertafel. She sang a solo and a duet with Armes Beaumont.

19 October 1885 Metropolitan Liedertafel concert in the thirteenth season, Melbourne Town Hall. She sang 'The Erl King' by Schubert, with orchestral accompaniment; 'Lo the orb of day' with orchestra; 'Qui la voce' – a solo and cavatina from *I Puritani* (Bellini); and a duet with Armes Beaumont, 'O that we two were maying', by Alice May Smith.

Christmas 1885 She was in Sydney and sang with the Philharmonic Society in their annual *Messiah* under Henry Kowalski. She also appeared with the Sydney Liedertafel. In the last weeks of 1885 she was engaged as soprano soloist at St Francis' Church, Lonsdale Street, Melbourne. She resigned the following year.

22 January 1886 After a short concert tour she sang at the Sydney Masonic Hall for the first farewell of her career. Governor and Lady Carrington were present.

on her death-bed. She had been with the choir only four months bu the members presented her with the elaborately worded illuminate address usually reserved for long-term associates. It may have been, a Agnes Murphy assumes, a mark of personal good-will towards Nelli herself, but it could also have been a gesture to David Mitchell wh had just been appointed Victorian Commissioner to the Indian an Colonial Exhibition in London and was taking Nellie with him. Th church was well aware that Mitchell's influence was considerable an that in honouring his daughter they might win the father's suppor at a time when sectarianism was rampant.

The Mitchell family must have had some months' notice of thei father's new post since Annie wrote on 31 July 1885 that she ha decided not to accept David Mitchell's invitation to go with him: 'h is too Scotty and would be very strict, so after due consideration think I prefer my liberty at home'.[20] However, she was to change he mind.

The London appointment was a great honour as far as Mitchell wa concerned. For Nellie it was a godsend. Whether or not her fathe had been given the position or had acquired it by influence partly fo her benefit, the fact remains that he not only offered Nellie the chanc to go with him but also granted her a year's tuition with the teache of her choice into the bargain. She was told to write to Charli Mitchell had summoned him to travel with his wife as a husban should. Two-year-old George was to join them and so were his aunt Annie and Belle. A respectable, united family front was necessary fo a man in the public eye and Mitchell intended that the Armstrong would do as they were told for his and the colony's cause, particularl since he was paying the bill.

At the end of the financially unsuccessful January tour Nellie gav a second farewell in Sydney, this time with a small profit. Back i Melbourne she sang at the town hall on 25 February under Charle Tait's management and again on 6 March, five days before she wa due to sail for England with her family, in first class, on the RM *Bengal*. The last of her four farewells was poorly attended, in spite c the presence of the Governor of Victoria and Lady Loch, and nette Nellie a mere £67 4s 8d.

At this point Pietro Cecchi is said to have stepped in and threatene to seize Nellie's luggage if she did not find 80 gns as payment for th twenty months of intermittent singing lessons he had given her sinc her return from Mackay. The memoirs give six weeks before sailin as the time of Cecchi's demand. Murphy sets it as after th 6 March concert, when he 'applied for immediate payment at ful rates'. The memoirs record that Nellie 'heard rumours that Signo Cecchi was threatening to seize [her] trunks if [she] did not pay hi bill before [she] left'. The early Murphy version of the story then say that Nellie was afraid that word of Cecchi's action would reach he amily, in particular her father, and revive his opposition to her career. he implies that Mitchell had no knowledge of the lessons, let alone hat she was in debt because she had wrongly believed herself capable f meeting costs from her concert fees. The 1908 version adds that Nellie, in 'a state of great mental embarrassment' raised the money rom a friend, paid Cecchi and thereafter 'refused to link his name vith one word of blame'.

By 1925 Melba had changed her tune dramatically.

> I went to see him and I shall never forget his small, dark, swarthy figure and the bright avaricious eyes that examined me coldly as he remarked; 'You owe me eighty guineas. That money must be paid before you leave'.[21]

The money from her farewell, she claimed, had gone to pay bills and hat she dared not go to her father because he had just paid her passage money:

> Had it not been for a dear old uncle and a friend, I might never have gone to England, but at last I raised the eighty guineas and stuffing them into my purse, I went to Cecchi and threw the money, purse and all on his table.[22]

he then told him that if she was ever a success she would never mention his name as having been her teacher. Cecchi shrugged his houlders and pocketed the money. Melba told the world that 'all hat he taught me I had to unlearn when I was privileged to study under Madame Mathilde Marchesi'. This was manifestly untrue. What vas more she states categorically that Cecchi died of apoplexy, 'talking of me and my ingratitude'.

Why Melba chose to bend the truth in quite this way is hard to understand, but bend it she did. For one thing she wrote to Cecchi in friendly terms four months after this final encounter, chattily telling him of her London concerts, her illnesses, accidents, and family, and asking for news of her friends. There is no sign of a break between teacher and pupil. As for Cecchi dying of apoplexy because of her refusal to acknowledge him, his obituary says he died of long-term heart disease on 4 March 1897. He had been in court as a witness that day and had shown signs of prolonged distress. As he sat down to dinner he began to talk not of Nellie, but of the lawsuit, then suddenly stopped, drew a deep sigh and died.

Why did Melba blacken his name after his death in this way? Possibly because Cecchi's bill almost brought down her father's wrath at a crucial moment in her life and nearly put a stop to her English adventure. She may have thought later that it was a premeditated act, but her teacher, like her father, may have honestly believed her concert engagements had paid well enough for her to find 80 gns. After all, according to her biographer Hetherington (and he has it from Waters),

22 February 1886 Second farewell concert for Mrs Armstrong. Given in St Francis' Church. Alfred Plumpton arranged it and his wife, Madame Tasca, played the organ. Haydn's *Imperial Mass* was given with Mrs Armstrong, Mr Williams, Mr Ramsden and Mr Daniels. Her last item was Gounod's 'Ave Maria'.

23 February 1886 Third farewell concert for Mrs Armstrong arranged by C. Tait in the Melbourne Town Hall.

she had earned £750 in her first year as a professional singer, money earmarked for overseas travel and study before Mitchell's offer materialised. Cecchi would have known the fees usually offered, and the number of times she had appeared. He would also have known that her rich father was supporting her, not her invisible husband. Who knows what debts Cecchi had himself? The usual excuse given for her accusations is that Melba was forced to repudiate all her earlier teachers in return for Marchesi launching her career. But there is an oddly false ring to the story. It was out of character for Melba to act spitefully towards anyone connected with her Australian youth. Was there a subplot; had rumours hardened into facts over the years; was it an unstated slander against her that she was speaking out against?

In the memoirs Melba records a second incident that came close to wrecking her hopes of a European career. Again it has an air of something left unsaid, a record being set straight. Apparently, she went to the theatre one night, shortly before the sailing date, with a male friend and his sister. When they came out their carriage was delayed. To while away the necessary time they went to a café nearby to eat oysters. The French husband of a friend saw her and told his wife she had been there with a man late at night. The friend told David Mitchell who was so shocked that he coldly informed Nellie he had made up his mind not to take her to London with him. He would not tell her why but urged her to examine her conscience. Some days later the Frenchman confessed to his wife that he had lied. The wife went to Nellie who urged her to go to Mitchell and tell him the story was a malicious invention. Mitchell heard the friend out, but all he said to Nellie was, 'I'm sorry, lassie'.

On 11 March 1886 the Mitchell contingent sailed from Port Melbourne. There were 3000 people on the wharf to farewell the 142 passengers. Mitchell was an important man and was ushered on board in proper style, his entourage trailing obediently in his wake. Nellie was simply a fashionably dressed eldest daughter seeing to his needs. That she was a singer of some small reputation made her a social asset which enhanced her father's position. That Nellie Armstrong was anything more, only she suspected.

Top left: Isabella Mitchell (née Dow), Melba's mother. *(Performing Arts Museum, Melbourne)*

Top centre: David Mitchell, Melba's father. *(La Trobe Library, Melbourne)*

Above: Nellie Mitchell. *(La Trobe Library)*

Far left: Nellie Mitchell. *(Performing Arts Museum)*

Left: Nellie Mitchell, 1880. *(The Age)*

Melba's birthplace, Doonside in Richmond, Melbourne. Except for a short period after her marriage, this was her home until she left for England in 1886. *(The Age)*

Madame Mary Ellen Christian was Melba's singing teacher at PLC. *(Performing Arts Museum)*

Pietro Cecchi, the Lyster Opera Company tenor who became Melba's second teacher in Melbourne. *(The Age)*

Charles Armstrong, Melba's husband. *(The Age)*

Melba studied singing in Paris with Mathilda Marchesi, then at the height of her successful teaching career. *(La Trobe Library)*

Melba with her son, George Armstrong. *(La Trobe Library)*

Lady de Grey, the London society hostess who acted as Melba's patron, and her husband, the Earl, who was an influential member of the Covent Garden board. *(La Trobe Library)*

Chapter 4

MARCHESI'S MELBA

'Grey skies ... dirty wharves' and a 'million chimney pots' greeted Mrs Armstrong on 1 May 1886 as she came up by steam train from Tilbury to London. 'How can I sing in such gloom?' she thought, looking out of her hansom cab at the sombre crowds. But the tulips were gold and crimson in Hyde Park and Melba's heart lifted as she came to the house her father had rented at 89 Sloane Street.

Three days later she heard Emma Albani sing 'Home sweet home' at the opening ceremony for the Indian and Colonial Exhibition. She told her father at the end of it, '*That's* worth coming from Melbourne to hear'.

She wrote nine days later to the German tenor, Rudolph Himmer, who had sung at her farewell concert in Melbourne:

Last Saturday I heard Albani whom I think has a truly magnificent voice Nillson who is very disappointing she sang *I dreamt I dwelt* just like a schoolgirl, Edward Lloyd Santley and Madame Patey, of course they all have beautiful voices and a pianist Vladimir de Pachmann who is a true artist, I never heard such playing in my life, it was simply beautiful. I have also seen Mrs Langtry, Violet Cameron and Sarah Bernhardt they are all beautiful women. Next week I am going to hear Rubenstein and Patti so I expect a great treat.

The opening of the Exhibition was a very grand ceremony; it was opened by the Queen and all the members of the Royal family were there. Albani sang *Home Sweet Home* beautifully, it went straight to my heart. I sang to Wilhelm Ganz his own song *Sing Sweet Bird* the other day and he was so pleased with my singing that he has arranged for me to make my first appearance in London on 1st June at the Princes Hall Piccadilly at a concert Emil Bach is getting up. I sing *Ah fors'è lui* with orchestral accompaniment Ganz conducting. It is rather a big undertaking but in for a penny in for a pound. I also sing on the second of June at which Ganz is conductor so he must think a good deal of me to bring me before a London audience so soon for he tells me that sometimes really good artists sometimes have to wait a year before they can even be heard. Do not tell anyone I am going to sing until you

hear whether I have success or not but I knew you would be
interested in my doings so that is why I tell you. I am going over
to Marchesi in about two months when I shall tell you faithfully
all she says of my voice. There is no doubt about it London is a
wonderful city and I hope I may be able to settle here eventually.
We are quite close to Hyde Park where all the youth and beauty
either ride or drive every day, what beautiful women one does see
such complexions. When we arrived in England the first news we
heard was that Mr Armstrong's mother Lady Armstrong was very
ill indeed so we had to hurry down to Sussex to see her fortunately
she is a little better now, but still very weak. I like all his connections
and relations very much, they are all very nice. We had lots of fun
on the *Bengal*, there were *many* musical people on board so we had
six concerts four balls and one fancy dress tableaux dramatic enter
tainments sports cricket etc. Have you ever been to Colombo? Are
not the curries there delicious and I have dreamt about them ever
since. And now I shall stop as I have many more letters to write
Hoping to hear from you soon. Give my love to Madame Pinchof
[Elise Wiedermann] and Mary Hume if you see her. With kindest
regards. Believe me, yours very *affectionately,* Nellie Armstrong.[1]

To Cecchi she wrote on 27 June:

It is already two months since we arrived in London. I have
commenced writing to you two or three times, but I have never
been able to finish them. I am charmed with London, and think it
is a beautiful city. I have heard all the great singers, viz: Patti, who
is divine, Albani, Nilsson (*I do not like*), Madame Patey, Trebelli
Mr Lloyd, Santley, Foli. I have been to hear Sims Reeves four times
but he has never sung once. Is it not disappointing? He was to
have sung at Patti's concert on Wednesday, but of course did not
appear, so Nicolini sang instead. I have also heard Rubinstein
Halle, and de Pachmann. The latter is a wonderful pianist. Sarasate
and Carrodus are wonderful violinists. It is really wonderful the
beautiful music one can hear in London.

You will be pleased to hear that I have already sung twice in
London, and had the greatest success, splendid critiques, and every
one predicts a great future for me. Herr Ganz, the man who wrote
Sing, Sweet Bird, has taken a wonderful fancy to me, and declares
my voice is more like Patti's than any voice he has ever heard. Vert
the concert agent, is working hard for me, so I am sure to get on
Antoinette Sterling [the American-born contralto] was singing at
one concert where I sang, and she was in a fearful rage because I
got a bigger reception than she did. The first concert I sang at I
had the biggest orchestra in London to sing to. I sang *Ah! fors'e
lui* and *Sing Sweet Bird*. Ganz conducted both.[2]

For a time David Mitchell was ill in Scotland but Nellie makes no mention of being with him. She told Cecchi that she had been ill herself for several days when she was knocked senseless leaping out of a moving train – she had caught the wrong one by mistake. But that was not all: 'I have also had bad toothache, so I have been in the wars altogether'. As for her husband, Charlie had signed on with the Prince of Wales Leinster Regiment (Royal Canadians) on 29 May and was commissioned lieutenant in the 3rd battalion. He resigned sixteen months later. Meantime his regiment was stationed in Ireland during July that year and Nellie was to join him, staying with her brother-in-law. However, she intended returning to be with her mother-in-law, Lady Armstrong, at Seconfield House, Littlehampton, in Sussex for a time.

The memoirs ignore all this. There Melba says that within forty-eight hours she was making use of her letters of introduction, determined to win some kind of recognition that would persuade her father, once and for all, to let her take up a singing career. Mitchell had already agreed to a year's tuition but Melba seemed to think he was still hesitating about backing her if the verdict of her concerts in London was unfavourable.

She records that when Charlie landed he was met with the news of his mother's illness and that they set off for Sussex at once. As it turned out, her mother-in-law took an instant liking to Charlie's Australian wife. So did the rest of the Armstrong family. Nellie remained on good terms with all of them even during the years of her open liaison with the Duc d'Orléans and the scandalous divorce action Charlie brought against her.

Forty-eight hours may have been an exaggeration, but certainly Nellie began her tedious and disappointing trek from one contact to another almost at once. She drew a complete blank with the first name on her list, Hubert Parry, then known as a choral conductor. He was already a member of the staff of the three-year-old Royal College of Music and choragus at Oxford but not yet knighted nor the distinguished director of the former and Professor of Music at the latter that he was to become. That season he was so bombarded with requests for interviews by so many aspiring musicians that in self-defence he refused to hear any of them.

Arthur Sullivan, who partnered W. S. Gilbert in the writing of comic operas and was later knighted, at least agreed to see her. She arrived at his flat in Victoria Street to find him at the piano playing 'a little tinkling tune in the treble with the soft pedal on'. She held her breath: 'Here at last was a composer, a man who created'. But Sullivan was plainly bored with the ritual of auditioning yet another unknown. He asked what she wanted to sing for him. Was there anything special he would like, she countered. No, he sighed, it was all the same to him. So she sang 'Ah! fors'è lui' from *La Traviata*.

At the end he was silent for a moment, then said: 'Yes, Mrs Armstrong. That is all right'. Melba's face fell. Then he told her that there were no openings in the Savoy opera company at the time but that if she liked to come back again after she had studied for another year he might find her a small part in *The Mikado*. And he turned back to the keyboard to play 'one of the little tunes which all London was later to be whistling', a putdown Melba waited nearly forty years to deliver.

The Brinsmead family of piano manufacturers was also on her list and though she gives an account of a meeting with one of them she fails to name which – the father, John, or one of the two sons, Thomas or Edgar. She was asked to play one of the new pianos. When she sang, Brinsmead compared the timbre of her voice to the timbre of his pianos. No doubt he meant it as a compliment, but Melba left more depressed than ever.

The following day she went to see opera composer–conductor Alberto Randegger, then at the peak of his career as a highly influential singing teacher at the Royal Academy of Music and the Royal College. She found this ' "beau ideal" of a singing teacher, beautifully dressed, very chic, very glad to see one, very complimentary'. He was charming, she was charmed. Her hopes rose: 'But no. He regretted with an exquisite shrug of his shoulders that he had no time to teach me', though perhaps, later . . .

By the time she got to Wilhelm Ganz, Jenny Lind's sometime accompanist and conductor of his own orchestral society concerts, her spirits were sinking. Without expecting anything she sent in her introduction from opera composer Alfred Cellier, an associate of the Savoy Theatre and assistant to Sullivan. Ganz agreed to an audition, heard her in rising excitement and offered to arrange a concert for her, presumably not at his expense.

On 1 June 1886 Mrs Armstrong made her first public appearance in London in Prince's Hall, Piccadilly, as she wrote to Himmer, at an Emil Bach concert. A summer fog failed to lift all day. The audience was minimal and applauded gloved and no one of any influence came. It was a bitter disappointment and hardly the success she boasted of to Cecchi. If Vert was acting as her agent he certainly did not seem to know his job.

But Ganz had not finished with her. She was engaged to sing at a dinner of the Royal General Theatrical Fund in the Freemasons' Hall. Then he arranged a meeting with Carl Rosa, the opera impresario, who pencilled the appointment time on his shirt cuff and forgot about it. Melba paced Ganz's Harley Street house for hours but Rosa failed to show up. Typically, she refused to make a second appointment.

Plainly London was not ready for Melba, but by then she had made other plans. Soon after her arrival she had used the introduction given to her by Madame Elise Wiedermann in Melbourne to approach

Madame Marchesi in Paris. Marchesi wrote back telling her to be ready to audition there in two months' time.

Without the Wiedermann introduction Nellie would have had little hope of seeing a teacher who was in such demand, but as an ex-pupil of Marchesi's who had become a prima donna with the Vienna Opera, Wiedermann could command her teacher's attention. David Mitchell, who knew Wiedermann as the wife of the Austrian Consul, Carl Pinschof, could not have taken her recommendation lightly. And so, with her father's reluctant blessing and his money safely deposited in her bank account, Nellie took George and set off for Paris.

Melba says that she had forgotten the Wiedermann letter until after the Ganz concert when she went to her father with it to plead for a last chance to prove herself. If Marchesi did not like her she would go home to Australia 'and try to be happy'. Mitchell is supposed to have patted her on the head and said, 'Very well. But this must be the last time'.

By her own evidence, the Himmer letter, Nellie had planned from the beginning to go to Marchesi. Certainly her father would have needed time to arrange money transfers and accommodation for her. And her poverty that first year in Paris was not as dire as she later made out. Someone had to be found to care for her lively toddler, for one thing. Either way there was money to meet the need, though probably not Charlie's, since he and Nellie spent his short visits to Paris quarrelling over George's Frenchification.

Early on the morning after she arrived in Paris, Melba went to Marchesi's house in the Rue Jouffroy. She was oblivious to crowds, shops, famous sights alike: she felt an urgency to act that she could not repress. She handed over the Wiedermann letter of introduction – according to the memoirs – and 'a resplendent footman' kept her on the doorstep for ten minutes then returned to tell her Madame could not receive her at the moment but would see her at 10 a.m. the next day. Melba bit her lip to prevent tears of frustration and hurried back to her rooms to prepare.

Next day at 9.40 a.m. she was shown into an ornate gilded drawing-room where she sat waiting, trembling with excitement, hands demurely clasped in her lap, watching the other pupils as they began to arrive. The inner door opened. Nellie was alarmed by the rigid uprightness of the severe-looking woman who stood framed in it. She was small, with grey hair pulled into a plain knot at the crown, her clothes somewhat less than elegant. Then she smiled 'and her whole face, with its long upper lip and its intelligent eyes, seemed to be transformed. I felt at last that I had found a friend', Melba wrote.

One by one other pupils stood, sang to Madame's accompaniment, sat down again. Nellie's hopes rose. She knew at once she could best any of them. Her turn came and she was told to stand on the student's minute platform, where she could be clearly seen by Madame, who looked tired and bored. Asked what she would sing Nellie chose 'Ah! fors' è lui', the aria from *La Traviata* she had sung for Sullivan. He, too, had been bored. Madame began the accompaniment. Nellie watched her intent profile. Suddenly Marchesi stopped, spun round on the piano stool and exclaimed, 'Why do you screech your top notes? Can't you sing them *piano*?' The novice on the platform was struck dumb. Madame struck a note – top B. Melba sang it, softly. 'Higher!' Marchesi struck C. Melba sang it, watching the old lady. There was an air of tension, a new look to her eye. Melba sang on to top E, pianissimo. Without a word Marchesi rushed out of the room, leaving Melba still standing by the piano, trembling. The rest of the students began to talk among themselves as if nothing unusual had happened. Nellie thought she had been dismissed as unbearable. Then Madame returned. The test was repeated. At the end Marchesi took her by the arm and led her out of earshot of the others, sat her on a sofa and said, 'If you are serious, and if you can study with me for one year, I will make something *extraordinary* of you.'[3] Months later her teacher told Nellie that when she left the room she had gone to her husband upstairs, snatched the paper he was reading out of his hands and cried, 'Salvatore, j'ai enfin une étoile!'. (The usual translation for this is: 'Salvatore, I have found a star!'. John Cargher, in his notes to the re-issue of the memoirs, suggests that more properly this should read: 'Salvatore, at last I have a star!'.)

Marchesi had not produced a great voice since soprano Ilma di Murska, who had retired six years before, and though many other great singers had passed through her studio most had been initially trained elsewhere, as Nellie had. Apart from Melba her four most famous pupils were Emma Calvé (1858–1942), Ilma di Murska (1836–89), Emma Eames (1865–1952), and Mary Garden (1877–1967). According to Cargher, Calvé was recommended by Marchesi to Milan's La Scala but was booed off its stage. Her career only blossomed after she changed teachers. Eames claimed in her memoirs that the Marchesi method was so bad that her voice deteriorated to the point where she was forced into premature retirement. Garden had only three weeks with Madame and refused to go back to her in spite of pressure from her patrons.

With so much hostility coming from such influential ex-students, Marchesi may have indeed needed to find another great protégé, but this time one who would never speak against her. Marchesi was 65 years old. She could hardly be blamed for wanting to see her good name upheld after her death and to be anxious to find a means to that end very soon.

Marchesi had the power to make Nellie's name and the young singer knew it. She was desperate for independence and for success. Marchesi offered her the means to an end and though Nellie must have known that Madame dominated her students to such an extent

THE VOICE

Mathilde Marchesi: 'Nellie Melba, mon amie chérie et l'éléve de mes rêves avant qu'elle fût mon idéal de l'artiste'.

Emma Calvé: 'A Nellie Melba. Comme une ange vous chantez avec votre voix divine'.

Joseph Joachim: 'As an exemplar of unaffected purity in vocal art, Melba surpasses all other great singers of our time'.

that many turned against her and that her methods of promoting her favourites were ruthless, if not unethical, she was prepared to trade her loyalty in return for being launched by the most famous singing teacher in the profession.

The list of great names Marchesi claimed as products of her method include, in the di Murska era and later, Caroline Dory, Antoinette Fricci and Gabrielle Krauss; in Vienna, Anna d'Angeri, Etelka Gerster, Katherina Klafsky, Emma Nevada, Rosa Papier, Caroline Salla, Caroline Smeroschi, Amalia Stahl and Wilhelmina Tremelli; and in Paris, Suzanne Adams, Emma Calvé, Emma Eames, Mary Garden, Melba, Sybil Sanderson and her own daughter, Blanche Marchesi. A formidable list.

Melba was right to put her trust in this woman. The evidence was there that she could carry out the promises she gave to her students. The price Melba paid was betrayal of Cecchi. Is it possible that Cecchi understood the bargain that was struck? Could Melba have warned him of what she would be obliged to say? After all, Cecchi knew the world Nellie was entering and he no doubt knew the gossip about her new teacher. He must have known, too, that the sometime German mezzo-soprano, Mathilde Marchesi (née Graumann), was herself a pupil of Ronconi, Nicolai and Garcia the younger, an impeccable teaching lineage. The posts she had held, singing at the Vienna Conservatory (1854–61 and 1868–78), and at Cologne (1865–67), gave her invaluable contacts in professionally influential places, while her carefully fostered entrée into high society provided her with access to the patronage necessary to employ the protégés from her private practice. How could a young Australian hopeful say no to any demand such a teacher could make? If Marchesi turned on her, Nellie would have found engagements almost impossible to obtain.

For a month after that first audition Marchesi taught her newest pupil apart from the rest of her students, a privilege not usually given to beginners at the studio. At the end of the month her teacher pronounced Mrs Armstrong a fit candidate for her opera class. Melba admitted:

it came about that I never had to study the exercises of the wearisome routine which it is necessary for most singers to study, as this clever woman saw that I did not require them.[4]

Cargher believes a year in this opera class was the minimum needed to grasp a basic repertoire. There was no place in it for voice training as such; that was supposed to precede it. If Melba was beyond it where did she acquire the training she displayed? Cecchi? Perhaps, but certainly not Marchesi alone.

For Nellie the tourist's Paris was forbidden. She worked on her studies eight hours a day, using her voice very little and her intelligence a great deal to master theory (emphasising techniques), history and

MARCHESI'S INFLUENCE ON THE VOICE OF HER STAR

'There is no doubt that Melba owed a great deal to Marchesi in methods of vocal polish and knowledge of phrasing; after all, she had already sung in London to absolutely no effect, and Hermann Klein testifies that Mrs Armstrong was not all that far "along the road to vocal sophistication". In London she heard Patti, Nilsson and Albani and realised that she had a lot to learn, but she also knew even then that her voice had an individual quality. . . .

'Marchesi pupils on records all have a good, clean, fresh tone and perfectly steady emission. However, some fail to demonstrate strong high notes and are taxed by the tessitura of Puccini operas, whereas their shrill Italian contemporaries show more stamina, rarely enchanting the ear, but at least not tiring. Certain uneasy moments in the records of Suzanne Adams, Miriam Licette, Frances Alda and Blanche Marchesi are noticeably absent from the records of Melba, who is triumphantly at home in the testing, high-lying stretches of Bohème, and whose high notes are rock-solid and radiantly beautiful. These Italianate qualities I believe to be Melba's inheritance from the teaching of Pietro Cecchi, reinforced by the all-important lessons in breath support that Jean de Reszke imparted to her.'[1]

Melba once claimed that 'The real study actually begins after one has come before the public, and it is to subsequent development that the most earnest attention should be paid . . . Learn from the very beginning to depend upon yourself. Your teacher can do no more than point out the way. You must walk along it yourself. Use your own ears and do not depend on anyone else's opinion'.

1. Michael Aspinall in the notes to EMI *Nellie Melba: The London Recordings 1904–1926*, RLS 719 (ed. Paul Holmes).

language. She came to Paris proficient in French in the schoolgirl manner, but though there were claims that she spoke it like a Parisian within a year and had mastered Italian within two years her accent continued to worry Marchesi for some time beyond her début. As it turned out the Wagnerian roles she coveted were beyond her capacity so she failed to acquire more than a working knowledge of German.

Marchesi once told Katharine Susannah Prichard: 'Nellie Melba, she was not stupid. Do you understand. It was her brain that made Melba's voice'. But if Mrs Armstrong had hoped her teacher would exempt her from the kind of rigorous control she forced on other students she was soon disillusioned. Quite early in the piece during training for the Mad Scene from *Lucia di Lammermoor*, Madame, though not for the first time, rounded on Nellie in front of the class and poured out a stream of corrections so severely phrased that the young woman left the room in tears, vowing she would never return to it or to Marchesi. Madame uncharacteristically went after her, threw her arms around her, exasperatedly exclaiming, 'Nellie, Nellie! you know I love you. If I bother you, it is because I know you will be great. Come back and sing as I wish'. Nellie, also uncharacteristically, obeyed. It was a near disaster for both of them but Marchesi had taken her pupil's measure and thereafter drove her at a more sensible pace.

At first Marchesi was unaware that Nellie considered herself to be living in poverty with 'nothing but the bare necessities of life to keep [her] going'. She was under the impression that David Mitchell had provided an allowance to keep his daughter and his grandson in modest decency until Nellie was able to support both of them. There was no reason to suppose that should she run short her father would not send more, or that her husband was incapable of adding something from the Sussex estate. But Nellie could be as close with money as her father at times and her fear of having to go through the humiliating ritual of begging for money from him kept her purse closed. She walked instead of taking the bus, went second class on trains, and spent nothing on her own clothes. She claimed she had only one winter dress, a thick blue and white striped serge, which she wore day after day. The message would have been hard to ignore; Nellie's sense of theatre tended to be over dramatic at the best of times. Marchesi eventually got tired of this game of conspicuous self-sacrifice for the sake of art and told Mrs Armstrong never to wear the offending dress again. When Nellie said she had no money for another, Madame snapped: 'Nonsense. You have a rich father. Go and order another dress and put it down to him'. But the blue and white stripes kept on appearing at the opera classes. Marchesi offered to let Mrs Armstrong's name be added to her bills at Worth's but still the serge dress remained, a silent reminder that Melba was no dilettante and that soon, very soon, she intended to claim her independence.

Marchesi dominated Melba in the studio, but outside it the younger woman stoutly resisted all attempts at interference. She was told singers did not wash their hair, they cleaned it with tonic and a fine tooth comb, otherwise they caught cold. But Melba washed, caught colds and risked a scolding in class. When she was invited to stay with Madame and her husband she discovered the bath was used by the Marquis as a boot cupboard. She found a tub for her room in which to wash herself, to Marchesi's protests. She was told riding was bad for the vocal chords, but this time she listened to the advice – anyway, in Paris it was too expensive a pastime.

In the Marchesi household the Marquis was under Madame's thumb, and, to a lesser extent, so were her three daughters, one of whom she taught singing. Blanche, like both her parents, was to become a distinguished singer and teacher, but though she always expressed respect for Melba as a singer she came to hate her for absorbing her mother's professional interest. Nellie and Blanche, who was two years younger, were thrown together in Marchesi's studio as subordinates, Blanche as the assistant, Melba as the focus of attention. Blanche was merely a good Wagnerian soprano, not a great one. Madame refused to permit a first professional concert until 1896. Blanche finally broke into the operatic field four years later, worked a few seasons with the Moody-Manners Opera Company and appeared at Covent Garden only in 1902, as Elizabeth in *Tannhäuser*. By then Melba was a legend.

By the end of 1886 Marchesi had allowed Mrs Armstrong to test herself in unpaid recitals at a few society parties and at minor concerts in the Rue Jouffroy drawing-room. Then, in December, Marchesi decided to exhibit her there before an invited matinée audience, which would include the critics. A stage was installed in the dining-room and electric light – then a novelty – was connected. For the first time Nellie Armstrong appeared under the name of Madame Melba, a change Marchesi thought necessary since the public was still convinced, even then, that only the Italians could produce great operatic voices. Nellie chose the name as a tribute to her home town. In her wake, to her annoyance, other Australian singers did the same – Austral, Stralia (versions of Australia); Benda (Bendigo); and Ballara (Ballarat) among them. There was, however, an extra factor involved in Melba's case. Since she was born on the anniversary of the proclamation of Melbourne as a town by Governor Bourke, her birthday and that of her birthplace coincided. She took it as a good omen.

Among Marchesi's guests for the December recital were Lapissida and Dupont, two directors of the Brussels opera house, the Théâtre de la Monnaie. Parts of Bemberg's *Elaine* were performed and Ambroise Thomas was present to hear Melba as Ophelia in the Mad Scene from his opera *Hamlet*, a part he was later to coach her in.

Figaro, *La Liberté* and *Le Sport* produced kind words about her the next day. But in a newspaper interview after her début at the Paris

MELBA THE DÉBUTANTE

On 24 August 1887 Melba wrote to Arthur Hilliger from Paris: '. . . everyone tells me my voice is pure gold and that I vocalise perfectly. Marchesi tells me she has never had such a pupil. My studies are nearly over now for I make my début in the beginning of October at the Théâtre de la Monnaie, Brussels in *Rigoletto*, I sing five operas in Italian and five in French and so you will see how hard I have worked, it is frightfully hard work; the next letter you write will you kindly address it to the Théâtre de la Monnaie. If you care to put another notice in the paper to that effect I shall be pleased . . . I could never live in Australia now, I do not know *why* the Australians are making such a fuss of Amy Sherwin, I don't think she has ever sung on the Continent and in London she only sings at second and third rate concerts. I have never heard her but I believe she sings out of tune very often . . . the doctor was very afraid for me about two months ago, but I think the worst has passed now. [She had just had three weeks' seaside holiday to recover from 'nervous headaches'.] Madame Elmblad [the pianist she suggested to Cecchi in letters from Mackay as her associate on tour] quarrelled with her husband in Prague, took a pistol out of her pocket and "blew her brains out". She was very young and pretty . . . Always be careful what you say in your letters because as you know my husband is frightfully jealous and I have not a very easy time with him – also impress this on Jack Moore please.'[1]

(Amy Sherwin (1855–1935) was called the Tasmanian Nightingale. A Strakosch singer in American companies, she was a concert singer of considerable reputation in America and in England. Her fame at the time of Melba's début was such that back home the critics were sceptical of the prophecies that one day Melba would outshine her.)

1. MS 1123, Mitchell Library, Sydney.

Opera on 8 May 1889, Melba said the recital which Lapissida and Dupont of the Monnaie attended was a charity concert at the Salle Erard, given under Gounod's patronage. Why she later told Murphy it was at the recital in the Marchesi house is a mystery, but at that recital there *was* one man present who was to take a hand in her immediate destiny.

Enter Maurice Strakosch, Adelina Patti's impresario, her brother-in-law and, according to Melba, the bad fairy at her own professional christening, her operatic début at the Monnaie. Strakosch had heard Melba one morning as he was enjoying a cigar with the Marquis in Madame's smoking-room. Melba was rehearsing 'Caro nome' upstairs. Strakosch forgot the cigar and the Marquis Castrone de la Rajata and listened in silence. He then said, 'I want that voice. I do not know whether she is short or tall, pretty or plain. I want her'.

At the special matinée recital Strakosch offered Melba his services. She needed money and signed a contract binding her to appear under his sole management at 1000 francs a month, an amount which was to double each year. In the memoirs Melba says Strakosch interrupted her lesson on the day he came to visit the Marquis, made her sing a few songs more, then took her aside and, without haggling, the deal was made on the spot, presumably in Marchesi's presence. Murphy puts the contract date forward to the time of the matinée. Melba was both Murphy's and Nichol's informant. Why, then, did she alter the story? Was it mere forgetfulness? Possibly not.

Murphy says the two Monnaie directors were at the recital, but Melba makes no mention of it. She claims they arrived one morning to audition the students one by one. After they had heard several they asked to hear the 'young Australian, who they say has a beautiful voice'. Marchesi had to tell them she was already signed up with Strakosch and could not audition for them without his consent. Melba decided they should hear her and sang, oddly enough, the Mad Scene from *Hamlet*, the same work Murphy says she sang before the same gentlemen some time earlier.

A hasty conference between the directors and Marchesi was held in the next room behind closed doors. Madame returned, all smiles, to tell Melba the Monnaie wanted to engage her at 3000 francs a month. 'But Madame, my contract with Monsieur Strakosch?' Marchesi waved it aside. 'That is nothing at all', she said. Wasn't she a friend of Strakosch? She would arrange it, he would understand. But unfortunately he did not. Or perhaps an offer from Madame to buy back the contract was not high enough to match the expectations he held for the voice he had coveted from the moment he first heard it.

Melba says there was a dreadful scene when Strakosch, purple in the face from five flights of stairs, invaded her rooms. For fifteen minutes he raged against Marchesi's double dealing before he 'blew himself out of the room'.

Under instruction, Melba acted as if nothing had happened and went to live in Brussels in 'a little house off the Avenue Louise' with George. Her father and at least one of her sisters had returned to Australia at the end of the 1886 season. In Brussels, and possibly in Paris, Melba's other sister, Annie, lived with her.

With remarkable timing Strakosch managed to have a legal order restraining Nellie from performing at the Monnaie served on her as she stepped out of her carriage at the stage door on the day of her first rehearsal. She went at once to the manager, Lapissida, who threatened and entreated, and sent telegrams right and left. Nothing worked, Strakosch was implacable. Rehearsals went on, and an anxious Melba tried to keep her mind on the job but day after day passed without any news of progress. She was sleepless and overwrought.

Then, on the Monday morning before the première, Lapissida came bounding up the stairs shouting to her: 'Strakosch est mort! Il est mort hier au soir, dans un cirque. Et je vous attends au théâtre à onze heures!' ('Strakosch is dead! He died last night at the circus. And I await you at the theatre at eleven o'clock!').

Strakosch died in Paris on 9 October 1887, to be precise, four days before Melba's début, an event which would not have occurred then or there had he not been so obliging. What Strakosch intended to do with Melba is a matter of conjecture. Since he managed opera groups in America with his brother Max he may have had plans to use her on that circuit.

It was raining on the morning of 13 October 1887 when Marchesi came to Melba early in the day 'fluttering and excited', trailing a solemn Salvatore wearing a huge boutonnière. Nellie paced the room thinking of the sun on gum trees. As the autumn day faded so did her spirits. Outside the Théâtre de la Monnaie a banner proclaimed in crimson letters 'Madame Melba'. Nellie felt 'a chill, almost of horror' as she looked at it on her way in. She sat stonily in front of the dressing-room mirror and allowed herself to be made-up, but refused to wear the blonde wig that was usually worn by Gilda and only later realised she had created a precedent out of pure nerves. On top of everything else there had been only three stage rehearsals.

After only nine months with Marchesi, Melba made her début in *Rigoletto* that night under the baton of Dupont and with Engel as the Duke of Mantua and Seguin in the title role. She wrote:

from the first note which I had to sing in the Second Act, there was a hush that hardly seemed human, a hush in which I heard my voice floating out into the distance as though it were the voice of someone other than myself. Nor shall I forget the thunders of applause which broke in after the end of the Second Act. I said to myself: 'This cannot be for me. They are clapping and cheering for somebody else.'[5]

THE MARCHESIS AND MELBA

In 1923 Blanche Marchesi, Mathilde's daughter, wrote: 'In this rather small house [Rue Jouffroy] my parents managed to give operatic performances with a stage, and here Melba sang Bemberg's *Elaine*, staged for the first time . . .

'Melba remained a student for many years after her career had started, and she rarely sang anything that she had not first worked at with my mother in Paris, even when she was at the height of her success . . .

'The most striking voice and finest quality of light soprano that my mother ever brought out was Melba . . . I must only mention that she was an ardent student, and also stepped straight from the classroom to the stage of the Brussels Royal Opera, keeping for my mother lifelong feelings of deepest respect and loving gratitude. Melba's friendship for my mother was one of her great joys; it made up for the forgetful hearts of many others. Needless to say the success of Melba created much jealousy among the students of the school, for unfortunately pupils often believe that success depends entirely on the teacher's managing powers, and that some are pushed and some neglected.

'Her voice always struck me as exclusively pure and quite specially religious. Often when hearing her on the stage I was struck with the contrast between the slight operatic music she sang and the value and beauty of her tones and her style of singing it. To explain my impression, she often appears to me as would a wonderful diamond set in brass.'

Blanche claimed that Melba influenced the management to exclude several singers from Covent Garden – the tenor Bonci, soprano Frances Alda, the baritone Ancona, and the soprano Parkina, also a Marchesi pupil. There was, she said, '. . . a certain reign of terror at Covent Garden, and that some powerful invisible spirits were hard at work to eliminate artists who might have easily settled in the heart of the public'.[1]

The Baron Podhragy Collection holds letters to Mathilde Marchesi from Melba; most of Melba's letters are undated and are in English with occasional lapses into French. This one was possibly sent from Brussels at the time of Melba's début there, since there is mention of going to an exhibition with Madame Gevaert. She writes: 'I am awfully afraid (entre nous) my husband is going to arrive very soon, I am most awfully uneasy as you know how afraid I am of him when he has one of his mad fits on'.

From Hôtel de l'Europe, Aix les Bains, where Melba was holidaying with Lady de Grey and Lady Gosford, possibly just after the d'Orléans scandal, she wrote: 'I suppose you have heard that my procès is finished. I am so happy. I shall tell you all about it when I see you, love Nellie'.

Post-dated 9 December 1895: Melba had had a great success in *Manon* with de Reszke and hoped to repeat it in Paris. She told Marchesi she was writing to Massenet and added, 'I am crazy about the part'.

At the end of the third act (though Murphy claims it was at the second performance) Melba records in the memoirs that she was summoned to the royal box to make her curtsy to the wife of King Leopold, which was as much a mark of the singer's duty to the Queen as a mark of the Queen's approval of a new singer and therefore of the judgement of the management. Still, the Queen had noticed her and Melba's career was launched. She told Robert Sherard in 1889:

I have special reasons for gratitude to the Queen of the Belgians, who was so very kind to me during my season in Brussels. She rarely missed one of my evenings until the death of Prince Rudolph, and whenever she came to the Opera she used to send for me to come to the royal box and talk with her. She is very good and clever about music.[6]

At the supper party after Melba's début performance Marchesi took the wind out of her sails by berating her loudly for forgetting two notes in the Quartette. Melba apologised in front of the guests, aware of Marchesi's need to be still seen as her mentor. Dupont leant across the table, shook his finger at Madame and said 'Don't bother her – she has had the most marvellous success of any singer in the world. Why don't you think only of that?'

The most marvellous success? Not quite. For one thing Melba sang the role of Gilda in Italian, not French, which was the official language of the Monnaie stage, a concession made by the management to her Australian accent, which was felt to be such a drawback in French that at the risk of offending the patrons it was thought wiser to let her sing it as in the original.

Next day the reviews were ecstatic. *La Chronique* called her 'the sensation of the day', her voice warm, velvety, superb, her stage presence distinguished and her trill mathematically exact. The *Indépendence belge* found her a 'revelation', the technique perfect, the voice unique, and complimented her on her intelligent acting. (Melba's acting was to come in for a lot of adverse criticism over the years but at the beginning the verdict was occasionally in her favour. One wonders which music critics were also devotees of the theatre and judged Melba's acting accordingly, and which never stepped over into the rival art form long enough to know the difference between the art of the actor and the dramatics singers were required to perform as an adjunct to their own art.) The *Étoile belge* dubbed her 'the young Antipodean with "the profile of an Empress" in the same category with Patti and Nilsson'. *Le Ménestral*, less overcome, noted that she sang with remarkable style and expression. *La Réforme* spoke of the purity of her voice, and *La Patriote* predicted accurately that within two years she would be known as La Melba.

Three weeks later, on 9 November 1887, Melba appeared for the first time as Violetta in *La Traviata* (Verdi), a part that taxed her acting skills to the limit. She remembered

the stage requirements were exceptionally exacting for a novice, and one of the newspapers in the next day's notice dwelt on my evident inexperience. This was the first paper I saw, and, although all the others were full of generous encouragement, I could not forget the one snub. I cried almost incessantly for a whole week at the recollection of this particular criticism. Then I took heart again, and threw myself into my studies with fresh vigour [and] resolved to work until I got to the top.[7]

Étoile belge's critic wrote:

Those who were at the last representation of *Rigoletto* were able to note the great progress made by Madame Melba in the scenic interpretation of the part of Gilda, and how this exquisite singer was asserting herself as a comedian [*sic*]. Even they will have been surprised at the really remarkable manner in which she has composed the part of the *Traviata* (The Frail One) . . . we could scarcely expect that she would have so completely understood and rendered its touching features, and the heart-rending conclusion. Not only is it Violetta the perfect Italian singer, but it is also Dumas' Marguerite Gautier. Her person and deportment are perfectly adapted to the portrait as depicted by Dumas.[8]

Violetta was followed by Lucia in Donizetti's *Lucia di Lammermoor*. The house was packed. The Mad Scene 'created an extraordinary impression', but it was an impression Melba was not able to repeat when she made her London début in the role a few months later.

Her fourth Monnaie opera, opening on 8 March 1888, was Léo Delibes' *Lakmé*. Delibes himself was consulted in advance. Should Melba risk singing in her accented French this time? Delibes, exhausted by the rehearsals, told the directors: 'Qu'elle chante *Lakmé* en français, en italien, en allemand, en anglais, ou en chinois, cela m'est égal, mais qu'elle la chante'. At that point Melba decided something had to be done about her French. She engaged a Mademoiselle Tordeus to teach her and began a crash course, working six hours a day.

In April, under the personal guidance of Ambroise Thomas, she gave her first performance of his *Hamlet*, the last of her Monnaie season. Seventeen years after the Brussels première Thomas called Melba 'the Ophélie of my dreams'.

In Marchesi's Paris house Melba had met only men her teacher thought necessary for her career – Charles Gounod, Ambroise Thomas, Léo Delibes and Jules Massenet among them. Marchesi continued to put her in touch with the influential in Brussels, this time with François-Auguste Gevaert, the Belgian musicologist, teacher, opera composer and one-time music director of the Paris Opera, then director of the Brussels Conservatory. Gevaert took a fancy to Nellie's son and

Post-dated 26 June 1896: 'I have had perhaps the biggest triumph of my career as Rosina [*Barber of Seville*] I am so happy about it and it is such a load off my mind. It appears that I have made quite a creation of it and that no Rosina has ever acted the part as I did – I sang *Una voce poco fa!* in *fa* as I formed it too low in *mi*. I also put in all the *staccato* notes, so you can see I was in excellent voice – I sang *Sevillana* (Massenet) at the lesson scene and the public were most enthusiastic. Then I sat down and played my own accompaniment to Tosti's *Mattinata* and the public went so crazy, I had to repeat *Sevillana* – at the end I sang Arditi's waltz and I believe I had twenty calls at the end of the opera'.

Undated: 'The other night Eames sang *Faust* and there were not 500 people in a hall which holds 9000, and it was a good lesson to her and she is in her own country here. HA! HA! God *is punishing her!!* [Possibly Melba believed Eames had spoken against Marchesi.]

From London: 'The article does not surprise me and the man who wrote it sent it you – This man *hates me* and always writes infamous articles about me because I won't subscribe to his papers – Tear up such rubbish dear Madame – Your pupil Parkina is having a great success and you can well be proud of her'.

From 30 Great Cumberland Place, London: 'Parkina is doing splendidly and having great success which makes me happy – She has such a charming nature, it is quite touching'. [Written at the time when George was studying for Oxford and the King of Spain had invited her to sing in Madrid.]

From Florence, possibly early 1898 but dated only 9 September: 'I arrived here last night after having studied *La vie Bohème* with Puccini at Lucca for nearly a week. It was *most interesting* and he is very enthusiastic at my interpretation. He sent many kind messages to you'.

From St Paul on 23 November, possibly 1905: 'I wonder if you realise how far I am away from you – out in the far west of America, I never felt so lonely in all my life, so I shall have a nice chat with my dear little Mother'.

From Hôtel de l'Hermitage and marked 'strictly private and confidential': 'Beloved Madame, I am writing to ask you about something which will interest you as much as it does me and also to ask your advice: but I must ask you to keep my secret and only tell Salvatore *no one else*. Gailhard came to see me yesterday and asked me to create Isolde in Paris next winter – Jean de Reszke will sing Tristan – of course it would be very interesting but do you think it would be injurious to my lovely voice. Of course it would be easier for me in French than in German – I told him I would consider it and let him know – Please write me what you think you ought as of course I will be guided entirely by your judgement. I wish you were here. The performance of *Bohème* will be splendid, it is beautifully mounted and my tenor Caruso is excellent'.[2]

often had him and his mother to lunch with him on Sundays. There was an introduction, too, to Emile Wauters, a fashionable portrait painter. Melba and her sister Annie, who lived with her for a time in Brussels, both had their portraits painted by the young Wauters. The portraits are now in the Charlier Museum, Brussels, fine examples of the society portraits of the day, romantic visions in luminous pastels, all innocent ripeness and rose complexions.

In his biography of 1932, Percy Colson wrote:

Melba's undesirable husband was still very much alive, and having, of course, heard that she was likely to become a star in the musical firmament, he came to Europe, and suddenly made his appearance in Brussels one afternoon when she was taking tea with a well-known painter, Monsieur Wauters. There was a terrible scene; the little boy was frightened out of his life, and poor Melba was at her wits end to know what to do, as Armstrong told her he would make life impossible for her. He even threatened to make a disturbance at the opera that evening when she was singing. She was naturally afraid to appear, and very sensibly went to the directors of the opera and explained the situation to them, begging them to interfere in some way. They fortunately succeeded in persuading Armstrong to leave Brussels. It is not known how and where he lived after this until the final denouement, but Melba and her child were henceforth able to live unmolested. She probably made him an allowance on the condition that he left her in peace.[9]

This is the sort of gossip Melba learned to ignore in silence but this particular story was told very shortly after her death by a man who claimed a long friendship with her. Was there any truth in it? Had she told this embroidered version of a fight with Charlie one afternoon when he disturbed her (and probably her sister) with the handsome Wauters? Had he heard rumours of Gevaert's affection for his son – and perhaps its extension to his wife? Possibly. But Charles Armstrong was not bought off. Whatever it was that set off the explosion that day in Brussels marked the end of negotiations between them. For a while there was a truce, but when the press began to link her name with that of the Duc d'Orléans some time later Charlie decided to take action. If his ambition was to put a stop to his wife's career, social as well as professional, he came close to achieving it, but that he was paid off seems improbable since the Armstrong family was not exactly impoverished.

1. Blanche Marchesi, *A Singer's Pilgrimage*, pp 48–57.
2. Baron Podhragy Collection, MS 2647, NLA.

Chapter 5

A RIGHT ROYAL AFFAIR

With the Brussels success behind her Melba could have chosen to appear in any number of European houses. Instead she accepted the reluctant invitation of Augustus Harris, the manager of Covent Garden, who had been pressured into making the offer to include her in his first season by Lady de Grey, a patron he could not afford to ignore. She had heard Melba at the Monnaie and was determined to have her in England. As the wife of Earl de Grey (later the Marquess of Ripon), a wealthy member of Covent Garden's committee of management, and as a leader of a social set that included the Princess of Wales, Harris had to listen to her. But Gladys de Grey was more than that. She was a devotee of opera, an aficionado, an expert. But her passion for opera was tempered by shrewd musical judgement. In Melba's case the judgement went in her favour.

The theatre built on the site of a convent's kitchen garden in Westminster had had a stormy history since 1732 when it was opened by John Rich. As Harry Trevor put it in the jubilee souvenir programme of 1908:

> When not engaged in ruinous competition from without, its multifarious impresarios, directors and managers have sought relaxation in quarrelling with their companies, evading the attentions of the bailiff man, and indulging in fisticuffs with their audiences. Naturally the pursuit of such pleasantries could only result in disaster, and, until comparatively recent years, disaster has been its record from time immemorial.[1]

The son of a former stage manager at Covent Garden, Augustus Harris had given a successful experimental season of Italian opera at Drury Lane as part of the celebrations of Queen Victoria's Golden Jubilee the year before. In 1888 he took up the lease of the dying Covent Garden, where standards had fallen to an abysmal level, to 'give grand opera a decent burial or resuscitate it'. It would have been an impossible task without royal patronage which alone could sell the house, boxes to pit, before the prospectus was printed. Royalty acted only through carefully chosen friends, in this case Lady de Grey and Lady Charles Beresford, both closely associated with the Prince and

Princess of Wales. In Gladys de Grey, Melba had suddenly acquired the most important patron in English society, not that it did her much good in that first season, spectacular as it was in other respects.

Harris opened on 14 May 1888 in a newly redecorated theatre. The Prince and Princess of Wales, seated in the royal box, were surrounded by 'the flower of British aristocracy in the stalls and three tiers of private boxes'. Fursch-Madi, Trebelli, Ravelli and Navarrini sang but Nordica, de Reims, Macintyre, Lasalle, Arnoldson, the de Reszkes and Albani appeared only later in the season. Melba was introduced in *Lucia* on 24 May, but Harris had failed to see to the usual publicity. Melba wrote:

> There had been no sort of announcement of my appearance in the papers; there had been none of the usual preliminaries which are necessary to arouse the public to any state of expectancy. I do not believe that the greatest critics had even bothered to look in at all.[2]

And why should they? She was still a nobody singing a role allotted to her and not the one of her choice – Gilda. Albani, the reigning prima donna, had first rights on the role and refused to permit the young colonial to compete in it; as first woman in the company, that was a perfectly proper stance to take. It was a disastrous début. There was one rushed-through orchestral rehearsal before Melba confronted the half-empty house where an air of apathy hung heavy over the stalls and boxes. The reviews next morning filled her with

> a feeling, first of indignation, then of astonishment, and then of amusement. Of my voice they said practically nothing. They seemed to be concerned solely with my powers as an actress, and of these they spoke in terms too generous for my capabilities.[3]

It was true that for her performances as Lucia and Gilda – she was finally permitted to play the part on 12 June – Melba was lauded as an actress in *The Times*, the *Daily Telegraph*, the *Daily Chronicle*, the *Morning Post*, *The Standard*, the *Pall Mall Gazette*, *Vanity Fair*, *The Globe*, the *Weekly Advertiser*, *The Queen*, the *Morning Advertiser*, *The Echo*, *The Era*, the *Lady's Pictorial*, *The Stage*, *The Musical Standard* and *St James' Gazette*. But her singing was also noticed. One of the greatest critics, Hueffer in *The Times*, wrote of the Lucia début:

> That Madame Melba will in the end be successful there is little reason to doubt, although the impression produced by her début was not an overpowering one ... although Mme Melba proved herself to be a talented and well-trained artist, who, for all one can tell, may be endowed with dramatic as well as vocal ability.[4]

Harold Rosenthal, the Covent Garden historian, adds that 'The other leading critics wrote in a similar vein'.

ba formed a lifelong friendship with the great violinist Joseph
him. *(La Trobe Library)*

Franchetti, Mascagni and Puccini, 1893. Melba was friendly with
many of the composers of her day, but none of them created a great
new role for her. *(La Trobe Library)*

Far left: Flautist John Lemmone in 1924. He
was Melba's manager, obbligatist and close
friend. *(The Age)*

Left: Melba at the time she met the Duc
d'Orléans. *(La Trobe Library)*

Left and far left: Louis-Philippe, Duc
d'Orléans, Pretender to the French throne.
His affair with Melba caused an international
scandal and almost ruined her career.
*(Performing Arts Museum; La Trobe
Library)*

Right: Melba, Milan, 1893. *(La Trobe Library)*

Below left: Melba *circa* 1900. *(La Trobe Library)*

Below centre: Melba during her first Australian tour. *(The Age)*

Far right: Melba as Aida, a role she disliked because of the 'blacking up' required. *(Australian Information Service)*

Above: Melba and Hermann Bemberg at the tea table. Haddon Chambers and Bertram Mackennel are standing. *(Performing Arts Museum)*

Right: Melba as Gilda in *Rigoletto*, Covent Garden. The audience lights have not been turned down, as was the custom at the time, allowing the social set to display themselves to the house. *(La Trobe Library)*

Albani had relented after the tepid press Melba had received for
ucia. She had had Ravelli (Edgardo), Cotogni (Enrico) and Navarrini
Raimondo) to pull her through on stage and Mancinelli to conduct,
ut even their experience made no difference. In *Rigoletto* she had a
ovice tenor, Giulle (the Duke), D'Andrade (Rigoletto) and Scalchi
n stage with Mancinelli again in the pit. The press still remained
ikewarm.

Melba went to see Harris two days later to try to better the situation:
nother opera, a more sympathetic conductor, anything. He offered
er Oscar in Verdi's *A Masked Ball*, which she hotly refused and
acked her bags and left for Brussels, determined never to sing at
Covent Garden again.

At the Monnaie she sang *Lakmé* in October, *Hamlet* on 3 November
nd then, late in February 1889, in Gounod's *Roméo et Juliette* with
Ingel as Roméo and Renaud as Capulet. It was a triumph and the
'aris Opera made an offer. The Monnaie management countered, but
here was little hope of retaining her beyond the contract for the
eason. There were charity performances in Liège and other towns, a
ew attempts at oratorio, a farewell evening, a diamond and sixty
ouquets at the Monnaie. On 14 April 1889 the King of the Belgians
resented her with the gold medal of the Brussels Conservatoire.

On 8 May, with two of her sisters in the audience, Melba made
er début at the Paris Opera as Ophélie in *Hamlet*. Madame Richard,
vho played the Queen, had been taken ill and the dates for *Hamlet*
vere changed several times, almost unnerving the débutante. To make
natters worse, at the last moment her lead, Lasalle, lost his voice. She
ang opposite a Hamlet she had never seen before and without an
orchestral rehearsal.

August Vitu of *Le Figaro* wrote:

Madame Melba possesses a marvellous soprano voice, equal, pure,
brilliant and mellow, remarkably resonant in the middle register,
and rising with a perfect *pastosita* [rich softness] up to the acute
regions of that fairy-like major third which is called *ut, re, ni* above
the lines. Her personal appearance was an advantage to her: tall,
slender, gifted with an expressive physiognomy. She was applauded
in her first duet with Hamlet, *Doute de la lumière*, then in the air
Mieux vaut mourir and in the second duet, *Ah! les serments ont des
ailes*, to which she gave a dramatic expression rare among our
Ophélies; but the occupants of the orchestra stalls, faithful to their
temperate habitudes, were disposed to regard it as somewhat ex-
aggerated. Madame Melba was, however, recalled after the fine trio
in the third act which drives Ophélie to desperation.

Up to this point all had gone smoothly, without rising above an
excellent medium. But in the fourth act the veil was thrown aside.
When Ophélie was seen in her white garments, garlanded with
flowers, Madame Melba was transfigured. It was Ophélie herself

HAMLET

French composer Ambroise
Thomas (1811–96) was best
known for his *Mignon* (1866).
His *Hamlet*, libretto by
Barbier and Carré, is based on
the Shakespearian tragedy. It
was first produced at the Paris
Opera on 9 March 1868 with
Nilsson as Ophelia and Faure
in the title role, which was
altered from tenor to baritone
to suit Faure. It was produced
at Covent Garden on 19 June
1869 in Italian as *Amleto*,
with Nilsson and Santley. In
America it first appeared in
the Academy of Music, New
York, on 22 March 1872
with Nilsson, Cary, Brignoli,
Barré and Jamet, but it met
the fate of most operas with a
baritone for the hero in
America – the indifference of
the public. It was revived for
Lasalle and by the Chicago
Opera Company for Ruffo.
Thomas became director of
the Rome Conservatory in
1871, as successor to Auber
(after the few days it was held
by Salvador Daniel, who was
killed in battle on 23 May).

PARIS AND TRIUMPH –
THE REVIEWS 1

As Pierre Vernon expressed it in *Le Charivari* on 10 May 1889: 'The singer, new to Paris, but acclaimed and consecrated in Brussels, is of Australian origin. She comes from the fine school of Madame Marchesi which so often shames our Conservatoire by comparison ... She is certainly one of the most complete Ophelias that Ambroise Thomas had found. Her début at the opera was the most triumphant for many long years. Although forced to perform with an extempore Hamlet and without previous rehearsal, Madame Melba, who had not been able to get together with M. Bernardi, was not troubled for a minute ... From her first appearance the audience set out to reassure her, and the bravos began a formidable crescendo ... Tender and dramatic in turn, Madame Melba has given proof of style as much as of virtuosity. After the Mad Scene, delight overtook the entire place ...The scene was sung and performed by Madame Melba with an irreproachable perfection which supports comparison with all – including the inaugurator of the role herself [Nilsson, 9 March 1868, Paris Opera] ... The débutante that Brussels has already acclaimed will long be remembered for this evening when the Parisian public gave her the supreme accolade of inscribing her name in the Golden Book of Art'.[1]

1. Kobbé, *The Complete Opera Book*, p. 585.

who charmed all eyes and touched all hearts while interpreting with supreme virtuosity that admirable scene ... That which ravished us was not alone the virtuosity, the exceptional quality of that sweetly timbred voice, the facility of executing at random diatonic and chromatic scales and the trills of the nightingale; it was also that profound and touching simplicity and the justness of accent which caused a thrill to pass through the audience with those simple notes of the middle voice, *Je suis Ophélie*. And when at length the echoes of the lake wafted to us the last high note of the poor young creature, an immense acclamation saluted in Madame Melba the most delicious Ophélie that has been heard since the days of Christine Nilsson and of Fides Devries. She was recalled three times after the fall of the curtain, and, as statisticians, we have calculated that three recalls like those in the opera at Paris are quite equivalent to seventy-five recalls in Italy at the very least.

We might explain this evening, parodying two lines of Voltaire 'Each people in its turn has reigned upon the scene; Australia's hour has come, as ours has been'.[5]

With this review the Melba legend came into existence. The Australian press at first simply translated and reprinted it then, in astonishment, began to comment.

Today Melba's meaning for her Australian contemporaries and the generation that followed seems to have been lost, partly due to time, but partly also, due to Dame Joan Sutherland's advent as well. The odds against two such voices appearing from such a small population must be astronomical. Historians ignore Melba, either because they believe everyone knows all there needs to be known about her and because they see her career as un-Australian and irrelevant, or because their own cultural background has not included music at the kind of level normal for an earlier aspiring Australian middle class. Manning Clark speaks of her only in the context of Australian women's education and then as 'a Lilydale gentleman's daughter, in whom the gods had planted both the gift of song and the madness of art'. Yet in 1934, musician Muriel Campbell could write that

the names of Melba, Ada Crossley and Mary Conly will be cherished amongst us forever. The triumphs they achieved in the world of music abroad were a source of pride and delight to their compatriots – they were the first and in their several fields have not since been surpassed.[6]

Composer Henry Tate, music critic for the *Age* until his death in 1924, eulogised:

Our singer, thrilled with the song of the gums and the sough of the wind, beating across the interminable ranges of the Never-Never, fought her Homeric fight against the sneering coteries of

European art circles by virtue of her innate Australianness and her unquestionable courage.[7]

Roger Covell, in the only systematic history of Australian music to date, *Australia's Music*, rightly calls this 'ultra-nationalistic' and 'pure tarradiddle'. Still, it was the way others beside Tate felt. Melba triggered something special in the Australian consciousness at a time when national heroes were needed. The us-against-them mentality of Federation Australia, with its need for reassurance that it was doing the right thing, focused on her as the woman who showed the world we were not only a civilised people but could outstrip all competition in a purely European art form where even the English failed to shine.

John Thompson in *On Lips of Living Men* says 'She was in her own day by far the most famous of living Australians'. The current *Grove's Dictionary of Musicians*, speaking of Melba in a wider context, says she was 'regarded as the most accomplished and most famous soprano of her time'. Paris was the beginning of that fame.

'Figaro's Gentleman of the Orchestra', a musical gossip column that followed the critique, wrote of the Paris début:

No subscriber to the opera since the days of Nilsson remembers to have seen the curtain raised three times, after the Mad Scene; not by the *mot d'ordre* of a splendidly trained claque, but in response to the unanimous demand of the entire audience moved to its inmost fibres and quivering with emotion . . . Before conquering her public as an artist Madame Melba had, from her first appearance, vanquished them as a woman . . . In that tall and handsome person, the look of profound trouble, the physiognomy so remarkably mobile, seem made to express dramatic passion. There breathes from her that perfume of romance without which there can be no true Ophelia, and that aristocratic grace which befits the fiancée of a King's son . . .[8]

The critics, from August Vitu, Johannes Weber, Victor Roger and Pierre Vérnon to Henri de Lapommeraye, Charles Le Roy, Victor Wilder, Louis Besson, George Launay, Léon Kersy and H. Izouard, praised her to excess. In a press interview the next day Melba said:

I am intensely happy. It was delightful. After the fourth act I was recalled three times, a compliment which they say has not been paid to any singer at the Grand Opera for over thirty years.[9]

Her salary leapt from 3000 francs a month at the Monnaie, a sum Melba thought almost extravagant at the time, to 6000 francs. The directors had offered 4000, to be paid only if her début proved she was worth it. Since the contract was unsigned at the time Melba's triumph left her in a bargaining position. She settled for 6000 francs. Madrid, Berlin and the Paris Gaîté offered her more at once but, she

PARIS AND TRIUMPH – THE REVIEWS 2

Arthur Pougin in *Le Ménestral* on 12 May 1889: 'The début of this young singer occurred in the most deplorable and unexpected circumstances . . . She appeared for the first time on the French scene, in a role as difficult and demanding as Ophélie, without having had an orchestral rehearsal. But even more she had rehearsed with M. Lasalle, who should have played Hamlet, and with M. Plancon who should have taken the part of the King. And then on the very day, M. Lasalle and M. Plancon both finding themselves suddenly ill, she was obliged to put herself through this dreadful test with two partners that she did not know, M. Bérnardi and M. Grasse. One can guess her fright at this news, and the tears which followed it.

'It is in these unfavourable conditions however, that Madame Melba scored a triumph such as we have not seen for a long time at the opera, and which literally enchanted the public. From her first appearance on stage, a flattering murmur welcomed her. Her pretty appearance, her natural distinction, her grace and elegance won her instant favour. In spite of the fears which at first choked her, the voice, pure and limpid, with an adorable timbre and perfect accuracy, emerges with the greatest ease. The articulation is precise, and there is hardly a moment when an unusual syllable reveals, in an accent which is light but not without grace, her Australian origins. (We know that Madame Melba is an Australian and that in Brussels, in recent times, she sang in Italian in the midst of her fellow performers who sang in French.) The whole Book Scene was performed not only with the great skill of a singer with rare taste and with great certainty of bearing, but with real dramatic purpose and with highly intelligent stage movement.

'From this moment, her success was assured. It continued through to the third act, during the beautiful trio with Hamlet and the Queen, where the replies were given with a rare assurance and in an accent touching and stamped with a broken-hearted sadness. But it was in the fourth act, in the Mad Scene, that the ovation was at its fullest and her triumph dazzling . . .

'Over the past twenty years we have seen many artistes succeed in the role of Ophélie, but, if memory does not fail us, Madame Christine Nilsson, for whom the role was written, and Madame Fides Devries are the only ones that we have heard sing this fourth act with such absolute and incontestable command.'

said, 'money is not everything, so I shall stay on at the Opera', which was what her by then signed contract stipulated anyway.

Melba went on to sing Gilda and Lucia but on 6 June 1889 she was back at Covent Garden for *Rigoletto*. Gladys de Grey had written to her while she was still in Brussels offering her Juliette. Melba refused. Lady de Grey wrote again to say the Princess of Wales had seen the London *Rigoletto* of the year before and had been deeply impressed, adding:

I know that things were badly arranged for you before, but if you come back I promise you that it will be very different. You will be under my care and I shall see that you do not lack either friends or hospitality.[10]

But London itself gave no sign of relenting. The audience was tiny and Melba was barely noticed. Then on 15 June she appeared with the de Reszke brothers in *Roméo et Juliette*, Mancinelli conducting. Harris decided that it should be sung for the first time at the Garden in French. His gamble paid off 'and at last', Melba wrote, 'at long last, there was a packed house'. This time the critics had nothing but praise for her.

A command performance at Buckingham Palace was arranged for the 28th but Melba developed a bad cold and, bitterly disappointed, she had to withdraw. On 2 July there was a gala performance at Covent Garden for the Shah of Persia. The Prince of Wales asked for Melba in 'Je veux vivre' from *Roméo et Juliette*. That request made Melba socially. Within days the society hostesses were vying with one another for her services. Her fees for such appearances rose astronomically. She wrote:

It was Gladys [de Grey] who gave me my first London party; that is to say, the first party to which I went after I became a somebody . . . Never shall I forget the succession of women who drifted into that room – the Duchess of Leinster, robed in white satin with marvellous sapphires round her neck, holding her head like a queen. Lady Dudley, with her lovely turquoises, so numerous that they seemed to cover her from her head to her knees; and Lady Warwick, then at the height of her beauty, the old Duchess of Devonshire, making somewhat pointed comments on those around her, the brilliant Duchess of Sutherland, Lady Cynthia Graham, Lady Helen Vincent, and many others.[11]

This roll-call of London society hostesses was no boast on Melba's part. She could have added dozens of other Debrett names within months. What it meant was that as long as she remembered she was there as a glittering prize and behaved as high society saw fit, she would be petted and paid. The moment she broke the rules her career would be at an end. Within two years she was to learn how easy it was to fall from grace and to stare ruin in the face because of it.

The Covent Garden season gave Melba two performances of *Rigoletto* and seven of *Roméo et Juliette*, though she made one unscheduled appearance during *Faust*, in which Margaret Macintyre, Lillian Nordica and Sofia Scalchi alternated. Melba was off-stage watching when the wings caught fire during the Study Scene; the audience, which clearly saw the sheet of flame suddenly shoot up the gauze, panicked. Melba stepped out when everyone else on stage seemed paralysed and calmed the lot of them as the fire was put out and the opera resumed.

The final Juliette, on 27 July, saw the royal box occupied by the wedding party for the marriage that day of the Duke and Duchess of Fife, including the Prince and Princess of Wales, the King of the Hellenes, the Grand Duke of Hesse and the Crown Prince of Denmark, all wearing wedding regalia. At the end of the performance the orchestra played the Mendelssohn *Wedding March* for the royals' exit.

The second half of the year Melba spent under contract to the Paris Opera. She left George at school in England on his father's insistence, so she said, but also because the career she now saw ahead of her had no place in it for a young boy. Better the barbarities of boarding school than the atmosphere of a soprano's house, even if it was 9 Rue de Prony near the Parc Monceau, just round the corner from Gounod's. Sarah Bernhardt and the Marchesis were near neighbours and Artot Padilla lived a few doors away. It was a very expensive, fashionable address which George saw only on holidays. It was there that Melba began her first essays into interior decoration with a bedroom containing a Marie Antoinette bed and chair, an art nouveau telephone booth, two telephones, silver candlesticks and old china on the ornate mantle, wall-to-wall carpet with Persian overlays, masses of small pictures on walls and shelves, and a brocade-clothed writing table holding her monographed writing box which stood in front of the bed. Her taste was neither original nor elegant, but it was no mere imitation of aristocratic fashion either. Her houses had an air of respectable opulence about them, nothing different, nothing out of place, but everything moderate good quality of its period.

Melba had met Gounod through Marchesi early in her student days and travelled back and forth from Brussels to study *Faust* and *Roméo* with him. Once installed in the Rue de Prony she became a frequent visitor in his house where the 70-year-old hypochrondriac was only too willing to spend hours explaining the roles in these operas to their greatest exponent. Melba had this to say about those sessions:

It was Gounod who taught me *Faust*, *Roméo* and *Mireille* [1864, 3-act opera, not often performed later], and while he was teaching me he would sing the other parts himself. At one time he would be the Nurse, at another the Devil, at another Romeo, and whichever role he sang, he seemed to adapt himself both in voice and

THE VOICE

The composers

Charles Gounod: 'A la chère Juliette que j'espère, à Nellie Melba.'

Jules Massenet, on her interpretation of the Infanta in *Le Cid*: 'Pleurez, pleurez, mes yeux. Heurex les publics, bien heureux les yeux qui pleureront, alors que Melba chantera cette scène; et j'en conserve une impression inoubliable'.

Sir Arthur Sullivan: 'So perfect is Melba's vocal utterance, that by the mere emission of tone, independent of all collateral aid, she can express the whole gamut of human feeling'.

Guetano Braga: 'Il vostro canto e una ineffabile carezza'.

Léo Delibes: 'Votre voix idéale avec un pureté surhumaine'.

Hermann Bemberg: 'Que je plains ceux qui n'ont pas eu la joie délicieuse d'être chanté par elle! Je ne me souviens pas d'une émotion plus intense que cela que j'ai éprouvé en entendant soupirer de cette adorable voix ces premiers mesures de l'aire d'Elaine! J'ai cru rêver, et j'étais éveillé. Puisse la réalité ne pas s'envoler comme un rêve et me donner l'incomparable bonheur de voir créer "Elaine" par l'artiste que je mets au-dessus de toutes – Nellie Melba'.[1]

Ambroise Thomas: 'the Ophélie of my dreams'.

1. Murphy, *op. cit.*, pp. 69–70.

FAUST

Gounod's *Faust*, the libretto by Barbier and Carré, was first produced at the Théâtre Lyrique, Paris, on 19 March 1859 with Miolan-Carvalho as Marguerite; at the Grand Opera, Paris on 3 March 1869, with Christine Nilsson; at Her Majesty's Theatre, London on 11 June 1863; and in Italian on 2 July 1863 at the then Royal Italian Opera, Covent Garden. An English version was done at Her Majesty's London on 23 January 1864 with Santley as the Valentine, and for whom Gounod composed what was destined to become one of the most popular numbers of the opera, 'Even bravest hearts may swell' ('Dio possenie'). The first New York production was at the Academy of Music on 26 November 1863 in Italian, with Clara Louise Kellogg (Marguerite). Henrietta Sulzer (Siebel), Fanny Stockton (Martha), Francesco Mazzoleni (Faust), Hannibel Biachi (Mephistopheles), G. Yppolito (Valentine), and D. Coletti (Wagner). At the Metropolitan Opera it opened on 22 October with Nilsson, Scalchi, Lablache, Campanini, Novera and Del Puents. The first Australian performance was given in Sydney on 3 March 1864, and on 2 May 1864 in Melbourne. *Faust* achieved popularity from its first night at the Academy, but it did not come fully into its own until the Maurice Grau regime at the Met. when it was sung in French by artists who were familiar with the traditions of the Paris Opera. As Faust, Italio Campanini, who sang the Italian version at the Academy with Nilsson as

temperament, to the character he was interpreting. He was exactl like a nurse, and he was positively Satanic as the Devil. And believe that had there been any listeners in that long room with i great organ and its innumerable photographs, they would hav thought that there were a dozen people singing, instead of onl Gounod and myself.

Gounod *saw* his characters as human beings. I remember hi telling me the difference between Marguerite and Juliette – Ma guerite, the simple peasant, but *Juliette etait une affrontée*. He adde that it was she who proposed to Romeo, not Romeo to her.[12]

Melba's near worship of Gounod has been read as a lack musicianship on her part, a matter of poor judgement. She certainl seems to have credited him with near divine creative ability, but th might have been merely the extravagant tribute of a grateful sopran to the man who created roles ideally suited to her voice. After all, sh knew him as the central figure in contemporary music, a man enjoyin great popularity and stylistically influencing a whole generation composers, though he was shortly to fall out of favour to such a extent that Saint-Saëns would speak of his musical style as 'of a impeccable elegance' overlaying a basic vulgarity, the usual verdi today. In Melba's era Gounod was treated with extravagant respe and was paid lavishly for his work; she was not alone in her hig opinion of him.

Gounod took a keen interest in Melba, attending her rehearsals an sitting in the director's box during performances, listening for th slightest flaw. When she pleased him, he would come smiling to he afterwards and throw his arms around her in front of the compan Pride of place among the collection of autographed photos on Melba drawing-room mantle was given to one of Gounod inscribed 'To th dear Juliet for whom I hoped – to Nellie Melba – Ch. Gounod Melba would show it to guests, saying, 'I thank God for having m and known Gounod. He awakened in me my artistic sense. He w so broad, so human, and had so much to give'.

The pity of it was that no younger composer of real worth foun a proper and original use for Melba and that she in turn did not g out of her way to commission work. She sang in works by Bember (*Elaine*), Puccini (*La Bohème*), Ambroise Thomas (*Hamlet*), Massen (*Manon Lescaut*), Goring Thomas (*Esmeralda*), Delibes (*Lakmé*), Mas cagni (*I Rantzau*), and Saint-Saëns (*Hélène*) and knew every compose of the day, yet she created only two leading roles – Elaine (5 Jul 1892 at Covent Garden and two years later at the Met., both wit Jean de Reszke) and Hélène (Monte Carlo, 18 February 1904). Neith opera was worthy of its star.

The reviews to this point had been full of praise for Melba's actin the doubts came later. Yet she went to the trouble of telling her fir biographer that before she appeared at the Paris Opera she was pressured into taking acting lessons 'from a certain teacher ... whose influence was considered paramount. No one had ever been able to make headway independent of this professor'. She refused to be pushed and replied, 'That may be, but I will not be coerced. I shall take my lessons from whom I like, when I like, and how I like, and I will also take the consequences'. She was implying that she did indeed take the consequences. From that point on her acting was found wanting and once that found its way into print she was unable to get it out again. In other words she was very sensitive about accusations of woodenness but felt that there had been, at least in the early days, a plot against her. Robert Sherard in *Twenty Years in Paris* hints that the person responsible may have been the theatre critic of an important Parisian newspaper. In the memoirs it is Sarah Bernhardt who coaches Melba and M. Pluque, maître of the ballet of the Paris Opera House, who gave her the name of a dancer who agreed to instruct the singer in how to use grease-paint. Melba spent a month with the make-up artist, a good deal less with Bernhardt.

Melba had seen Bernhardt in *La dame aux camélias* and at Marchesi's insistence went to ask her help. Melba found Bernhardt's rooms gave the impression 'more of a circus than of the *salon* of a great theatrical star'. The place was thick with dusty curtains, animal skin rugs, stuffed hunting trophies including horns, a tiger, a bear, and even a snake. There were busts of Sarah, mythological characters, pictures on easels, tapestries, dying plants and a huge neglected bowl of water holding overweight goldfish. Sarah came in late and 'jumped on to a sort of box which stood in a corner of the room and sat on it, waggling her legs like a schoolgirl, and talking with extreme rapidity and a wealth of gesture'.

Melba elected Bernhardt to teach her one role – Marguerite. The character as Gounod gives it is particularly silly and Melba plainly had trouble swallowing the idea of a girl victim so cheaply won. She was puzzled. She felt Gounod had nothing further to offer, hence her need for Marchesi's advice.

Colson records that 'Sarah greeted her with a torrent of words. Did she like Paris? Did she like Marchesi? Who had brought her there? Above all, did she like Sarah Bernhardt?'. Melba adds:

And then without more ado she started to go through with me the part of Marguerite in *Faust*. It was a revelation. Little points of character which I had overlooked were made to live before my eyes . . . For instance she said: 'When on the death of Valentin, he curses you, and tells you that owing to your sin with Faust your white hands will never be called upon to spin any more – what must you do? You must hide your hands behind your back, terrified, ashamed, as though you wished that you might cut them from your body.

Marguerite, was remembered for a generation for his exquisite phrasing in the romance 'Salve dimora casta e pura!' ('Salut demeure chaste et pure'). The greatest American Faust was Jean de Reszke whose inborn 'chivalry of deportment' made him a lover after the heart of every woman and whose 'refinement of musical expression' clarified every role he sang. Christine Nilsson, Adelina Patti, Melba, Eames and Calvé are among the famous Marguerites heard in America. Nilsson and Eames, it was thought, had too much natural reserve for the role, but then the libretto made Marguerite more refined than Goethe's Gretchen. Patti acted the part with great simplicity and sang it flawlessly. Melba's 'type of beauty' was judged too 'mature' for the character, but her voice was perfect for the role. Calvé's was a logically developed character, first to last, and one of the most original interpretations. At the Met. Sembrich and Farrar were Marguerites of note but not in the same class as Melba. As Mephistopheles, Plancon outshone all his rivals.

Michel Carré and Jules Barbier, the librettists, concentrated on the love story of Faust and Marguerite, ignoring the rest of Goethe's *Faust*, a love story which was not part of the original legend. Because of this the opera is called *Margarethe* in German, not *Faust*. In the ten years between the first performance at the Théâtre Lyrique and the first Paris Opera *Faust* there were only thirty-seven performances. In 1887 it had had 1000 performances and from 1901 to 1910 it was given 3000 times in Germany alone. The score, declined by several publishers, was brought out by Choudens who paid Gounod 10 000 francs for it and still made a fortune. Gounod sold the English rights for a mere pound and that only on the insistence of Chorley, the translator.

See!' – and she whipped her hands behind her back, staring me straight in the face with an expression in her eyes of such utte torture, that every time in the years to come when I listened to Valentin singing those words *Sois maudite* called up the vision of Sarah Bernhardt.[13]

Colson put it slightly differently. He gives this as:

And she whipped her hands behind her back, with a look of tortur that haunted Melba ever afterwards when she heard Valentin sing the words *Sois maudite*. Alas! Melba herself was never able to cal up a look of tragedy more intense than that of a lady who ha forgotten the name of the gentleman who is taking her out to supper and doesn't want to hurt his feelings.[14]

Agnes Murphy gives the sober rider:

The great French tragedienne, after explaining and suggesting th possibilities of the part, was always careful to add: 'You must no imitate me. Do it your own way. You must be natural. Be yourself'.

This second Paris season included Donizetti's *Lucia* in the Decembe of 1889. The primo uomo, Cossira, lost his voice almost as soon a he came onto stage. The house was packed. If Cossira went off s early – there was no understudy to take his place – the managemen would have lost heavily through refunds. Melba signalled that sh would carry the tenor's recitatives for him and, as far as possible, som of his heavier work, but by the time the duets appeared the audienc had realised what was going on and the curtain had to be brough down. The directors rushed to the stage. Everyone stood about i confusion as Cossira apologised and the directors swore. Then Melb remembered that the Brussels tenor, Engel, was in the audienc occupying a seat up front that she had arranged for him.

The critic for *Le Ménestral*, H. Moreno, observing what happene next, said dryly that there was 'no longer any security for Frenc citizens; not even in the auditorium of the opera during a performance He had just seen a peaceable spectator

who seemed a good bourgeois and a family man, dragged out o his seat by the director's hirelings and manhandled through th theatre, whereupon he was handed over large boots and stockings a plumed hat that came down over his ears was thrust on his heac and he was pushed on stage with the threatening words: 'Come on you *have* to sing *Lucia*'.[16]

The man in question was M. Engel who had sung the role twenty five times but had auditioned unsuccessfully for the Paris Opera onl a few weeks before; the artistic director thought his voice would no get beyond the first three rows of seats. What Moreno saw was Engel argaining for a contract. In their hour of need

our worthy directors, downing their bitter cup, had had to admit that M. Engel had been audible as far as the balcony of their theatre, so much so that after the second act M. Ritt, moved to tears at his narrow escape, had slipped his saviour a note for a thousand francs.[17]

Moreno praised Melba's performance that night as much as any of he critics, but though he recorded the ovations from the house he dded: 'let us wish that in spite of Madame Melba's triumph the ther night, that we could see her soon applying her marvellous talents o work of more modern and lively artistic interest'.

In the bi-monthly *L'Art musical* A. Landely sounded a similar note. He praised 'the limpidity of her voice, the light and dark of her inging', but while he was charmed, he also confessed to 'vague nisgivings' about the Donizetti – which he claimed were not due to under-rehearsal as it had had ten weeks' study – but to the work itself nd the waste of such a voice in its service.

Shall we always see her imprisoned in the art of the past, captive of the frivolous and the convenient, a talent that poetry caresses with its warmest rays? . . . Madame Melba is worth more than her actual roles. If she agrees to give them up, if she wants a career as an artist and not the career of a simple virtuoso, the composers should hurry to her side. The place of Star in the artistic firmament is empty. May Madame Melba consent to fill it.[18]

ronically, ninety years later the same lament was being heard over Melba's modern alter ego, Dame Joan Sutherland.

The second Paris season was broken for Melba early in 1890 by an ngagement at Monte Carlo. Her contract with the Paris Opera made t possible for her to take advantage of outside offers if the fees were empting enough, hence Monte Carlo in the winter season and Covent Garden in mid-1890 when she appeared in *Roméo et Juliette* (3 June), Lohengrin (10 June), *Lucia* (16 June), *Rigoletto* (26 June), *Esmeralda* 12 July), and *Hamlet* (21 July) in Harris' Royal Italian opera season. She was due to sing Micaëla in *Carmen* on 28 July but 'as often happens when prima donnas are cast for secondary rôles she was ndisposed'.

The Goring Thomas opera, *Esmeralda*, was given on 12 July and was performed for the first time in French, and included a new scene hat reminded everyone of the prison scene in *Faust*, as well as a number of other last minute alterations that taxed even Melba's ability o learn a role in record time. As it was she gave a second-rate performance in it. Based on Victor Hugo's *Notre Dame de Paris*, Esmeralda has been described as 'a flow of doggerel', but its 'emasculated libretto' was suited to Thomas' 'graceful, elegant, French

ROMÉO ET JULIETTE

Gounod's five-act *Roméo et Juliette* (libretto by Barbier and Carré after Shakespeare) was first produced at the Théâtre Lyrique on 27 April 1867 and revived in January 1873 when it was taken over by the Opéra-Comique. It appeared at the Paris Opera only on 28 November 1888. The first production at Covent Garden (in Italian) was on 11 July 1867; at the Academy of Music in New York on 15 November 1867 (with Minnie Hauck as Juliette); at the Met. on 14 December 1891 (with Eames as Juliette, Jean de Reszke as Roméo and Edouard de Reszke as Frère Laurent); and in Chicago on 15 December 1916 (with Muratoe as Roméo and Galli-Curci as Juliette).

The original Juliette – also the creator of Marguerite – was Madame Miolan-Carvalho. The opera was more popular in France than elsewhere. Like *Faust* it took its place in the American repertoire only after it was given during the Grau regime at the Met. by singers familiar with the traditions of the Paris Opera.

Eames is remembered in America as the vocally and histrionically superior Juliette; Capoul, Jean de Reszke and Saleza as fine Roméos, Edouard de Reszke for his Frère Laurent. Adelina Patti, then married to the Marquis de Caux, sang the role opposite Nicolini, who became her second husband. There was a startling night at the Paris Opera when the two exchanged no less than twenty-nine impassioned kisses on stage during the performance, the audience counting as they went.

influenced music'. The happy ending of the original was replaced in this French version by a tragic denouement, but the work was not well received. As Shaw said of Thomas Goring, 'he always seems to be dreaming of other men's music'.

On 4 July 1890 Melba was summoned to sing before Queen Victoria and the German Empress Frederick at Windsor Castle. Melba says she went up by the 3 o'clock train with Jean and Edouard de Reszke and Paolo Tosti, the composer who taught singing to the royal family and the usual accompanist for command performances; Murphy gives the accompanist as Mancinetti. There was some mistake made about which train was to be met by the castle's carriage. Melba and her party had to hire a ricketty old cab and a bewildered driver who took them from gate to gate until, at 4 p.m., they finally found the right entrance and the little waiting-room reserved for visiting entertainers. They were left to cool their heels for a leisurely half-hour. Melba, staring at the wallpaper, began to fret aloud that they would never get back in time for that night's performance at Covent Garden. At 4.30 p.m. an attendant came to tell them that the Empress Frederick had gone for a drive and had not returned yet. The Queen had waited for her but now wished to hear Melba's party in spite of her guest's absence.

A tiny figure in black with 'smooth silvery hair' and 'heavy eyelids', received them, shaking hands and looking directly at each performer as she did so, her ladies-in-waiting hovering behind. Years later Australian artist Cyril Dillon, a close friend of Melba's, remarked to her that she looked very like the Queen. Melba tartly replied, 'Don't say that! I hated the bloody woman'. What was more she had come, by then, to hate the Germans.

At 4.45 p.m. the Queen gave the signal to begin. There was no sign of the Empress. Melba sang 'Caro nome' and the waltz song from *Roméo et Juliette*, the duet from *La Traviata* with Jean de Reszke, and ended with the whole of the last act from *Faust* (though it was reported in the press next day as only the trio). At 5.30 p.m., just as they finished, the Empress came in. To Melba's horror the Queen said, 'What a treat you have missed. We must have more for you!' Like it or not the concert party hurriedly repeated the trio from *Faust*. Jean de Reszke sang the 'Preislied' from *Die Meistersinger von Nürnberg*. The Empress expressed great admiration for this, saying it made her long to hear the whole opera. There was a moment of panic, but no, they were not asked to attempt anything more. Refreshments were offered in another room and they were dismissed, but there was no time to eat. As they swept out of the castle Miss Minnie Cochran handed each a little parcel; in the train which they just managed to catch they opened them. A brooch of pearls and rubies for Melba, gold cufflinks for Jean de Reszke, a gold pencil for Tosti and gold and platinum links for Edouard – hardly equal to the kind of fees

Melba and the de Reszkes could command at a society dinner, and here at least they were properly fed. The curtain went up fifteen minutes late on a very hungry Gilda who remained, for the rest of her life, contemptuous of a Queen who paid so little for so much. She was reported next day as saying all the correct, obsequious things expected of her. In Australia she was written down as a snob, when in fact she was simply being careful not to antagonise the source of her toast and caviar.

Melba had had one warning already of how easy it would be to fall out of favour. She had been commanded to appear before the Queen on 26 June, not in the less formal surroundings of Windsor, but at an official event at Buckingham Palace in the presence of the royal family and the court. The programmes were usually selected from the older Italian repertoire and the atmosphere was forbidding. Melba quite genuinely had laryngitis and failed to appear. A week later she was snubbed by the Prince of Wales at a party at Lady de Grey's, and in despair Melba went to her hostess next day to ask why. She was told the Prince had heard she was seen enjoying herself on the Thames when she should have been at the Palace. Never one to accept defeat, Melba got a doctor's certificate and an audience with Edward via Lady de Grey. She drove to Marlborough House and was shown in to the Prince's rooms. With her usual bluntness she asked why she had been snubbed; the Prince told her. She offered her certificate. He waved it aside. 'Oh, I don't want to see that', he said.

Two nights later, going in to dinner at Mrs Ogden Goelet's house, the Prince asked Melba to sit at his table. There was a sudden silence. Edward announced, 'Madame and I have had a little misunderstanding. But we have made it up now, and we are going to be great friends again. Madame Melba, I drink to you'. Her career was saved, but only by royal favour.

And then, in that first aura of success, she met Tip – Louis Philippe, Duc d'Orléans – the great-grandson of the last French king, and pretender to the throne of France. He was 20 and a few months; she was 29.

The Duc was born in England at York House, Twickenham, in 1869, the eldest son of the Comte de Paris. He returned to France as a 2-year-old and remained there until he was exiled at 17. The French had shown too much royalist fervour when the Comte's daughter married Don Carlos of Portugal. The French government sent father and son to exile in England where the Duc finished his education at the Royal Military College at Sandhurst, following it with a year in India in a British regiment. There were more military studies in Switzerland, then a defiant return to Paris to serve, under the law, the three years military service obligatory for all French males. Since he was infringing the exile laws he was arrested and sentenced to two years' imprisonment. He was pardoned after a few months, returned

THE DE RESZKES

The de Reszkes were a Polish family of singers, the most notable of whom were Jean (tenor), his younger brother, Edouard (bass), and Josephine (soprano), their sister. She sang as Giuseppina di Reschi, making her début at the Paris Opéra in 1875 and appearing there season after season for a decade. In 1885 she married Baron Leopold de Kronenberg and retired. History is inclined to remember only the brothers.

Jean (1850–1935) studied as a baritone, first with his mother, then with Ciaffei and Cotogni. As Giovanni di Reschi he made his début at La Fenice, Venice, in 1874 as Alfonso in Donizetti's *La Favorita*, repeating it for his Drury Lane début later that year. After the season there he went to Dublin, then, as Jean de Reszke, to Paris for his début as Fra Melitone in *La Forza del Destino*. In December 1876 he sang for the last time as a baritone as Figaro.

Jean became convinced that he was really a tenor. He retired from the stage to study with Sbriglia. In November 1879 he and his sister Josephine appeared in Madrid together in *Robert le Diable*, Jean for the first time as a tenor in the title role. He was a flop. For four years he refused to take the stage again. But on 1 February 1884 he scored a triumph in the Paris production of Massenet's *Hérodiade* as John the Baptist at the Théâtre-Italien. In 1885 he created the role of Rodrigue in *Le Cid* at the Opera, where he remained on contract for the next five years. He sang in London as a tenor for the first time on 13 June 1887 as Radames at Drury Lane. Nine days later he sang his first Wagnerian role in *Lohengrin* – in Italian. His Covent Garden début occurred the following year.

On 28 November 1888 *Roméo et Juliette*, rehearsed and conducted by Gounod, was premièred at the Paris Opéra with Jean, Edouard and Patti in the cast. Which is why Melba tried to teach all her Roméos the technique Jean developed; she felt it was the only authentic version, since Gounod had supervised it. The following June *Roméo et Juliette* was repeated at Covent Garden with Melba.

Jean went on to make his American début in Chicago in 1891 on 9 November. Five weeks later he gave his first American Roméo in New York, following it with a string of the weightier Wagnerian roles.

His last appearance at Covent Garden was in 1900 and in New York the following year. His last new role was Canio in *Pagliacci* in 1902 in Paris. He became a teacher in Paris and Nice, producing such students as Louise Edvina and Maggie Teyte. His career as the handsome, sensitive tenor, capable of the lighter French as well as the great Wagnerian roles, was distinguished and influential.

Edouard (1853–1917) studied with Steller and Coletti and made his début as the King in the first Paris performance of *Aida* at the Opéra on 22 May 1876. He had two seasons at the Théâtre-Italien and made his Covent Garden début in 1880. He appeared with Jean in *Le Cid* and in *Hérodiade*.

to England and there met Nellie Melba. He was a romantic hero, six feet two, educated, entertaining and enchanted with life and with the newest of the great prima donnas.

On 11 December 1890 Melba made her first appearance at the Opéra-Comique in Paris in a Bizet memorial matinée. The opera was *Carmen* with Galli-Marié, who created the role, in the title role and Melba as Micaëla. She elected to sing this secondary role at Covent Garden in 1891 and later in America with Zelie de Lussan. The reason remains obscure.

Melba left immediately afterwards for the Imperial Opera at St Petersburg, where she and the de Reszkes were to sing in *Lohengrin*, *Faust* and *Roméo et Juliette* at the invitation of Tsar Alexander III. A certain young nobleman followed at a discreet distance.

Melba claimed that she was the first to sing in a language other than Russian in the Tsar's Theatre and that it was a concession only made after long negotiations. However, Cargher counter-claims that though it was true that Tsar Paul banned performances of operas in Italian in St Petersburg theatres after 1798, an Italian opera company played regularly in the Imperial theatre after 1843, Verdi's *La Forza del Destino* was premièred in 1862 in Italian and when Patti toured in 1871 she did not sing in Russian. Why Melba made the claim remains a mystery.

The Imperial summons was hard to resist. Even the Paris Opera was persuaded to let Melba go for six weeks in the middle of the winter season. With all her personal costumes in the baggage car, Melba set off for what she plainly thought of as high adventure. She soon found it.

The route lay via Vienna. There, as Eugène Clisson of *L'Evénement* wrote,

> it is the custom . . . to go to the opera at 5 o'clock. One dines at nine after the performance, sitting down to it in ordinary evening dress . . . that's the fashion. So Viennese society was very surprised in the course of the performance to see in one box, a conspicuous woman covered in diamonds and very décolleté, truly a gala toilette, accompanied by a young, fairhaired man, correctly dressed . . . In Paris this departure from the norm would have passed unnoticed. In Vienna it created a scandal. The Court party itself was upset and it was discreetly made known to the Duke that his conduct was the cause of unfavourable [royal] comment.[19]

Colson has it that Van Dyk, the tenor in that night's *Lohengrin*, knew Melba from Brussels and was behind the curtain idly looking through the small opening that allowed the performers to scan the house. He spotted the conspicuous lady and her companion and, titillated, like everyone else, identified them for a friend who was backstage, a journalist from the *Vienna Tageblatt*. At supper the journalist met Blanche Marchesi, who was by then married and living in Vienna, and told her what he intended to publish. Colson says she begged him not to but he would not listen. She had no way of warning Melba since she had no idea where the couple was staying. Next morning when Melba walked in before breakfast Blanche showed her the morning paper, telling her to pack up and leave before the scandal got out of control. But, as it happened, Melba was due in St Petersburg and had no intention of staying on in Vienna anyway. As was her wont, she ignored the storm she had raised and refused to comment on it to anyone.

At the Russian frontier the 'fiery eyed' customs officers tossed over her travelling trunks, holding no respect for artists whose names as guests of the Tsar had not preceded them. Melba was woken from an exhausted sleep at the darkening snow-bound station to find her *Lohengrin* cloak lying on the ground close to the feet of soldiers who were stamping about to keep warm. She stormed out to rescue it; today it graces the Performing Arts Museum of the Victorian Arts Centre in Melbourne.

In St Petersburg Rubinstein wrote to her saying he was too ill to come to the theatre but asked to meet her. For hours she sang everything he asked for, Rubinstein accompanying her in spite of his failing eyesight.

Melba was entertained lavishly by the Grand Duke Alexis and was given 'a little souvenir', a bracelet of diamonds and sapphires, while the Grand Duchess Paul presented her with one of turquoise and diamonds. The Tsar outdid both with a bracelet consisting of engraved diamond cubes and large pearls strung on gold and platinum. Melba loved its arrogance and wore it as a mascot, prizing it nearly as highly as the diamond solitaire given to her as a fee in Berlin by a kinsman of Mendelssohn. She said publicly that she preferred pearls to other jewellery, but Melba did not mean the modern cultured pearl; she meant the wild matched pearl necklaces that society women wore at one another as badges of financial rank.

And then, the Paris press reported, at the end of one of Melba's arias during *Roméo et Juliette* one night

> suddenly, in the orchestra stalls, someone rose to his feet shouting bravos and applauding wildly. The Tsar was at the performance and it is he, as one knows, who must give the signal for applause. He found out who the 'claquer' was and sent one of his aides to ask him to quit the theatre. The Prince refused, saying he had paid for his ticket and intended to stay. When the envoy insisted: 'That's alright,' the Duc said, 'I'm going to explain myself to the Czar', and he was preparing to do just that when he was stopped at the very door of the Imperial loge through the intervention of a Grand Duchess. The following day, by order, the Duc left St Petersburg.[20]

Thereafter the brothers' careers were intertwined in London, Chicago and New York. Edouard was a huge man with a huge voice, a natural for the big Wagnerian roles in which he had such success. He retired in 1903, shortly after Jean.

Melba left also after an extravagant farewell at which she had t
ask for a chair to be placed in the wings so that she could rest betwee
recalls. Students tied handkerchiefs into a long line and waved
across the theatre from the gods. Outside a band of young Russia
aristocrats spread their coats on the snow for her to walk on from th
stage door to her carriage, which she found filled with orchid
Autograph hunters refused to let the horses move and she signe
hundreds of autographs with a borrowed pencil. When she returne
it the owner was besieged by his friends for a Melba souvenir. He b
the pencil into pieces and divided the spoils. The crowd still presse
close, many trying to shake her hand. To distract them long enoug
to clear the horses she took off her gloves and threw them int
outstretched hands. The carriage was away, the gloves torn into relic

In Paris the gossip grew. Sherard recalled:

> There was a rival prima donna on the Opera stage – an America
> – who waged war in the press on the Australian singer. One da
> Melba called at my house to show me with great indignation, som
> very offensive paragraphs which had been printed about her in th
> Australian papers, and to ask my advice as to the best way o
> answering these attacks. I told Melba . . . that an artist like herse
> had no need to trouble about criticism of that kind – 'Il n'y a
> Madame, que les petits hommes qui redoutent les petits écrits'
> said.[21]

Melba left for a command performance at Covent Garden schedule
for 8 July 1891 in celebration of the State visit of the Germa
Emperor and Empress. The royal route down Pall Mall was lined b
illuminations on the façades of the naval, military and political club
The Coldstream Guards formed a guard of honour before the Ope
House. Flowers lined halls, boxes, balconies and doorways and frame
off the royal box where the Prince and Princess of Wales, the Duk
and Duchess of Edinburgh, the Dukes of Clarence and Cambridg
the Duke and Duchess of Fife, Princesses Victoria and Maud of Wale
the Duchess of Albany, Princess Henry of Battenberg and the Duche
of Teck sat with their guests.

The programme was the usual royal mishmash: a compressed fir
act of *Lohengrin*, a shortened fourth act of *Roméo et Juliette* (Melb
with the de Reszkes), the last scene of *Orfeo*, and the fourth act o
Les Huguenots. The evening ended at half past twelve but it was
wonder the night occurred at all since the French contingent refuse
to have anything to do with it. The de Reszkes agreed to go on onl
after energetic persuasion.

1891 was Harris' best year, with a sixteen-week season and ninet
four performances of twenty operas, beginning on 6 April. In tha
season Melba appeared in *Carmen* (Micaëla), *Lohengrin*, *Lucia d
Lammermoor*, *Rigoletto* and *Roméo et Juliette*, but not *Faust* whic

Eames and Janson shared.

That summer one of Charles Armstrong's brothers heard it said openly in a London club that Melba was the mistress of the Duc d'Orléans. With family honour in mind he went to talk to her during rehearsals at Covent Garden and found the Duc in one of the boxes. When he confronted Melba she told him it was all lies, that the Duc was 'only a child who was obsessively following her everywhere'. She promised she would not permit it to continue and so he wrote to his brother.

But Charlie had already seen reports in an Australian newspaper and had written to Nellie to tell her he was returning to Europe where he meant to settle things with the Duc. When he arrived he went straight to his wife who told him the whole thing was false, and that Emma Eames was trying to blacken her name through professional jealousy. Charlie plainly didn't believe her. He delegated his brother to challenge the Duc to fight a duel and, being the offended party, Armstrong chose firearms. The Duc was willing but his father stepped in to remind the two hot-heads that those of the blood royal did not fight commoners. Charlie had to accept this, but *his* blood was up and he told *Le Temps*: 'I will horsewhip him – which will be better', and instructed his lawyers to file for divorce on the grounds of adultery, naming the Duc as co-respondent.

The Duc tried to avoid having the papers served on him and kept on the move round Europe, protected by his retinue. But at Vienna, as he stepped off the train, a man, apparently presenting a petition, somehow got through. The Duc presumed his aides had already decided the man was safe but he found he had accepted, not a list of names to some special request, but the dreaded divorce papers. Once they were formally served the matter was in the open and Melba's reputation was to be torn to shreds much as her gloves were in St Petersburg, the remnants tossed to the souvenir hunters.

In Paris, Melba took refuge with the Marchesis. There, on 1 November 1891, the divorce papers were served on her as opera fans and journalists crowded round the door. *L'Evénement* reported:

> She was extremely affected by it, so much so, that for an hour she was prostrated with a violent attack of nerves, followed by a long session of crying . . . The action today is, they say, provoked by the particularly interesting situation of Madame Melba. It is this complication that has determined M. Armstrong to break his silence.[22]

M. Armstrong, it said, was demanding 500 000 francs damages from the Duc. Bets were laid in the clubs as interest quickened, and the press grew daily more insistent that they talk to Melba, the Duc, their servants, anyone from stage-hands to hotel bootboys. The Duc's lawyers played for time, taking every legal step possible to delay a hearing.

But Charlie was determined to wrest custody of George from Melba who had taken steps at law to prevent his spiriting their child out of her reach and had kept the boy close to her for some time. Armstrong's lawyers, however, counter-petitioned, then had a few questions asked in the right quarters. They discovered that not only had Melba and the Duc occupied the same suite at the Hotel Sacher in Vienna in February 1891 but that in August 1890 they were together at the Beauséjour Hotel at Ouchy, the Duc under the name of M. Revelle. They were accompanied by 8-year-old George and by Nellie's 14-year-old brother.

When this got out Nellie accused Charlie of cruelty. If her conduct meant she might be seen as an unfit mother she was not prepared to let Charlie go unchallenged. She made sure he was seen as at least equally unfit for the guardianship of a child. Months passed and suddenly the case was dropped without explanation. Was it British diplomatic intervention? The matter *was* creating awkwardness with the French government. Whatever weight was brought to bear, it worked. In October 1892 the name of Armstrong was dropped from the English divorce lists. The Duc was sent off on a two-year African safari. In 1896 he married the Archduchess Marie Dorothea, daughter of the Archduke Joseph, son of the last Palatine of Hungary, and not his cousin, the Princess Marguerite, daughter of the Duc de Chartres, to whom he had been engaged at the time he met Melba, and whom he repudiated in consequence. There were no children from this marriage. The Duc became an explorer in the north-east of Greenland, and in Arctic and equatorial waters. The support he won from French royalists forced the Republic to regard him as dangerous and he was left in exile. When he died of pneumonia in 1926 his request to be buried in France or buried at sea in French waters was refused.

There were rumours, now and then, that the singer and the prince still saw one another. When he was 50 he wrote to Melba from the Ritz Hotel, Piccadilly, on 25 March 1919:

My dear Nellie, what can I tell you of the tender emotion that I have felt again after so many years? It seemed to me that it was yesterday that I said au revoir to you and that I found myself near to you the same, in spite of the age I then had nearly thirty years ago.

I was so happy to find you in spite of your sufferings moral and physical the *same Nellie* who has never changed and who remains in my life, sometimes so sad, the only constant and faithful friend towards whom — even in the delirium of death that I so closely escaped — my soul and heart reached across space. For you know me and understand me! In spite of all the world has done to separate the one from the other. I am satisfied because the confidence you gave me is my recompense. Thank you for the few moments in which you have really made me happy in evoking the past year

Top left: Melba in the title role of Saint-Saëns' *Hélène*, one of the few roles she created. *(La Trobe Library)*

Top centre: Melba as Ophelia in Ambroise Thomas' *Hamlet*. *(La Trobe Library)*

Above and bottom: Melba as Nedda in Covent Garden's 1893 production of Leoncavallo's *Pagliacci*. Fernando de Lucia is Canio. *(La Trobe Library)*

Far left: Melba as Massenet's Manon. *(La Trobe Library)*

Left: Melba as Delibes' Lakmé. *(La Trobe Library)*

Top left, top right and centre left: Melba as Marguerite in three different productions of Gounod's *Faust. (All La Trobe Library)*

Above centre and below left: Melba as Violetta in Verdi's *La Traviata. (Both La Trobe Library)*

Above right: Melba as Rosina in Rossini's *The Barber of Seville. (La Trobe Library)*

of my youth that I have relived through you and with you. I count the minutes that separate me from the moment when I will see you tomorrow evening, I hope for longer than this evening? I have so many things to say to you that I cannot write. But that tomorrow evening will come of themselves from my lips when I am near to you. I hope you will give me time to tell you all that I have in my heart. Meanwhile, my dear Nellie, I kiss most affectionately your pretty hands and am always your old

Tipon.[23]

Chapter 6

A TOAST TO MELBA

The royal affair came close to ruining Melba's career. To offend high society's code of conduct at that time was box-office suicide. Queen Victoria had already rejected her for a *Faust* at Windsor Castle in favour of Albani. The message was clear enough. Melba bowed to the conventions, remained discreetly silent and sent the Duc away. Charles Armstrong divorced her in Texas in 1900 on the grounds of six years desertion. She denied this through counsel.

George Armstrong was sent to a preparatory school at Littlehampton in Sussex, Hetherington says at the age of 10 or 11, that is in 1893 or 1894, and that some months later George's father and his uncle Montague arrived without warning. He was told he was to go on a long journey. His bags were packed hastily and with the school's acquiescence, but without Melba's consent, George was shipped out to America where his mother had no right to claim him.

Melba finally traced the boy to Charlie's farm in Texas but it was ten years before he saw his mother again. By then he could ride a horse as well as his father, but his general education had been sadly neglected. If Hetherington was right, why did Melba, who spent considerable time touring in America, decide not to see her only child. Possibly because she felt an adolescent boy had more to gain from life with his father than she could offer. To interfere could only lead to arguments with Charlie which the boy could well do without. In any case George had been reared at an English-style distance from his mother from the start. Nursemaids and school matrons would have known more about him than Nellie. The bond could hardly have been strong. Besides, Charlie would have been quite capable of raising yet another storm had she gone against him. The acid of the gossip columns would have re-opened old wounds and jeopardised her career yet again. This was the one thing Melba would not tolerate.

But there is later evidence than that available to Hetherington. In 1971 the National Library of Australia acquired the Baron Podhragy papers from Vienna. Podhragy was Marchesi's grandson. Among his Melba letters are some which give George's age when his father removed him from Melba's custody as eight and which indicate that George was restored to Melba in his late teens after Charlie had taken him to hear her sing in Portland, Oregon. Anne Fairbairn, the archivist ho negotiated the transfer of the collection, writes:

One night Charles took young George to hear his mother sing in Portland, Oregon. His famous mother stood, glittering with diamonds, and George was hypnotised. He could not resist the temptation of her invitation to go and live with her. Charles was so lonely without his son that he sold his farm in Texas, and died in 1946, a recluse, in Victoria, British Columbia, having never given his side of his tragic marriage even to his family in Ireland. Melba was the world's most famous opera singer, but to her husband, however difficult, she gave a life of sorrow ... When George came back to live with her, Melba gave much time to him. She wrote to Mathilde Marchesi: 'I have decided not to work so hard in the future and devote more time to my beloved George who is an angel'. In another letter she wrote: 'George is very well and sends you both his love. He is very busy studying for Oxford'. But Nellie was a domineering mother. She lavished money and affection on George and organised his life, and his first marriage, which she planned, ended in divorce. He then found happiness with a wife of his own choosing.[1]

The Charles Armstrong of the Fairbairn portrait is the same man f whom Melba wrote to Marchesi at the height of the d'Orléans candal: 'I am awfully afraid (entre nous) my husband is going to rrive very soon, and I am awfully uneasy as you know. How I am fraid of him when he has one of his mad fits on!'. And it is the ame domineering mother who befriended George's second wife, Evie, nd suffered with her when Evie's first child died.

But she was saddened by the parting with the Duc and never quite ecovered. It was not her habit to reveal her deepest feelings to anyone, ut the press, sympathetic to her romantic cause, frequently reported er look of loneliness, her air of emotional fragility.

In the spring of 1892 Melba sang *Lucia* at Nice as part of a tour f distraction, won first prize for the best decorated car in the annual Battle of Flowers carnival and was fêted by the Prince and Princess of Monaco. By then the public had forgiven her and the opera was acked.

In Sicily she sang *La Traviata* at Palermo where she found Gaetano Braga, a fashionable composer of unfashionable operas, was staying in he hotel room next to hers. He was playing the cello late at night nd she recognised the music and began to sing. He demanded to see er at once. Melba said no, she was in bed, but Braga persisted. His ge, she said, tempted her to let him in. What harm was there in a amous old man talking to a famous young woman in the middle of he night? But Nellie had learned caution. At 63 years old Braga, it eems, was still not to be trusted, much less the hotel staff. They met next day at 2 p.m. and Braga presented her with an armful of flowers.

THE VOICE

François-Auguste Gevaert: 'Melba's art is as spontaneous as the murmur of the brook. She sings because she must sing'.

Comte de Fontenailles: 'Combien je garderai bon souvenir, chére Madame, de ce joli matin de mai où je vous attendais dans votre petit salon, la fenêtre ouverte, en écoutant les oiseaux chanter dans les grands arbres du jardin ... Vous êtes arrivée ... et vous avez chanté ... et les petits oiseaux se sont tus, furieux de la concurrence et charmés par votre voix'.

Sarah Bernhardt: 'A la plus charmante femme; à la plus délicieuse artiste; à la voix de pur cristel, la plus vive sympathie'.

Emmanuel Bourquet: 'La prima donna incontestée de notre Academie nationale de musique [Paris]'.

Melba formed a number of friendships with men, some of the
more than platonic, but for the rest of her life she was wary of publ
displays. Wechsberg quotes one of her oldest friends as saying:

Nellie handled her private life with the poise of a great lady. W
would die with curiosity but no one would have dared ask her
question. She had a wonderful way of getting rid of people whe
she expected company that we were not supposed to know of. Sl
would say, 'What are you doing tonight?' which was our exit cue

A second friend told Wechsberg:

I once had a terrible row with Nellie on the Riviera. She had bee
seen constantly with a man there. People talked and I opened n
mouth. I told her she was still married though she certainly ha
no husband. Nellie got mad and gave me a piece of her mind, an
she gave it to me straight. When she got mad even with her be
friends she would let them have it! Afterwards I never said anythir
again. Melba simply wasn't the sort of woman who talks intermir
ably about her romantic days when she gets older. She didn't hav
to escape into the world of her youth, because her entire life w.
full and rich. She had, of course, her moods of nostalgia an
moments of depression, but who hasn't? At any rate, Melba ke|
them to herself.[3]

A third recorded that:

Melba never talked about the men in her life but we knew whe
she was getting involved. In those times her voice had an incar
descence and she would sing with much deeper feeling. She hac
as the French say, 'a tear in her voice'. On such an evening peop
would go home after a Melba performance with great warmth i
their hearts though they couldn't explain what had been differen
It was simple: Melba was in love, and she made everybody fall
little in love with her. Of course all of us knew about the Du
d'Orléans and none of us talked about him. He was the only ma
in her life who was really important. I am sure she never forg∈
the Duc. It was *La Traviata* all over again – the beautiful woma
who loses the man she loves because his family steps in. A corr
story, and one of Melba's most famous parts – on and off stage.[4]

After the Duc, Melba's name was linked with a string of successor
among them Haddon Chambers, then a fashionable London play
wright. He was an Australian, born in Sydney a year before Nellie,
former clerk and jackaroo who failed to make a go of it in Englanc
When he was 21 and was returning home he met a group of music:
entrepreneurs on board ship. With the contacts they gave him he wa
able to find work around the London theatres. His first three play
failed to be noticed. In desperation for a star to launch his work, h

followed Beerbohm Tree into a Turkish bath, locked them both in and read his script of *Captain Swift* to the imprisoned actor. Tree liked the play, took the lead in a production at the Haymarket and Chambers was made.

He went on to produce fourteen plays, the last in 1917, four years before his death. As a writer of the new *fin de siècle* society play he was the vogue, and kept his name consistently before the public with up to 200 performances of each London production but never achieving more than a nod from historians of the English theatre. In retrospect some critics have categorised him with Arnold Bennett and the early Somerset Maugham.

Chambers embodied Australian dreams of success, just as Melba did. Both were practitioners of European high art forms, both had achieved fame and fortune. But where Chambers became to all intents and purposes an Englishman, Melba never lost sight of her origins.

She met Chambers in 1895 when a mutual friend, Henry Russell, invited them both to supper to ease Chambers into a discussion of a libretto adaptation of one of his plays as a vehicle for Melba. Russell recalled:

> Few people knew more about the stage at that time than Haddon, and Melba realised at once how much she could learn from her talented compatriot. The friendship grew and the diva undoubtedly benefited by the care that Haddon bestowed on every new role she learnt, teaching her gradually to be an intelligent actress. I remember Melba telling me how grateful she was for his assistance and how she considered her art had improved by her association with him.[5]

But Chambers' name does not appear in the memoirs.

Unfortunately Chambers' ardour warmed as Melba's cooled. In the end she had some difficulty shaking herself free. The Australian sculptor Bertram Mackennel and the song writer Bernard Rolt were seen as often in her company as Chambers at one time. The friendship with Mackennel lasted for life; the fine marble bust of Melba in the National Gallery of Victoria remains as a tribute to it. Rolt was nowhere near such a successful artist as Mackennel or Chambers. In fact Melba, only too well aware of his needs, left him £100 in her will.

Chambers and Mackennel were both personable men but they were eclipsed by composer Hermann Bemberg. He was Melba's age, the Parisian-born son of an Argentinian banker and his Spanish wife, an amateur singer of some ability. He had wealth, was highly gifted musically and was physically very attractive to both sexes — tall, graceful, sometimes referred to as faun-like, with wit and the kind of *joie de vivre* that won Melba on sight.

I was sitting in my little 'salon' in the Avenue Victor Hugo when

MELBA THE PRACTICAL JOKER

At one time the composer Hermann Bemberg began to regard Melba's Covent Garden dressing-room as his cloakroom, leaving his coat and hat and other belongings there during performances. To teach him a lesson, 'I cut his hat almost completely round the rim, covered the inside of it with black grease paint, cut his umbrella so that it would fall to pieces when it was opened, and put two eggs in his overcoat pocket.

'At the end of the Third Act, Bemberg rushed round for his hat and other belongings, telling me that he had to hurry to Lady de Grey's box, where there was a particularly august assembly of persons waiting for him.

' "Eh bien!" I said, "I hope you enjoy yourself".

'I do not know whether Bemberg did enjoy himself, but Gladys de Grey told me afterwards that he arrived in her box with a face like a nigger, and that when he took off his hat it fell down at her feet.'[1]

1. Melba, *op. cit.*, p. 57.

MELBA THE PRACTICAL JOKER

The Comte Charles de Mornay sent Melba twenty letters in various languages one April Fool's Day. They were all proposals of marriage from legendary noblemen, including de Mornay himself. Melba enjoyed the joke and went out driving. When she got back she found a huge box in her bedroom. She opened it, and as she did there was a piercing noise from inside. It was a turkey which tried to bite her. A second box and the Baron de Saint-Imand, a very sober old friend, were later shown in together. Nervous of what might happen next, Melba asked the Baron to open the box. He obliged. Out jumped a large rabbit. 'The Baron was absolutely horrified because, at the same time as the rabbit, his own card fell out of the box. "Ma carte – c'est une infamie!" I tried to explain to him that it was only a practical joke, but he was so obsessed by the insult that he would not listen to reason and vanished in a cloud of indignation.'[1]

That night de Mornay and his accomplice, Bemberg, dined with Melba. As they settled to the table, a servant came in and asked what he was to do with all the cakes which kept arriving. Not only had he run out of money to pay for them, but he had also run out of space. Without turning a hair Melba said: 'Give them to the concierge, and when he has had enough give them to another concierge. There are plenty of concierges in Paris'.

The party set off for the opera, only to find the box piled with oranges. Again

very slowly and softly the door opened. I could not imagine what it was, and I was just going to shut it when through the crack there was pushed a magnificent bouquet of orchids. This was decidedly intriguing. 'Qui êtes vous?' I cried. The door opened, and I saw a very handsome young man, who advanced towards me, precipitated himself on his knees, and said: 'Only Bemberg'. I began to laugh. It was then noon, and I went on laughing the whole afternoon and most of the evening until midnight.[6]

On 5 July 1892 Bemberg's opera *Elaine*, his only large-scale work of the kind, was given at Covent Garden with Melba and the de Reszkes (to whom it was dedicated), Pol Plançon, Marie Brema and Mathilde Bauermeister, but it was a *succès d'estime*, nothing more. Bemberg withdrew it. The revised version of 1893 went somewhat better, but the truth was that his was a light-weight talent. He had studied with Bizet and Henri Maréchel, Théodore Dubois, Gounod and Massenet, and he was awarded the Rossini prize. His one-act opera *Le Baiser de Suzon*, to Paul Barbier's libretto, was produced in 1889 at the Opéra-Comique, and he was the first to write music for Oscar Wilde's *Salome*. But in spite of the auspicious beginnings Bemberg remained simply an ornament in musical society, his ambition, as Melba put it, 'clogged by a large private fortune'.

Melba's friendships with men, as opposed to her liaisons, sometimes took odd forms. There was the Baron de Saint-Amart whose hobby it was to take up new prima donnas and promote their cause. He had worshipped Albani and Patti and helped launch the three Emmas – Eames, Nevada and Calvé. He favoured Sibyl Sanderson and Gabrielle Strauss. Melba was next. She was grateful, but she disliked his grand manner and his meanness – he never so much as sent his protégés a bunch of flowers. On his side there was no question of physical intimacy. Colson says not only was he very religious but 'he suffered from a nervous complaint which rendered impossible any "crisis d'amour" ', letting himself go only in verse.

Alfred de Rothschild, an intimate of Patti's, became equally enchanted with Melba. He was a little man, obsessed by fears of illness and death, but he loved the opera and idolised the prima donnas. At his parties these women sang without fee, knowing full well that he would send them gifts far in excess of the sordid money that was the usual thing, and, like Melba, they profited from his financial advice at little gatherings for lunch in the Rothschild offices where a £100 note slipped into the singer's table napkin was the usual hors d'oeuvre.

Hetherington called Rothschild a fop, a hypochondriac, something of a poseur but a financier who would afford his own symphony to conduct with an ivory baton banded in diamonds. Colson dubbed the orchestra 'a private band', which he kept with a small circus at Malton, his estate near Wendover, where, dressed as a ringmaster, he would stand in the ring cracking his whip, 'a queer little figure' no one dared laugh at.

For Melba, Rothschild's friendship was crucial. Her income from investments made on his advice eventually made the money she earned from her singing a comparatively minor matter. She makes no mention of Rothschild's orchestra in the memoirs though the circus and the dog kennels rate a paragraph describing the ritual Sunday inspection, the guests in elegant little pony carts, the host followed about by the animals. Rothschild believed his menagerie loved him. Melba thought the affection had something to do with the sugar, apples and carrots he carried in his pockets.

It was at Rothschild's that she dined with Cecil Rhodes, whom she had long wanted to meet. When her host told her Rhodes, an infrequent visitor to London, was coming, she dropped everything. He turned out to be a disappointment, however. After a few conventional words he fell silent. Two courses later Melba gave up and turned to her neighbour. Suddenly Rhodes intoned, 'Which is it that appeals to you most, the art or the applause?' Melba, tried beyond politeness, snapped, 'How dare you ask me such a question?' There was a flurry of muttering. Then Rhodes whispered, 'I apologise. After all, it's the *power* that we like – the power!'

Joachim, Kubelik, Paderewski, the French actor Coquelin, millionaire John Jacob Astor – the list of Melba's conquests is endless and most of it probably apocryphal. Her admirers felt life-long devotion, but for those she failed to win over the effect seems to have been equally fervent and long lived. The American novelist Marion Crawford was reduced to tears once as Melba sang to him in private. To ease him out of the embarrassment she asked him to write in her autograph book. Crawford had long since lost any feeling for women when a youthful affair ended in rejection. He wrote in the book: 'Credo in resurrectionem mortuorum' (I believe in the resurrection of the dead). Their friendship never looked back.

Among the disaffected was the Australian baritone Peter Dawson who knew Nellie as a colleague. In the mildest Melba passage of his autobiography he wrote that

> there is no doubt that she possessed a glorious voice. The trouble was that she was unable to get 'down to earth' again after her rave notices. From the nice Australian girl she became the spoilt social snob of the musical world.[7]

John Lemmone, her Australian business manager and associate flautist over a period of forty-seven years, was her closest male friend. It was presumed he was also her lover but neither party ever admitted to it.

At Covent Garden the 1892 season saw Harris' introduction of a series of German operas sung in the original language. He imported,

Melba ordered them to be given away and pretended that nothing had occurred. The next day payment for the cakes arrived. Not a cheque but a sticky mass of one centime stamps, so large that Melba said she could have papered her bathroom with it.

A year later Melba had her revenge. Every quarter of an hour she sent the fastidious Bemberg a bath, beginning at 8 a.m. and ending at midday. At noon a Professeur de Memoire arrived to give Bemberg lessons and refused to leave, saying Bemberg had forgotten that he had sent for him. By mid-afternoon Bemberg, almost in tears, was at Melba's flat crying quits.

1. Melba, *op. cit.*, pp. 59–61.

in effect, the whole Hamburg Opera with its recently appointed Kapellmeister, Gustav Mahler, then 32 years old. With expenses for Wagner's *The Ring* at an all-time high the seven-performance series prices were set at £42 for pit and grand tier boxes, and scaled down to £4 18s for balcony stalls. The regular Italian and French series held their audiences but the Germans attracted not only the German colony but many of the Jewish city merchants who knew Harris as a sheriff of London. The regular box holders always hesitated over a new series. The merchants, eager to join high society by imitation, snapped up the boxes. The end result was a subtle change in the Covent Garden audiences as the merchants infiltrated the regular series, and though the aristocracy still turned out, especially for Melba nights, the nobility faded from the house. Prices and language problems may have lain at the root of it, but so too did the trend towards taking opera seriously. When electric light was added to the auditorium that year, gas was kept for the orchestra pit in order to let the players see their parts but the main lights were lowered and silence enjoined after the continental custom. Jewish seriousness and scholarship in music very slowly added its weight to such practices. Ladies who dressed to be seen, opera buffs who bought libretto booklets at the door to follow during the performance, and fashionables who liked to gossip during the boring bits were put out at the stringency of the new order, but opera as an art form rather than a social one had arrived at Covent Garden.

Melba sang in *Elaine, Faust, Lohengrin* and *Roméo et Juliette* in the Royal Opera season from May to July, and in *Aida, Faust, Lohengrin, Otello* and *Rigoletto* in the autumn–winter season beginning in October and stretching on into early 1893. Emma Calvé made her début that year at Covent Garden. She, too, was a Marchesi pupil with a Brussels and Paris reputation. She created the role of Suzel in Mascagni's *L'Amico Fritz* in Rome in 1891 and the first Paris Santuzza in *Cavalleria Rusticana* the same year, repeating both very successfully in the Covent Garden season. Hermann Klein, the *Sunday Times* critic, acclaimed Calvé:

> we felt we were listening to the opera [*Cavalleria*] for the first time . . . indescribable was the impression created by the strangely poignant tones of Calvé's voice, the extraordinary charm of her expressive singing, the tragic power and the intensity of her acting. Criticism for once was silent; enthusiasm broke forth only after the curtain had fallen. We realised that we were in the presence of a new and towering genius.[8]

Melba was faced with a genuine rival. When she countered with Bemberg's *Elaine* on 5 July, Klein wrote: '. . . we could easily have been spared novelties so dull; but both composers [Bemberg and de Lara, whose *Light of Asia* appeared on 11 June] had friends on either ide of the footlights'.

Melba was too ill to appear in the Ben Davies' *Faust* début on 25 uly but sang Elsa in the closing *Lohengrin* three days later with Louise Meisslinger, a pupil of Viardot. In August she holidayed at Aix and accepted several 'Continental engagements'. On 4 November she sang her first *Aida*, 'displaying greater energy as an actress than ever before, and [with] faultless vocalization', though it was generally thought the costumes were ugly and the 'black ropes that served for hair' hideous. On 23 November, with only four days' study, she appeared as Desdemona. Her memory failed her for a few bars in the ensemble of the third act. The critics noticed. Calvé's shadow grew larger.

Colson says Calvé, the de Reszkes and Melba were summoned to Windsor Castle to perform *Carmen* before Queen Victoria, with Melba as Micaëla to Calvé's title role. A bizarre event, surely, considering the subject of the opera and the Queen's tastes. Calvé did not appear as Carmen at Covent Garden until 1893. After the Windsor performance the two divas embraced affectionately, and if Colson is right this makes it an even more bizarre occasion.

In the memoirs Melba states that she was engaged to sing in New York in 1892 and that when she arrived in Paris from the Sicilian tour she was greeted with the news that the Metropolitan Opera House had been burnt down and the engagement was cancelled. (In fact she sang in the Covent Garden summer season before the fire occurred on 27 August 1892.) She says she refused to press for the money owed under the contract, telling Henry Abbey and Maurice Grau, the Met.'s impresarios, she couldn't expect to be paid if she hadn't sung. However, she only had £200 in the bank and no immediate engagement was in sight. Knowing Grau was holidaying at Nice, she booked herself and two maids into his hotel, the best in town and one she could ill afford. Grau asked her if she would sing at Nice for 4000 francs a night. She waved him away with supreme indifference: 'I wouldn't dream of singing for less than 5000', she said, and got it – 5000 francs of bluff. For whatever reason, Melba was singing in Nice before the May start to the Covent Garden season; it had nothing to do with the fire at the Met.

In December Melba was in Paris for the professional jubilee of the singer Marie Zieger Alboni. In March 1893 she made a serious bid for the favour of the Italians. Without that additional conquest, Calvé's claims might have outweighed Melba's. She could no longer afford to let her rival outshine her on any field. Milan's La Scala was her target. She was to open in *Lucia di Lammermoor* on 16 March, but Patti, the long-term house favourite, had appeared there in January, followed only weeks later by the première of *Falstaff*; the enthusiasm of the regulars seemed exhausted. After so much excitement a foreign soprano without claim to Milanese loyalty stood little chance of rousing La Scala from its refractory state. To make matters worse, after the first

THE LA SCALA DEBUT, MILAN 1893

On 17 March 1893 Aldo Noseda, critic for *Corriere della Sera*, wrote of Melba's début at La Scala: 'It was a true and genuine success. Who expected it? No one, or almost no one. The public this year is not in an optimistic mood. To nibble now and then at a bit of soprano, to take a mouthful of tenor, is its regular function – in Lent almost a first necessity. The betting might have been ten to one that almost all the spectators went to La Scala last evening with a certain fear, mingled with ill-concealed flattery that they were about to offer on the holocaust of the diva Melba the complete annihilation of *Lucia*, the said annihilation to terminate with the sanguinary sacrifice of the diva herself. When, at the end of the first act, the public realized that its gloomy expectations had melted away in the warm light of reality, it seemed as stupid as an elephant before a corkscrew. . . .

'Madame Melba won a great battle yesterday. Many are the stars who have fallen on the stage of La Scala, and how much greater was the fame which preceded them, how much more were we led to expect from them! Yesterday evening's success counted as one of the most gratifying to the *amour propre* of an artist, and, let us frankly say, was flattering to the reputation of our public, who discerned, with the fine taste of a connoisseur, the exceptional qualities of the singer, who left little to be desired even as an actress.

'Amongst the useless things which the so-called wisdom of

rehearsal rumours spread that her début would be a fiasco. The musicians who might normally have called to pay their respects to a distinguished visitor hesitated, all but the composer–poet Arrigo Boito who went to her as soon as the first whispers began. Things looked so bad that a Venetian impresario approached Melba's agent at La Scala and suggested she leave at once for Venice where he had everything underway for *I Rantzau*. Threatening letters began to arrive – she would be poisoned, her hotel lift would malfunction if she used it, there would be a stiletto waiting for her if she walked in the streets. If it had not been for the calm good sense of her secretary, Louie Mason, Melba said she would have panicked.

When at last, heart throbbing and in a state of extreme anxiety, Melba stepped on to the stage at La Scala, she found herself uncharacteristically looking at the audience, only faintly visible to her close to the footlights and above in the boxes where the musical experts habitually sat. To her dismay she saw nothing but backs turned to her. But the seating in these boxes was angled so that the occupant had to turn towards the stage against the rigidity of the seats. What Melba saw was the end of conversation that her entry stirred up. Within moments she had everyone's attention. The experts fell oppressively silent, then turned. The act ran to a steady crescendo of 'Bravos', ending in a ten-minute standing ovation after the Mad Scene. Melba was completely unnerved by the unexpectedness of it.

The Milan début led to offers from all over the country. She agreed to Florence, Turin and Genoa, taking with her some of the soloists and the orchestra of La Scala in a triumphal procession across Italy. In Milan she met Verdi briefly, and was impressed by his simplicity and his reserve. At a later date she worked with him on *Rigoletto* and *Aida* (her favourite Verdi opera) and possibly *Otello*, not, as she claimed in her memoirs, at that time. Verdi died eight years later, although Melba says 'not long afterwards'. Leoncavallo and Puccini were also paraded for her and duly said all the correct things. Leoncavallo asked if she would be the first London Nedda. *I Pagliacci* was to be premièred at the Teatro del Verme in Milan on 17 May 1892. Melba introduced the opera at Covent Garden on her 32nd birthday and on 11 December 1893 in New York at the Met.

In April she toured to Lyons, Marseilles and other French provincial cities where her Ophélie was the role in demand, but she was back at Covent Garden for the opening of the season on 15 May with *Lohengrin*, followed by *Faust*, *Roméo et Juliette*, and a single performance of the new Mascagni, *I Rantzau*.

The *Roméo* was a special performance to celebrate the marriage of the Duke of York and Princess Mary of Teck (later George V and Queen Mary). The house was massed with roses, a contingent of Beefeaters in full regalia formed a guard of honour along the crimson lined corridors, and for the first and only time before the Great War a complete opera was performed – rather than the usual excerpts – for a royal occasion.

Calvé's triumph in her first *Carmen* that season outdid Melba's in *I Pagliacci*. In need of new conquests where Calvé was no competition, Melba set off that autumn for her first tour of Sweden and Denmark. On 31 October she sang Juliette at the opera house in Stockholm and later gave Elsa, Marguerite and scenes from *Hamlet* and *Lucia*. Like Milan, Stockholm had its house favourites – this time Jenny Lind and Christine Nilsson.

Dagens Nigheter's critic wrote of Melba's first Swedish appearance in a Wagnerian role:

Melba *is* Elsa; Melba, who by competent judges is said to have her greatest strength in pure *coloratura* parts, and whose voice might really be classed as soprano *légère*; Melba whose dramatic talent does not yet exist, if we may take the word of the English critics. Well, as dramatic understanding does not reach very high in England, one can scarcely wonder, perhaps, if she did not trouble in that country. That, when she wishes, she can even in dramatic work satisfactorily render the most difficult parts, it has pleased her to show to our public. Everyone who sees her as Elsa is soon convinced that the famous singer is also a great actress.[9]

This was welcome praise after the *Daily Telegraph's* laconic opinion of the same role at Covent Garden five months previously: 'There were moments . . . when her embodiment of the least dramatic of Wagner's heroines seemed a trifle too pronounced'.

Later opinion set Melba down as no better and not much worse than most opera singers, ignoring the early reviews. Her efforts with Bernhardt and Chambers reaped no rewards, but if she learned anything from them it could only have been a style of acting no longer in use in the theatre by the time she was in mid-career. Praise in the 1890s may have been for a gallant try at an accepted technique. The subsequent dismissal of Melba as an actress could also have signalled the rejection of the acting style of a previous era kept intact by an ageing star who did not find it necessary to re-learn her craft.

Towards the end of the season an unexpected royal command performance for the King of Sweden disrupted Melba's plans for her first American tour. Grau, her manager on both sides of the Atlantic, had to put everything back a week. King Oscar asked for an arduous night's work – the second act from *Lohengrin*, the Balcony Scene from *Roméo et Juliette*, the Mad Scene from *Lucia* and the last act of *Faust* – but he was so swept away by the performance that he twice rose to his feet to applaud, taking an astonished and uncertain audience with him. Melba was summoned to the palace the next day to be decorated with the Order of Literature and Art. As he moved to attach the order to Melba's dress the King discovered there was no backing pin

a nation burdens itself by transmitting from one generation to another is the foolish aphorism, ''comparisons are odious''. The devil they are: but how if the values should be relative, and everything not come up to the same standard? Well, then, the typical singer on whom we who write are forced to base our criterion of judgement, and therefore our comparisons, is Adelina Patti. She remains for us the most perfect exponent of the great art of singing. How many times last evening we told ourselves that for marvellous facility of production, for the finished art of modulation, for pureness of intonation, Madame Melba again renewed in us the intense enjoyment experienced so many years ago when listening to the diva Patti! Who else now, may we ask, can sing like Melba? It is true we have not, so far, seen her in strongly dramatic parts – not in the great roles of the repertoire of new operas – neither as Elsa nor Isolde; but, then, who suggested that as yet she has her harp completely slung? Ah, but to bring close to our hearts' ears the magic of the inspired melodies of the old Italian masters – no one now interprets them as she can. We may add that the facility and good taste with which she showed she could play with what to others would be stupendous difficulties – technique, perilous leaps, scales of the most perfect limpidity, the purest trills – gave to this somewhat out-of-date music a witchery and fascination entirely novel.'

and asked Melba if she had one. She said she had nothing but a hat pin. When an equerry provided a sewing pin the King, remembering the old superstition, said, 'But this may cut our friendship if I don't give you something in exchange' and kissed her fervently.

In Stockholm the King's pleasure in the prima donna had its usual effect. Five thousand people turned out to see her off at the station, 'all singing their divine Swedish folk tunes', the memoirs gush.

Three years later 'an enormous man' confronted Melba's butler in London demanding to see her. The butler, flurried, burst into the sitting room to tell his mistress some lunatic calling himself the King of Sweden was forcing his way in. Oscar was right behind him: 'I've come to have some tea with you – I'm absolutely dying for a cup of tea', he announced. It was produced. 'Now, let's sing', he commanded, flinging open the *Lohengrin* score from Melba's library. To her surprise the King turned out to have a 'fresh, sweet tenor voice'. They sang duet after duet.

According to Murphy, foreigners were not permitted on the stage of Denmark's only opera house, so Melba's Copenhagen appearances were limited to two concerts, the first on 12 November. By then her European reputation was established, but when she sailed for America late in 1893 she was not yet the supreme diva, the marker by which all others had to be measured. She was one of several great singers, all competing for top billing, top fees, and contracts for the places and the choice of roles that would enhance their status and clinch the bookings for years ahead.

Her voice was fully developed, the experiences of life had matured its use as an expressive tool of trade, her health supported it, and her musical judgement as far as the use of that voice was concerned was informed and, after one major mistake, reliable. She was shrewd in business matters; Mitchell and Marchesi had served her well.

The voice itself she described as 'like a glorified boy's voice'. Its range was from B flat below middle C to the F sharp above high C, if Wechsberg is to be believed; B flat below to F[111] if you accept Rosenthal and Warrack's data. Some authorities claim the recordings are not to be relied on in the matter since the technical problems of early discs and their deterioration over time make even the originals faintly pitch-suspect, though it can only be a matter of minute change.

Opinions about the quality of Melba's voice are legion. Every critic who heard her attempted an analysis and the writer who sat through even a single performance had something to say about it. So did her friends, her enemies, her colleagues and her pupils. Their verdict was unanimous – a unique, silvery voice, pure and seamless, with the power to sweep the listener to emotional heights and near-religious ecstasy.

Melba left from Le Havre for New York and her first American tour late in 1893. The winter crossing was exceptionally rough. She was exhausted from seasickness and unable to rest in the steam-heating of the Waldorf Hotel, suffocated by an unaccustomed luxury her lungs could ill afford.

Her contract with Abbey and Grau included performances at the Met. but it also provided for appearances in Boston and, more importantly, in Chicago, where the World's Fair promised audiences of a size no entrepreneur could afford to ignore. She was to sing *Lucia di Lammermoor, Semiramide, Roméo et Juliette, Tannhäuser, Faust, Hamlet,* and *I Pagliacci* (11 December – the first time it was staged in America) at the Met. There had been no opera in New York for a season after the fire and audiences, swollen by a huge influx of World's Fair visitors, were in the mood for new voices and all the glitter of what was most grand in opera. For a career almost at its zenith it was a challenge and a necessity. If the Americans accepted her, Melba could step up from first class to world class. If she could sustain the reputation gained through the American connection there would be no one to touch her – she would stand alone.

Opera in America began in colonial times with imported English ballad opera, followed by other European comic styles. In the 19th century first Italian opera, the French grand opera and finally German music-drama went in and out of fashion. There were tentative and unsuccessful efforts by native composers, most of it imitative of whatever style was the vogue, with librettos at times self-consciously centered on so-called American themes, the Indians and the Puritans being the most popular subjects. Prizes were offered, new operas, some of them genuinely experimental, opened with a flourish, closed shortly afterwards and were set aside and forgotten. The public wanted sumptuous settings for established European operas sung by imported stars.

Some American sources give the first opera performance date as 1703, though there is some uncertainty about this even among musicologists. Certainly ballad operas were playing in New York by the mid 18th century and there were fairly regular seasons for the next fifty years. In fact the number of performances in proportion to population was greater than at any period since.

The first season of regular Italian opera in New York was given in 1825, the company led by Manuel Garcia. The American music lover of the early 19th century was familiar with operas by Paisiello, Mozart, Beethoven, Weber, Boieldieu, Auber, Donizetti and Bellini. Entrepreneurs often took up new works with alacrity. Rossini's *The Barber of Seville* played in New York in 1819, three years after its Italian première and six months before it was first staged in Paris. Weber's *Der Freischütz* (1821) appeared in New York in 1825, and excerpts from Wagner's *Tannhäuser* (1845) were given by the Germania Society in 1852, at a time when Wagner was not heard much in most of the European musical centres.

THE VOICE

The critics

Henry Krehbiel, from the *New York Tribune*, wrote on Melba's American début: 'There is no need to mince matters here, and therefore no exception be made even in favour of Mdme Patti. Mdme Melba is at the zenith of her powers. Her voice is charmingly fresh, and exquisitely beautiful, and her tone production is more natural, and more spontaneous than that of the marvellous woman who so long upheld the standard of bel canto throughout the world.

'Mdme Melba is not obliged to seek her means or to guard against possible failure. All that she wants lies in her voice ready to hand. Its range is commensurate with all that can possibly be asked of it, and she moves with greatest ease in the regions which are most carefully avoided by most of the singers of today. To throw out those scintillant [*sic*] bubbles of sound which used to be looked upon as the highest achievement in singing seems to be a perfectly natural mode of emotional expression with her. Concerning the reasonableness of such a method of expression we are not concerned now. It is enough that Mdme Melba comes nearer to providing it with justification than anybody who essays the task on the contemporaneous stage, unless it be Madame Sembrich.

'Added to all this, she has most admirable musical instincts, and these we have been taught to admire more than ever, even while we have been learning to give the reverence due to the dramatic elements in the modern lyric drama. It was small wonder that the audience last night (not so numerous an audience as might have been expected under the circumstances, but evidently one able to appreciate good singing) gave Mdme Melba such enthusiastic tokens of approbation as to convince her that she was permanently established in the good will of our public. It was a superb greeting, superbly deserved'.[1]

W. J. Henderson, from the *New York Times*, wrote on Melba's Wagner failure: 'Too many considerations for dismissal at this time surround the first essay of Mdme Melba in German opera. She appeared, of course, at a late hour, and there were evidences that even her experience and self-confidence were not proof against the assaults of nervousness. It is undeniable, and may as well be said now as later, that the quality of her voice and her style of singing are not suited to a complete embodiment of Brünnhilde, and she can be praised now only for her conscientious effort and for her ambition, which was more potent than wise.

'The performance as a whole was a splendid success, and its one grave shortcoming may be dismissed kindly at this time'.[2]

1. William H. Seltsam (ed.), *Metropolitan opera annals.*
2. *Ibid.*

The Metropolitan Opera House at Broadway and 39th Street, where Melba was to make her American début on 4 December 1893 in *Lucia*, dated from 1883. The fire of 1892 meant extensive rebuilding but not demolition.

On opening night Melba faced a new audience in a new house and a new country. Dufriche, who was to sing Enrico, was taken ill and replaced by an Enrico who had no time to rehearse the part. It was enough to unnerve any soprano. On top of this Melba was to sing a role that had been Patti's American property at a time when Patti herself was touring the United States. And, finally, Melba faced a social set in the Met. boxes which was unlikely to be won over by a a mere entertainer. As she said:

> In London if an artist made a great success, he or she was received on a footing of absolute equality with the most 'exalted' people in the Capital. Not so in New York. An artist was an artist, and although she might be the subject of amazing hospitality, though innumerable kindnesses might be showered upon her, there was always a subtle difference between her and the rest of society . . . However, I was too much interested in my work to bother much about anything so material as the Four Hundred.[10]

And the Four Hundred had no friendly leader to play Lady de Grey's role for her in New York.

Colson claimed that at the time no singer who had not had a success at Covent Garden had a hope of a Met. engagement. Local artists – Nordica, Eames, David Bisphan – had to make their New York débuts via European opera houses. Melba was coming in with all the right credentials.

The audience for *Lucia* on 4 December was cold. When some of the occupants of the best boxes applauded the house refused to follow, suspecting foreign sympathies in company members who spent too much time abroad. After the Mad Scene there was some enthusiasm, but next day the *New York Tribune* was one of the few critical voices in her favour. Friends tried to console her, saying she had come on too late in the season when both her rivals, Eames and Calvé, had already won their following weeks before. Melba, nothing daunted, said: 'If it's been Madame Eames and Madame Calvé at the start, it'll be Madame Melba at the end'.

She set out to upstage both women. A Sunday evening concert series by artists from the opera had been running in the season but had failed to pick up an audience. The stars turned their backs on it Melba decided to use the concerts as a show-window and a month after her début turned the series into a popular success. The press and the opera public began to pay attention.

On 19 January 1894 she appeared as Juliette, this time to overwhelming applause, but the critics regarded Nedda and Ophélie as unsuitable roles for her, although they were prepared to warm to her ill-prepared first Elizabeth in *Tannhäuser* (in French on 29 January with Vignas as Tannhäuser and Ancona as Wolfram, with Mancinelli conducting), and to her Elsa in *Lohengrin* (in Italian on 6 February with Vignas as Lohengrin, Ancona as Telramund and Edouard de Reszke as the King). Melba maintained that this was her first *Tannhäuser*, learned in three days, the result of having the performance announced while she was in Washington and her feeling that she was infected with the American spirit of getting things done'. She read the announcement in the *New York Herald,* accepted it as a *fait accompli* and tried to learn the part – though not successfully. Of course it could all have been a fine piece of audience tease, a way of getting publicity. The role was, after all, one she had heard in at least two seasons at Covent Garden and the score of which she undoubtedly owned and studied.

The official Met. season ended with a triumphant *Faust* on 23 February, with both the de Reszkes. At the end of the performance the brothers responded to demands for a Melba encore by pushing a piano onstage so that Jean could accompany her in 'Home sweet home'.

In Chicago it was *Lucia* again, but this time the cold New York reception was not repeated. The *Herald* said:

> It is idle even, through fear of appearing over-enthusiastic, to deny the self-evident fact of her commanding superiority. There is but one voice belonging to the generation with which Melba's may properly be compared, and that is the voice of Patti as it was known to us and admired a dozen years ago, when in the full glory of its prime. It exhibits the same faultless timbre, the same purity and smoothness throughout a wide range, the same electric quality, the same elasticity and flexibility, the same richness and colour. And yet there is a tinge of added warmth to give it individuality. Her faculty of execution is a marvel. The stage has seldom known a finer example of tone production, or a voice more persuasive and enchanting. Such a triumph so magnificently rounded out and complete is almost without parallel in the history of our stage.[11]

The Chicago *Record* described her in *Semiramide* (with Scalchi and Edouard de Reszke) as 'the greatest artist of the time'. For *Roméo et Juliette* the town turned out in spite of it being Holy Thursday. At the end of the Balcony Scene the applause spilled over into Jean de Reszke's succeeding number, forcing him to stop twice until the conductor could regain control of his audience. Melba seemed inspired by the adulation. She surprised everyone with a perfect Elizabeth in a banner-night *Tannhäuser* and sent the fashion writers into a frenzy over the £500 costume she wore in the second act.

In Philadelphia she sang a near-fatal Gilda, almost falling off the

THE VOICE

W. J. Henderson, critic for the *New York Times*, later of the *New York Sun*, who heard Melba at her best in the ten years after the American début of 1893, wrote: 'No words can convey to a music lover who did not hear Melba any idea of the sounds with which she ravished all ears . . . One could say, "It's the unique voice of the world". This writer never heard any other just like it. Its beauty, its clarion quality, its power differed from the flutey notes of Patti. Melba's voice has been called silvery, but what does that signify? There is one quality which it had and which may be comprehended even by those who did not hear her; it had splendour. The tones glowed with a star-like brilliance. They flamed with a white flame . . .'[1]

'. . . and they possessed a remarkable force which the famous singer always used with continence. She gave the impression of singing well within her limits.'[2]

'The Melba attack was little short of marvellous. The term "attack" is not a good one. Melba indeed has no attack. She opened her mouth and a tone was in existence. It began without ictus, when she wished it to, and without betrayal of breathing. It simply was there. When she wished to make a bold attack, as in the trio of the last scene of *Faust*, she made it with the clear silvery stroke of a bell.'

'From B flat below the clef to the high F . . . the scale was beautifully equalized throughout and there was not the smallest change in the quality from top to bottom.'[3]

1. Joseph Wechsberg, *Red Plush and Black Velvet*, pp 55–6.

2. Notes to *Nellie Melba: The London Recordings 1904–26*, RLS 719 (EMI 1976; ed. Paul Holmes).
3. *The New Grove Dictionary of Music and Musicians*.

back of the railless stairway set and as a result cutting short the trill that climaxes the scene out of sheer fright. It was no wonder that she preferred to sing season after season in houses where the conditions of rehearsal and set design were known quantities; the near-misses were enough to make any singer want to stay at home. Most of it was due to the too well-known last-minute theatrical syndrome, alias inefficiency, in the face of the running demands of too little time and no contingency plans to deal with it.

Back in New York for the supplementary season, Melba found *Lohengrin* replaced by *Semiramide* when three of the possible Ortruds – Fursch-Madi, Domenech and Guercia – were *all* taken ill, but her *Lucia* (26 April) reversed the response it received when she made her Met. début. At the end the audience refused to go home. Melba was obliged to give up trying to shed her costume in her dressing-room, put on a wrapper and appeared on stage in it for the ritual of the wheeled-on piano and the 'impromptu' 'Home sweet home'. The same thing happened at the end of the final polyglot programme that involved Nordica, Calvé, Scalchi, Eames, Arnoldson, Bauermeister, the de Reszkes, Lasalle, de Lucia, Vignas and Carbone. Melba's Mad Scene from *Hamlet*, saw the audience on its feet, recalls with Abbey and Grau, and 'Home sweet home'. The orchestra and most of the box-holders followed her to the Savoy Hotel afterwards and serenaded her as she stood on a balcony overlooking the lobby. Like di Murska before her, she invited the lot of them to supper in the hotel dining-room where the toasts went on for hours. So, though it had been Calvé and Eames at the start of the season, the Australian was right – it *was* Melba at the end.

By May 1894 she was briefly back at La Scala, then at Covent Garden for a revised and impoverished *Elaine*, a *Lucia* and *Rigoletto*, *Roméo* and, paired with Eames, *Lohengrin* and *Faust*. By that time the critics were noting the added power of her lower register. In mid-season Melba sang at the Handel Festival in the Crystal Palace – 'Let the bright seraphim' and 'L'allegro ed il pensieroso'. But the Palace turned out to be no place in which to sing and Melba stormed off, swearing her first appearance there would be her last, which it was.

The second time around, Melba had the shrewdness to let her presence in New York be known well ahead of the Met. season. This time she did *not* avoid the inquisitive, personalised interviewing of the press; the questions about the Duc ignored before were parried now. Her 'melancholy expression' was played up for all its romantic worth, while she herself remained discreetly silent.

Henry Abbey ran pre-season concerts featuring Melba and by 19 November, when she appeared in *Roméo* with the de Reszkes and Plançon, she was the Met.'s acknowledged star, accorded the reigning prima donna's right to first and last of that season's performances. She made concert appearances in Washington, Boston, Providence, New

Above left: Melba as Juliette in a New York production of Gounod's *Roméo et Juliette, circa* 1893. *(La Trobe Library)*

Above centre: Melba as Juliette in Gounod's *Roméo et Juliette.* The mauve cloak is now in the Performing Arts Museum, Melbourne. *(La Trobe Library)*

Above right: Melba as Desdemona in Verdi's *Otello. (Melba Memorial Conservatorium)*

Below left and right: Melba as Juliette in Gounod's *Roméo et Juliette. (Both La Trobe Library)*

Melba as Mimi in Puccini's *La Bohème*.
(Melba Memorial Conservatorium)

Melba with Dino Borgioli in *La Bohème*
performed in Melbourne during the 1924
Melba-Williamson season. *(Melba Memorial
Conservatorium)*

Above right: Melba as Desdemona in a 1924
production of *Otello*. *(National Library of
Australia)*

Right: Covent Garden, 1908, during Melba's
heyday. *(Melba Memorial Conservatorium)*

Melba in the café scene of *La Bohème*, during the 1924 J. C. Williamson season.
(Sonia McKillop)

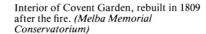

Interior of Covent Garden, rebuilt in 1809
after the fire. *(Melba Memorial
Conservatorium)*

Haven (where the Yale students serenaded her under the window of her hotel for half the night), Baltimore (to begin her long association with the Boston Symphony at the opening of the New Music Hall), and Chicago (where her suite was occupied by a lady who refused to vacate it for her and who was held to ransom by gunmen who wanted the fabled Melba jewellery).

She sang Lucia and Desdemona with Tamagno as Edgardo and the Moor; Micaëla to Zelie de Lussan's Carmen; with Jean de Reszke in *Tannhäuser* and *Lohengrin*; the title role in *Lakmé*; the revised *Elaine* (19 December 1894); as the Queen in *Les Huguenots* (26 December 1894), with a rare combination – Nordica, Scalchi, the Reszkes, Plançon and Maurel; and on 25 January 1895 in *Semiramide* with Scalchi, a Patti opera in which the critics conceded Melba had outstripped the older singer.

In Philadelphia a stock character in the Melba legend appears – the faithful fan, the little old lady who greets the great singer outside the opera house in the snow and asks for a souvenir, a flower, just one rose, from Melba's armful of curtain-call bouquets. The generous hearted lady gives the humble woman *all* the flowers. Through tears the devotee whispers – 'God bless your beautiful heart'. There was a set of verses written to commemorate the act and published all over America. The trouble is that the same little old lady pops up in too many memoirs of those who knew Melba and in too many publicity pieces. Surely there could not have been so many little old ladies (variously said to be ex-flower-sellers outside Covent Garden fallen on hard times, old family retainers and Australian girlhood friends, even ex-rivals) in so many snow drifts outside so many opera houses begging for so many flowers (sometimes it is roses, sometimes it is money). What was probably a cynical publicity exercise for a dull patch in the season became sentimental truth the next day and legend thereafter. Of such stuff are most of the Melba stories made.

Melba's reputation as a hard-swearing, callous, egomaniac is made of the same stuff – a mixture of truth and wishful thinking. Tall poppies incite the envy of ground cover. Melba swore. Did it make her less of a singer or more human? The criticism was intended to cheapen her by contrasting the earthy woman and the ethereal voice, to divorce the god-given talent from the vulgar mind.

She insisted that stage-hands wore noiseless shoes backstage. This has been translated as a dictatorial act, which created strong resentment among the workers. It seems strange today to think that any management would be so slack as to allow noise of any kind backstage during a rehearsal or performance. An egomaniac? What successful singer has not been accused of that? Melba had a career that could only continue if her contracts were renewed each year. The renewal depended on her performance and that of her rivals. Of course she used her friendship with Lady de Grey and later her box-office influence with other

THE MYTH: RECEIVED WISDOM

'She was singing one summer evening at a house in Grosvenor Square. In one of the upper rooms in a house near to it, a man was lying so dangerously ill that he was not expected to recover, so ill indeed that he had prayed to die ... the sound of an exquisite voice came floating through the night into his open window. He said: "If there is such beauty on earth as that voice, let me live". From that moment he began to mend, and eventually recovered his health completely.'[1]

1. Colson, *op. cit.*, p. 219.

THE MYTH: RECEIVED WISDOM

' "Her voice", he said, "you tell me that I never heard it at its best. And yet – there was a morning in Venice some five years ago when a miracle happened. It was an exquisite morning of early spring. The canals were veiled in a haze, and the whole city seemed poised like a silver bubble between this world and the next. Melba and I were sitting on the steps of an old 'palazzo'. She saw a friend passing in a gondola and hailed him. He was a pianist. Impulsively she suggested that we should all go to her 'salon'. She wanted to sing. She sang as I had never heard her sing before. Every trace of age seemed to have left her voice. One felt that there must be some strange harmony between the morning and the song. The mists were lifting from the city, leaving it bright and sparkling; the mists were lifting from her voice, leaving it brilliant and golden. There was indeed a quality of light about her voice. She sang 'Voi che sapete'. It was like a moonbeam stealing into a darkened room. We were all crying when she had finished. I would give a lot to cry like that again." '[1]

1. Beverley Nichols quoted in Colson, *op. cit.*, p. 239.

managements to head off the competition. She knew how and when to exert that influence, like any successful businessman. It was her constant vigilance and her unerring judgement in advancing her career and her attendant finances that her less gifted rivals could not forgive; it was condemned as ungenerous, heartless and unwomanly behaviour.

But as the years went on and Melba remained at the top of her profession the tide of ugly tales began to wash away the sticky sentimental ones and coat the reputation of the most conspicuously successful Australian of the times with indelible muck.

She has been accused of being a snob, of boasting of her acceptance by high society, of sucking up to money and titles and looking down on the rest of us. Most of the evidence for this seems to be in the Nichols–Melba memoirs and the after-effects of Nichols' novel *Evensong*. In the American pages of the memoirs the name-dropping is endless: 'Mrs Paran Stevens, whose daughter was Lady Paget'; and 'Mrs Ogden Mills, the mother of Lady Granard' gives way to, 'I remember W. K. Vanderbilt's house, which was full of divine treasures'; and 'Astor's parties were of course magnificent'.

But the book was meant to sell on both sides of the Atlantic and it was not so much Melba's snobbishness that was being exploited by Nichols as the snobbishness of his potential buyers. Nichols' forte was the tale told against the great but which put his subject in a good light. He deliberately overplayed this act in what appears to be pure mockery of Melba. She comes out of the book as a conceited social climber of monumental petty mindedness. The book's effects were maximised when extracts were syndicated world-wide. Confronted daily by this form of public relations exercise, a public that might never have met the woman or heard her sing, felt free to think badly of Nichols' female Frankenstein.

Melba herself had a bad habit of thinking any publicity was good publicity. Bernard Heinze remembered Sir Edward Cunningham of the *Argus* in Melbourne telling him that Melba once upbraided the press baron for not giving her enough space: 'I don't care what you say', she told him, 'for me or against me, but for heaven's sake say something *about* me'.[12]

She was not above inventing the odd story either. One trip from Melbourne to Sydney was so tediously normal that she had no news ready for the waiting journalists, who expected her to hold forth on the coming opera season (1924 Melba–J. C. Williamson). Instead she launched into a hectic tale of being bitten by fleas in her carriage. She got the headlines she wanted and let loose an investigation of railway hygiene by the authorities that went on for weeks. Such little inventions were harmless enough but Nichols' kind of publicity was destructive. Melba failed to understand this. She liked Nichols. He was, like Bemberg or Chambers, the fashion and keeping up with the fashion had always been one way to keep ahead of her rivals. Nichols was

od company and Melba seldom thought badly of anyone who could
nuse her.

What is not said in the memoirs is that the North American tour
as the kind of success Melba needed to make it possible to bargain
on her own terms – her way into season after season thereafter on
th sides of the Atlantic. She went from summer seasons in London
winter seasons in New York, trailing an entourage fit for minor
yalty, living in grand hotels and expensive rented mansions (often
e property of hard-up members of the nobility), dining with the
eat and singing at their parties for enormous fees, ablaze with
amonds and fame. It gave her the final boost to the top that had
en necessary. From that point onwards she was alone and, for a
ne, unassailable.

The New York season of 1895 ended for her on 4 May. She
urned to Covent Garden for *Faust*, *Huguenots* (Marguerite de Valois),
ucia, *Rigoletto* and *Roméo*, and a management-enforced Micaëla to
alvé's brilliant Carmen before the Duke of Saxe-Coburg-Gotha and
e Crown Princess Stephanie of Austria. She was outshone. But it
as the year of Patti's return and in spite of the American publicity
alvé and Melba were eclipsed.

Melba stepped round the Patti onslaught by repeating the American
ncert manoeuvre. With Arthur Nikisch conducting, she appeared at
ueen's Hall before the Crown Prince and Princess of Romania and
e Grand Duke and Duchess of Hesse. It did little more than keep
er name from being totally swamped in a rare season.

She tried the 'stage accident' story as a publicity diversion. The
ueen in *Huguenots* has a court scene in which she talks to her ladies
audibly while the music goes on for others. Melba got caught up
the mime and missed her cue, then forgot the next phrase in her
onfusion. After a minute gap which the audience failed to notice,
e improvised, ending with a florid cadenza. Plançon, as St Bris, was
ue to meet this with 'Madame I will go and bring my daughter',
ut he was so amused he joined the act and sang, 'Madame I will go
nd tell Meyerbeer', almost breaking up the conductor, Mancinelli,
ho had to bury his face in the score to stop laughing. The story got
pace, as all Melba stories did, but it was only one in the hundreds
f such snippets any singer had on file for a press-neglected rainy day.
ome were invented, some deliberately made to happen, and some of
nem were possibly as real as this one.

That summer Melba spent time in Paris, studying Massenet's *Manon*
ith the composer. He was a perfectionist, never letting a flaw pass,
emanding a phrase be repeated over and over until Melba had it as
e wanted. She found him charming but 'what a devil he was for
ork!' *Manon* was premièred at the Paris Opéra-Comique on 19 January
884 and on 23 December 1885 at the New York Academy of Music.
Melba first appeared in it on 27 January 1896, in the winter season

at the Met., when her sister Annie and brother Ernest were in th
audience.

For Christmas 1895, Melba brought out from London the fiancé
her secretary, Louie Bennett, and gave them a wedding at St Patrick
Cathedral, New York, on 14 January. At the reception Nordica, Calv
the de Reszkes, Plançon, Maurel, Cremoni, Bevignani, Ancona an
Adamowski – the top bill of the Met. in fact – lined up for Melba
entry with Archbishop Corrigan, she in mauve to upstage his purpl
The singer was apparently none the worse for having had her fur cloa
catch fire from an old metal and charcoal footwarmer in the carriag
that took her to a singing engagement in Brooklyn the night before

On 20 April she gave a Polish lunch for Paderewski amid grea
publicity and four days later left for England, the press captioning he
picture with, 'An American singer going to Europe on vacation'. Thre
days after she reached London she set off for Paris and rehearsals fo
Hamlet which she gave on 21 May at the Opéra. By 13 June she ha
sung the role there seven times. There was a hectic social and profes
sional round of parties where she appeared sometimes as a guest (c
the Duchess of Manchester) and sometimes as a performer (for th
Prince de Sagan and for the Countess Jean de Castellane), all of i
spaced out so that her name was constantly in front of the readers o
the social pages. The income was considerable but so was the exposure

On 19 June (1896) she opened in *Roméo* at Covent Garden befor
the Grand Duchess of Micklenberg-Strelitz and the Duke and Duches
of Fife; the stars' game of feeding the box office by netting the bigges
social catches of the season was on again, with Melba, as usual, in
the lead. But on 22 June, Augustus Harris died of heart failure. A
first Melba refused to go on in *Rigoletto* the following night; she ha
lost a friend. But she had also lost an ally. From that time on sh
had to fight harder to persuade the new management – under Mauric
Grau – to her point of view. She was obliged to swallow her grie
and get on with the job. Again there was no sign of personal traum
in the Gilda she sang that night.

Harris had not only managed Covent Garden – he had influence
much criticism in some peculiar ways by modern standards. He ha
won over Bernard Shaw who became one of his most able publicists
particularly in his campaign to have Wagnerian opera sung in German
but he also had enemies in Fleet Street, particularly on the *Referee*. I
retaliation Harris had bought the *Sunday Times* for which Herman
Klein had been music critic since 1881. Unofficially Klein used t
advise Harris on plans for his seasons. Officially he was not onl
Harris' employee as a critic for the *Sunday Times* but wrote criticism
for its rival, the *Illustrated London News*, and to quite some effect.

Friendly critics were always of importance to Melba, but in Londo
they were central to her career. With Harris and his influence gone
she was suddenly more vulnerable than she cared to admit. To sta

it the top would require a little more vigilance.

Melba prefaced that year's American season with a concert at the Music Hall in Boston with the Boston Symphony Orchestra on 6 November. Hundreds of 'matinée girls' – regulars who came armed with bouquets to throw to their favourite performers – gathered at the hall door to chant and applaud. On 16 November she opened at the Met. in *Faust*, followed by *Roméo* and on 21 December gave her first American Violetta. And then, on 30 November, she made the greatest mistake of her professional life – she sang, only once, as Brünnhilde in *Siegfried*.

Murphy says that at the time Melba attempted this role she was suffering 'a severe attack of blood-poisoning'. She was also suffering from her worst bout of musical misjudgement. Melba's voice was supremely well suited to bel canto opera, but the operas written as vehicles for coloratura display were considered in the 1890s to be outdated and often light-weight. On the other hand the cult of Wagnerian opera, a weighty matter in every sense of the word, seemed to be about to out-distance both the old operas and the values and voices they enshrined. Anxious, as ever, to keep up with the fashion of her day, Melba decided to risk a Brünnhilde where it could create the best effect and be most readily accepted – New York, where the Wagner cult was still new and the judgement more likely to go in her favour than might have been the case at Covent Garden where the German seasons had already refined audience response.

Melba had already sung *Lohengrin* and *Tannhäuser*, both with some success, but she sang Elsa in French and Elizabeth in Italian. Brünnhilde she sang in German, a language she had found too difficult to cope with before. But under the influence of Jean de Reszke, whose enthusiasm for *The Ring* she caught, Melba took advantage of her box-office power to persuade the management of the Met. to reserve the role for her. De Reszke later said he encouraged Melba to try the Forest Bird, not Brünnhilde. Melba herself said that in spite of Marchesi's warnings on the subject she got Kniese over to Paris to coach her for Brünnhilde well in advance.

Lilian Nordica, enraged at being shut out of a part that would naturally have fallen to her lot at the Met., spread rumours that Melba had intrigued with de Reszke to see she was not engaged for that season. Nordica later apologised, perhaps unnecessarily. Melba's failure in the role meant no suitable replacement was contracted when the remaining five scheduled performances fell due and were cancelled; the season was put in jeopardy by Melba's selfish demands. The performance was a near disaster. As one of the critics wrote:

That the music wearied her was painfully evident long before the end of the one scene in which Brünnhilde takes part in *Siegfried*. Never did her voice have the lovely quality which had always

THE MYTH: RECEIVED WISDOM

This undated review presumably refers to Melba's one attempt to sing Brünnhilde at the Met. on 30 December 1896. Melba cancelled later performances due to vocal damage.

'Madame Melba's collapse is politely enough explained here as physical. That is Mr Grau's adjective, and Mr Grau is nothing if not tactful and sympathetic. But there are mental factors that contributed largely to it, that were probably at the bottom of it.

'Her virtual failure as Brünnhilde was the first source of irritation. For six months she had been working on the part, and she expected a triumph. A lark might as well have sung in a canonade. Instead of an ovation, she was forced to hear and read the apologies of her friends – made, none will dispute, with an ingenuity that might have been successful with the public had she been a little more politic in concealing her chagrin, or, rather, in not revealing it by explanations that did not explain.

'Another unpleasant feature has been the withdrawal from her, one by one, of operas she had come to regard as her own. It was bad enough when Eames took one; it was worse when Calvé took another; it was worst when at an hour's notice Clementine de Vere-Saplo took *Hamlet* then *La Traviata* and, mirabile dictu, offered to take *Lucia*, mad music and all.

'And the irony of the situation was that Melba was compelled to submit to the very logic she had used at the outset of the season to justify her own assumption of roles which Nordica had been inclined to regard as hers.

'Pique is the real trouble with Madame Melba. There is nothing the matter with her voice but 'nerves' and 'blues' and both come from temper. The public will not be humbugged by medical certificates to any more serious effect ... Wagnerian opera she cannot sing in a style worthy of herself or Wagner. It is the Latin music, not the Teutonic, of which she is mistress.

'The Svengali who looks into Melba's throat will see no streams of pearls and diamonds flowing toward Bayreuth. All the roads there lead to Rome.'[1]

1. Clipping, n.d. [19 January ? 1897], Melba file, New York Public Library.

characterized [it] in the music of Donizetti and Gounod. It lost i euphony in the broadly sustained and sweeping phrases of Wagne and the difference in power and expressiveness between its highe and lower registers was made pitifully obvious. The music, more over, exhausted her. She plunged into her apostrophe with mos self-sacrificing vigour at the beginning of the scene, and was prodiga in the use of her voice in the early moments, but when th culmination of its passion was reached, in what would be calle the 'stretto' of the piece in the old nomenclature, she could no respond to the increased demands. It was an anti-climax. Wagner' music is like jealousy; it makes the meat it feeds on if one be bu filled with its dramatic fervour ... There is one glory of the sun and another of the moon, and another glory of the stars, for on star differeth from another star in glory ... Madame Melba shoul have been contented with her own particular glory.[13]

Her friend, Percy Colson, believed: 'She had neither the temperamen nor the type of voice called for; the music did not lie within he voice, and she was not of the heroic mould necessary to give convincing portrayal of that formidable damsel'.[14]

Henry Krehbiel in the *New York Tribune* later summed up:

The sincerity of her effort was admirable. A large party of th public went to hear her in a heroic role, and she has won such encomiums as her laudable and plucky experiment deserved .. But the music of the part does not lie well in her voice, and if sh continues to sing it, it is much to be feared there will soon be a end to the charm which her voice discloses when employed in it legitimate sphere. The world can ill afford to lose a Melba, even i it should gain a Brünnhilde. But it will not gain a Brünnhilde.[15]

And neither it did. As she left the stage that night Melba sent fo her manager. In her dressing-room she ordered him to 'Tell the critic that I am never going to do that again. It is beyond me. I have bee a fool'. Later she wrote:

The music was too much for me. I felt as though I were strugglin with something beyond my strength. I had a sensation almost o suffocation, of battling with some immense monster ... I learn my lesson, but it was a very expensive one, for even this one performance did very great harm to my voice, and though I wa able to appear once or twice after it I gradually found that I wa not singing at my best, and I was told that if I went on withou a rest, I might never be able to sing again. And so in the middle of the season I threw up all my engagements and went back to Paris, where I kept an enforced silence for nearly three month more. And may I, having told this story, implore young singers no to attempt to sing roles which are beyond their power.[16]

Chapter 7

HOME SWEET HOME

Melba did not appear at Covent Garden in 1897 until 23 June at a command performance for Queen Victoria's Diamond Jubilee. The Queen herself did not attend, but most of the English royals and their European cousins did, along with diplomatic representatives and Empire heads of state. For once the fresh flowers that usually festooned the theatre for grand occasions were missing; the smell of them had been found too overpowering for audiences and cast alike, so artificial roses took their place. The Jubilee audience got the second act of *Tannhäuser*, the third act of *Roméo* and the fourth act of *Les Huguenots* in the usual tasteless manner of royal occasions. The only other role Melba sang that season was Marguerite on 28 June.

The rest of the summer she recuperated at Fernley, exploring the river country and resting her voice on the advice of her laryngologist, Sir Felix Semon. In other years she took Quarry Wood Cottage on the Thames near Maidenhead as a summer house. The *Siegfried* episode may have left very little physical trace in the long run, but it left a permanently bruised ego. Sir Milsom Rees, the London ear, nose and throat specialist who attended to Melba for years, thought he detected a weakness of the vocal chords towards the end of her career that might have been due to the American disaster, but it was not something that showed up in Melba's prime. The bruised ego did. Her dislike of other sopranos who could take Wagnerian roles was well known, but the voice she aspired to turned out to be owned by a fellow Melburnian who was born in the same suburb of Richmond and who took lessons at the Albert Street conservatorium in 1914, just before Melba returned home to create her own singing school there.

Florence Austral (alias Florence Fawaz) was a pupil of Elise Wiedermann and defected with her teacher when Wiedermann joined Marshall-Hall at the University Conservatorium. Melba was to set up in opposition to her. She cut Austral whenever they were obliged to meet before the girl left Australia in 1919, and she kept up the snub for life, though she admitted admiration for the voice that took Covent Garden by storm as her own star was fading. Part of the reason may have been, as has since been assumed, pure jealousy, but it may also have been due to Austral siding with a pro-German group at a rival

THE MYTH: RECEIVED WISDOM

Peter Dawson, the Australian baritone who knew Melba as a colleague, claimed that: 'The trouble was that she was unable to get "down to earth" again after her rave notices. From the nice Australian girl she became the spoilt social snob of the music world. Only to fellow Australians did she remain – more or less – her natural self. But that vanished after a few years. I cannot forget how she grumbled to me at length when she heard about the success of Florence Austral, that magnificent soprano who made a sensational overnight success when she appeared in *Aida* at Covent Garden ... Melba's reaction was not against the success of Florence, but against her use of the name Austral ... "Why the devil can't they keep to their own names and stop copying my idea?" was her angry remark.'[1]

1. Peter Dawson, *Fifty years of song*, p. 190.

THE MYTH: RECEIVED WISDOM

'When singing at Covent Garden she was in the habit of chewing a little Australian "Wattle" gum. It was very soothing for the throat. In the wings was a small piece of plate glass, on which she would deposit the piece of gum while she was singing. When she had finished her *aria* she would put the gum back in her mouth. Unfortunately, she had made herself very unpopular with the stage hands, particularly because she insisted that they must wear plimsolls during their work because the noise of their shuffling upset her.

'One night she took up her piece of gum as usual, but screeched and spat it out; she flew into a furious temper and stormed and raved about the stage. Someone had replaced the gum with a quid of tobacco made up to look exactly like the gum.

'To make matters worse, Caruso went into peals of laughter when he heard about it. Melba demanded the dismissal of all the stage hands. They were dismissed; but the next day they turned up as usual, the manager making the excuse that he was unable to engage any others.

'After this the gum was guarded by a dresser, a woman who afterwards said, "I'd like to have put something stronger than tobacco in its place, but she'd 'a known 'oo it was" '.[1]

1. Dawson, *op.cit.*, pp. 22–3.

conservatorium at a time when Melba herself was setting up an anti-German, non-university school during the First World War. There was also the social question of being associated with a woman living openly with a married man – John Amadio.

In the autumn of 1897 Melba was asked to sing at Bergamo for the Donizetti centenary festival. With Joachim and one of his nieces, Robert von Mendelssohn, Piatti and von Kendel, she wandered about the local countryside, invading peasant houses to eat spaghetti, which she learned to cook in order to inflict it on her guests as an unexpected quirk. At the festival exhibition, which she saw with Joachim, she found Wagner's copies of Donizetti scores displayed, done for a copyist's pittance: 'I sat there looking at those copies with Joachim, wishing I had known Wagner in those days', she wrote. Not Donizetti – whose work she sang – but Wagner.

Madame Alva was one of the musicians engaged for Bergamo. The London press ignored her, praising Melba and Joachim. Alva wrote to the *Daily Telegraph* asking why she was being discriminated against. The *Telegraph* printed her letter in full, much to her annoyance. She decided Melba had kept her out of the papers to begin with and plotted to ridicule her later in the season by this exposure. It was the kind of story that haunted Melba. Half of such accusations were probably true, but which half no one ever really knew.

The 1897–98 season was made under the management of Walter Damrosch and Charles Ellis. Ellis had managed Melba's first Boston concert with such efficiency that she had made him her sole American manager. Damrosch, already mentioned, was the composer-entrepreneur who founded his own opera company in 1895 but returned to the Met. from 1900 to 1903. For the long tour across America, Damrosch and Ellis provided Melba and her travelling party with a special luxury coach capable of housing six guests and able to be attached to any train, main lines or country branches, whatever the private company. The Pullman company christened it *Melba* and her name was duly emblazoned on the side. This elaborate gypsy caravan was destined to be her hotel for some time and came equipped with its own conductor, porter, chef and waiter. Melba brought along her own servants as well. The rent and moving charges for the tour were $3500. The chef cost $200 a month, the waiter $75, the conductor $75 and the black porter $50; food and tips were extra.

At the end of the usual Met. season Melba set off across America to Boston, Chicago, Denver, Washington, St Louis, Philadelphia (where she gave her first American *Aida* on 13 January 1898), Salt Lake City, Minneapolis, and across country to San Francisco.

The city of the Golden Gate had a few surprises in store for its headline-making visitor. To begin with she was knocked unconscious by a falling bronze bust at a crowded party. The press reported her as ill, dead and then buried. Melba retaliated by utilising the gift of

ree telegraphing rights given to her by John Mackay, the co-
founder of the Commercial Cable Co., to send off a flurry of cables
world-wide to reassure managers and family that she was far from
dead.

The American–Spanish war was declared on 21 April, the day
Melba was scheduled to sing in *The Barber of Seville*. It was too late
to change the programme for something less inflammatory. All night
Melba went nervously from scene to scene expecting the audience to
let loose with the hostility she sensed was being barely kept in check.

Earlier in the tour she had followed the tradition of an interpolated
number in the lesson scene by giving 'Still wie die Nacht', 'Sevilliana',
'Mattinata', 'Home sweet home', the Mad Scene from *Lucia* and 'The
old folks at home'. But with the audience in such a mood she decided
to chance her arm and gave 'The star spangled banner'. Britain sided
with America in the line-up of allies but had been very quiet about
it. Melba's gesture was taken as a signal from diplomatic quarters that
the American–British alliance was complete. Before the end of the
first verse the whole house was on its feet. At the start of the third
verse Melba and most of the audience were in tears. *She* lost control
and faded off. *They* roared their approval. Sixteen years later she was
to take this new-found gift for whipping up patriotism via music to
absurd, profitable and disturbing heights during the First World War.

But Melba's first coast-to-coast tour ended in fire when the same
theatre that had witnessed 'The star spangled banner' episode went
up in flames. It was one of those bits-and-pieces nights that were
often inflicted on end-of-season audiences and European royals alike.
There were strange knockings below stage and an unusual amount of
backstage traffic. Just as Melba was about to go on for the Mad Scene
from *Lucia* she saw flames leap through the gallery windows. There
was a scream of 'fire', a scuffle and the promise of panic from the
stalls, but the occupants of the boxes sat tight. Melba stepped forward
and shouted, 'Please – go out quietly. There is no danger'. But there
was. A figure suddenly loomed in front of her. Bimboni, the orchestral
leader, was clambering his way out over the footlights. Melba ordered
him to stay where he was, but 'the Bimboni' was not in the mood
to listen to a mere woman, so Melba lent forward 'and gave him a
resounding crack on the head'. He sank back in his seat, stunned.

The theatre burned to the ground, but no one was killed. Melba
wrote:

I always think that is a wonderful tribute to American discipline.
But I thought it an equally wonderful tribute to American energy
to discover on leaving the theatre, that the newspapers had already
brought out a special edition about the fire, containing a great deal
more information than we knew ourselves. And so – home to our
hotels in all our war-paint – some as Mefistofeles [*sic*], some as

Lucia, some as courtiers, some as soldiers. But all of us must hav
looked clowns.[1]

There was a brief 1898 London season for Melba – *La Traviat*
(with Patti, one of the great Violettas, listening from Alfred d
Rothschild's box), *The Barber of Seville* (before the Princess of Wales
and *Roméo et Juliette*. There was a charity concert at Stafford Hous
where Joachim played the violin obbligato for her *Il Rè Pastore* an
a private entertainment for the Queen of sections of *Siegfried*, Melb
singing the music of the Forest Bird, not Brünnhilde.

In the summer of 1898 Melba spent six weeks at a hotel in Lucc
where Puccini coached her for her first *La Bohème*. For two hours
day over ten days, he shyly explained the music to her and made nea
little annotations on her score.

La Bohème had been premièred at the Teatro Reggio in Turin o
1 February 1896, in Manchester (in English as *The Bohemians*) o
22 April 1897, and in English on 2 October 1897 at Covent Garden
Melba sang Mimi for the first time at the Academy of Music
Philadelphia, on 29 December 1898. Initially the opera was a failure
It only began to pick up after the third production at Palermo i
1896. In was left to Melba to make the opera her own.

There were sixteen recalls after the Philadelphia performance. Gra
and Ellis suddenly realised they had a success of a very special kin
on their books. *La Bohème*, as Melba's special vehicle, went into th
1898 tour – Chicago, Boston, Buffalo, Rochester, Kansas, Denve
Baltimore and San Francisco, though it was not in the Los Angele
season.

From the start Melba recognised that *La Bohème* was a better oper
than anyone believed. She also knew that Mimi was the perfect rol
for her. Its music fitted her voice with a rare ease and grace. Whe
she realised that here at last was a front-rank composer in sympath
with her needs, she decided she must have a role of his to create
Murphy writes:

> Subsequently, in England, she advised Puccini to see [David] Be
> lasco's pathetic Japanese play [based on John Luther Long's shor
> story] and discussed with him its possibilities, which he eventuall
> utilized in his opera *Madame Butterfly*, in which it was at firs
> anticipated she would create the title role.[2]

Melba stated later that Puccini actually wrote the part for her.

Wechsberg says Melba took Puccini to the play (at the Duke o
York's Theatre), which, being in English, he did not understand, bu
he liked the central character. Melba studied the role with Puccini i
Venice but found Cio-Cio-San too dramatic a part. Her friend an
neighbour, Lady Stracey, once stepped into the library just as Melb
hurled the score across the room shouting, 'Damn the thing, I shal

never learn it!' Puccini, at the piano, muttered unhappily, 'Patienza, cara signora', but Melba had no patience left and the 'damned thing' remained unlearned.

There may be another explanation for this singular inability of Melba's to learn a new part. Puccini's music for *Madame Butterfly* is harmonically complex in a way that *La Bohème* is not. This may have given Melba pitching uncertainties that she did not care to test in public. The trickiness of a part beyond her acting skills, which also demanded acute musical concentration throughout, eventually made her back off, which is a pity.

In contrast *La Bohème* was to remain in her repertoire until the end and was the last opera in which she appeared, yet when she gave the first of the Met. Mimis (26 December 1900) Henry Krehbiel of the *New York Tribune* thought the role not suited to her voice and denounced *La Bohème* itself as 'foul in subject, and fulminant but futile in music' – words he was to live to regret.

Melba sang Mimi to many great Rodolfos over the years, but by far the most famous was Enrico Caruso. They began their stage partnership in Monte Carlo in 1902, but off-stage there was little love lost between the two. Melba thought Caruso an uncouth peasant and made no secret of it. For his part, Caruso regarded her as too much the grand lady. To take her down a peg or two, he resorted to practical jokes. Singers often had spirit lamps or portable stoves backstage to cook the odd essential snack at odd hours. One night Caruso heated a sausage which he took on stage with him. As he began the aria 'Che gelida manina' ('Your tiny hand is frozen') he took Melba's hand, turned her so that she faced the audience while he was in profile, moved the captive hand well below his waist level and pressed the warm sausage into it with some ardour. Melba jerked back and the sausage went bouncing off across the stage, to the audience's puzzlement. Melba hissed through her teeth, 'You filthy dago!' But Caruso held on to her and when the first break came he whispered, mock-hurt, 'English lady, you not like to have the sausage?'[3] But if he had thought to shock Melba he had missed his mark – Nellie was well-nigh unshockable. What annoyed her so much about the episode was the unprofessionalism it revealed. She was not above the odd practical joke herself, but on stage – never.

At Covent Garden the Carl Rosa Company produced *La Bohème* twice after the Manchester première in 1897, but it failed to attract much interest. When Melba insisted that she wanted it revived she was obliged to offer a security against loss in the form of one or other popular scene from another opera to be sung by her after *La Bohème* until the new opera was established. She got her way. On 1 July 1899 *La Bohème* played to a packed house and was never out of the repertoire again.

Melba's winter season for 1899 began in Holland in November.

CARUSO'S MELBA

Early in 1902 Raoul Gunsborg, the impresario at Monte Carlo, presented Caruso and Melba in *La Bohème* in order to attract the English audience that was always in a majority at the Casino Theatre.

Caruso first saw Melba in the casino at the roulette table, ablaze with diamonds that filled the near-indecent *décolletage* of her Worth gown. To him she appeared disdainful and not at all the beauty who had scandalised Europe over the d'Orléans affair, but he approved of her splendid teeth, her musical laugh and her flawless skin. She was 40 and twelve years his senior. She was not a tall woman but her bearing made her seem so. The tenor Bonci wore built-up shoes to cope and Caruso, out of nervousness, thought he should do the same, but Gunsborg talked him out of it. Melba was a stickler for punctuality and travelled everywhere with several alarm clocks, each synchronised to the minute. Caruso had the sense to arrive at rehearsals on time. Melba unbent and showed the newcomer how to move less stiffly on stage, and though she kept reminding him that 'darling Jean [de Reszke] did it like this', Caruso held his tongue. She even let him smoke his strong Egyptian cigarettes between acts when no singer at Covent Garden would have dared to do so in her presence. She surprised everyone by openly delighting in Caruso's voice and accepting the chubby tenor in place of the romantic de Reszke. Soon she was responding to his lyrical power in their love duets.

Caruso in turn was lost in admiration of her clear phrasing and silvery timbre which, he admitted, challenged Tetrazzini.

Melba found him simple and lovable but vulgar, deploring his taste in clothes and his table manners; but 'when I sang with Caruso in *La Bohème*', she said, 'I felt as if our two voices had merged into one'.

Caruso was ill at ease in the glamorous casino society and felt provincial in his badly cut tailcoat after seeing Melba breezing out of the white building in an immense ermine cape, surrounded by a pride of Russian nobles. He preferred to slip away to the gardens and to eat spaghetti with his friends and rarely ate at the luxury hotel with Melba who introduced him there to her favourite dish of plover's eggs stuffed with caviar. But in spite of his manners it was Melba who saw to it that Grau lured him to Covent Garden.

Their personal disenchantment with one another gathered pace with the years, but the ecstatic vocal flights they inspired in one another went unimpaired.

THEY SAY

'Clara Butt and Melba lunched together one Sunday at Sir Arthur Sullivan's riverside house. When it came time to leave all the men kissed Melba and would have done the same with Clara but she pulled back, objecting. "Don't give yourself airs", Melba said. "What's the harm in it?" '[1]

1. Colson, *op.cit.*, p. 230.

She gave *Faust*, *La Traviata*, *Rigoletto*, *Lucia* and *Manon* at Amsterdam and Rotterdam, but the young Queen was not interested in music and the usual royal cachet was missing along with the social set and the attendant box office. There was a repeat of the same narrow repertoir in Germany and Austria. In Berlin she gave her first concert at the Philharmonic Hall, Joachim playing obbligato again for the Mozart *Il Rè Pastore* and later presenting her with a miniature ebony violin 'in mourning over her departure'.

In December Melba sang Lucia at the Imperial Opera House, Berlin, before the Emperor and Empress. She told Agnes Murphy that the imperial pair were 'both most gracious' to her when she was summoned, still in the costume from the Mad Scene, to their box. She found the Emperor 'very musical, and he discussed with me variou methods of obtaining certain vocal effects'. He ended by asking her to sing often at the Opera House. With this bit of publicity fed the press her scheduled four performances were extended to nine. Yet on the other side of the First World War the memoirs recall that the Emperor had left her abruptly after this conversation on the performance and snapped his fingers for his wife to follow, which she did 'rather in the manner of a puppy dog', an unspoken apology 'on her tired face'. Pre-war and post-war publicists bent whatever facts Melba fed them into fashionable shapes for her in an effort to put their client in the best possible light. It was her misfortune that Murphy was a sycophant and Nichols a poseur. Her judgement of *them* was what la at fault.

In Austria her patron and box-office bait was the Emperor Franz Josef, for whom she sang *La Traviata* on royal command at the Imperial Opera House, Vienna, on 19 January. He created her Chamber Singer to the imperial court in return. At Leipzig she sang at a Gewandhaus orchestral concert under Nikisch and before the King of Saxony. At Monte Carlo, where she resumed her usual contracted opera routine, the holidaying British contingent who loyally turned out for her included Countess de Grey, the Duchess of Marlborough, Lady Erskine, Countess Miranda and Mrs Hwfa Williams whose house in London Melba rented from time to time. The Prince of Monaco came with the French social set and on off nights Melba was to be seen in the casino gambling at the tables in their company. She enjoyed the betting and the people – the publicity was effective even when it was directly generated by Melba. She once told the press that she and Lady de Grey had been mistaken by a Frenchman in the casino for cocottes and that both the ladies had enjoyed the experience.

On 28 August she was in Dublin to launch a protégé, Australian contralto Regina Nagel, at the Royal University Hall. As the guest of the Lord-Lieutenant of Ireland, the Earl of Cadogan, Melba attended horse shows, did a little betting at the Leopardstown races and took home as a souvenir a screen designed by the Royal Irish School of

Art and Needlework, presented to her by the Earl. Even this little aside was reported with Melba's co-operation; anything that would keep up her reputation in the eyes of society was to be encouraged.

The Germanic tour had prevented the usual American appearances but after a small Covent Garden season and a number of private parties, for which her going rate was 500 guineas, Melba was back on circuit for the winter of 1900-01. Covent Garden, a holiday in Scotland at Dunrobin Castle as the guest of the Duke and Duchess of Sutherland, Ireland again as the guest of Lord and Lady Rossmore, Monte Carlo, Switzerland, Paris and back to Covent Garden, a round of Sunday musical parties at her town house to launch protégés – it was a life of constant and very public activity with not a move wasted.

The parties in the coronation year were ceaseless and socially and vocally demanding – Rothschild's at Seamore Place where Edward was staying, a dinner at which Melba sat between Lord Kitchener and General Lucas Meyer (then leaders of opposing armies), the Astors' in honour of Princess Christian, at Dudley House for J. B. Robinson, at Lady Cooper's in Grosvenor Square where Melba and Bernhardt sang and recited the vocal parts of Bemberg's *Ballade du désespéré*, at Coombe, Lady de Grey's house where there were regular Sunday gatherings, and for charity at Stafford House for the Duchess of Sutherland.

When Elgar was commissioned to write an ode for the coronation, Melba was asked to be the lead vocalist but the huge celebratory coronation-eve gala performance was cancelled when Edward was taken ill. She was philosophical about it – the ode had nothing to offer a soloist of her calibre anyway. Her biggest pomp and circumstance involvement was at a concert in aid of the King's Hospital Fund at the Albert Hall on 11 June which began with a fanfare from the silver trumpets on loan from the King and heralded his entrance to the royal box. Melba sang the first verse of the National Anthem, Clara Butt sang the second, and for the third the audience stood to sing, unfurling miniature Union Jacks which they waved wildly 'in an ever-increasing tumult of sound'.

There was a contingent of Australian soldiers in London for the coronation. They were Empire window-dressing, the biggest and the best looking men available. They had planned a demonstration for Melba at the cancelled gala concert but sent their tribute instead to the stage door after *La Traviata* one night at Covent Garden – a huge bouquet with the regimental badges won in the South African campaign attached to its ribbons. On 28 July these men were in the audience for her last appearance of the season and cheered her until they were hoarse, not only because she was the most famous Australian of them all but because now, at the peak of her career, she was coming home.

Melba came home to Australia in 1902 for the first time in sixteen

MELBA'S WILD CATS

'Paris, 5 April – Mme Melba recently tried to emulate Mme Bernhardt in having savage household pets – like the divine Sarah's panther. So she bought at Marseilles from a sailor a pair of caged wild cats. The experiment was abandoned yesterday and the only result was a large bill presented by the Ritz Hotel management for damage done by the escaped carnivores.

'The wild cats had been smuggled into her apartment a week ago and been fed by Melba's chambermaid – much to the girl's distress. Yesterday while the cage door was ajar to introduce food, one of the beasts clawed terribly the hand of the servant, who fled shrieking, leaving the wild cats in possession of the rooms. The brutes were on a rampage for two hours, climbing curtains, upsetting bottles and crockery and tearing valuable tapestries to shreds.

'Finally some attendants at the Zoological Gardens were telephoned and they captured one wild cat in a net and killed the other.'[1]

1. *The World*, New York, 6 April 1902.

CLOTHES BY WORTH

Melba's stage clothes as well as her personal wardrobe were mainly designed by Worth, the first of the great Parisian fashion designers. Born in 1825, Charles Frederick Worth was an Englishman who in 1845 migrated to France. After twelve years as a fabric salesman at Gagelins, the firm permitted him to set up a small dressmaking section in their shop in the Rue de Richelieu where Worth realised his own designs. He married a saleswoman, Marie Vernet, who became his collaborator and the first live mannequin. When the designs won a gold medal for France at the Great Exhibition of 1851, business boomed for the Maison Gagelin. In 1855 the success was repeated at the Paris World Fair.

Worth felt he was being exploited by his employers and in 1858 he set up his own establishment in his home in the Rue de la Paix. With the building of the Opera House the area became fashionable. The House of Worth, with its elegant and original designs and its displays of new fashion worn by live models, caught the fancy of the aristocracy. In 1860 the accolade of royal approval was won when Marie Worth persuaded Princess Pauline Metternich to order two crinoline gowns and to wear them at the Tuileries Palace before the Empress Eugénie. The Empress became Worth's most famous patron, though his clients eventually came to include nine European queens. From that time on he was the undisputed leader of European fashion.

years. She left as part of her father's entourage, a talented headstrong daughter with ambitions, barely noticed in the crowd. She returned as a world figure. The Melba myths travelled with her, a burden she was never permitted to put down. In Australia what had been a fabulous, shining image of success, trailing a little intriguing scandal, was to be tarnished permanently. What had been previously discounted as malicious gossip and jealous fabrication, to be expected as part of the price of fame, was to be accepted as received wisdom and handed on to another generation as if it were an heirloom. That 'wisdom' has taken some curious forms, then and now; the mirrors are legion, but the image that is thrown back reflects more of the imperfections of the surfaces used than the subject herself.

Two or three times a year rumours circulated that Melba was about to visit Australia. She would publish a vigorous denial. It happened so often that in the end no one believed she would ever come home. The Australian press ran cartoons and verses about it. Then in November 1901 Melba cabled the daily papers that she would pay a professional visit to Australia in 1902 after the London season. She selected George Musgrove to be her manager for a series of concerts to be given in Melbourne, Sydney and Adelaide during September, October and November and told the London press:

I believe that on many occasions rumours have been published of my going to sing in my native country, but they have never been authorized by me, as until now the difficulties appertaining to such a venture have proved insurmountable.

Now that these difficulties have been removed, I cannot tell you how delighted I am in looking forward to a visit so full of potential pleasure to myself in the renewal of old friendships with the people among whom I was born and brought up; and if by the exercise of my art I am able to add some joy to the lives of my countrywomen and countrymen, my happiness will be complete. Nellie Melba.[4]

She cabled to Australia: 'I shall sail from England in August', but on the 22nd of that month she left from Vancouver aboard the *Miowera*, nicknamed 'the weary Mary', and was due to berth at Brisbane early on Sunday 14 September 1902. Melba wrote:

Never shall I forget that voyage. Four times in the middle of the sweltering Pacific we broke down and lay heaving on the burning waters for hours and sometimes a whole night at a time. Those were before the days of wireless, and there was no means of letting my friends in Australia know that I was safe. Consequently, as I was to find on my arrival, the most alarming rumours spread all over the country – that we had been wrecked, that we had disappeared, that we had sunk. I should not have minded the delay and discomfort had it not been for the fact that my father was an old man, and I feared that the agitation which this delay must be causing him was not only agonising but dangerous.[5]

On the morning of Wednesday 17 September there was news that the *Miowera* was wrecked in Moreton Bay. At 2 p.m. a cable reached Brisbane from Cape Moreton that the ship was safe. When Melba saw this first landfall she curtsied three times to the crumbling bluff 'for luck', as she told a friend on board.

Some time after 9 p.m. the ship docked at Pinkenba, some miles downstream from Brisbane and the official welcomes began. The mayor, George Corrie, and his wife, carrying a sheaf of wattle, had jumped the gun hours before by persuading the Health Commissioner to take the official launch out early to meet the *Miowera* midstream for the regulation inspection. All the way south it was the same – people trying to get to Melba outside the official receptions, the roped-off actual presentations. The train stopped for speeches and flowers at Toowoomba, Newcastle, Hornsby and a series of other smaller towns. Even on the flower-decked whistle-stop stations crowds gathered to wave as she passed slowly by. It was the same out of Sydney.

The day before, David Mitchell, then a frail 74-year-old man, had travelled to the Murray River border town of Albury, 191 miles north of Melbourne, travelling in the State car the Victorian Railway Commission had sent to bring the diva home. Nellie had been joined by one of her sisters on board the train coming south. When they got to Albury the packed crowd parted to reveal not her father, but a doctor who had come to tell them Mitchell had had a stroke and was lying paralysed in a Mrs Griffith's house nearby. Melba wanted to stay with her father but Mitchell insisted she go on to Melbourne. After an hour's delay the pilgrimage south resumed. At Wangaratta, Euroa, Benalla, Seymour – where her other siblings came on board – and at a dozen other stations covered in greenery, flags and wattle, the patient crowds cheered her on, lining up for hours for the merest glimpse of her.

At Spencer Street station the chanting mob, topped by press photographers on portable towers, demanded flowers from the bouquets heaped up in the carriage. Melba tore the mounds of flowers apart and threw them in every direction. There was a brawl under the horses' hooves as men fought for souvenirs of daffodils and violets. Small boys dashed in for what was left, then sold them as Melba mementoes to the crowds further along the packed streets. It was a slow progress, handkerchiefs waving at every window along Collins Street, members of the Stock Exchange throwing their hats in the air as she passed, a halt before Allan's music shop where a band played 'Home sweet home' and stops all along St Kilda and Toorak Roads on the way to Myoora to accept flowers from the women who came out into the

Within a few years Worth was employing over a thousand cutters and a great luxury industry was in the process of creation. He lived and entertained lavishly, showing his collections in a palatial atmosphere and selling designs to stores, manufacturers and dressmakers in Europe and America. A visit to Worth's became an essential outing for American ladies making the Grand Tour.

The Franco-Prussian War forced many of his wealthiest clients abroad and the supremacy of the 1860s was lost as rivals began to appear and technical change brought mass-produced fabrics into the market. Worth's sons, Gaston and Jean-Philippe, and later his grandsons, controlled the firm after Charles' death.

Marchesi introduced Melba to Jean-Philippe Worth at the time of her début. Melba felt indebted to him for his constant help and advice, not only on what to wear off-stage but also for making her realise how important it was for her career that her stage clothes were of a quality that lent glamour to her stage presence. Melba later went to Jacques Doucet and others in Paris and London, but Worth remains the name most associated with her stage, as well as her personal, clothes.

path of the horses to hand up their posies.

The official welcomes were overwhelming. In short order she wa
presented to 2000 citizens at a mayoral reception, entertained by th
national and state viceregals and given a sell-out matinée of *Swee
Nell of Old Drury* (25 September) by Nellie Stewart, the darling o
the Australian theatre and George Musgrove's putative wife. Th
audience for *Sweet Nell* stood to sing 'Auld lang syne' as Melba too
her seat in a bower of wattle and gumleaves complete with a cage
magpie as centrepiece. Her old school, PLC, received her with a guar
of honour of girls in white and a ladies' band playing 'See th
conquering hero come'.

Melba gave her first return concert on 27 September in the Mel
bourne Town Hall. Ticket prices soared from hour to hour as th
scalpers got to work. Police reinforcements were brought in from th
suburbs to control the crowds waiting to see her pass to the stag
door. The applauding audience refused to let her begin for a quarte
of an hour, as she stood stock-still, staring down at them, tall, sombre
apparently emotionless. At the end she played and sang 'Home swee
home' to an overwrought hall. The next day the papers ran no
columns but pages on the event. At the second concert, which he
father attended, she sang a first encore of 'Comin' through the rye
for him. She had told the press in advance that he had taught he
the ballad. This was almost too much for the reporters who poure
out an astonishing amount of pure schmaltz next day to entertain
public gone suddenly mad with Melba-fever.

Possibly the absurd peak of it all was reached in a speech given b
the Ormond Professor of Music at the University of Melbourne, wh
said:

Madame, we all of us, professors and students alike, feel that it i
very charming of you to pay us a visit in this our little 'Poets
Corner'. You may perhaps, hardly any longer now understand th
singular sensations that pass through us artists, dreaming our dream
in this remote, quiet, isolated nook of the universe, when suddenly
like some northern comet, you flash through our silent heaven
bespattering it with brilliancy – flash, and are gone.

You represent to us all the possibility, the promise, the glamou
of that rich imaginary world which each one secretly in his hear
of hearts dreams attainable, if not by him- or her- self, at least b
others more gifted and more lucky. And it is good for us, in thi
trite, vulgar, prosaic modern world to now and again surrende
ourselves to such youthful sweet illusions; it is good that in th
height of success, fame, and triumph you should descend on us –

'A lovely apparition, sent
To be a moment's ornament;'

ba's dressing-room at Covent Garden, 1906. She always
the same room and kept the key herself. No other artist
allowed to use it. *(Melba Memorial Conservatorium)*

Melba decorated this car for a charity procession and won first prize.
(The Argus)

Royal Box, Covent Garden, 1908. *(Melba Memorial
nservatorium)*

The property room backstage, Covent Garden, 1908. *(Melba
Memorial Conservatorium)*

Far left: The tenor Enrico Caruso, Melba's
most illustrious stage partner and rival.
(La Trobe Library)

Left: A satin programme for a command
performance on 23 June 1897 with Melba
as Juliette surrounded by top-line names.
(The Age)

A Covent Garden gala performance *circa* 1908: the boxes are laden with roses and the royal family is in the centre. *(Melba Memorial Conservatorium)*

Melba welcomed by the Women's Choir at Spencer Street Station, Melbourne, on her first visit home in 1902. *(La Trobe Library)*

Far right (top, centre and bottom):
Programmes for London concerts by Melba. The inset picture shows Melba as Violetta. *(La Trobe Library)*

Melba during her 1902 visit at her father's quarrying site at Cave Hill near Lilydale. *(The Age)*

a living image of that ideal phantasm which lurks deep in our souls, and which represents our secret aspirations to all that is free, beautiful, and joyous in life. With romantic delight we regard your royal procession through the city, your military guard of honour at our capitolium, the illuminations and acclamations that greet you everywhere. For to us you represent more than a particular person, charming though we acknowledge that person to be: you represent an idea – nay, the idea to which we have devoted our lives and energies, the idea of art – art, the supreme manifestation of joyous strength. In your triumph art triumphs; in your honourment art is honoured. Your living presence has compelled this immature, partially cultured, somewhat unintellectual city to dimly feel for a moment that presence of that occult divine power which in higher states of civilisation is openly worshipped. And in these few inspired moments of joyous enthusiasm which you have awakened their dulled, unenlightened souls pay homage to, even though they are unable to understand, those subtler, more lasting, more forceful elements of life which become preponderant only in the rare blossoming times of the world's history, which constitute the 'heroic,' and which art – art, the memory of humanity – preserves in everlasting freshness, to remind us in times of physical and intellectual weariness of the splendid traditions of our race. Was it not in the days of Lodovico Sforza that the conqueror, at the head of his army, rode into Milan, a great general at one bridle rein, a great poet at the other – himself the great intellectual force that knew how, when and where to utilize both? And you, madame, who come from these historical seats of the ancient splendour, power, and culture of the human race, seem to waft with you something of their aroma, of their beauty, their traditions, in the presence of which even modern, plebeian, democratic Melbourne becomes animated, festive, and joyous. You are to us the ambassadress of that far romantic ideal world of art, of beauty, and of adventurous hope to which we vaguely aspire; as such we offer you what humble welcome we can, and pray your acceptance of this little memorial of our good-will.[6]

Embarrassing as this overbloated flattery appears now – and it was embarrassing to Melburnians even then – it still reflects something of the rapturous response of the Australian public to Melba's re-appearance in 1902. Murphy included the speech in full in her 1909 biography, but by then she was using it as a commendable, if ineffective, counter-claim in the face of the Norton scandal which eventually closed the tour. Melba's triumphal progress, with all the attendant hype, went unchecked until then.

The obligatory pilgrimage to scenes of childhood took Melba to her father's Lilydale estates via his wine-cellars at St Hubert's where

THEY SAY

'Someone once asked a State Governor's wife how Melba showed up as a house guest.

' "Delightful!" the governor's lady said ... "You know, she does allow you to feel so much at home in your own house!" '[1]

1. John Hetherington, *Melba*, p. 203.

THEY SAY

'If only the Australians could have heard how Melba herself used to rail against her own country! If only I had possessed a gramophone record of the mocking, bitter invective which she poured out upon Australia and everything Australian! By comparison, Mrs Trollope's assaults on Victorian America were the sweetest milk of human charity.

'I found myself in the curious position of having to defend her own countrymen against her onslaughts.

' "They may be crude", I would say, "but they're incredibly warm-hearted and hospitable, and they're anxious to learn".

'She brushed such protests aside:

' "They're hopeless ... hopeless!" '[1]

1. Beverley Nichols quoted in Hetherington, *op. cit.*, p. 217.

THE MYTH: RECEIVED WISDOM

'Stories naturally collected around her, some of them malicious, for a woman in her commanding position inevitably created envy as well as admiration. She could be impatient, but she was immensely generous: to her protégés; to stage-hands; and to the many unknown people who wrote to her daily, telling of their hardships and asking for help. It has been estimated that while she earned £500,000 for herself from her singing, she earned £200,000 for charity, apart from her liberal, personal gifts. The figures may be inaccurate, but the proportion is probably near the truth.'[1]

1. Geoffrey Hutton, 'Melba' in *Great Australians*, p. 29.

THE MYTH: RECEIVED WISDOM

'I heard that our own Dame Nellie Melba had signed a contract with Covent Garden which precluded the appearance of any other soprano without her consent! I understood that this embargo was held by Melba for over 20 years. Another clause in her contract stipulated that no other artistes were to receive as much payment as herself. When Caruso was at the zenith of his career an arrangement had to be made whereby he received £1 less than Melba for each appearance he made. Melba's fee was £400, Caruso's £399.'[1]

1. Dawson, *op.cit.*, p. 21.

the Nellie of another era surfaced briefly to tear round the carriagew. in her brother's dogcart. At Lilydale her drag was met by an esco from the local hunt which led her into the little town through triumphal arch of greenery and flags. Blue and gold-sashed scho children sang her into the rotunda to hear yet more speeches. Shop houses, bicycles, carriages, dogs and horses all sported the Mitche colours and even the local paper, the *Lilydale Express*, was issued blue paper with gold lettering. At Cave Hill, where she was phot graphed with a kangaroo, her father gave her a huge picnic and night a brass band and torchlight procession escorted her to the railwa station.

The Sydney, Brisbane and Adelaide concerts were even more su cessful than the Melbourne season. For the third Sydney appearan she was paid a net £2350, to that date the highest fee ever paid singer for a single engagement. Jenny Lind held the previous recor of £2000 for her first concert in America when Barnum, of circ fame, whipped up public interest by holding a public auction for th tickets. Melba had no need of such tactics.

The question of Melba's fees began to interest the Australian pres So did her response to the drought-stricken country she watched pa monotonously by in the thousands of miles she travelled by train. Sh wrote to the Victorian press offering £200 to seed a drought-reli fund for the ruined small settlers of her home state, but she mad the mistake of announcing that she had also appealed to 'a few my friends in England and America, who happen to be blest wit wealth and influence'. The Council of the Melbourne Chamber Commerce met in a flurry and issued a statement of disapproval. The argued that Melba was suggesting outside intervention that coul damage Australian credit.

What started as a fairly mindless but good-natured gesture intende to keep her stocks up with the locals soon looked as if it could en with Australian stocks falling on the international share market. rallying call from Melba could have that kind of effect. The Prim Minister, Edmund Barton, stated in the House that he accepted th views of the Chamber. The Victorian Parliament discussed Melba motives at some length. She was obliged to withdraw her offer bu the public, expecting her to stand her ground and carry through h defence of the underdog, was disappointed. Within days she left fo New Zealand. At that point John Norton began his campaign destroy her reputation.

Norton ran the weekly scandal-sheet *Truth*, originally a Sydne concern which later established offices in other states. He had the ea of the nation. He was a middle-aged Londoner with a reputation the worst order. Hetherington called him

a strident bully, devoid of scruples, whose path to affluence wa paved with lies, violence, blackmail, seduction and empty whisky bottles . . . a man who made a profitable business of character assassination and just-within-the-law pornography.[7]

He was four times a member of Parliament, three times an alderman; and a collector of Napoleonic relics. As a young journalist in Constantinople he was once caught in a harem and given the option of surgery, being sent to the bottom of the Bosporus in a weighted sack or taking the first boat home. He chose to ship out to London and shortly afterwards, in 1884, to Sydney. He had nothing when he arrived. When he died in 1916 he left an estate of £100 000. Cyril Pearl said of him:

> He had been publicly denounced many times as a thief, a blackmailer, a wifebeater and an obscene drunkard, without ever refuting the charges; and he had been accused of killing his oldest friend in a drunken quarrel . . . Norton was a Fascist when Mussolini was a schoolboy . . . he assumed the title of 'the people's tribune' and by violence, skilful, and cynical demagogy, persuaded thousands of Australians that he was their champion.[8]

Hetherington adds 'at least half his victims were men and women whose only sin in his eyes was that they had become respected public figures . . . He was a man seething with insensate hatreds . . . obsessed with drunkenness'.

Melba completed her first Australian tour in Sydney in March 1903. The final stages included a sea journey to Western Australia and Tasmania. Concerts were advertised for Launceston and Hobart, where she originally intended to change ships for New Zealand. Late in the piece Norton got hold of a series of gossip items put together by a journalist in London, a woman whom Melba had deeply offended by giving her a piece of her mind in the course of this work. Melba, she said, was a drunkard, promiscuous and a morphia addict. Norton now found the moment to build on these claims.

The entrepreneur for the Launceston concert, a Mr Thompson, guaranteed £1000 return on the night. The only way Melba could keep this engagement was by crossing Bass Strait from Melbourne by paddle steamer. She set off across one of the wildest stretches of water in the world in a vessel incapable of dealing with it. The result was violent sea-sickness. Her throat was so torn and inflamed that she could barely speak, let alone sing.

Elva Rogers, then a 19-year-old contralto engaged in Melbourne as an associate artist, recorded the voyage:

> It was an awful trip. We were all sick. The captain said it was the worst crossing he had ever experienced. As soon as we were settled in the Hotel Brisbane, in Launceston, Melba called me and said, 'Miss Rogers, I don't think I'll ever be able to sing again. My

throat is bleeding after the dry retching. Come and listen! I can't even get high C.' We went to the piano and she sang a few scales. Anyone, much less a singer, could have told that her vocal mechanism was in bad shape. The doctor ordered her to bed, and she stayed there until next day, when we took the train to Hobart.[9]

Melba herself said the doctor told her 'that it would be madness for me even to attempt to sing for several days, and gave me a certificate to that effect'. The public was notified at the last minute that the concert was cancelled and that Melba had left on the first available train. No explanation was offered. A rumour spread that guests at the hotel had seen her arrive, order a bottle of champagne and down it on the spot. At the station 'a few disappointed and infuriated holders of tickets [came] to hoot me as my train steamed out of Launceston station', a fact that 'was magnified until it seemed as though the whole city had turned out to execrate me'.

As it happened John Norton was in Tasmania at the time. He cabled a feature to *Truth* accusing Melba of bad faith and hinting that he had a bigger story to break later which would reveal the real reasons why she had failed to sing in Launceston.

On Sunday 28 March 1903 *Truth* published an open letter to Melba from Norton. It occupied the better part of four columns of the broadsheet format. In it he brushed aside Melba's claim that she had been too ill to sing, putting it down to another cause.

> Your powers are ripe; your reputation is made; all the world asks of you is the privilege of paying to hear you, and applauding you. What more could woman wish or desire? What woman with a heart or soul would rashly risk such rich gifts and golden opportunities as yours by wantoning in wine? The careers of great divas, some of whom have died drunk and destitute [possibly a reference to Ilma di Murska] – who have caressed the cup and drowned their songs in strong drink, should cause you to look upon champagne with a shudder, and to shun it with a shiver so long as God shall give you leave to sing. Your voice will not last for ever; it should be cherished like chastity, and not submitted to the risk of ruin that banquets and drinking bouts entail.

He went on to accuse her of mean and bad tempered behaviour to her fellow artists, and of 'raking in the shekels by charging prices probably higher than she could ever obtain or average in London or on the continent of Europe'. He admonished:

> Surely you have made enough money out of your offended and outraged countrymen and countrywomen, and given so little of your easily gotten superfluity to the deserving charities of your native land, to enable you to deal not only fairly but liberally with the few second-rate artistes who accompany you, and with two such

reasonable and deserving attendants as your private secretary and your personal companion. It is altogther too bad to add to the truculence of the termagant, the vagaries of the virago, and the proclivities of the poculant pocharde those of a miserable miser, who, while revelling in wealth and swigging champagne, balances and buncoes dependants who have kept better faith with her than she has kept faith with the public who have paid her so liberally, and generously forgiven her so much.

He ended with a challenge:

Perhaps now that I've done with you you'll think it about time to begin with me. Be it so, but be sure you count the cost before commencing; and consider well who will gain most by a public investigation by way of cross-examination in the courts – you or your legal advisers. I tell you frankly that I court such a contest, and feel confident that if it is commenced that I shall come off more than conqueror.

Melba seems to have been forced to agree with him as no action was ever taken. For one thing to press libel charges in Australia at that time could have meant abandoning her career for months in order to be present for the trial. It is doubtful if she could have pleaded *in absentia*. It was too great a risk to take. She could have lost as much as £50 000 in earnings alone. Even had she been able to fight solely through legal representation without a personal appearance there were other matters to consider. Any challenge to Norton would necessitate his letter being publicly refuted in detail and some of the detail would have required re-opening issues Melba thought better left as they were.

It was true that the tour had not gone smoothly for her associates or for herself. Few touring groups hit it off all along the line. But the Launceston group included the Melbourne tenor, Walter Kirby, an emotional young man who suffered openly when Melba's exasperation at his ineptness, rather than his singing, got the better of her and she indulged in the kind of acerbic remarks most of us would like to use for such occasions but seldom do. Melba never hesitated. Kirby was likely to be called as a witness.

The references to champagne, chastity, banquets, 'deserving charities' and 'faith with the public' would all have to be examined. Would such an examination have entailed reports on her visit to her father's vineyards, her London lifestyle, her relationships with colleagues, Lemmone included, and, perhaps, even with the Duc? Her divorce was only two years behind her. Would it have meant exposing her financial affairs to public scrutiny, or a rehash of the sensitive Chamber of Commerce issue to the embarrassment of the party in power? And would all of it find a distorted way into the European and American press?

THE MYTH: RECEIVED WISDOM

'Singing was a way out of being a woman. Singing was a way to enforce equality of admiration, adulation and approbation from the male. She hated the [*sic*] female company. She hated female colleagues and would destroy them as ruthlessly as her dad would blast a quarry face. She turned herself into a one-woman European aristocracy, but all her life specialised in the tactical use of the Great Australian Adjective just to let it be known that she was a male macho at heart — a sort of singing bikie. When she had rare attacks of insecurity, she'd gather the stage hands around her and give them a song. Free. And the grafters would concede that Melba was a really beaut bloke. She was never known to sing free for the girls ... The adulation she received from Australia satisfied the need she had required from a father. Irrational, because he was a loving dad as far as idiosyncratic dads go. Thus, from the simple conditions of a semi-pioneering Australia, uncouth and cheerfully sexist, the world got one of its greatest singers. Australia got the most famous citizen it has produced in all its history.'[1]

'She was the all-Australian world champion bitch ...'[2]

'She was demanding, dictatorial, ruthless, appallingly snobbish, imperious, vain, capricious, inconsiderate, childish, tight-fisted, stingy, mean, ungrateful, pathologically jealous, publicity-hungry and supremely egotistical.'[3]

'She made her voice out of will, work and ruthless ambition. Her acting was

Melba was wise enough to refrain from taking legal action but she could not resist trying to refute Norton's claims when the time came. She returned to Australia in 1907 to see her father. Her manager, John Lemmone, arranged for a Launceston visit. She wrote warning him to book on the steamer across Bass Strait: 'Last time I went I had to cross in a paddle boat, and I was so utterly prostrated that I could not sing'.

Armed with this letter Lemmone went to the local club, 'the stronghold of prejudice', as Melba calls it in the memoirs: 'John stood up in the centre of the room, facing the serried rows of self-satisfied faces'. When he asked if it was true they were spreading it about that Melba would be hooted out of town if she tried to give a concert in Launceston, they replied that it was, backing it up with all the old accusations of Melba leaving Thompson in the lurch at great personal cost because she had been too drunk to sing. Lemmone told them they were a pack of ignorant provincials. He told them Thompson had had £400 compensation and that Dr Hogg had provided Melba with a certificate to prove her illness. Both men lived in Launceston. He demanded to know why they had not been questioned. He then produced Melba's letter and read it, showing the postmark. 'There', he said, 'that's an honest letter, isn't it?' Grudging apologies were offered. Lemmone, not satisfied, took the letter to the local paper which printed it with an article of explanation. It was reproduced nationally. At the end of the Launceston concert some of her audience took the horses out of the carriage and fought to drag it and Melba through the crowded streets to her hotel.

But it was no use. The muck clung. In 1909, the year of her whistle-stop tour through the Australian outback, she was forced to retreat halfway through one concert because of a sore throat. As the announcement was made Lemmone, stationed at the back of the hall, heard remarks about her being drunk again. In 1911, during her first Australian grand opera season, ticket-holders repeatedly rang her hosts in Melbourne, Edward and Kate Fanning, to ask if she would be sober enough to sing that night. During the Sydney season she went down with laryngitis and was off for several nights. She wrote to her press agent, Claude McKay: 'Isn't it disgusting? The people say I am drunk. What can be done about it? Yours, heartbroken, Nellie Melba'. McKay had the letter published in the *Sydney Morning Herald*, to Melba's delight. When she reappeared on stage some time later the house stood and cheered for minutes on end. McKay remembered, 'She always said that this was the reception that moved her most deeply of all'.

But then there was the night in Ballarat when Melba's fans gathered outside her hotel after the performance chanting, 'We want Melba, we want Melba'. But Melba was not to be seen. The shouting attracted the attention of three Melbourne reporters in town for a conference of the Australian Natives' Association and finishing their day's work in the bar. One of the three decided that Melba ought to put her followers out of their noisy misery. Donning a floral dressing-gown and with a towel wrapped, toque fashion, round his head, he stepped through the French windows of his room onto the upper verandah and stood there, swaying. The apparition caused an unexpected silence to fall, into which a slurred voice shrilled, 'I wish all you buggers would go home and let me get some bloody sleep!'

And of such stuff are legends made. For the rest of her life Melba was pursued by Norton's malice. It was useless, to protest that no singer who was drunk could perform to schedule as Melba did. Even now, when the idiocy of such an accusation has long since been established, the rest of the mud splashed by Norton is still visible on Nellie's tarnished image. To the Australians of her day it was as if the Worth creation they had admired at a distance for so long, had turned out, on close inspection, to be nothing but theatrical tat.

abysmal. And many critics found her singing impersonal, lacking in heart, emotionally sterile. It was the quality of the voice that conquered the world. George Bernard Shaw grudgingly conceded its "superhuman beauty". Sarah Bernhardt described it as a "voice of fine crystal". It got as close to disembodied perfection as the human voice can become when it is controlled by an iron will. But some of the most respected later critics weren't all that impressed by technical perfection. Ernest Newman said it was "uninterestingly perfect and perfectly uninteresting". Neville Cardus acknowledged "the flawless vocalism pure and simple. But never in my experience did it enter the deeper world of music". Even so, it was a voice so wondrous that she ruled Covent Garden with all the subtlety of a bosomy Adolf Hitler from 1892 to 1926."[4]

1. Max Harris, *The Unknown Great Australian and Other Psychobiographical Portraits*, p. 31
2. *Ibid.*, p. 26
3. *Ibid.*, p. 27
4. *Ibid.*, pp. 27–8

Chapter 8

MANHATTAN VERSUS METROPOLITAN

THE MYTH: RECEIVED WISDOM

The American Wagnerian baritone Clarence Whitehall met Melba in 1899 when she was touring in America with Campanini who brought the younger singer to meet the great diva. Whitehall told the press, in all innocence: 'We approached Mme Melba's apartment and I heard sounds of tussling within, terminated by a wham, as a body was thrown against a door. "What sort of rough-house is going on?" I said to myself. The next moment we were admitted and I had my first glimpse of Melba, a sturdy creature, her hair somewhat dishevelled and flopping over her eyes. She had, when we interrupted her, been wrestling with her conductor, later Sir Landon Ronald! And she had just pinned him down when we came in!" '.[1]

It was true that Melba rolled on the floor, often publicly, as a weight control exercise. It did not work. Given her partner on this occasion, it seems unlikely that she was simply exercising.

1. Clipping, n.d., Melba file, New York Public Library.

Melba had left Covent Garden after the summer season of 1902. During it she had appeared as Gilda to Caruso's Duke at the Italian tenor's London début. She had sung earlier with him at Monte Carlo and 'reported enthusiastically' about him to the Garden's management but he was not an overnight success. It was only when he sang Rodolfo to Melba's Mimi on 24 May that the box office began to respond. Blanche Marchesi sang Elizabeth, Leonora, Elsa and Isolde in the autumn season.

When Melba returned in 1903 it was to find Titta Ruffo making his début on 5 June as Enrico in *Lucia* but unfortunately for him he created such an impression at the dress rehearsal of *Rigoletto* that Melba, sensing the competition was too strong, protested that he was too young to play her father. He was removed from the cast and never sang again at Covent Garden. Years later, when he was a celebrity, he took his revenge on Melba at another opera house. This time it was Ruffo who did the objecting – this time Melba was too old to play his daughter.

On 6 July 1903 there was a command performance at Buckingham Palace to entertain the President of France, Monsieur Loubet, and a gála for him the following night with the royals and the French contingent present. Two days later Melba gave a huge society party at her house in Great Cumberland Place, singing the Bach-Gounod 'Ave Maria' to Kubelik's violin, her protégé Ada Sassoli's harp, and Landon Ronald's piano accompaniment. Ronald was *répétiteur* at Covent Garden in 1891 when Melba asked for a pianist to come to her hotel to study Massenet's opera *Manon* with her. He had the piano score almost from memory in a single night and so impressed Melba that she promoted his career at every turn, as he freely acknowledged later. He toured America as her accompanist in 1894 and played for her frequently thereafter, publicly and privately. Sir Landon Ronald, as he became in 1922, was also a distinguished conductor and critic, and a minor composer, no mere background support for a prima donna, though some of that support – on her early recordings – is historically significant.

In October there was an extensive Canadian–American tour with Sassoli in tow, but the second half of the concert season was cancelled when Saint-Saëns summoned her to prepare his *Hélène* which was to be premièred on 18 February 1904 in Monte Carlo. The role was written specifically for Melba but, as usual, she had the bad luck to find herself allied to yet another second-rate work by a minor operatic talent. It surfaced again for a London début on 20 June but it made no real impact.

In March there was a tour of the English provinces. April was spent in Paris, replacing the costumes lost when the hold of the *Saxonia* was flooded on the journey home out of Boston. The scores of *Aida*, *Rigoletto*, *Faust*, *Roméo et Juliette*, *Hamlet* and *Lakmé*, all marked in detail by the composers, were ruined. Melba cried for two days.

In June, at the height of the Covent Garden season, there was a command performance for the Austrian Archduke Franz Ferdinand at Buckingham Palace where the Order of Science, Art and Music was conferred on Melba and her private recordings, made in Australia in 1902 for David Mitchell ('Caro nome', 'Sweet bird' and 'Ah! fors' è lui'), were displayed.

At the end of that summer there was a holiday with New Zealand cousins, Melba happily tripping about Europe with all the usual verve, but in Paris disaster hit. Her chauffeur-driven car, the diva in the back seat, ran down and killed an old man who had stepped onto the road unexpectedly. The driver was exonerated but Melba found she could not get the incident out of her mind. Her mental health deteriorated rapidly. She cancelled engagements and took to her bed, but there was a contract for the New York winter season to fulfil and against doctor's orders she set off, brooding and despondent. After a single appearance in *La Bohème* she came down with pneumonia and lay dangerously ill in her rooms at the Waldorf Astoria.

The rest of her engagements from December to March were cancelled. She worried incessantly over the effect on her troupe who had already lost work over her bid for *Hélène*. It was only when George Armstrong came to her rescue that she began to heal. By the end of March she was on tour again in America. In London, when she sang at the Albert Hall for Prince George's Union Jack Club, the audience, including a team of Australian cricketers and the King, got to its feet in a solemn welcome home. A few days later she resumed her place at Covent Garden in *La Traviata* to the bejewelled applause of a typical Melba night and later sang four numbers at Cliveden for Astor at 500 guineas a song. Her powers of recuperation were, and remained, extraordinary.

By this time the first of her recordings had come onto the market, ostensibly as a teaching aid. Melba's discography forms an appendix to this book, so I will not go into details here, except to point out that the test discs for the Gramophone Melba Records were made

SOME COVENT GARDEN RECEIPTS

The extent of Melba's fees at Covent Garden is indicated by seven receipts for separate and sometimes collective performances which were itemised. They are signed by Melba or by her agent, C. Gill. The managing director at the time is given as Maurice Grau.

1. Audit dated 28 May 1902. £200 each for *Rigoletto* (22 May 1902) and *La Bohème* (24 May 1902).
2. No date. £200 for *Roméo and Juliette* (10 June 1902).
3. 23 June 1902. £200 for *Rigoletto* (20 June 1902).
4. 29 July 1902. £200 for *Roméo and Juliette* (29 July 1902)
5. 25 June 1907. £1250 for *La Bohème* (21 May 1907), a Gala (11 June 1907), *La Bohème* (16 June 1907), *La Traviata* (18 June 1907) and *La Bohème* (21 June 1907).
6. 20 May 1914. £750. Audit dated 26 May 1914. For *La Bohème* (20 April 1914), a Gala (11 May 1914) and *Rigoletto* (20 May 1914).
7. 5 June 1914. £1000 for *La Bohème* (26 May and 6 June 1914), *Rigoletto* (29 May 1914) and *Otello* (4 June 1914).

THE VOICE

Michael Aspinall, a recording expert, wrote in 1976: 'The voice may have been that of the hermit thrush, but the woman was of sterner stuff: "In my own path great obstacles were placed, but I do not think anything in the world could have hindered me from becoming a singer". Or anything else she wanted to be, she might have added. The ruthless stamp of her driving ambition is clearly revealed just by the sound of her records; *Caro nome*, for instance, is destitute of feminine frailty and charm, and the aggressively assertive Gilda seems bent on bullying her audience into submission with cascades of dazzling runs, brilliant staccati and vibrant, flawless trills. At times she wields her angelic voice like a club to stun her hearers. The strange Providence that imprisoned the hauntingly pure and ethereal voice in the frame of such a canny, worldly woman was not perhaps ill advised; many a fragile, limpid voice has failed to achieve its early promise for lack of the hard wisdom of Melba, inherited from her Scottish father'.[1]

1. Michael Aspinall, Notes to *Nellie Melba: The London Recordings.*

in March 1904 at Melba's house in Great Cumberland Place b the Gramophone and Typewriter Company. Melba's response wa damning:

'Never again' I said to myself, as I listened to the scratching screeching result. 'Don't tell me I sing like that, or I shall go awa' and live on a desert island, out of sheer pity for the unfortunat people who have to listen to me.' The records were therefor destroyed.

But the gramophone people [with whom the Victor Talkin, company were now associated] persisted. Never have I known suc courtesy combined with such persuasion. They simply would no leave me alone. They said that no great artist, with the exception of Tamagno, had ever sung for the gramophone, and that if I woul only give them another chance, with their greatly improved appa ratus, they were sure that I would be delighted.

I did and I was.[1]

The use to which she put the test recordings – playing them to th royals and having the fact universally reported, playing them t journalists as personal mementoes of her time in Australia wit 'Daddy', and making it known that teachers everywhere were writin, to her clamouring for discs to back up lessons – had its effect whe the 1902 private recordings were redone as tests for the 1904 run.

Melba's recording career and indeed the whole recording industr boomed. But the monetary return was not the only attraction for he She said to Agnes Murphy, if the stilted language her secretary use is indeed Melba's:

Only think how extremely interesting it would be for me to b able to go to the British Museum and hear Jenny Lind sing the a from Mozart's *Il Rè Pastore*, with violin accompaniment by Joachim He has presented me with the cadenza which he arranged for Jenn Lind, and I always use it.[2]

Today that sense of history and of continuing tradition has give generations of musicians an insight into a style and method whicl was thought of then as the final flowering of the long period of be canto development. The Melba recordings give access to and perpetuat a great deal more than one singer's voice; behind them and discernibl in them lies at least two hundred years of changing practice anc creativity. Melba knew the significance of the trust she was placing i a primitive technology. She risked her reputation then as now, anc we cannot be anything but grateful.

In October she sang in the autumn opera season, at the Bristo Festival and at Windsor Castle for the Greek royals and, in November for the relief of Calabrian earthquake victims.

Early in 1906 she attended the wedding of the Infanta Maria Teresa sister of King Alfonso of Spain, then toured the country at the King's invitation. At Malaga a bloodless bullfight was staged for her (she had protested at all the goriness of the usual variety), and at a charity concert she walked in over an elaborately woven carpet of flowers, a tribute usually reserved for the royal family. Caged doves were released at the end of the night as the 200 best families hurled bouquets at her feet. Her spirits, like the birds, soared.

That summer she holidayed at Coombe Cottage at Kingston Hall, a house associated with the Empress Eugénie, Queen Victoria and the Rothschilds and rented from Lord Charles Beresford, the spokesman for the coterie which brought Augustus Harris to operatic power and Melba to the light at Covent Garden. It was this house that lent its name to Melba's retirement home in Australia.

She was at Coombe for her birthday on 19 May when the Covent Garden season resumed and when she was in the process of recovering from a bad cold, an annual event for her because of the biting east winds, so she thought. Her car broke down near New Malden with no help in sight. Her maid, her coat and therefore her support system had gone on ahead. Eventually a butcher's cart trundled into the remote little lane. Melba hitched a ride on the exposed front seat to Malden station. She was dressed for a quick ride in a heated car and by the time the curtain went up for *Rigoletto* that night she knew that the cold wind and the long cold ride sans maid, sans coat had done their worst. She spent the next two weeks in bed, her appearance cancelled yet again. (Like the flower-seller in the snow, the ride on the butcher's cart turns up in odd places. There was one man who swore, on tape, that it was he who drove her – but in 1926 down St Kilda Road in Melbourne.)

Late in the year George Armstrong married Ruby Otway, the daughter and heir of millionaire art collector Sir Jocelyn Otway. Melba had opposed the match as she thought both parties were too young, but when an elopement was threatened she gave in, settling $10 000 a year on her son, with $4000 of it secured in a marriage settlement. George had been living with his mother, dividing his time between London and Melba's country property at Otway on the Thames. The newly-weds set up together in an apartment at the Great Cumberland Place house. Romantic titbits on their supposedly idyllic marriage were fed to the press at regular intervals but in 1908 George began divorce proceedings against Ruby, who countered the action. George was also named co-respondent in a second suit.

A divorce was granted to Ruby on the grounds of 'extreme personal cruelty and misconduct'. On the stand 'the wife told a most pitiful story of abuse, violence and infidelity on the part of her husband'.[3] Melba's name was kept out of the proceedings and the London papers made no mention of her in their reports of the suit, but the American press went to town on it. It was believed that her Australian tour of

the time was extended so that she would be out of England during
the hearing.

In the period between the first and second visits home, new rival
and changing managements at Covent Garden and the allied Metro
politan began to take their toll. Melba was in her mid-forties, meno
pausal, her health a little uncertain, her figure beginning to spread
her voice not yet affected by time but its pre-eminence threatened by
younger, fresher voices in newer roles and by the slow change of public
taste. How to command attention, to remain the star, became a
necessary obsession and like everything else she did, Melba worked
hard at it.

From 1904 on, the Garden seasons began to lengthen and the
repertoire to expand under the growing influence of Pitt, Richter and
Forsyth, though the Melba faction, Lady de Grey and Higgins, re
mained in control. That year saw the advent of Emmy Destinn and
Selma Kurz, another of 'that galaxy' of Marchesi students then singing
in London. Kurz reappeared for the 1905 season but she failed to
become a permanent member of the company – she was far too
popular in the Melba repertory for the ruling diva's taste and she saw
to it that life was made just a little too difficult for Kurz to negotiate
a long-term contract.

Melba was at the peak of her career, though aware that time was
against her. In 1905 the London *Telegraph* wrote of her return in *La
Traviata* on 17 May, a role she sang dressed in a succession of Worth
creations before a full turn-out of London society:

> Melba carried away many of her audience by the roundness, the
> purity, and the sympathetic charm of her singing . . . it was a
> typical Melba night. The new Alfredo Constantino, is scarcely a
> singer of the highest distinction . . . some of the minor characters
> were in weak hands; but no-one takes them keenly into account
> when Melba is of the company.[4]

The popular press wrote: 'The house last night was crowded with
well-dressed women and jewels galore . . . on such a night it is almost
difficult to say who was not present – all London seemed in evidence'.[5]

At this moment the antithesis of a John Norton appeared in Melba's
life – the extraordinary Oscar Hammerstein. Why she accepted his
offer to sing in a new opera house set up as a shaky rival to her
established trans-Atlantic circuit house, the Met., where her future
seemed guaranteed, is still something of a mystery. Why she liked
Hammerstein is not – they were birds of a feather.

Oscar Hammerstein I was a playwright and composer, an inventor,
a builder and an impresario in love with opera. He was an aggressive,
stubborn, human dynamo and a formidable opponent. Melba called
him 'the most American of Americans, and the only man who ever
made me change my mind'.

On 23 February he fired the first shot in the most sensational operatic 'war' in the history of the American theatre with the announcement that he, a mere David, intended to compete against the Goliath of New York, the Metropolitan Opera Company. He had no stockholders, no advisers, no partners, no board of directors and no rich patrons. He had been a bankrupt. He had built theatres that failed as often as they succeeded. And now, with the proceeds from vaudeville, he proposed a season, not just of grand opera, but of the greatest opera ever heard or seen. It was pure ballyhoo and so the music critics of the day told him, loudly, publicly and frequently. Henry Edward Krehbiel, in *Chapters of Opera*, said some of them looked upon his enterprise as quixotic, down to the very day of the opening of his house'.

That house was the second Manhattan Opera House which Hammerstein was then building on West 34th Street between Eighth and Ninth Avenues. Over ten years before, his first Manhattan also went up on West 34th, but between Broadway and Seventh Avenue, the site Macy's department store later occupied. The new building was four stories high, the structure itself 200 feet deep and 105 feet long, its façade decorated along the 34th Street side where heavy stone pillars at the entrance gave way to pilasters and a pediment above. The interior could only be described as Louis XIV Theatrical. It had a capacity of 3389 seats; this was later modified to 3100. The Metropolitan held 3800 but it was supported by $400 000 worth of subscribers and the long-established Astor–Morgan–Vanderbilt directorate, with its Wall Street backing.

Hammerstein let it be known that Jean de Reszke would appear at $3500 a performance and his brother Edouard at $1000. No contracts had been signed. He promised a repertoire of twenty-five Italian and French works and to introduce Charpentier's *Louise*, Bruneau's *L'Attaque de Moulin* and Debussy's *Pelléas et Mélisande*. He was unaware of rights being bought up behind his back. The chorus, recruited from the New York voice studios, was something new in American opera – an integrated stage force.

Hammerstein said to a reporter from the *New York Herald* shortly before the opening night:

Look at them – note the different types. Do you not see that they are wholly different from an Italian chorus, in which every woman looks the same and every man seems to be built on the same lines and both men and women appear never to have learned more than four gestures? Wait until you see these young men and women on the stage.[6]

But there were yet more enticements offered – an auditorium constructed with clear sight lines and a design that gave a sense of intimacy with the stage (something that was lacking in the vault-like

THE INCREDIBLE OSCAR HAMMERSTEIN

Oscar Hammerstein was German born, the son of a building contractor, a real martinet of a man. At 15 Oscar ran away to sea and arrived in America in the middle of the Civil War. His first job was making cigars but it was his inventions for the tobacco industry that gave him the finance to publish the *United States Tobacco Journal* in 1874. He composed and wrote plays in German, much of which was produced by the Germania Theatre. In the 1880s he became a builder. In 1889 he opened the Harlem Opera House and a year later the Columbus Theatre. In 1893 he was challenged to write an operetta within forty-eight hours, with original words and music. He won the bet, then had *The Kohinoor*, as it was called, performed successfully. In 1895 he built the Olympia, but went broke shortly afterwards. Everyone said that was the finish of him but Hammerstein borrowed against his inventions and built a vaudeville house, the Victoria, the most successful of his theatres. Within nine months he was again a rich man.

The great love of his life and the reason behind his relentless drive to make money was the production of grand opera. In 1908 he wrote: 'Grand opera is, I truly believe, the most elevating influence upon modern society, after religion . . . I sincerely believe that nothing will make better citizenship than familiarity with grand opera. It lifts one so out of the sordid affairs of life and makes material things so petty, so inconsequential, that it places one for the time being, at least, in a higher, & better world . . . Grand opera is more than music, it is more than drama; it is more than spectacle; it is more than a social function . . . It is the awakening of the soul to the sublime and the divine; and this, I believe, is the true mission of grand opera'.[1]

1. Oscar Hammerstein, 'The mission of grand opera' in *The North American*, grand opera edition, Philadelphia, 17 November 1908.

shape of the Met.), 5000 lights to produce a brilliant night scene th Met. could not rival, realistic stage-settings and effects, historicall accurate costumes that blended into the *mise-en-scène*, and a stag discipline that would ensure that the accidents so common at the olde house (bungled lights, failed curtains, backstage noise during perform ances, disorder during scene changes, and collapsing sets) could no occur.

Hammerstein believed that opera as given at the Met. was a disgrace He thought Heinrich Conried, the director since 1903, was incom petent. In earlier German seasons, and later under Henry E. Abbey Maurice Grau and John B. Schoeffel, vocal standards had been of th highest. In the seasons between 1891 and 1903 it was said all th great singers of the times appeared at the Met., yet the production were marred by the lack of good supporting casts, second-rate chora and orchestral forces, a ballet 'little short of absurd' and inconsisten stage management. Grau's policy had been to produce nothing nev since he believed the audience came to hear the star, not the opera Year after year he gave his patrons the casts and the operas to which they had become accustomed. So long as the supply of stars continued he could afford to ignore the relatively few demands for change Conried, like Grau, knew little of music or of singing. He wa essentially a theatrical manager. To cover for his inadequacies he adopted a high-handed manner that rapidly made enemies for him a the Met., among them Melba. She had not sung there since 1(December 1904 and then, due to illness, only once, as Mimi, and had been absent for four years before that. She may have been simply bored under Grau, whom she had learned to manage, but Conried was another matter; a single season was enough for her.

Hammerstein maintained that the difficulties he ran into during the period when he was assembling his Manhattan company were due to Conried's backstage manoeuvres. In 1906 on a recruiting expedition to Europe, Hammerstein found agents who had welcomed him with open arms only days before would suddenly decide he was a danger to their relations with the Met. and refuse to trade with him. He found Conried had secured production rights to all the Puccini operas He made a bid for Jean de Reszke's services at $3000 a performance and tried, unsuccessfully, to contract Toscanini. Jean de Reszke, like Toscanini, eluded even Hammerstein who left, discouraged, for Milan but Conried's telegrams had preceded him and neither agents nor singers would open their doors to the man out to ruin the Met. Then unexpectedly, an old and now wealthy friend, Bianca Lescout, who had sung for him at the old Manhattan, decided to lend him her influence in the Italian musical world. Agents and singers began to receive him. Cleofonte Campanini, the darling of La Scala, had just resigned, dissatisfied with conditions there. He was at the peak of a distinguished conducting career that had included the Met. early on

He left because he did not believe millionaires and society wives should dictate artistic policy. When he accepted Hammerstein's offer with enthusiasm the impresario at last had the kind of company that could support the one person he now needed – the pre-eminent star, the artist who could attract more attention, sell more seats, create more excitement than anything the Met. had to offer. There was only one – Melba, 'the greatest singer in the world'.

Melba was in demand by every major opera house on both sides of the Atlantic and, it was presumed, the property of the Met., where she had won the right to refuse to sing if her fee was not paid in cash before the curtain went up. (This, incidentally, was not meanness on Melba's part, as this used to be interpreted, but a relic of a once necessary precaution against the failure of an opera company. As a girl Melba would have known the fate of quite a few penniless opera singers stranded in Australia because of a company's inability to pay its personnel at the end of a season. Even in Edwardian times it was not an uncommon event for an opera company to declare itself bankrupt and for its less influential members to go unpaid while its stars, secured by pre-production guarantees, were cushioned against the fall.)

According to Melba, Hammerstein set siege to her in Paris in a way no prima donna could resist. He got a letter of introduction from Maurice Grau and when she turned down his original offer of $1500 a night called, wrote and telephoned with offers. On one occasion, as Melba recorded in the memoirs, he managed to get as far as her bathroom while she was in the bath and began battering on the door:

Hammerstein: 'Are you coming to America?' Myself (between splashes.): 'No.' Hammerstein: 'I'll give you two thousand five hundred a night.' Myself: 'Go away.'

So it went until he finally broke in while she was reading *Le Figaro* over breakfast and carpeted the room with thousand franc notes. Still she refused. When he had gone she gathered up the money and deposited it at the Rothschild Bank with instructions that it was to be kept for Hammerstein. He refused to take it back. In the end she gave in and went to America to give ten performances for $30 000 because, as she said, 'I love a good fight'.

Hammerstein's less well-known version of this legendary tale from opera's history is quite different and much more convincing, given the characters involved and minus Nichols as the literary go-between. The Hammerstein account was published in New York in *The World* a month after the event:

Everywhere I had gone I found hostile cablegrams had preceded me and an icy reception was awaiting me. But one by one I had gathered together artists who more than fulfilled my desires. I say

I gathered them in, but technically I hadn't. In every contract was
a punitive clause by which, with the payment of a forfeit, I could
withdraw. I had made up my mind that if I couldn't get Mme
Melba I would be obliged to drop the whole grand opera under
taking.

It was make or break with me, and I decided there was no time
like the present. So I got into fresh linen, brushed my travel-stained
clothes, called a cab and at 6 in the evening headed for Mme
Melba's home in the Boulevard Malesherbes. It was a big project
that I had on my hands, and I had reached the point where I had
to trust to luck.[7]

The maid who answered the bell told Hammerstein that Madam
was entertaining at dinner and might not like to be disturbed. Ham
merstein stood his ground. The maid disappeared: 'Three minute
later I heard a great rustling on the stairs and in came Mme Melb
with a great sweep and flourish'. She knew at once what he had come
for. She told him to come back next day, she had guests, it was th
wrong moment. 'Tomorrow is impossible', he said, 'I am going to
Berlin. I have a great list of artists, but my contracts are punitive and
I have made up my mind that without you I must give the whol
thing up'. 'Ah, that would be unfortunate indeed . . . You must not
do that', Melba replied.

Hammerstein begged for just ten minutes. Melba hesitated, swep
off to excuse herself to her guests, and was back in an instant. 'Now'
she said determinedly, 'what do you want?'. When Hammerstein
named his singers and outlined his plans Melba interrupted him with
'I know all about that. See here'. And she went to her desk to display
a bundle of cablegrams. 'I have been annoyed to death with des
patches', she exclaimed. 'My time is open next season, and perhaps
would just as soon sing under your management as anyone else's, and
so end the whole matter.'

Hammerstein asked her terms. She named the figures and condition
in a snappy, business-like way, warning him that she was a wealth
woman: 'I need not sing unless I want to – therefore I come high'
Hammerstein recorded: 'She certainly did come high!' He asked for
ten minutes to think it over, bowed himself out into the Parisia
night and began to walk round the block. Before he got half-way th
decision was made. No matter what she cost he would have her. Back
in Melba's parlour he told her he accepted her terms. She said sh
would help him to his success by her influence and that he was to
return in the morning to sign contracts. Unwilling to take any furthe
risks, Hammerstein asked for a line of acceptance there and then
Without hesitation she opened her desk and wrote the note.

'That's settled', said I . . .
'Not quite', she replied dryly. 'You know, Mr Hammerstein . .

...dale's welcome to Melba in 1902 included a stop for speeches in the bandstand. ...nd her on the steps is her father. *(La Trobe Library)*

George Armstrong and Melba in 1908 photographed at Del Monte, California. *(La Trobe Library)*

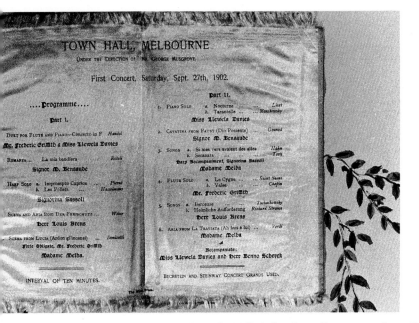

...ve and below: The programme and the audience for Melba's first Australian concert of ...902 visit on 27 September in the Melbourne Town Hall. *(La Trobe Library)*

Below: Melba on the concert platform of the Melbourne Town Hall, 7 October 1902. *(Performing Arts Museum)*

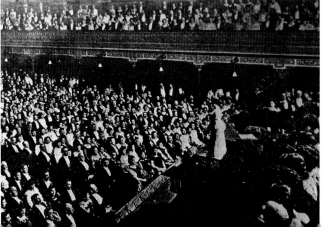

Melba had postcard pictures made of her Paris apartments. This view was sent to her student, Beryl Fanning, inscribed 'A little corner of my Paris home'. *(Sonia McKillop)*

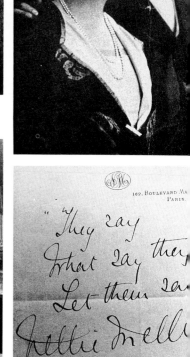

Melba's bedroom at her home in Great Cumberland Place, London, with a telephone on each side of the bed. *(La Trobe Library)*

Top right: Melba with the composer Hermann Bemberg *circa* 1914. *(Melba Memorial Conservatorium)*

Right centre: Melba's defiant response to gossip. She refused to refute recurrent slanders in the press, sending this quote in response to requests for comment. *(Sonia McKillop)*

Right: The final page of the diary of one of Melba's earliest Australian students, Beryl Fanning. The little book traces the progress of her lessons with Melba. *(Sonia McKillop)*

Far right : Melba at Bairnsgate, England, 1900. *(Performing Arts Museum)*

I always require a guarantee, no matter for whom I sing – whether for Conried or Covent Garden or . . .'.

'Certainly', I answered. 'How much must it be?'

'Twenty thousand dollars deposited wherever you desire – preferably in the Credit Lyonnaise', said she, without a quiver.

'Why not deposit it with you and avoid all the red tape of recording it?'

'That's asking too much', she exclaimed, with a surprised look.[8]

ut next morning he laid out the money on her desk. She swept the le into a drawer without even counting it and turned the key.

'And now,' said she, 'we must work together, and I shall do all in my power for you. Last night you told me you could not get Renaud. You must get him, for he is the greatest baritone in France. Yes, you must – we must – get Renaud. I will get him for you. In three days you will receive word at your hotel to meet him and sign the contracts.'[9]

he was as good as her word.

And so, for $3000 a performance, her travelling expenses and ermission to engage for concerts outside New York whenever she was ot singing at the Manhattan, Hammerstein secured the most famous nger of the day. There was a lot of speculation about Melba's motives r accepting such a contract with a fledgling company when she could ave re-engaged for the Met. Wechsberg says she was a proud woman ho loved power. This contract pitted her against one of the world's reat opera-houses, not just another soprano. She was challenging a ystem that denied her the place she held at Covent Garden – as rima donna assoluta. Hammerstein gave her that rank, with all the uthority that went with it. She wrote:

If I had been one of the regular staff of the Metropolitan, I should have had to sing when and where they wanted. My roles would have been dictated for me. I should have been at their beck and call. No artist gives her best under those conditions. I said to myself: 'I am Melba. I shall sing when and where I like, and I shall sing in my own way.'

It may sound arrogant, but arrogance of that sort is not a bad way to get things done.[10]

Hand-in-hand with authority went controversy:

Battle was in the air when in December, 1906, I arrived in America. I had realised, before I left England, that there were stormy times ahead. Hammerstein had sent me a sheaf of cables, and the whole trend of them was to show me that we were in for a fight. After all, this was natural enough. For years the Metropolitan Opera

House had stood unchallenged. Like a lodestar it had attracted all
the great artists of the past. It had had no rivals; in fact, it might
almost be described as a national institution. And now a new Opera
House had sprung into being.

It was already, after only a few weeks of existence, on the verge
of collapse. Candid friends in America had cabled me, time and
again, that it would be madness for me to come out, and to
associate myself with such an obvious failure. The receipts had
fallen and fallen, until, on 12 December, they stood at the ridicu-
lously low figure of barely over £200. It seemed that the Metropolitan stood supreme, unchallenged, that the fat financiers of New
York, whose interests were so largely bound up with that of the
old house, had won.[11]

But had it? *Was* the Manhattan 'on the verge of collapse' when
Melba arrived? *Did* she rescue it, as she claims? Murphy says that ten
days after it opened the Manhattan's receipts had fallen to $1100 (not
£200) and implies this meant the house was near ruin. She also says
rumour had it that Melba had no binding contract with Hammerstein
and if she withdrew the Manhattan's fate would be sealed. J. F. Cone
in his history of the company, admits that Hammerstein had problems
well in advance of the opening – a court case aimed at preventing
him from producing Melba in *La Bohème*, a broken contract with an
outraged Edouard de Reszke (whose voice Hammerstein found had
deteriorated beyond repair since he had signed him, and who blamed
Melba for his exclusion), and an unfinished building which necessitated
shifting the opening from 19 November to 3 December. There was
trouble over paying the chorus for three weeks' rehearsals, the conductor, Campanini, took a dislike to the concertmaster and demanded
he be replaced, Hammerstein fell on the opera house stairs, and a
strike by the carpenters and steam fitters was called off only in the
nick of time. As it was, the last of the seating was installed only
hours before the first night audience arrived and patrons later found
evidence on their finery that they had arrived shortly after the painters
had left.

The opening itself was a sensation, in spite of the lack of high
society. The reviewers were delighted with Bonci – the tenor brought
in to rival Caruso at the Met., rejoiced in the chorus, the orchestra,
Campanini and the house. Thereafter, as was expected, the size of the
audiences varied, depending on what was on at the same time at the
Met, and the state of play with the press. Murphy's figure seems to
refer to the take for a single night, however, not to the first ten nights
of the season. It could be that it was a way of underlining the Melba
figures she gives later – a top of $11 500 at her farewell *Bohème* on
25 March 1907, and never below $10 500.

Cone gives no indication that the Manhattan was on the brink of xtinction when Melba made her first appearance – in *La Traviata* – 1 2 January 1907, but though she did not rescue Hammerstein's ouse from bankruptcy she certainly brought in the audiences he eeded to ensure a second season.

On 19 December 1906 Melba cabled Hammerstein that she agreed o appear first as Violetta since her own choice, Mimi, had to be put ide until the courts settled the matter of production rights. It was ported that her costumes for *La Traviata* would be copies of 1848 esigns, not the usual mock 17th-century versions, and that she would e wearing a quarter of a million dollars worth of jewellery, including five-strand diamond necklace once owned by Marie-Antoinette. On e pier Hammerstein and two hired detectives took Melba and the iamonds into protective custody. She refused to be photographed. Iammerstein persuaded her to pose. She was affronted by the outra-eous questions she was asked. Hammerstein whispered something to er. She smiled and answered. No, it was not true that she had agreed sing at the Manhattan because her voice was gone and she could ot get a Met. contract; she was in the best of health and her voice as perfect. Hadn't they seen the reviews of the season just finished Covent Garden?

At the St Regis Hotel the constant ringing of phones and doorbells, nd the barrage of visitors, flowers, presents and letters, drove Melba distraction. At the Manhattan she had to rehearse against the noise f hammers as extra seating was put in to accommodate the audience hich had over-booked the house. By the time the curtain went up n a crammed society audience, both she and Hammerstein were aking with emotion. She wrote:

> The orchestra struck up the overture, the curtain rose, and from my position in the wings, I could see many familiar faces that were pillars of the Metropolitan. They had deserted their old home to hear me. Very well then, I should sing as I had never sung before. I stepped on to the stage, and, contrary to all operatic custom, a storm of applause burst out like a clap of thunder. Silence again, and I heard my voice ring out. In thirty seconds . . . I knew that I had won. The rest of the performance was one long triumph, and when it was over, I walked through the corridors full of massed bouquets. I felt the emotion which Cecil Rhodes described to me as the supreme sensation of life – power![12]

he next day she moved into a furnished apartment in West 58th treet, cabled to London for her linen, plate and servants and settled 1 for the season.

Melba appeared in a second *La Traviata* on 19 January 1907, in *Rigoletto* on the 11th and 31st, in *Lucia di Lammermoor* on the 28th. he *Rigoletto* of the 11th had a superlative cast – Melba, Bonci and tenaud, a trio unparalleled at the Met. In February she sang in *Faust* (on the 8th), *Rigoletto* (the 14th and 25th), *Lucia* (the 16th) and *L Traviata* (the 23rd). In March she gave *Rigoletto* (the 20th), and *L Bohème* four times (the 1st, 6th, 11th and 25th).

The *Bohème* of 1 March 1907 was given in a glare of publicit unrivalled in the history of American opera. Negotiations for the righ to perform Puccini's operas had gone on for a year. Hammerstei swore he made a verbal agreement with George Maxwell, the America agent for the Italian publishers, Ricordi and Co., before leaving i March 1906 for Europe. He understood that he could produce any c the operas, with the exception of *Madame Butterfly*, for the same fe as Conried – $150 a performance. He then conferred with Ricordi i Milan, asking his advice about artists, then went ahead with orderin costumes and scenery. On 25 July Maxwell wrote to remind him c the copyright, but he failed to mention that Conried had been grante an exclusive contract for all the Puccini operas. In court Maxwe denied there had been a verbal agreement with Hammerstein, bu said he had refused to contract with him until all the artists wer selected. Hammerstein had agreed to notify him when this was don but since he had failed to do so Maxwell had contracted with Conriec Ricordi filed an injunction on 19 October to restrain Hammerstei from producing *La Bohème* – Melba's greatest drawcard. On 3 Januar 1908 Judge Townsend refused to grant the injunction. The followin day Ricordi appealed. Hammerstein went ahead. It was only on 1 April 1908, after Melba's fourth Mimi, that he consented to a nev injunction. By then Ricordi (and the Met.'s) victory was nullified Hammerstein had a triumph.

Puccini was in New York while the argument was at its height (s were Camille Saint-Saëns and Ruggiero Leoncavallo, both of whon visited the Manhattan) but he took no part in it, preferring to sav his energies for the Met.'s first *Madame Butterfly* on 11 February witl Farrar, Caruso, Scotti, Homer and Reiss. As it was, he found Vign – the conductor – asinine, Farrar intractable and Caruso indolent, anc complained of having to direct as well as advise for want of someon capable. He thought the performance 'lacked the poetry' he had writter into it. Publicly the composer and the Met. seemed to be in clos partnership. Possibly Puccini felt he could not risk the anger o Conried, Melba, Campanini or Ricordi and was taking refuge in silence

Puccini did not, incidentally, provide the score of *La Bohème* fo Hammerstein as was rumoured at the time. Ricordi guarded the numbered manuscript copies very carefully. A frantic search began fo a damaged manuscript that the publishers might have discarded. A it happened the Del Conti Opera Company, touring from England had such a manuscript. Murphy, obviously on Melba's authority, say this was the score Hammerstein used, but the *New York Times* o 2 March 1907 said it was the one Clementine de Vere used on tou in America years before. But whichever it was, it was incomplete

Campanini wrote in the missing parts but, like Puccini, he feared the power of Ricordi and would not conduct it in public, letting Fernando Tanara take his place. The press read his absence as the result of a quarrel with Melba over her interpretation of Mimi.

On the night before Melba's first Mimi for the Manhattan, the Met. gave *La Bohème* with Caruso, Cavalieri, Alten, Stracciari and Journet in the authorised version. Maxwell issued a statement on the afternoon of the Manhattan performance which read:

> Mr Hammerstein's presentation of the opera *La Bohème* is without the authority and consent of the composer, Giacomo Puccini, or ourselves as owner of the copyright. It will be given with an unauthorized orchestration, and we would request all who attend the performance not to hold Signor Puccini as composer or ourselves responsible for it.[13]

Murphy interprets this as a claim that an adequate performance of *Bohème* that night was an impossibility. She says that

> terse announcements to the same effect were circulated among the critics, professional musicians, amateurs, and every other interested section of the New York public. Rumours were current that, if the performance went on while the appeal to the highest court was still pending, Madame Melba and Mr Hammerstein would be committed for contempt of court, and even as late as half an hour before the curtain went up representatives of the opposition coterie assembled in the vestibule of the Manhattan and loudly voiced their opinions, so that all might hear.[14]

For all that, the night was a resounding success, with Melba singing more beautifully than she [had] done anything else this season in New York'. According to the memoirs and to Murphy, it was Melba who dragged Hammerstein back from the brink of failure, but this was not quite the case. Her colleagues – Maurice Renaud (baritone), Allesandro Bonci (bel canto tenor), Charles Dalmorès (dramatic tenor), Clotilde Bressler-Gianoli, Regina Pinkert (lyric coloratura), Vittorio Arimondi (bass), Giannina Russ (dramatic soprano), Eleonora de Cisneros (contralto), Charles Gilibert (basso buffo), Mario Ancona (baritone), and Mario Sammarco (baritone) – were hardly nonentities, and the repertoire included first-rate performances of *I Puritani*, *Mignon*, *Dinorah*, *Don Giovanni*, *Un Ballo in Maschera*, *Aida*, *Fra Diavolo*, *Martha* and Verdi's *Manzoni Requiem* as well as the Melba operas.

Meantime back at the Met. the major attraction and Melba's real rival, Caruso, was in trouble. Early in the piece Hammerstein had fed a fake publicity story to the papers that Caruso had challenged his opposite number at the Manhattan, Bonci, to a duel. The public was disappointed when nothing came of it, crying coward, but it was a

THE VOICE

In Boston in 1907 Phillip Hale wrote Melba's favourite review: 'There is still no voice like unto that of Madame Melba, and no-one of her sisters on the operatic or concert stage uses voice with the like spontaneity and ease. Thirteen years have gone by since she first gave delight to this city, but charmed and applauding time has constantly enriched her. When she first visited us, her reputation was that of a brilliant ''coloratura'' singer, with a voice of unsurpassable beauty. Impersonating Mimi eight years ago, she showed that she was more than a singer of dazzling bravura. Her tones had a warmth, a sensuous quality, that some had denied her. Those who were so fortunate as to hear her memorable performance of Marguerite's music in *The Damnation of Faust* at a Cecilian concert a few years ago were struck by the richness of her middle and lower tones, which were in themselves expressions of womanly and tender emotions.

'To-day this voice is still brilliant in florid passages, it still has the freshness, the ''girlish quality'', that has always characterized it, and set it apart from those of other singing women; but it now has a fullness, a richness, and a sumptuousness that are incomparably beautiful. The voice of Madame Melba would work a wondrous spell even if the artistry of the singer were not uncommon, thrice admirable. And perhaps the most striking characteristic of this voice as it is today is its impersonal nature. It is not so much the voice of a perfect singer as it is the ideal voice

of song. The hearer revels in the tonal beauty. The tones themselves are charged with emotions of which, perhaps, the singer is not always conscious. The voice is like that of the hermit thrush apostrophized by Whitman:
"O liquid and free and
    tender!
  O wild and loose to my
    soul! O wondrous
    singer!" [1]

1. Agnes Murphy, *Melba: A Biography*, p. 265.

mere tiddler of an affair compared to the whopper which the pres landed in November 1906 and which almost capsized Caruso's career On 16 November the great tenor and a Mrs Hannah Stanhope were in the monkey house in Central Park Zoo where Caruso 'annoyed' the lady to such effect that she laid charges. Caruso was arrested and convicted. For a while it looked as if the Met. was going to have an early retirement on its hands. It was said that Conried's chagrin was such that he had a nervous breakdown.

But he was in for much worse. Accused of conservatism in the Met.'s repertoire, Conried had taken up the challenge with a vengeance He decided to give Richard Strauss' *Salomé*. New Yorkers were so shocked that it had to be withdrawn after one performance and a great deal of money was lost.

The first battle of the opera war had gone to Hammerstein; to everyone's astonishment there was a distinct possibility that next time he could bring down the elephant of 39th Street.

On 25 March 1907 Melba farewelled the Manhattan for the season in her fourth *Bohème*. (Two days later – 27 March 1907 – Emma Calvé made her Manhattan début in a notable *Carmen*.) It was her fifteenth appearance with the company, though she had contracted for only ten performances. She had extended her time twice in order to concertise out of town, make recordings and to take advantage of the success of the Manhattan itself. At the end of the night she sang the Mad Scene from *Lucia*. The audience stood cheering for forty minutes while Melba took twenty-three bows. At the end she called for the usual piano and sat down to accompany herself in *Mattinata*. It was the signal for even wilder demonstrations; but Hammerstein had the lights dimmed so that the audience had to grope its way out while caterers set up tables on stage for a supper party in Melba's honour. Thirty-five musicians entertained the guests with *Memories of the Manhattan Opera Season* composed by Hammerstein himself. The menu included '*suprème de volaille Hammerstein*' and '*pêche Melba*'.

Melba says in the memoirs that Escoffier invented that much-abused dish and had it sent up to her room while she was lunching alone at the Savoy. She gives no date. She enjoyed the confection and asked its name. Escoffier said it had none – could he perhaps name it in her honour? Melba gave her permission. The chef's other Melba specialties included *poire* and *fraises Melba* but only the peach dish took the public's fancy. Escoffier's recipe instructs the cook to poach the peaches in vanilla-flavoured syrup, then to dish them in a timbale on a layer of vanilla ice-cream and to coat them with a fresh raspberry purée. Escoffier wrote that he created the dish in 1894 after Melba sent him two orchestra stalls tickets for a Covent Garden performance of *Lohengrin* in which she appeared with Jean de Reszke. The next day she gave a party for the Duc d'Orléans at which Escoffier presented *pêche Melba* in a large silver cup placed between the wings of the

Lohengrin swan, which was made of ice. It became popular only after the opening of the Carlton Hotel in London, where Escoffier was chef, in 1899.

Melba liked oven-dried Melba toast but does not mention it in the memoirs. She made no profit from any of the soaps, ribbons etc., which bore her name and once tried to stop a perfume being named after her but was told she had no more right to the name than the manufacturer. She then patented her own name. She kept a supply of Melba cigarettes in her house to offer guests, but she did not smoke herself.

In her first speech at her farewell Melba said of Hammerstein: 'His pluck appealed to me from the first, and I leave as I came, his loyal friend and admirer'. When Hammerstein was asked why, after all the trauma, he still wanted to be an opera director rather than a manufacturer of cigars, as he had been, the redoubtable Oscar replied, 'Ah, but the tobacco business is prose, this is poetry – you know? It's more fun to make Melba sing than it is to make a cigar'. But, as *Town Topics* put it, there was another reason: 'gold poured no more lavishly from her throat than it piled up in the box office'.

In the week preceding this farewell Melba made a 22-hour train journey from Chicago to Philadelphia on the Monday; sang on the Tuesday; returned to New York and sang at the Manhattan on Wednesday; made a ten-hour train trip to Pittsburg and sang on Friday; sang and then took the overnight train to New York on Saturday; and on Sunday began a week's recording. For that week's work for the Gramophone Company she was paid a cash bonus of $50 000 with royalties to follow. Like her earning capacity, her stamina was incredible.

On Friday 22 February Melba accepted a box at the Met. for a morning performance of *Parsifal*. She had never heard the work and for hours afterwards found it difficult to shake off the effect it had on her. Wagner was still the god of the musical public at the time and Melba accepted the verdict that his entire output was worthy of respect and *Parsifal* a source of infinite musical wisdom. Murphy says that that night Melba could not be drawn out by her house party but seemed to be in some kind of abstracted state. Late at night she said to her secretary 'in a sort of soliloquy': 'How great this work, how great! And yet here am I going to sing in *Traviata* tomorrow. How can I do it? Heaven, how can I do it?' Then she added:

I remember, when I went to Bergamo for the Donizetti Centenary in 1897, I was shown some of the Italian composer's manuscript which had been copied by Wagner. Carefully and clearly written out by Wagner, as a means of earning his bread! The tragedy of it! I should think Wagner's heart must have almost broken in the task.[15]

Next morning she sent for the score of *Tristan und Isolde* and spent the day studying it.

The flirtation with Wagner and her envy of singers with heavy voices able to cope with his demands was not over. *Tannhäuser, Lohengrin* and the fatal *Siegfried* had all had their day with her but in 1907 she began to toy with *The Flying Dutchman*. Fortunately she never tried it before the opera-going public.

At Cherbourg after the Atlantic crossing early in April 1907 Melba decided to come ashore in the tender during the trans-shipment of the mails. There was a delay and she stood exposed to the weather for a long time and landed chilled to the marrow. Bronchial pneumonia set in, affecting the right lung for some time thereafter. Engagements at Brussels were cancelled but she sang as well as ever that season at Covent Garden. On 8 June she appeared at Buckingham Palace and again on 11 June at Covent Garden for the celebration of a Danish royal visit. *The Times* described the ease and polish of her performance as 'miraculous'. On 30 July she finished the season with *La Bohème* before Queen Alexandra. She had already let it be known that she was going home to Australia for a private visit and the usual Australian contingent that turned out for Melba nights to shout 'coo-ee' from the stalls was at the stage door to cheer her on, its more athletic members running beside her carriage until it crossed Long Acre.

The private visit, ostensibly to see her father, did not remain private for long, though she took the precaution of booking her passage under her family name. George and his new wife, Melba's secretary and her servants embarked separately. The Australian press was asked to play down the whole affair. The truth was that Melba was ill and needed rest. She spent several weeks at Ercildoune, Sir Samuel Wilson's country property near Burrumbeet, not venturing into Melbourne until 14 September when she and her father attended one of Clara Butt's concerts. Melba was recognised as she went in. The crowd applauded until she was forced to stand in acknowledgement. Without singing a note Melba had upstaged the English contralto. Unfortunately Dame Clara was not inclined to forget it.

In 1928, at the height of the last Melba–J. C. Williamson opera seasons, Butt's biography appeared, written by Winifred Ponder for Harrap and Co. of London. In it Miss Ponder says that Kreisler, Tosti, Butt and Melba appeared together at Windsor shortly after Edward VII's accession. The party was discussing Butt's proposed first Australian tour on the train back to London. Ponder writes:

> Melba naturally, being Australian, was particularly interested. 'So you're going to Australia?' she said. 'Well *I* made twenty thousand pounds on my tour there, but of course *that* will never be done again. Still, it's a wonderful country, and you'll have a good time. What are you going to sing? All I can say is – sing 'em muck! It's all they can understand.'[16]

As has been said many times since, the forcefulness of the phrases has the true Melba ring to it.

In Sydney a reporter showed Melba the offending passage. On 7 August, after a series of cables between Melba, Butt and the publishers had put a gleam in the eyes of several lawyers, Ponder's agent announced that Harrap had prohibited further sales. Too late. In spite of Dame Clara's protests that Miss Ponder had misquoted her and Harrap's frantic editorial surgery on the remaining 3000 copies of the edition, some 1150 had already found their way into the hands of the public, though only 150 of these had been sold, intact, in Australia.

By the time the expurgated version had appeared the press had made the most of it and turned Dame Clara's unguarded moment with Miss Ponder into the sensation of the day. Miss Ponder swore she had reported her subject accurately. To this day the Australian vernacular still includes 'sing 'em muck' as a term of contempt. Melba was never forgiven by her countrymen in spite of her flat denial that she had ever said such a thing.

Her rest at Ercildoune had helped control her health again, and Melba gave in to the demands to appear at charity bazaars and balls, dinners and receptions. She leased a Melbourne town house and went to the races, the theatre and cricket matches. At PLC there was a repeat of the 1902 welcome home; this time she went to the annual garden party as president of the Old Collegians' Association only on the understanding that no operatic airs were to be played and that her speech would be read by the Reverend Dr Alexander Marshall from her prepared script. There is a curious sentence in the middle of this homily:

> There are few things in this world which realize what we hope of them, and our greatest successes and achievements are often far less to ourselves than they seem to others, because we know how much more we aim to do, and the labour, often great and bitter, has been all our own.[17]

A bitter labour? For all her robust assertiveness, her reputation for having no patience with fools and tolerating no opposition to her will, Melba was never seen as a woman acting out of bitterness. Her vulnerability is briefly exposed in this little speech. It is unexpected and somehow uncharacteristic. Melba's private feelings usually remained just that – private.

In November she gave a series of concerts in Melbourne and Sydney. She was with her father for morning service at Scots Church on his eightieth birthday on 16 February 1908, and was guest of honour next day at the University of Melbourne Conservatorium of Music. Four days later Melba left Melbourne by train for Adelaide and the *Orontes*, bound for London. At Spencer Street station 1500 choristers from the Women's Work Exhibition Choir dressed in white with corsages of wattle, somehow found out of season, sang 'For she's a jolly good fellow', 'Home sweet home', and 'Auld lang syne'. In London she told the press:

> Imagine 1500 women singing together, and producing a vocal effect so charming, so harmonious, that it is impossible to describe. It touched my heart-strings, and I felt very proud at being one of them – an Australian woman.[18]

At Naples she left the ship for a motor tour along the Riviera but her car broke down before she got as far as Rome. She had to take the train to Paris where she began an intensive study of *La Tosca* in anticipation of the London season, but she was not to appear in the title role then or later. On 11 June she took part in the Paris Opera gala *Rigoletto* in aid of the Société des Auteurs et Compositeurs Dramatiques, with Caruso as the Duke and Renaud as the jester, arguably the greatest soprano, tenor and baritone of the day.

Though she had lived in Paris for the first fourteen years of her professional life, Melba had not sung at the Paris Opera for six years because of Covent Garden contracts. It was in some sense a try-out after the illness of the year before, but it was also a way of getting the press to report on the state of her voice at a safe distance from Covent Garden where she was about to undertake her twenty-first season and where, in her absence, a new rival had stolen a good deal of her thunder.

Luisa Tetrazzini was ten years younger than Melba. Her sister Eva, nine years older and also a soprano, was the wife of Cleofonte Campanini, then Hammerstein's chief conductor. Campanini promoted his sister-in-law wherever he went and had chosen his moment to launch her at Covent Garden carefully while Melba's back was turned in order to minimise the chance that the older soprano would block the move. He may have disliked Melba, he may even have set out deliberately to oust her from Covent Garden, as Hetherington claims, but primarily his aim was to bring forward one of the great voices of the century. Campanini was a fine musician and recognised the potential of such a voice. Why would he have ignored or suppressed his sister-in-law's right to be heard out of consideration for a star of equal magnitude but whose power was just discernibly waning?

Tetrazzini made her début at Covent Garden on 2 November 1907 as Violetta. She was hailed as the new Patti, just as Melba had been. The younger singer had a showy voice, and a warm personality that endeared her to her audiences. Melba's cool quality and majestic command were in direct contrast to the Italian's bravura style that could reduce her audiences to a state of near hysteria. The house was sold out whenever she appeared for the rest of that autumn season and she was re-booked for the main season of 1908. She sang the Melba roles – *The Barber of Seville, Rigoletto, Les Huguenots, Lucia d.*

Lammermoor and *La Traviata* – and added *Les Pêcheurs de Perles*. She alternated with Melba as Gilda and Violetta. It was a victorious procession of parts, so the younger singer thought, but Melba rallied in the alternations as Mimi and Desdemona. As with Calvé and all the other challengers, Melba kept up a public pretence of friendship with her opponent and seldom let slip what she felt about her professionally or personally.

Tetrazzini returned to Covent Garden every year until 1912, but thereafter she opted for an American career and left Covent Garden to a battle-scarred Melba. The fortune she made in her heyday was gone by the 1920s, as was her voice. When she died in Milan on 28 April 1940 she was nearly penniless and nearly forgotten.

Melba, on the other hand, took good care of the fortune she made and the voice that made it. Unlike Tetrazzini she did not give money to every beggar who found her door. Claude Kingston, who was associated with the management of the 1924 and 1928 Melba–J. C. Williamson opera seasons, recorded that she would come into his office regularly with a pile of begging letters, weed out the leeches and set aside money for those she considered deserving. The amount she sent off was usually between five and fifty pounds each but at times she would stipulate a certain amount to be paid weekly over a period of time. Kingston says she insisted that no one was to know that she did this. On a single day he saw her give away £400 in this manner, which seems to put the lie to later accusations of meanness but, unlike Tetrazzini, she was careful about who got what.

Tetrazzini made her Manhattan début in *La Traviata* on 15 January 1908 to rave reviews. Melba was still in Australia. When she returned to the Manhattan on 14 December 1908 it was as a highly nervous, overweight and ageing Mimi who was aware she had to regain the territory that had been hers before Tetrazzini's advent. However, she had a first-rate cast with her – Zenatello, Trentini, Gilibert, De Segurola, Sammarco, and Gianoli-Galletti – and the Manhattan audience remained loyal, bursting into wild applause the moment she appeared.

On 15 December 1908 Henderson of the *New York Sun* wrote of Melba's voice:

> what it has lost in silver it has gained in gold. It is still youthful and a warmer, more winning, more touching voice today than it ever was before; and better than all, it is backed by a more beautiful sincerity and a more rounded musicianship.

With almost the same cast, Melba played Mimi at Hammerstein's new Philadelphia Opera House on 17 December. (The local press claimed that she had sung this role in Philadelphia on 30 December 1898, but in fact she had not been seen there in opera since 1904.) It was a sell-out and 'beyond question the most brilliant social event

THE VOICE

The critics

The critic from *The Times*, London, wrote on 19 June 1908: 'Madame Melba is, perhaps, the only singer who can delude her hearers into believing for a moment that *Traviata* is a work of beauty or of real importance, and she did it again on Wednesday. How this is accomplished and how this most tedious of operas reaches in her hands almost the level of real music drama can hardly be guessed, for it is certainly not in any appreciable degree due to great or even convincing acting. The secret would seem to be in the singer's marvellous power of giving expression to the voice itself without altering the purity of its quality or the exquisite finish of its style. Such eloquently expressive phrasing as she gives us in "Ah! fors' e lui" and elsewhere is worth all the gymnastics upon which most singers depend for making their effects. These gymnastics are, of course, executed with the ease, certainty and delicacy that have always distinguished Madame Melba, and her singing of scale passages is as astounding as it has ever been; but in comparison with the magical power of her cantilena and her musical phrasing, vocal tricks fade into insignificance, however admirably accomplished'.

MELBA THE SUFFRAGETTE?

'Madame Melba is the latest notable adherent to suffragism. She says she has been compelled to join the movement for humanitarian reasons. She visited recently Glasgow, Liverpool, Manchester and other large industrial centers where the poverty of the working women touched her heart. It compelled her to believe that their condition could be bettered if the influence of women were used in the selecting of members of Parliament. She also sees political justice in the demand for women suffrage. She believes strongly in the wisdom of lawmakers in Australia who have enfranchised women. "There is also", she adds, "the familiar claim that women like myself should not be denied the power which is given to our butlers and grooms".'[1]

1. *Los Angeles Examiner*, London datelined 4 November 1908.

of the winter season'. Tetrazzini was getting a run for her money and Melba was ecstatic. Coming off-stage at the end of the first act, she said to Hammerstein who was sitting in his usual place, the habitual cigar in his mouth: 'I have never sung in such a house. It is simply delightful. All one has to do is to open one's mouth, and the house does the rest. You are a wonder. But how dare you smoke in my presence, you beast?' Hammerstein did homage and removed the cigar. Melba burst into laughter and dropped the imperious manner, exclaiming, 'Oh smoke away, you old fraud!'

In the four weeks she remained with the Manhattan that season Melba appeared in ten performances – three of *La Bohème*, three of *Otello* and one of *Rigoletto* in New York, with two performances of *La Bohème* and one of *La Traviata* in Philadelphia. On 11 January 1909, the final night in New York, *Rigoletto* was performed, attracting the largest house of the season. There was no doubt that – Tetrazzini and the newest drawcard, Mary Garden, notwithstanding – Melba was still the reigning diva.

But on 5 January Hammerstein quarrelled with his financial adviser, G. Heide Norris, who had offered the Manhattan as security on a loan to keep the Philadelphia house operating. Hammerstein said that he had never authorised such a move and that he refused to have the Manhattan jeopardised in that way. He declared the Philadelphia adventure over and announced that the last performance would take place on 23 January.

There was an uproar when Melba, riding to the rescue, summoned the press so that she could make a statement deploring the loss of the house and declaring Hammerstein a genius. She kept up these news items until she left for Europe, ending with:

> Tell the people of Philadelphia that Melba says it would be a disgrace for them to sit idly by and see the splendid opera house closed. Tell them that I expect greater things of them, individually and collectively.[19]

At a time when private subscription supported opera rather than State subsidy, Melba's request was, in fact, directed at wealthy Philadelphians who could step in to guarantee Hammerstein against loss. Norris and two other members of the opera committee, Andrew Wheeler and C. Hartman Kuhn, then approached a friend of Melba's, Edward T. Stotesbury, a member of Drescel and Company and associated with the banking house of J. Pierpont Morgan and Company. On 13 January Hammerstein was given the $400 000 he needed with only the Philadelphia Opera House as security. After her Philadelphia farewell and the final press interview of 9 January, Melba went to supper at Stotesbury's. She left for Europe on the day the loan came into effect and it was generally thought that she had used her influence to save the day for Hammerstein, although it was also said that

Stotesbury acted for the interests of the Met. in its efforts to oust Hammerstein. Neither Melba's help nor the Met.'s interference has ever been proved.

The war with the Met. now shifted to Philadelphia from New York where both houses were still trying to poach from one another's casts, Conried buying Bonci and making an unsuccessful bid for Campanini, Hammerstein failing to get Caruso but winning over Nordica and Schumann-Heink. Early in 1910 the Met. announced it would produce opera in Philadelphia without a guarantee. Hammerstein's recent artistic success with *Salomé*, *Electra* and *Pelléas and Mélisande* had not been matched with financial success and he announced he would accept the Met.'s offer to buy out the Philadelphia Opera House. For a time the older house made no move to accept.

There was a brief Manhattan season in Boston (28 March to 2 April 1910) after which the company there disbanded. On 11 April Hammerstein met with the Philadelphia opera committee in Stotesbury's office. It seemed the opera-goers of the city were not prepared to underwrite opera of any kind that season, whether Conried's or Hammerstein's. On 16 April Hammerstein left for Europe, leaving his power of attorney with his son, Arthur. Ten days later Arthur sold his father's operatic interests to the Metropolitan for $1 200 000, of which Stotesbury took half in repayment of his loans on the Manhattan and the Philadelphia houses.

The Metropolitan's successful bid was made possible by Otto Kahn and W. K. Vanderbilt who had contributed heavily to the Met.'s finances over the Hammerstein period in order to keep it afloat until its rival was in a weakened position. The settlement, announced on 28 April 1910, spelt the end of the Manhattan and of the Melba–Hammerstein alliance.

As for Melba and the Metropolitan, she was to appear in their cast lists again only for *Rigoletto* on 24 November 1910 and for a *Traviata* five days later. The rest is silence, since she did not appear in the main seasons there again.

Chapter 9

SINGING 'EM MUCK

In 1909 Melba took what she called a 'sentimental tour', a journey of 10 000 miles that took her from Glen Innes, Dubbo and Orange in New South Wales, to Townsville, Mount Morgan, Charters Towers and Gladstone (but not Mackay) in Queensland, and to the little towns of Tasmania and New Zealand. She could have made more money by singing only in the State capitals, but she was determined that this time she would sing for the poor as well as the rich. She certainly made a profit, but that was not all there was to it.

Melba began in Melbourne with a concert in the town hall on 9 March with Frederick Ranalow as her associate and the Marshall-Hall orchestra supporting her in the Mad Scene from *Hamlet*, the 'Willow song' and 'Ave Maria' from *Otello* and 'Sweet bird' from Handel's *Il Pensieroso*. The organ gallery behind her was filled by the white-robed Women's Choir.

There was a second concert on 13 March, again with the Marshall-Hall orchestra, but this time with the women of the Melbourne Philharmonic Society choir in white as a backdrop and the Mad Scene from *Lucia* as the centrepiece. There was a third (and final) concert on 20 March when Melba, struggling with the flu, repeated the Mad Scene from *Hamlet* and added extracts from *Idomeneo* and *Marriage of Figaro*. The fourth (and absolutely final) concert a week later included Landon Ronald's song cycle *Summertime*, Bishop's 'Lo! Hear the gentle lark' and, yet again, the 'Willow song' and 'Ave Maria' from *Otello*. At the end Melba was presented with a floral dreadnought by twelve of the passengers who had travelled out with her in the *Orontes*.

Melba's motives in returning home to sing during the summer season at Covent Garden that year were queried publicly. Was she at the end of her career, her voice gone and the Garden no longer interested? Was she a has-been trying to conceal her dwindling fees with publicity gimmicks and nationalistic hyperbole? Her manager, John Lemmone, was moved to write to the editor of the *Argus* that his client's fees had been published by the Covent Garden Syndicate some months before. The lists showed that during the previous twenty years only two artists had received upwards of £250 a night – Patti and Melba. Statements by the Manhattan and the Metropolitan in

New York showed that Melba received $3000 (600 guineas) a night, which was $1000 more than anyone else in the company of either house. The average fee since Patti's retirement thirteen years before had increased so enormously that, on the figures quoted, Melba had become the highest-paid singer ever known. At the Royal Albert Hall in November 1908, a hall with a 10 000 seating capacity, the house had been sold out a week in advance. Melba, her loyal flautist-manager was saying, was still supreme, but the fact that he had to remind his readers that Melba had established a world record in 1902 in Sydney when her nett share of a single concert had reached £2360 meant that the winds of criticism were beginning to blow just a little cold.

Lemmone, Melba's some-time manager and life-long friend, began life as the son of John Lamoni, a Greek gold-miner. At twelve he bought his first flute with gold he had panned himself. In 1874 his family moved to Melbourne where he became principal flute with Lyster's Royal Italian Opera Company. He was a fellow débutant with Melba at the Elsasser concert of May 1884 and thereafter toured Australia and Asia with the Australian soprano Amy Sherwin, and later with Janet Patey, Charles Santley and the violinist Pablo Saraste.

In London in 1894, his name changed to Lemmone, he was engaged as Melba's flautist. That contact put him in line for work with Adelina Patti and a South African tour with Amy Sherwin. In 1897 he returned to Australia to become a concert manager, notably for pianist Mark Hambourg and the singer Marie Narelle. He was Melba's personal and business manager for the 1902 tour as well as her associate artist. In 1904 he was Paderewski's Australian tour manager. In 1910 he scouted for singers for the Melba–J. C. Williamson season of 1911, then toured with Melba to New Zealand, America and Europe. He remained with her for the fund-raising concerts of the war years. In 1918 the *Bulletin* described him as Melba's 'devoted chum' and the general presumption was that their friendship was something more than platonic, but though Lemmone was unhappily married (he married Isabelle Stewart in Sydney in 1889) he enjoyed an enduring relationship with Sydney soprano and singing teacher Mabel Batchelor and was a director of her family's furniture business. When Isabelle died in 1943 Lemmone, then 82 years old, married the 58-year-old Mabel.

On 5 April 1909 Melba, the Governor's wife, the Countess of Dudley, and Lord Richard Nevill left Spencer Street at 6.50 p.m. for Lilydale and the first of Melba's country concerts. The fire tower, the streets and the hall of Lilydale were hung with Chinese lanterns. Her father was in the vestibule to receive her and the townspeople stood en masse to 'cheer her to the echo'. Melba sang 'Ah! fors' è lui', 'Comin' through the rye', Tosti's 'Goodbye', 'Se saran rose', the Mad Scene from *Lucia* with John Lemmone as flautist, 'Home sweet home' to the diva's own accompaniment – it was all familiar, predictable and pure schmaltz. Una Bourne and Frederick Ranalow were the associates and, if Melba's remark to Clara Butt held any truth at all, she was certainly taking her own advice, a feat only exceeded by Ranalow who sang 'A sergeant of the line', 'I know of two bright eyes' and 'The little Irish girl'. It was the kind of programme Melba gave the length and breadth of the country and her Australian audiences loved her for it, curious as that may seem now. She had judged her mark with supreme accuracy. At the end of this first step out into the land of the ordinary Oz, Melba's party was led to the station by the local brass band and the now-obligatory torchlight procession. All along the route in the six months that followed there were similar displays. She wrote:

> I never had a more appreciative audience. From outlying stations they came, from remote homes in the wildness of the bush, in carts, in trucks, and often enough on foot, over distances of hundreds of miles. At every stopping place the village halls were packed, and at each place where I arrived they gave me a reception of which even royalty could not have complained.[1]

In little puffing trains, coastal steamers, stately mayoral carriages and once even in an undertaker's antique mourning coach, Melba slowly made her way permanently into the hearts of a generation. Every town's newspaper blossomed with fabulous stories about her, every hall she sang in was crammed, at times literally to the rafters since the roof and the space under the stage were often occupied by those who could not squeeze in through the doors. Once the stage collapsed from white ants, once a landlady bought a new bedroom suite in Melba's honour – then put its price on the bill, once a silently listening crowd locked out of the hall was let in and wrecked the place in a mad stampede, and once she met an old man waiting for her outside the hall who said, 'I've walked eighteen miles to hear ye. And it was worth it. You're all prizes and no blanks. And mind you ... I know a bit about singing. I was in a circus meself once'.[2]

But if ingenuousness was the order of the day up-bush and programmes were tailored to it, Melba had the sense to realise this was not possible elsewhere. In Sydney, and in the final two concerts she gave at the Royal Exhibition Buildings in Melbourne, Rossini's *Inflammatus* (*Stabat Mater*) was the drawcard. In Melbourne the Philharmonic and the Marshall-Hall orchestras supplied the setting. For the concert on 16 October sixty members of St Francis' Church choir were her guests. Their conductor Signor Rebottaro presented her with a huge horseshoe decorated with her racing colours – white, mauve and green, the suffragettes' tri-colour that lit up with electric globes. At the second concert on 23 October her entourage presented her with a silver laurel wreath mounted on velvet, its centre a silver map of Australia with all the towns she had visited that year traced on it. As

... farewell supper given by Oscar Hammerstein for Melba on the stage of the Manhattan ...ra House, 25 March 1907. Melba and Hammerstein are ninth and tenth from the right. *...Trobe Library)*

...ba laying the foundation stone of the New Gramophone Factory, Hayes, Middlesex,
...land (probably 1913). *(La Trobe Library)*

Above and below: The Melba–J. C. Williamson programme for the 1911 opera season given in Melbourne and Sydney. *(Melba Memorial Conservatorium)*

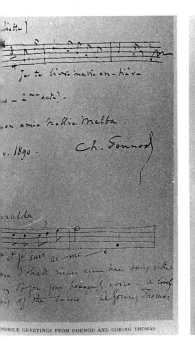

...etings to Melba from two composers
...ose operas she sang — Gounod and
...ing Thomas.

A charcoal drawing of Melba by the Duchess of Rutland. *(Australian Information Service)*

Melba with violinist Jan Kubelik. Together they toured English provincial cities, the U.S. and Canada from October 1912 to March 1914. *(Melba Memorial Conservatorium)*

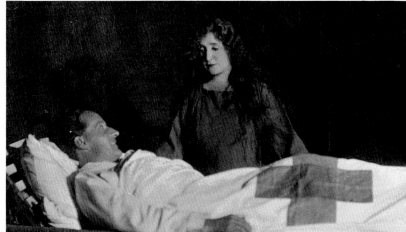

Melba and Ellen Terry share the platform at a war relief concert in Melbourne, September 1914. *(Performing Arts Museum)*

Jim Styles, a wounded soldier, was wheeled onstage during Melba's war-time concerts. *(Performing Arts Museum)*

The programme for the concert with Ellen Terry. *(Melba Memorial Conservatorium)*

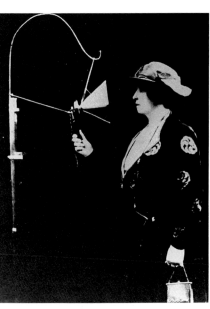

Melba recording by the 'Wireless Phone', Chelmsford, England, 1920. *(National Library of Australia)*

The 1913 line-up of female soloists at Co Garden, including the prima ballerina. M as the London hostess is on the left of the centre panel. *(La Trobe Library)*

an encore she sang 'Preghiera' from *La Tosca*, but though she seemed at the time to be trying out key parts of the opera on her concert public, the opera itself remained outside her repertoire.

Melba's visit in 1902 had been a journey to her own past, but her reception at home drew her back for the private visit of 1907 and for the bush tour of 1909 in a continuing search for permanence. In those seven years she had gradually come to the conclusion that she wanted a home in Australia and a place in Australian life. To that end she bought an estate at Coldstream and began negotiations with J. C. Williamson to produce a season of grand opera on a par with Covent Garden's. Nothing like it had been seen or heard in Australia before and she intended its effects to be lasting.

In 1909 she bought Dooley's farm, four miles from Lilydale and the Mitchell limestone quarries. The area became known as Melba country. John Grainger, the father of composer–pianist Percy Grainger whose London career Melba had helped launch, was the architect for the house built around Dooley's farmstead. Melba christened it Coombe Cottage after the house at Kingston Hill in Surrey, 12 miles from London, which she had rented from Admiral Lord Charles Beresford for one idyllic summer.

By 1911 Grainger had the place ready for her. He wrote to his son that Melba had no sooner arrived in Melbourne than she insisted on going to see over the estate. She was delighted with what he had done: 'she was as happy as a linnet and kept thanking me again and again for having given her such a delightful home – I have kept everything as plain as a clean sheet of paper and I've just hit it'.[3]

Grainger had built her a large, sprawling single-storey, flat-roofed box of a house with a Hollywood-style swimming pool and a roof garden, covered in trellis, with an outside stair. Beyond were stables and a stucco-fronted garage with a little tower, visible from the highway, on which 'East. West. Home's Best' was picked out in dull black letters.

William Guilfoyle, who retired as director of Melbourne's Royal Botanic Gardens in 1909, offered to design gardens for the grounds some time the following year, but it is not known if the actual plans followed were entirely his. Edna Walling managed the garden for Melba during the 1920s and supervised a number of changes. The grounds in front of the house are in the typical Guilfoylean manner but the main garden is rectilinear. Tall, dense clipped cypress hedges and herbaceous border walks enclose the pool garden and the Italian garden, a rose garden, an acre of kitchen garden and two tennis courts. Although the design is related to Sissinghurst and Hidcote in England, with sections in differing styles, it predates those famous gardens by ten or possibly twenty years. The National Trust considers it one of the finest garden designs in Australia and of world significance.

In 1909 David Mitchell still owned Cave Hill and St Hubert's

COOMBE COTTAGE

Lady Vestey, Melba's granddaughter wrote about Coombe Cottage: 'In the mornings she would have me sit on the bed with her and talk to me. She spoiled me, I know. All day long you'd hear her singing around Coombe. She never bothered to try to conserve her voice, even in her later years. She used it all the time – singing, humming, giving impersonations of people she knew.

'Coombe was her home, her base, the place where she could relax. Elsewhere she mostly lived in rented places overseas – places that weren't really her own. Coombe was different. In Melba's day there would be five gardeners and a butler and a footman in green livery, but even so, Coombe was never a grand place. Famous people – singers and conductors and people like that – would come to visit us for a day, but seldom stayed longer.

'It was essentially a retreat, and not a place where the great prima donna regularly held court.

'I can remember her putting on jazz records – she was intrigued by that sort of music – and trying to teach me how to dance the Charleston. Actually, though, she wasn't particularly good at it. As a child she had been strictly taught to walk with her toes turned out, but the Charleston had these steps with the toes turned inwards.

'I remember the dinner parties she gave, usually for up to about 18 people. Nothing elaborate, but she would order the food herself and sometimes check on how the cooking was going. In the afternoons before dinner parties she would always go away to rest. That was the way she had. "I always do what I like", she would say.'[1]

Tommy Cochran adds: 'Her first *home* was Coombe. She returned to it whenever she could, kept adding treasures to it, and to its wonderful garden . . . There was very little formality about life at Coombe when one was a guest there. . . .

'There was no ordered programme for guests, but with the early morning tea tray would come a little note, mostly written in indelible pencil, suggesting a function for the day, perhaps a picnic in the hills. Often such a note would be subscribed "B.G." meaning Bush Girl; at other times "C of C." It was a laughing affectation of Melba to name herself Countess of Coombe . . . On other occasions a morning greeting from the hostess would be scribbled across the face of a postcard showing Melba in one of her opera roles.'[2]

Ian Marshall concludes: 'Today the house is still owned by members of her family, but it is more of a museum than a home. The world is shut out securely. The iron gates that guard the grounds are barred. Caretakers watch over the silent, lofty rooms with their paintings, rich furnishings, thick carpets . . . Thousands of motorists heading into the hills have seen the gates and the high, immaculately trimmed hedges that guard the ghost of Coombe . . . The house itself, at the end of a short gravel drive, is unpretentious enough – a single-storey place, white-painted, with shady verandahs and lived-in look.

winery as well as other grazing land in the district. At a later date Melba bought 500 acres of the farming land around Coombe, in spite of warnings from friends who thought it unwise of her to settle in the district where her family still lived and, more particularly, where her brother, Charlie Mitchell, who was at Cave Hill, managed his father's quarries. He was regarded as a wild ass of a man, inclined to extravagant practical jokes and ocker behaviour. He once shot out the gatepost lights at Coombe's entrance simply because he happened to be passing with a rifle in his car. Nellie threatened to sue but nothing came of it.

In May 1910 the *Argus* announced that Melba would return to Australia in 1911 for two months, bringing the soloists needed for an opera season arranged in conjunction with J. C. Williamson on an equal share basis. She sang in the summer seasons at Covent Garden in 1910 and 1911, missed the 1912 season to stay in Australia for concerts but in 1913 and 1914 appeared there again. The Met. saw her in November 1910 and there were the usual concert tours and publicity stunts. Just to take one example – on 18 August 1910 she was on the *Campania* out of Liverpool to launch a scientific experiment in sea-current mapping in the mid-Atlantic. At latitude 41.54 N longitude 56.10 W, she threw overboard one of twelve huge globes with her name engraved in the copper in Old English characters. She offered a reward for its return, saying prophetically that she wanted it back as a souvenir because:

> It doubtless has a long, lonely journey before it, and I cannot but feel interested in the fact that my name will for many months – perhaps years – be tossing about on the restless seas. There is romance in the thought, and everyone, I suppose, is romantic, more or less.[4]

Agnes Murphy turned agent for Melba that year to arrange a Canadian tour for the autumn and winter of 1910–11, beginning in Halifax and taking in a half-dozen eastern-states cities near the border, west of the Great Lakes, before travelling across Canada, east to west. The itinerary was to take in a number of the new prairie towns, among them Edmonton and Prince Albert, the northernmost main-line railway stations on the continent. It was called a 'fur-coat frontier tour', because of the expected 40° F below zero temperatures and the names of some of the stopovers – Rat Portage, Medicine Hat and Pile o' Bones among them.

In August 1911 Melba arrived at Fremantle by the *Osterley* with her son, her butler, her chauffeur, her lady's maid and four Italian maidservants, and announced the make up of her first Australian opera company. It included the Irish tenor John McCormack, a pupil of Sabbatini of Milan and a rising star at Covent Garden and the Met.; bass Edmund Burke, a Canadian with Covent Garden and continental successes; and Polish dramatic soprano Jeanne Wayda (Janina Koro-lewicz-Waydowa), who was billed as having been prima donna assoluta at Covent Garden, Warsaw, Lemberg, Cracow, St Petersburg, Moscow, Berlin, Lisbon, Padua and Venice and as having created the part of Ulana in Paderewski's opera *Manru* in Warsaw. Wayda was currently engaged for the season at the Met. in New York and Chicago. Marie Axarine, known as the Russian Patti, was the lyric soprano; Eleonora di Cisneros, a La Scala product with Covent Garden experience, was the contralto; and the dramatic tenor was Francesco Zeni from the Imperial Opera House in Warsaw. The rest of the imported principals failed to make the press but it was clear, even from those names Melba singled out, that this was no colonial circuit opera troupe. As she told reporters:

We want Australia to realise that we have done our best. I have been at this work for two years now, and at last my dearest hopes are on the way towards being realised. It has always been my ambition to present grand opera in Australia – grand opera such as is given in Covent Garden – and I trust that the people here will all be pleased. We shall open in Sydney on September 2 and show there for two months. We shall not show outside Sydney and Melbourne. We tried very hard to make a tour of the whole of Australia, but the expenses of staging were found to be so great that it was quite out of the question. However, I am going to try to arrange for reduced steamboat and train fares throughout Australasia, so that people all over the Commonwealth and New Zealand may be enabled to see the performances.[5]

On 12 August Melba and her entourage were met at Spencer Street station by the Women's Choir and their conductor, Georgina Peterson; the opera season's choirmaster, Sacerdote; and the conductor, Giuseppe Angelini, who had come on ahead to select and train the Australian chorus and orchestra. Melba announced that she would open in Melbourne on 28 October and that the company would sing in Italian, with the exception of *Roméo et Juliette*. The repertoire was also to include *La Bohème, Rigoletto, Madame Butterfly, Lucia, Otello, Tosca, Faust, Carmen, Lohengrin* and *Samson and Delilah*. With violets and orchids in her hands and an escort carrying the presentation baskets of boronia and primroses, given to her by her fans, Melba tried to get to her car but found her way barred by a photographer. She was hemmed in and instead of escaping, as she usually did, she was obliged to submit to a dozen press pictures being taken, but also, the *Argus* reported, 'somewhere amongst the purring motor-cars was heard the whirring of a cinematograph handle'. This is the earliest known record to date of Melba's existence on moving film in Australia. Having escaped the crowds, she went first to Doonside to see her father, then to stay with her sister, Mrs Charles Lempriere, in Toorak.

'The original Coombe Cottage, small and square, is more than 100 years old and you can still trace its outlines at the centre of the rambling, multi-winged Coombe that the prima donna, with imperious waves of her hand, caused to be created.

'She would say, "We must have a new wing", a member of her family recalls. "And it was done. . .".'.

'The Quilter walk, paved with stones given to Melba by the composer Roger Quilter, is free of weeds. The cypress trees stand tall and handsome in the Italian garden Melba designed herself. Her tennis courts are ready for play. Her swimming pool is filled with fresh water.

'Her old opera costumes – Mimi, Manon, Rosina, Marguerite, Lakmé – still hang in locked cabinets in the Melba wing, the richly furnished, four-room section of the house she used . . .

'On a verandah wing an aged white cockatoo she bought in the old Paddy's Market in Melbourne in the twenties still cackles and grumbles and screeches in his original cage.

'The walls are still hung with her extensive collection of Australian art, including half a dozen or so rare Hans Heysens. Heysen was once her protégé and at her command he painted her garden, her son, her glittering green parrot. In the Melba wing you still find her writing desk, her porcelain, hand-cranked telephone, her bathroom with its marble bath demurely hidden in a discreet, mirror-fronted cabinet, her four-poster bed.

'Polished wooden chests and trunks here are still

crammed with scores and fan letters and concert programmes and snatches of music scribbled out in her own hand.

'Open any one of these drawers and the triumphant past comes tumbling out. Presentation scores with faded silk covers and tarnished silver edgings; working scores with her own notations; flowery illuminated letters acknowledging her appearance at charity concerts; sepia-tinted portraits signed by guest singers and composers "in homage and admiration". In the guest suite everything still stands ready and there is a sunken marble bath fit for an emperor or a visiting prima donna.

'The proud monograms – sometimes the single M as on the gates, sometimes a commingled M and N and sometimes a tangled M and N and G and E in honour of other members of her family – are everywhere around the house, on doors and on linen and even on an out-of-tune four-note miniature harp fixed to the door leading into the Melba wing . . .

'Since Melba's death, there have been few changes at Coombe. Some of the living lushness of rich old fabrics – curtains and quilts and hangings in Melba's bedroom – has faded and gone. There's bareness in places now. But for the rest, everything is in good order, polished and dusted and cared for, as if awaiting the singer's return from Covent Garden or La Scala or the Metropolitan Opera.'[3]

1. *Herald*, Melbourne, 4 March 1972.
2. Cochrane, *op.cit.*, pp. 241–2.
3. Ian Marshall, quoted in the *Herald*, Melbourne, 4 March 1972.

That afternoon she motored to Lilydale to inspect the progress of Coombe Cottage. A few days later she left by train for Sydney.

The rest of the cast was still at sea in the *Mooltan*, due at Sydney within the week, among them the principals whose names Melba had forgotten in Perth, the basses Vito Dammacco and Alfred Kaufmann, baritones Angelo Scandiani and Guilio Christiani and the contralto Marie Ranzenberg.

In Sydney, and later in Melbourne, J. C. Williamson's advertised auditions for the chorus. Over a thousand applications were received; a third of these were rejected on the spot. It was reasoned that 'Badly composed and badly spelt letters were fatal, for the grand opera chorus it is necessary to have a certain amount of intelligence and education'. Henry Bracy heard the rest and selected 150. Bracy and Williamson listened to these and selected fifty for Sacerdote. Four of them found learning twelve operas in a foreign language too much and retired. Sacerdote then rehearsed the women in the morning and the men at night until a standard was reached that permitted joint rehearsals. Most of this Australian chorus had no stage experience; they had voices but no understanding of the theatre. They were well-known concert singers and teachers who joined for the sake of observing Melba's cast and its technique at close quarters. Frank Rigo, the stage manager, had the nerve-racking task of teaching them 'the art of graceful inactivity' and to 'look natural when 1500 pairs of eyes are staring at one'.

At 8 a.m. on Saturday 2 September, the gallery audience arrived to camp in the lane beside Her Majesty's Theatre in Sydney, the women bringing camp stools and picnic baskets for two meals. By noon the place was like a side-show alley. At 2 p.m. the morning rehearsal was over and the crowd raced up the stairs to fill the top of the house. Mrs Hugh Ward sent up a piano for the six-hour wait and at 4 p.m. followed it with tea and sandwiches. A collection was taken up for two bouquets, one for Mrs Ward and one for Melba. Thousands were turned away from the £1 standing-room queues and when Melba sang her first lines in *La Traviata* that night she stopped the show. Afterwards the stage door crowd tore her dress in its frenzy.

Melba went on to sing three times a week as Violetta, Juliette, Mimi, Desdemona, Gilda, and Marguerite, but not as Elsa, Delilah, Cio-Cio-San, Aida, Carmen or Tosca, though she had intended to attempt the latter for the first time in Sydney. She had recorded 'Vissi d'arte' from *Tosca* in 1907, but was daunted by the histrionics required for the opera itself. In 1911 she fell ill, first with an ear infection, then bronchitis, just before the announced *Tosca*. Madame Wayda took her place to such effect that Melba declined the role for the rest of the season.

In Melbourne *La Traviata* was again the opening piece. One critic wrote that:

the evening was a succession of ovations. Yet the opera was Verdi's antiquated work *La Traviata*. No-one seemed to resent its disjointed and unintelligible story; the mechanical staginess of its characters offended no fastidious taste; the inconsiderate instrumentation excited little adverse criticism ... the applause was so long and pronounced that a modern French or German audience would have been as scandalised at the interruptions as the outburst of exuberant barbarians.[6]

Towards the end of the season the bass, Vito Dammacco, died after a month in the Melbourne Hospital. He was 28 years old and left a widow and a child. The company, which had planned a cricket match against Fitzroy Cricket Club for the day, found itself instead rehearsing for a solemn requiem at St Patrick's Cathedral, the men providing the Gregorian, led by John McCormack. Melba attended the highly ornate funeral and sent the wreaths laid on the coffin.

Years later Madame Wayda wrote in her autobiography that Melba had turned the widow away with the equivalent of less than a pound when she came, grief-stricken, to ask what her financial position was as far as the company was concerned. Why Wayda decided to give vent to her dislike of Melba in this way is obvious – Melba was long since dead and had no come-back. Such a gesture on Melba's part seems illogical given both Melba's known generosity to the really needy, the blaze of publicity surrounding the funeral, and Melba's profits from the season; she was hardly such a fool as to risk just the kind of gossip Wayda implied was circulating.

At the end of the run George Tallis, for J. C. Williamson's, reviewed the six-week Melbourne season:

Grand opera is always in every country of the world something of a hot-house flower. In every other part of the world it is subsidised. For an eight week's season in the Metropolitan opera-house in New York £160,000 was subscribed last November before the doors opened. At Covent Garden the money is, for the most part, guaranteed. And prices are considerably more, too. At Hammerstein's new theatre, in London, the boxes cost £1000 for the season. The Metropolitan opera-house in New York draws as much as £6,000 audiences. Here in Melbourne our highest – the first night – was £1,800. The house tonight is full, but the difference is nearly £1,000 – due to the difference in prices.

The attendances have, taken all round, been excellent – better than anything ever recorded before for grand opera in Australia. The first night here was a record for the house, I do not know any city of the same size which could have done better in that way. In Chicago, with its million and a half people, they only ran an eight or ten week season. With the exception of the first three weeks here the houses have been filled and the enthusiasm had been constant. The smaller audiences at first may have been due in some measure to the [Melbourne] Cup [racing] season. The result, at all events of the six weeks is this, that more money has been taken here than for the first six weeks in Sydney. But it is not considered that grand opera is an enormously paying proposition. The expenses are enormous. Roughly speaking the tour costs £4,000 a week; yet it has paid its way better than the last company in which Signor Dani and Signorina Bassick sung, which cost £2,000. We dropped £8,000 on that company, and have lost on every company in grand opera since the time twenty years ago, when we gave *Pagliacci* and *Cavalleria*. This has therefore been a notable exception. It was encouraging to note the educative effect of the series. Men and women who came with the idea of seeing one or two frequently became so fond of opera that they never missed one afterwards.[7]

Melba herself felt that the Melbourne season, begun with red carpets to the doors and footmen on the footpath, had been so successful that the company should return to Sydney where she had not been heard at her best because of her illness in the first weeks there. The smaller house in Sydney meant that there was less profit in a sell-out, even on Melba nights. In fact the refurbished Her Majesty's in Melbourne had more seats than Covent Garden. On Melba nights the take was £1900 and amounted to £8600 for the last week. In Sydney the other nights slumped after the first ten days. The season was shortened to ensure against loss, a matter Melba regretted when the tide turned in her favour; for in spite of Tallis' claim that Melba 'did not do this for any possible money benefit', her half share of the house, £46 000, could have been considerably increased by a return season and Melba was not the woman to ignore it. Still, the company had contracts to be filled elsewhere and there was no holding it together beyond mid-December. In London it was reported that she had intended to appear during the last six weeks of the Covent Garden season but her father's health had deteriorated. He was 83 years old and Melba felt she could not leave him; at least she had fulfilled a life-long ambition as far as he was concerned – he had been seated in the front row of the circle for the opening of the Melbourne season. At the final curtain that night Melba declared: 'I have never felt so happy as I do tonight.'

In Australia the 1911 Melba–JCW season had been part of Williamson's elaborate celebration of the jubilee of his first appearance in the colony as an actor. On 22 May 1913, back in England, Melba celebrated twenty-five years at Covent Garden with a sell-out *La Bohème*. Two days before, Caruso had returned in *I Pagliacci* and after 'Vesti la giubba' had received eight solo calls. The critics were ecstatic, saying no singer of the times ever made a more triumphant return and though Melba's Mimi opposite a new Rodolfo, John McCormack, oused the expected enthusiasm, Caruso undoubtedly upstaged her.

On 23 June Caruso and Melba, both then engaged at £500 a night, according to Rosenthal, gave *La Bohème* before the royals who also turned out for her Juliette to McCormack's Roméo on 22 July. McCormack was a gauche actor, like Melba, though he sang the music with grace and elegance. The combination of an aged Juliette who could not act and a young Roméo equally inept must have tested the credulity even of George V and Mary of Teck. On the other hand McCormack, realising where the crux of Melba's success lay, said, 'I believe – in fact, I know – that I sing better with Melba than with any other soprano', a belief shared by Jean de Reszke and Caruso.

The Caruso–Melba *La Bohème* was a tumultuous success. Stanley Jackson, Caruso's biographer, called it 'an acclaim more explosive than anything Caruso had experienced even at La Scala premières under Toscanini's baton'. Jackson quotes Osbert Sitwell who was in the audience and wrote that the famous pair were 'fat as two elderly thrushes, trilling at each other over the hedge of tiaras'. Even he succumbed to the magic of Caruso, if not Melba, whose voice he described as 'not invariably true, having about it something of the disproportion of the Australian continent from which she had emerged'.

On 5 August Melba made her first concert appearance in London for eighteen months, taking the platform at the Royal Albert Hall with Eugène Ysaye, Wilhelm Backhaus and Edmund Burke as associates and Landon Ronald and Hermann Bemberg as her accompanists, a combination of celebrities with considerable box-office impact. In the inevitable Bach-Gounod 'Ave Maria' she had Backhaus as her accompanist and Ysaye to play the obbligato.

It was the opening gambit in a tour that took her party round Great Britain for several months of concertising. The provincial tour was a necessary evil in most soloists' lives – there was money in it. To Melba it was a highly profitable way of life, and she made it as comfortable as she could, in spite of the constant travel, by limiting her programmes to a few old favourites and boosting her chances of success by taking on board some illustrious stars to make and share the augmented take, in this case Ysaye and Backhaus and, for the American–Canadian tour that followed, Jan Kubelik. Melba had toured Canada, America and the British Isles before, so neither the English nor the American tour was unique, other than the stars they brought into conjunction; but they serve as examples of what a performer's professional life is like, even now.

Her programmes were chosen from a very limited list: the Mad Scene from *Lucia di Lammermoor*, 'Vissi d'arte' (*Tosca*), 'Elsa's dream' (*Lohengrin*), the 'Jewel song' (*Faust*), Mimi's farewell (*La Bohème*), the 'Waltz song' (*Roméo et Juliette*), the 'Willow song' (*Otello*), 'Se saran rose' (by Arditi) and Tosti's 'Goodbye'. Late in the tour the Mad Scene from *Hamlet* and Louise's aria from *Louise* were added.

THE VOICE
The critics
Richard Aldrich, critic for the *New York Times*, wrote in 1913: 'Madame Melba is still – and her singing yesterday afternoon again attested it – one of the greatest singers of a school that seems almost inevitably destined to neglect and extinction; the school that cultivates the highest beauty of pure vocalism, of pure vocal style, of completely mastered vocal technique. It is well, therefore, that her reappearance on the New York concert stage should be recognised as an occurrence of great significance . . . The legato was beautiful; her phrasing of delightful finish. Madame Melba did nothing finer, in some ways, than the two songs by Duparc, in which her delivery of the sustained melodies had poignant eloquence and a true nobility of style. Madame Melba could not always have sung them so well. She touched, too, much of the profound beauty of Desdemona's "Ave Maria". There was much brilliancy and elan in her singing of Ophelia's air – and this, perhaps, she could once do better than she can now. Finally, the lovers of Mozart could rejoice to hear such a performance of the "Voi che sapete", such purity of style and finish of phrasing. And in all Madame Melba's singing, in whatever tongue, French, Italian, or English, it was good to hear the clearness of her diction and enunciation which then was seen to be an essential part of the finest and most artistic singing, and not an ornamental adjunct to it'.[1]

1. Wechsberg, *op. cit.*, p. 311.

Encores usually included 'Comin' through the rye', 'John Anderson my Jo', Bemberg's 'Les anges pleurants' and 'Home sweet home'. She did not go beyond this except at Margate when she sang 'Ah! fors' lui' (*La Traviata*)and gave the first performance of Liza Lehmann's 'Magdalen at Michael's gate'.

The concert party consisted of Melba, Backhaus and Ysaye, Edmund Burke, Gabriel Lapierre – the accompanist, and Phillipe Gaubert, flautist. In Newcastle they were joined by violinist Joska Szigeti and Ysaye left. At Hanley pianist Suzanne Morvay joined and Backhaus left, returning at Birmingham, Brighton and Eastbourne. At Lancaster cellist Arnold Trowell joined and at Southport Frederick Ranalow deputised for Burke. Una Bourne was the 1913 associate pianist and Marcel Moyse was that year's flautist. At Guildford Joseph Cheetham, a singer, joined. It is easy to see how the dovetailing of tours was something that had to be planned years in advance. To have the illustrious trio of Melba, Backhaus and Ysaye together for a season was not quite the aim of the exercise. A core itinerary was devised that allowed each soloist to leave to join some other tour, then return. In Melba's case she left to fulfil her opera contracts at the Garden.

It was a long tour, from 5 October 1912 to 31 August 1913, broken only by Christmas and the summer opera season. On 4 May 1913 Melba and Kubelik appeared together at London's Royal Albert Hall as a curtain raiser for their American tour, the London press being quoted in publicity there.

The American concert party consisted of Melba, Kubelik, Edmund Burke, Marcel Moyse and Gabriel Lapierre under the management of Laudon Charlton by arrangement with Melba's London agents, Schulz Curtuis and Powell. Melba landed at Quebec late in September and the tour began on 29 September 1913 in Montreal. It ended five months later in New York and for that period Melba again held to a very restricted programme of the tried and true.

Some of the figures related to Melba's earnings for this American tour, the preceding English tour and the Australian opera and concert season found their way into the American press, and though they are now difficult to translate into modern currency they still make fascinating reading. For the twelve week Australian opera season her receipts were given as the equivalent of $410 000. The best of the Sydney Town Hall concerts drew $13 340. The best nine concerts in Australia brought in $105 000. The Royal Albert Hall concert of 5 November that marked her return to London in 1912 returned $10 065. The English provincial tour drew $110 000. The Hippodrome concert in New York on 2 November 1913 set a record for that hall – $11 150 – for an audience of 7000, one thousand of whom bought standing-room tickets. In Cleveland she set a record for the house with an $8000 take.

In June that year the Duchess d'Orléans brought an action for

eparation against the Duc. His affair with Melba was back in the
news and what the Duc termed 'outrageous fables' were circulating
that he had given his wife's dowry to his mistress. He published an
official denial, saying the $240 000 dowry had never been in his
possession. It had been in a London bank and had recently been
removed to Austria by the Duchess' agent. Two years before the
Duchess had decided to leave her home at Wood Newton to visit her
mother. She would not return, but the Duc had no wish to live with
his mother-in-law. The Duchess then asked for $16 000 extra support,
which the Duc declined. The action at law was an attempt to force
him to pay.

Matters between the Duc and his wife had never been easy. His
engagement to his cousin Princess Marguerite, the daughter of the
Duc de Chartres, was broken off when he refused to sacrifice Melba
to the royal cause. But on his father's death in 1894 Philippe became
the putative incumbent of a lost throne. He married another cousin,
the Archduchess Marie Dorothea, in the chapel of Schönbrunn castle
in the presence of the Emperor of Austria and half of Europe's royalty
in 1896. The evening before the ceremony the Duc was told that his
bride was almost certainly sterile and the main aim of the match
unobtainable. The Duc decided to keep his word and married his
duchess. When she became ill he took her to her mother's castle at
Alksuth and resumed his bachelor life. The defect or disease that
made Marie an unsuitable wife was not named publicly.

After Melba and marriage, 'less illustrious charmers'[8] won the Duc's
favour, among them Ninette des Melays, who influenced him so
strongly that the Duc dismissed the chief of his political bureau,
Baron La Regle and other old royalists 'whom she called dotards and
called in a younger generation'. As a reward for acting as his adviser,
Philippe made Ninette a present of family jewellery, usually the
property of the heir's wife, that is, had there been a throne in France
still, the Queen. The Austrian Emperor publicly reprimanded the Duc
and took up a collection to buy back the heirlooms at an outrageously
inflated price. The Duc then broke with Ninette but in no time at
all he had rented a château at Putdael near Brussels for a French
aristocrat, Madame Haufmordt, where the lady presided at his political
dinners. Ninette had been no real threat to the Duchess; like Melba
she was a commoner, but the Haufmordt was another matter, well
born and fertile. The Duchess sued and while she was doing it the
whole Melba–d'Orléans scandal was rehashed in the press. Melba
herself refused to comment.

War was declared on 4 August 1914. Melba was already in
Australia, drawn home by her father's illness before the end of the
London season. For a while she concentrated her efforts on the local
scene, raising money for war charities by giving concerts for which she
accepted no fee. Late in 1915, when the war situation showed no sign

of an early settlement, she took ship for America and Canada to continue her patriotic fund-raising on an even larger scale, appearing in opera wherever she could; Covent Garden was closed for the duration. On her own reckoning she raised £100 000 for war relief over the 1914–18 period and it was for this that she was finally made a Dame Commander of the Order of the British Empire.

On 27 April 1915 she raised £6100 at a concert she organised in the Melbourne Town Hall for the Belgian relief fund. Arc lamps were installed to dramatise the entrance and the stage, which was draped in the red, black and yellow flags of Belgium, with gum leaves edging the platform. Melba came on in a storm of cheering, leading a bulldog. This was Jellicoe from the British Bulldog Club of Victoria, resplendent in a diamond-studded harness complete with a Union Jack back rug. The programme was selected from the same list that was used for the American Kubelik tour. Then Melba got down to the real purpose of the evening – auctioning the flags. Her ability to goad her audiences into giving turned out to be phenomenal. She got £120 for a Polish flag when she reminded her victims that Paderewsky was a Pole, but it was upped to £200 when she said she would be too ashamed to cable him such a figure. Two Australian flags sold for £60 and £40 apiece, but Melba exploded: 'Forty pounds for Australia! Why, the Germans would give more than that!' and the flags were re-sold. As she unfurled the final piece, a Belgian flag, she announced, 'This flag I hold in the deepest reverence. The whole world knows from what it saved us all'. She got £1600 in £100 lots from the biggest names in Melbourne business; her father was the first to bid.

For the next four years Melba used variations of this process to fund every known charitable organisation from the Red Cross to the victims of local disasters. She would make the news by demanding Australian women be conscripted for munitions work and by volunteering to work fourteen hours a day herself on the assembly line just to get attention for an auction sale of the seats to one of her concerts. She would play on her audience's sympathies, telling them that on her last birthday she had twenty-two couples to dinner and of the twenty-two men, seven had been killed at the front and seven wounded within the year.

After Gallipoli, when even *her* sterling gaiety began to falter, Melba took up the cause of wounded Australian soldiers. It was no longer a game with flags but a fight for the morale of young Australians shattered by the reality of war. For her first effort she had the Melbourne Town Hall's balconies covered in red, white and blue swathes, and wattle offset huge floral flags of the Commonwealth. Her students from the Albert Street Conservatorium formed the choir, some distributing flags to the audience. When fifty-three veterans were shown in, the audience stood to attention. When Melba waved *her* flag, they waved theirs, and a pipe band played in the viceroyals. Her 'girls' sang a chorus in praise of their teacher. The Governor presented her with a sapphire brooch and her fans pelted her with flowers. She was having a wonderful war.

Melba's first wartime concert party included the English actress Ellen Terry, then in her sixties. She was Melba's guest at Coombe at the time, stranded by the war, as Melba was, and unable to resume her professional life. Melba deferred to her, publicly and privately, a rare mark of respect on her part for any other woman, let alone another stage presence. For her part Terry admired Melba, saying:

She is a splendid woman – always working and doing everything herself – at home, I mean; goes to bed early, gets up early; eyes everywhere, always using her senses: her profile (when you get to know her face) is very fine, and she has a grand eye. She is full of fun, and yet is very serious. She expects a lot from people – useful service, but gives so much herself . . . So entirely self-forgetting, she compels one to disregard one's bodily discomforts, weariness, pains, morbid thoughts, and to 'press on' and do one's utmost. Bless her! [9]

Both Ellen Terry and Melba were frequent guests at Government House in Melbourne where Adelaide, the adolescent daughter of the Governor, Lord Stanley, met them both and wrote:

I can remember Ellen Terry sitting in the garden with my mother, her face all covered with powder and rouge, and dressed in flowing garments. Pamela [her sister] recited a poem to her and Ellen Terry praised her accent. My mother was much gratified.

Madame Melba often came to the house. She and my mother became great friends, although I don't think my father cared for her too much. He was bored by her aggressive prima-donna airs. We loved her as she was kind to us and gave us wonderful grown-up presents. To this day I have a smooth white Copenhagen china cat, curled up asleep, which she gave me.

She was a stocky woman of middle height, rather coarse-complexioned, with an imposing singer's bust. With men she was inclined to be tom-boyishly flirtatious, and she had an arch habit of pirouetting round on her heel when she wished to be specially fascinating and which I believe used to embarrass my father. She had a jolly sense of humour and an impulsive and basically generous nature. I think she was more often loyal to her friends than they were to her. Her speaking-voice as I remember it was rather strident and gave no hint of the pure and flute-like quality of her singing.

Sometimes she came and practised her roles in the drawing room at Government House, and we were allowed to listen . . . But what we liked best was when she lost her temper with Mr Carruthers, the accompanist. She would scream abuse at the wretched,

THEY SAY

'She makes money with her dairy and digs potatoes for her health.'

Melba: 'I make a hundred dollars every month from the milk alone on my farm . . . then I raise vegetables, some of them for market – lots of times I have dug potatoes and it's excellent exercise for the health . . . Besides my farm I have several shops in Melbourne where I sell furniture to the emigrants who come to that country in such great numbers. I have seen how difficult it is for them, practically penniless and with their goods tied in a kerchief, to make homes, and so I thought of a plan by which they could buy their household goods on the instalment plan . . . '[1]

1. Clipping, 23 October 1915, Melba file, New York Public Library.

squirming creature in between roulades and trills, and sometime even box his ears. She used to walk about the room gesticulatin and acting as she sang, and we would gleefully watch the accom panist flinch as she approached the piano during these peregrina tions.[10]

In early August Melba shipped out for an American war-funds tour Robert Parker, an American baritone, was her associate and Frank S Leger her accompanist. In spite of the exhaustion that had mean cancelling her last two patriotic concerts, she claimed to have alread raised $145 000 in Australia, a figure that kept her just ahead o Clara Butt's record. Apart from the American–Canadian war relie concerts that year she also sang for the Chicago Opera Company, with the Boston Symphony Orchestra in New York, and as a touring artis in her own right: not every performance was a non-profit affair fo her. Everywhere the form of the Australian concerts was repeated though the Stars and Stripes took pride of place and Red Cross nurse took over from her singing students. The Americans turned out to like the idea of an Australian touting for money from an erstwhil colony to help old England. Melba played on this, introducing Percy Grainger's 'Colonial song', a piano solo, into Frank St Leger's pro gramme, then singing an apparently impromptu obbligato to it from her seat in the audience. Grainger was by then an American citizen and acceptable to both sides. This was such a success that she repeated it even in Australia. Of Grainger she said: 'He's a genius. There i always something fresh and charming about Grainger's compositions' With the condescension of the high-art musician she claimed, 'It i not surprising that he has been so strongly attracted to the folk musi of different countries. There is something in his own personality and in his music of the same quality of morning freshness'. But more to the point she went on:

> His father and mine, you know, were closely associated in building in Melbourne, and when some fine place in the city reminds me o the fact I often think that Percy Grainger is a builder of Australian art. In my own way I aim to be one too. My students are coming along splendidly. I have little groups of them – little nurseries, like a gardener's – all round Australia and now they are rewarding me by the fine progress they have made as a result of steady work.[11]

Grainger wrote:

> Myself, I never liked Melba at all, I thought her rough and intender [*sic*]. But I loved her voice as truly as I disliked her person. Her voice always made me mindsee Australia's landscapes, her voice having some kind of a peach-fur-like nap on it that made me think of the deep blue that forms on any Australian hill if seen a mile or more off.[12]

THE VOICE

Percy Grainger, the Australian composer and pianist, whose career Melba helped launch in London: 'I think she had a very high standard of workmanship. She herself worked very hard at anything. Knew all details and had mastered, I think, every technique of her art. Her voice, of course, was a very distinctive one. Oh my goodness it was. I'm not particularly fond of opera singers as a rule, but I must say I have never heard anything to compare with the beauty of Melba's voice, in any branch of singing. The top notes of course were very ringing and telling, as they are with a good many fine sopranos. But the curious thing with Melba was that her lower notes and middle notes were equally telling. They had a quality of their own; and even when she was singing with a big orchestra, she was never wiped out. She had a tremendous carrying power and a tremendous beauty of tone and very great refinement of workmanship in everything she did'.[1]

1. John Thompson, *On Lips of Living Men*, pp. 16–17.

At the end of the first American wartime tour Melba turned for home again. In Melbourne her father underwent surgery for papilloma of the bladder, haemorrhaged and on 25 March 1916, died. Melba's ship did not dock until a week later. By then David Mitchell was buried in the Melbourne General Cemetery. At a frail 87 years old his death could hardly have been unexpected, but Melba was still deeply affected by his loss, though she resumed her teaching and touring in rapid order.

When America joined the allies late in the war, Melba spent a considerable amount of time praising the newcomer's roads, architecture, theatres and its know-how. The Melbourne Consul even declared that 'no-one had done better propaganda work for America in Australia and for Australia in America than she'.

She tried to set an example by travelling in old clothes, saying: 'I can't afford new garments until every suffering man, woman and child has food and shelter', and by declaring her Paris flat at 91 Avenue Henry Martin an army hospital and supporting its 200 beds with a $200 000 endowment. This bit of selflessness inspired the Americans to found the short-lived Melba Home Hospital circles. She began to auction her own jewellery at her concerts and soon had society matrons falling over themselves to offer their tiaras. For publicity she posed with a 'ferocious denizen' at Universal Studio's zoo in Hollywood, met the first Rin-Tin-Tin, and made a film clip with Charlie Chaplin on the set of *Taking the Cure*. In it she slaps Chaplin's face and chases him around a room. The aim of the exercise was to produce yet another gimmick for fund-raising back home. She found Chaplin 'a charming Englishman – a very interesting man, and really good-looking'.

But in spite of all her generosity, her good intentions and her hard work there was still a section of the press that, Norton-like, continued to treat her badly. When she announced she would holiday for three months in Honolulu between tours because of exhaustion, one columnist, whose words were subsequently syndicated, wrote:

One feels inclined to wonder that so much is said about her present need of a 'holiday'. The mere pastime to her of superintending some of the lessons of pet pupils at Melbourne Conservatorium is not 'work' as the Red Cross toilers understand the word. One long day standing packing up stuff for our soldiers would give our great singer a really tired feeling. She has been a prodigious worker in rough shaping and hewing her wonderful career. But now? There are no new worlds of song to conquer, and Melba is, or appears to be, getting a little weary – even of her greatness. Usually in women, it goes, as shadows lengthen, with loneliness. [13]

She was by then a large 56-year-old matron. She had outlived and outdistanced all the rivals of her generation, but when she said so publicly the gossip columns pounced on her statements gleefully showing them to a new generation of singers for comment:

> Those dear, delightful prima donnas are sounding the 'anvil chorus' again. Madame (Colonel) Melba in a long interview recently informed the public that, exclusive of herself, there are no more great opera singers. Nordica and Eames are dead, Sembrich is through with grand opera and only Col Nellie Melba remains as a constellation in the musical heaven – that was the way Madame Melba described the situation.
>
> Whereupon Geraldine Farrar casts her gauntlet into the arena with the stinging retort: 'If ever I live to sing "Marguerite" and weigh 300 pounds at the time, I shall ask to be excused for any foolish statements I may make in the press.'[14]

To Fritz Hart, her director at Albert Street, she wrote a long stream of letters chronicling the American wartime tours and reflecting every mood of every moment with all the verve that was the essential Melba 300 pounds or not:

> I shall be in New York for Xmas [1917] – far away from my cherished Coombe, but still I have good friends there and know they will do everything they can to make me happy. I am having wonderful success. I wish you could have heard *Bohème* and *Faust*. I have been in this country 7 weeks. I have had a cold, four accidents (one nearly fatal) and I have sung ten times in opera and given six concerts. *Not bad* I think – and God only knows how many more I have to give. Next week I sing at Springfield and Boston, the week after I sing with the Boston Symphony Orchestra four times. Philadelphia, Washington, Baltimore and Brooklyn and so on. I had a very tempting offer to go and sing at Monte Carlo but I have refused because it would be too sad for me in Europe just now. So I shall be in California in March and very likely return by Japan.[15]

Of America she wrote: 'This country is wonderful in many ways but oh! it is so *vulgar* and the press is *beneath contempt*. Of course America is going to win the war!!!! Need I say more? It makes one <u>mad</u>.'[16]

In public Melba seems to have been a simple-minded patriot of the 'hang-the-Kaiser' school. She – or rather Nichols – retold her meeting with the Kaiser in her memoirs of 1924 so that that gentleman came off very much the worse for the encounter, as suited the times:

> Kaiser [to Melba after a command performance of *Faust*]: Don't you think, Madame Melba, you took the Jewel Song at much too fast a tempo?
>
> Melba: No, your Imperial Majesty. I do not. I sang the part of Marguerite according to the instructions of the composer

himself, M. Charles Gounod, who was pleased to express his entire satisfaction with my interpretation and to compliment me on it.

(Exit the Kaiser, bristling, snapping his fingers for the Empress to follow him.)[17]

By 1918 she was certain that Germany had declared her public enemy No. 1 and that enemy agents had been sent out to kill her. It was true that she had had a number of accidents. She listed eight in the *Vancouver World*. A pole had fallen on her from the flies as she began the vision scene in *Faust*. Her left wrist was broken and she was unconscious for fifteen minutes. She was in two auto crashes, one where the other driver broke both legs and his ribs, the other in which a pedestrian was killed. The engine of her train exploded, and on another occasion her private carriage was uncoupled and careered off out of control. On yet another she was thrown to the ground by sudden braking. A bomb exploded near her box at the Chicago Opera House and finally she became so nervous that she fumbled making tea one night and her nightgown caught fire. The bomb seems to have been genuine, though it was faulty and its aim more political than operatic. The train incidents were the normal hazards of the American system, and the stage accidents were sheer incompetence. As for the man killed in the car crash, he seems to belong to a much earlier Parisian era. Still, it suited Melba to use these incidents in the cause of knocking the Kaiser and she made the most of it.

Early in 1918 she was awarded the DBE. She was parked overnight in her private railcar near Walla Walla, Washington, when the local newspaper bearing the news was delivered to her over breakfast. As she passed her secretary Freda Steinberg's table she dropped the paper in front of her. 'You like newspapers. Here's one for you', she said, and went to her room. Steinberg read the news and followed her. She found Melba stark naked capering about exclaiming: 'I'm a Dame! I'm a Dame!'[18]

In London, after peace was declared, Melba was given a reception by Katherine Goodson and her husband Arthur Hutton at their house at St John's Wood. London society greeted her with applause as she came over the threshold and the band played 'See the conquering hero comes'. Dame Nellie Melba had arrived. Exit the opera star, enter the Grand Old Lady. It was a welcome, but also the first of the farewells. Melba's world, the glamorous Edwardian world of titles and diamonds, of Society was swept aside by the war. She came home to a very different world and she was only too well aware of it. Yet, in 1919, Selwyn Rider could write in the *Melbourne Triad* of this raddled old woman, this left-over of another era who insisted on sweeping into concert rooms all over the English-speaking world and demanding attention as she bade it farewell over and over again:

I sat in the Town Hall, well back. I was surrounded by all sorts of people who clucked and blithered audibly, till in the end, or long before the end, I was forced to admit that they knew even less about music than I do. And so I heard Melba.

Did I enjoy Melba's singing? Why, of course. Did I enjoy the concert so greatly that the night will stand in my memory as something altogether exceptional and wonderful? No. Melba's voice stirs me to almost passionate admiration, but admiration isn't joy; admiration doesn't satisfy, there is no easy ecstasy in admiration. Melba's voice – how shall I put it? It pleases my brain without stirring my blood or in any way touching my heart. It is beautiful, it is even strikingly beautiful; but it is beautiful as a white camellia might be beautiful in Heaven, and I never could get thrills from white camellias.

There was very much in Melba that appealed enormously to the showman in me. I think she must appeal enormously to the showman in each of us. There is her confidence, the something of an extraordinarily delicious insolent charm with which she accepts all homage as her right, her perfect poise, her undisguised contempt for the herd that snuffles. It appealed to me tremendously, all that . . . I am afraid I enjoyed all that much more than I enjoyed the singing, because it got beneath my brain to the real place where I live . . . l'inévitable, c'est Moi.

And so I am led to the conclusion that a great part of Melba's marvellous popularity is due to her prodigious personal pull. People like her . . . the real people. It seems to them, as that night it seemed to me, that she is fine, individual, human. Here, you tell yourself, is a real fellow.

You don't have to know much about music to understand that, or to understand me, when I say that I enjoyed Melba vastly more than I enjoyed Melba's singing . . . I know nothing of Melba the actress, for I have never heard her in opera. There, I am told, one comes upon the real Melba. I can well believe it. The gift is operatic. On the concert platform – although, of course, I know nothing whatever about it – I would sooner hear Mme Kirby Lunn, sooner a dozen times so far as the singing goes. But in Kirby Lunn it is the singing only you enjoy; you do not enjoy the woman, as you enjoy the woman Melba.[19]

Left: The gates of Melba's country home, Coombe Cottage, at Lilydale, Victoria. *(La Trobe Library)*

Below: Rupert Bunny's 1902 portrait of Melba which hung for many years in His Majesty's Theatre, Melbourne, and is now in the National Gallery of Victoria. It bears little physical resemblance to Melba. *(The Age)*

Spencer Shier portrait of Melba in tiara and furs. *(The Age)*

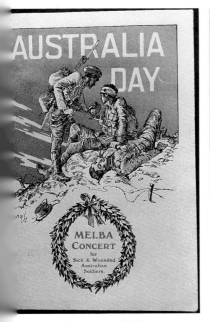

rogramme for a concert Melba gave to se funds for the wounded men of orld War I. *(Melba Memorial nservatorium)*

Melba's best known Australian protégé, Stella Power — the Little Melba. *(Melba Memorial Conservatorium)*

The marble bust commissioned by Melba from Sir Bertram Mackennel and completed in 1899. Melba herself presented it to the National Gallery of Victoria. *(The Age)*

Melba (*seated, second from right*) received her DBE from the Governor-General, Sir Ronald Munro-Ferguson, at Admiralty House, 1918. *(Performing Arts Museum)*

Melba at Coombe Cottage outside the main block which was designed by John Grainger. *(Melba Memorial Conservatorium)*

Melba and her students en route to a concert at Lilydale just after World War I. *(Melba Memorial Conservatorium)*

The gardens of Coombe Cottage in 1918. *(Melba Memorial Conservatorium)*

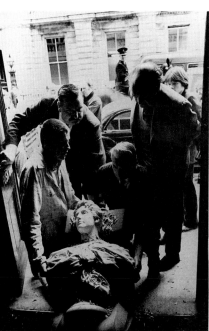

Moving Covent Garden's copy of the Mackennel bust in 1970. *(Performing Arts Museum)*

Melba meets the first Rin-Tin-Tin in Hollywood, 1918. *(The Age)*

Chapter 10

MELBA'S GIRLS

In January 1919 Melba returned to London to prepare for the first post-war Covent Garden season. It was one of the coldest months she had ever known and the once luxurious liner in which she sailed from New York prophetically offered her little comfort with its war-worn paintwork and broken portholes. She was physically and emotionally chilled. She found London a 'new, untidy, haphazard metropolis, so grey and so strange, from the London which I had known'.

As she made up her face in her old backstage dressing-room on opening night she found herself aware of other changes.

'It is not you', I said to myself as I peered into the glass. 'It cannot be Melba. It is somebody else. So many have gone, so many new faces have come – it can't be that you have remained.'[1]

It was 12 May 1919 and for the reopening that night Thomas Beecham was to conduct *La Bohème* before a post-war audience that bore little resemblance to the Edwardian splendours displayed at the Garden on other Melba nights:

I had the feeling that I was singing to an audience of ghosts. Lady de Grey had gone. Alfred de Rothschild had gone, and so many others, all gone, and yet I felt them there . . . and it was for them rather than for this great audience that I sang . . . It was that night at Covent Garden that made me realize the full extent to which London had changed. There was little of the old brilliance. Can you imagine in the old days, men walking into Covent Garden on a Melba night, or on any other night, and sitting in the stalls in shabby tweed coats? Yes, that is what I saw on this night, and though I have no objection to brown tweed coats or to shabbiness, I could not help feeling a sensation almost of resentment, that men who could afford to pay for stalls, could not also afford to wear the proper clothes.[2]

Bohème, Faust, Roméo – she sang in nothing new. She did not return until the 1923 season when she sang Mimi and Marguerite. On 8 June 1926 she gave her last performance at the Garden in Act 2 of *Roméo et Juliette*, the opening of the last act of *Otello*, and Acts 3 and 4 of *Bohème*. Melba – the greatest diva of them all – was fading

was told that it had been specially invented for her that very evening and was to be named after her. She was delighted. The surrounding tables stared, fascinated, till she flung her napkin over her face and besought her host to "stop them!" I have never seen anyone enjoy herself nor make others enjoy themselves so much.'[1]

1. Quoted in Hetherington, *op. cit.*, p. 202.

into legend, but Melba herself was not inclined to accept retrenchment. For years she had been developing her teaching skills and laying the foundations for a school of singers and teachers she intended should disseminate her methods for at least another generation. She saw herself as having inherited the Marchesi–Garcia method. She intended to pass it on, redefined and reshaped as her own, an invisible legacy for Australian culture. The school was not an arbitrary affair, not something forced on an otherwise musically inert, still-colonial society. Its history, in fact, had 19th-century origins.

Opposite St Patrick's Cathedral in Albert Street, East Melbourne there is a small bluestone-fronted building dating from 1892 and still known, as it was then, as the Victorian Artists' Society. Before the First World War it was the centre of Australian art, its exhibitions important events in the life of the Melbourne intelligentsia. It was also the hub of its musical life and, since all things cultural were then Melburnian, the national centre of musical development.

Late in 1890 the University of Melbourne reluctantly appointed its first Professor of Music when philanthropist Francis Ormond laid out £20 000 to found a Chair in opposition to the public demand for a Conservatoire. The university felt embarrassed that the gift was attached to what they misconstrued as a subject not amenable to academic discipline.

The first Ormond Professor, George William Louis Marshall-Hall, an English composer and conductor, was obliged to lecture in borrowed rooms on campus. Late in 1891 he met Arthur Streeton and through him the artists of the Heidelberg School. In 1892, with George Allan, he founded the orchestra which bore his name, inheriting the resources used by Frederick Hymen Cowen during the 1888 Centennial Exhibition. Cowen had been imported from London by a gold-rich society to produce a six-month-long festival of music at a personal fee of £5000. The conductor had no wish to come to Australia but was seduced when, to his astonishment, the colonies met his deliberately inflated price. He brought in his wake sixteen key instrumentalists to supplement the local players hand-picked from around the country and already in rehearsal under George Weston. With seventy-two players and an SATB choir of over seven hundred drawn from the Melbourne Philharmonic Society and the Liedertafels, he gave 244 concerts of 265 major works, including thirty-five symphonies, thirteen large choral works, ninety-one overtures and whole slabs from opera. The average concert drew nearly 2000 to a hall designed for 2500. At a time when Melbourne's population was 432 350, the total attendance figure was 467 299. Cowen later wrote that the concerts were 'a succession of high-class performances that I believe to be unparalleled in the history of music'.

Public enthusiasm ran so high that the Victorian government was persuaded to provide an unprecedented £3 000 to set up the orchestra as a permanent body. The result was the ill-fated Victorian Orchestra, which failed after a further 184 concerts, the victim of the economic collapse which ended the boom years. In spite of appearances by visiting celebrities of the calibre of Sir Charles Hallé, its conductor, Hamilton Clarke, was unable to hold thinning audiences and rebellious players together. Clarke thought the Australians were beneath him. The Australian instrumentalists in turn stubbornly refused to co-operate with him and he shipped out abruptly. It was left to Marshall-Hall to retrieve the Cowen scores, the self-respect of the players and an audience then counting its change before committing its odd guineas to subscription concerts.

The Marshall-Hall orchestra ran from 1892 to 1912. The English philanthropist and author, Archibald E. J. Lee, wrote of it:

And suddenly Melbourne found itself in possession of something like the Leipzig Gewandhaus, a fully-fledged orchestra collected from all quarters, and a conductor endowed with ideas and ambitions. What Mendelssohn once had done for Leipzig and all North Germany, Marshall-Hall now did for Melbourne and all Australia. Letting no difficulty stand in his way (and the difficulties were great and numerous) he gave to the Australian people all that was best in music.[3]

When Melba returned to Australia in 1902, 1907 and 1909 this was the orchestra which dominated the local scene, not, as is often claimed, the Melbourne Symphony Orchestra, an amateur body dating from 1905. By the time she returned in 1911 the Marshall-Hall orchestra had been destroyed by union action and its disillusioned conductor was about to leave for Europe and the abortive London production of his opera *Stella*. The Melbourne Symphony Orchestra, under Alberto Zelman jun., was no substitute for the older orchestra and did not emerge as a force until the early 1920s.

But in 1894, after years of haggling, the University of Melbourne agreed to lend its name to the establishment of a practical school of music. The University Conservatorium opened on 28 February 1895 in the Queens' Coffee Palace on the corner of Rathdowne and Victoria streets, Carlton, with Marshall-Hall as the lessee. The university did not feel inclined to dip into its own pocket for such an adventure and left it to the professor to find the rent. Its parsimony turned out to have monumental repercussions which were felt even by Melba when she elected to throw in her lot with the musicians of a comparatively small society.

In March the professor offered Streeton studio space in the Coffee Palace and its concert hall for an exhibition. The liaison between artists surrounding Streeton (notably Tom Roberts, Phillips Fox, Ernest Moffit and the Lindsays) and musicians allied to the university's conservatorium grew stronger. Some three years later the depression left the management of the Coffee Palace bankrupt. Because of his connections Marshall-Hall was able to re-house the conservatorium in rented rooms at the Victorian Artists' Society's premises in Albert Street and there it remained until 1900.

Marshall-Hall was no mild-mannered academic, but a rampageous bohemian composer who made no bones about publicly challenging the wowsers of Melbourne society. He was a declared atheist in a Christian city for one thing but, much worse, he lived openly with a woman who was not his wife and who had borne his bastard son. In 1898 he published a book of satirical and anti-clerical poems called *Hymns Ancient and Modern*. A vicious campaign was mounted against him which resulted in a public scandal. The musical as well as the general public divided into pro and anti Marshall-Hall factions, and a counter campaign in support of free speech kept the issue alive for years. In 1900 the university refused to renew Marshall-Hall's tenure. In retaliation the ex-professor announced that since he paid the rent at Albert Street he would continue to teach there. His students and staff remained loyal to him. What had been the Conservatorium of the University of Melbourne began trading in 1900 as the Melbourne Conservatorium of Music, its links with the university severed, to everyone's confusion, but to most Melburnians it was known as the Marshall-Hall Conservatorium or later simply as Albert Street.

Meantime the university had to find a new professor, new rooms and a new source of income from which to pay the rent. Professor Franklin Sievewright Peterson, the second Ormond Professor, introduced an Australian-based music examination system to replace the rival English systems which had long monopolised what proved to be a highly lucrative business. In 1906 a project fund for a new on-campus conservatorium was begun and on 26 November 1909 Melba laid the foundation stone for the new building. In 1913 the Governor-General, Lord Denman, opened Melba Hall, the concert area built with proceeds raised by Melba.

Melba's involvement with the two rival conservatoriums during her first Australian tour in 1902 was limited to attending the formal receptions each gave in her honour, but during the 1909 visit there was noticeable jostling for her musical favours. Melba was well aware of the power she wielded but she had the wisdom to play one institution off against the other for the common good. For a time she supervised singing students at the university conservatorium on an informal basis. Her provincial touring schedule prevented much time from being devoted to the cause in any case.

Melba had arrived in Australia late in February and gave four concerts over six weeks in the Melbourne Town Hall. She used what was advertised as a 'grand orchestra' but which was, in fact, an amalgam of orchestral and theatre-pit players conducted by Marshall-Hall and selected with an uneasy eye on the reaction of the Musician's

nion that was then objecting to any orchestra that bore the ex-
rofessor's name. His own orchestra was under fire from the union for
sing amateur (female) players alongside professionals (male), hence
e euphemism; neither Marshall-Hall nor Melba's manager, John
mmone, was prepared to risk trouble in that quarter, though most
 the players were in fact Marshall-Hall regulars. But though the
rchestra was associated with the Albert Street conservatorium, the
orus used for the opera excerpts came from the Women's Choir,
e group associated with the Women's Work Exhibition of 1907
hen it was founded by its conductor, the wife of the second Ormond
rofessor, Georgina Peterson.

Melba had shown interest in Australian orchestral matters long
efore this encounter, however. If there was ever to be a Melba opera
eason in her native land she knew the question of orchestral support
ould have to be resolved years in advance. It was not just a matter
f importing what was required. That was a possible, if expensive,
ay out, but she wanted something more – an orchestra was only
art of it.

For almost a century the pitch at which instruments and therefore
oices performed in European opera houses had been rising, possibly
ue to the snowballing effect of technological changes in stringed
nstrument manufacture, producing bigger tone for new concert halls
nd larger opera houses. The trend was blamed for ruining voices,
orced up by accompanying orchestras; the obvious remedy of tuning
own was resisted because of the expense involved in re-tuning organs
nd purchasing new woodwind and brass instruments if a standard
itch was adopted universally. In Adelina Patti's day at Covent Garden
erforming pitch had approached $a^1 = 450Hz$, but the then reigning
oprano brought such pressure to bear on the management that French
iapason normal ($a^1 = 435Hz$) was adopted for the 1880 season. This
as the pitch Melba worked at and which she meant to have duplicated
n Australia.

It was essential that Melbourne be won over first since it was certain
hat if the decision went in her favour there, the rest of the country
ould follow, the 1902 tour had made that clear. In 1906 she gave
50 to the university's orchestra to initiate reform when Professor
eterson appealed to her for help in the campaign he began in 1901.
Normal pitch ($a^1 = 440Hz$), as it was known, was accepted by the
ducation Department of the state that year and a set of 'standards'
basic fixed frequency devices) was ordered by the Minister of Edu-
ation, Mr Sachse, to be kept at the university by Professor Lyle. In
October 1907 the university ordered a complete set of normal pitch
rchestral instruments at a cost of £260, the Victorian Government
ssisting with a £100 grant. The set arrived in April 1908 but there
as no attempt to allow Marshall-Hall access to them. In October
Melba donated a set of normal pitch wind and brass instruments to

the Marshall-Hall orchestra – two oboes, four clarinets, one ba
clarinet, one piccolo, two bassoons, one contra bassoon, one cor angla
three trumpets, one bass trumpet, four horns, three trombones, o
tuba (but apparently no flutes) – a gift of considerable value ar
significance since it enabled the ex-professor to perform pre 19t
century orchestral and chamber music at close to the original pitc
The move towards authentic reproduction was credited to Melb
though it originated with and was carried through by Peterson. Mel
certainly had a vested interest in seeing it succeed, but she was al
aware that her gift would have far-reaching educational implicatio
for professionals, the public and even the schoolchild. She literal
facilitated a major shift in the direction Australian music took. T
university had the money but not the orchestra for the instrumen
needed for the change to be properly utilised. Marshall-Hall had t
orchestra but no money. Melba's gift ensured that normal pitch w
heard by a large public. Once heard it was accepted; once accepte
an opera tour could be planned.

On 6 March 1909 Melba and some 120 musicians gathered at t
Paris Café in Collins Street for the official handover of the twenty-fi
instruments left heaped on a table. A flashlight photograph was take
and the *Argus* duly reported that for once rivalries were put asid
though Peterson and Marshall-Hall can still be seen at opposite en
of the room. To save her voice Melba handed her speech to Sir Jam
Barrett to read:

> I ask you to accept these instruments, not only as a souvenir of m
> deep interest in your future achievements, but as an evidence of m
> gratitude for the splendid service you have already given to music
> art in my native city. The works of the great masters, which yc
> have so successfully presented to the Victorian public, were pract
> cally all composed for performance at the low pitch, and I am gla
> to think that in making these masterpieces still more familiar
> the people, who must necessarily be exalted by their ideal interpr
> tation, you will be able to perform them under the conditior
> intended.
>
> I hope that very soon some enthusiastic Victorian will con
> forward to provide the money necessary for the lowering of t
> Town-hall organ pitch, and that this example will be followe
> throughout the Commonwealth, so that Australia, which has alreac
> made such a wonderful showing in the service of the various art
> may hold a proud place in the world's musical advancement, a
> advancement very dear to your heart and mine.[4]

But Marshall-Hall's reply was less gracious. In no uncertain term
he told Melba he did not care what pitch the orchestra played at s
long as it played and this it could not do without more money
bolster the Lady Northcote Permanent Orchestra Trust Fund. His ple

was direct and personal and Melba was stung into action. She wrote
to the *Argus* with a guarantee of £100 a year for five years if nineteen
others would match her offer. She wrote:

> The ennobling inspiration which great masterpieces of music conveys
> to a people can never be known in Australia until we have an
> orchestra capable of giving these works at least reasonable interpre-
> tation. Such interpretation is utterly impossible with an orchestra
> hurriedly assembled, numerically unbalanced, and subject to con-
> stant change of personnel. Where even the elementary necessity of
> adequate rehearsal is hindered by these ever-varying, and ever-
> harrassing conditions, there can be no hope for that union of spirit
> which is an absolute essential for the expression of the composer's
> message.
>
> During my own concert tour, just finished, the impossibility of
> securing proper orchestral support was a depressing revelation to
> me. It was only possible to perform many of the selections by
> borrowing instrumentalists from the orchestras of the theatres and
> other places of entertainment by courtesy of their respective man-
> agements. Often it was not possible, even under these circumstances,
> to get the required players, and it never happened that all who
> took part in the final performance could attend the necessary
> rehearsals. Many of the numbers selected for presentation to the
> public had to be abandoned altogether because the essential com-
> plement of instrumentalists could not be got together under any
> conditions. One of our concerts depended entirely on a player for
> whom I had to send a motor thirty miles, who could not attend
> rehearsal, and to whom whatever remuneration he demanded had
> to be paid.
>
> In the face of heart-breaking difficulties Professor Marshall-Hall
> has worked wonders with the means at his disposal, and were
> reasonable material at his command, he would be able to render to
> the State labours of incalculable educational value.
>
> I refuse to believe that Australians are less patriotic, less zealous
> for the intellectual well-being of their country, than the people of
> the United Kingdom, Europe and America, where, even in com-
> paratively small centres, permanent orchestras have been established
> and maintained to the great artistic and commercial benefit of the
> communities interested. I say commercial advantages advisedly, and
> I think this side of the matter should be kept in view, for I am
> convinced from experience in America and elsewhere that the suc-
> cessful establishment of any great artistic attraction stimulates a
> corresponding measure of commercial advance. What a fine public
> spirit has made possible in Boston, where the unrivalled Symphony
> Orchestra stands for triumphant musical progress, should be ap-
> proximately possible in Melbourne and Sydney, which in population

and trade offer a fair basis for comparison.

To many dwellers in the Commonwealth Australia pours out mineral, pastoral and agricultural riches with a prodigal hand, and I am constrained to believe that those who owe their splendid affluence to the development of the natural resources of the country will not refuse a generous contribution towards a movement destined to develop the infinitely more important field of intellectual wealth. I therefore, appeal particularly to those whose prosperity has come from the products of our wonderful mines and pasture lands.[5]

But this direct approach brought little response. On 15 December she wrote again, this time widening the appeal to include all 'lovers of music' and committing herself to channel all contributions into the Northcote Trust. In effect she was promoting the Marshall-Hall orchestra as the only group in the country with the potential she needed.

By the time of her third visit in 1911, the first opera tour, there had been a downward shift in Marshall-Hall's fortunes. The Musicians' Union had refused to allow amateurs to appear with professionals. Marshall-Hall, believing his amateur women players were as good as his professional male players, resisted. In the uncertain atmosphere this created, personnel fluctuated and the standards of the orchestra dropped. It ceased to be effective early in the year but struggled ignominiously on until October 1912. By the time the Sheffield Choir arrived in July 1911 there was no orchestra to support it. Reports of the failure travelled with the famous group and the ex-professor's reputation was undermined. By then he was in Sydney conducting *Lohengrin* for the Melba–J. C. Williamson season. In Melbourne his opera *Stella* was produced at Her Majesty's on 4 and 12 May 1912 and the Balcony Scene from his *Romeo and Juliet* on 14 December. Their success induced him to try his luck in London and on 21 February 1913 he left. This left the Albert Street conservatorium without a director.

Melba was already in London by October 1912 and could not have seen *Romeo* though she must have been aware of the success of both operas. When Marshall-Hall arrived in London a meeting was arranged with Melba. It may have been through her interest that the score of *Stella* came into the hands of Thomas Beecham who had thoughts of taking it on for Covent Garden if it succeeded at the Aldwych. There was a successful season at the Palladium in June 1914 but the war put a stop to the progress of *Stella* almost immediately and Marshall-Hall gladly accepted the reinstatement as Ormond Professor that was offered to him when Franklin Peterson died suddenly. He returned in triumph but six months later was hospitalised for an emergency appendectomy and died in agony of peritonitis.

Marshall-Hall's return had caused problems at Albert Street. When he left in February 1913, Edouard Scharf had deputised as director.

The English composer and JCW conductor Fritz Hart took over Marshall-Hall's lecturing schedule, but a year later Marshall-Hall wrote asking that Albert Street be closed, and Scharf defected to the university conservatorium. The rest of the staff refused to budge and Hart became the elected director. Marshall-Hall found himself in the ironic situation of being in opposition to his old conservatorium.

When Marshall-Hall reappeared, some of his former Albert Street staff switched institutions to be with him – Edward Goll, Miss Goode, Mrs Patten, Emily Dyason and Madame Elise Wiedermann, the former star of the Vienna State Opera and student of Marchesi who gave Melba her letter of introduction. The professor brought in organist A. E. Floyd and the voice-production specialist in relaxation method, Otto Fisher Sobell – an Adelaide man who had had thirty years of London teaching experience. But at the same time Alberto Zelman jun. and his singer wife, Maude Harrington, left the university conservatorium.

Attempts were made to amalgamate the two conservatoriums but though there was a faction at Albert Street eager to go over to the university, the group in favour of remaining separate with Hart as director suddenly found its hand strengthened when Melba decided to give Fritz her support. Any thought of amalgamation was dropped. Melba's name was taken as a guarantee of success. There were two reasons for Melba's decision – rivalry with Elise Wiedermann and Melba's own re-emergent nationalism in a time of war.

Melba declared herself pro-British and anti-German from the moment 'poor little Belgium' was overrun and threw herself into anything that could support the war effort. She saw Albert Street as part of the campaign, but her staff there could not match skills with Marshall-Hall's acquisitions. She realised that what Fritz needed was a popular cause if the student body was to increase and multiply, so she took to pointing out the virtues of British music (in which she included Australian music) and to the sterling names of Hart's staff. Somehow she managed to tar the rival institution as pro-German because of the national origins of surnames on the appointments list. At first glance the names appear anything but German – Laver, Coutts, Nickson, Scharf, Dyason, Goll, Lebens, Janson, Sobell, Malyon, Patten, Goode, Truebridge, Delpret and Wiedermann in 1915, but it was Elise Wiedermann who was the target in fact, not the Czech Goll or the German–Jewish Sobell. In the context of public hysteria and academic campaigns against German (read Jewish) lecturers, she found willing and influential ears.

Wiedermann came to Australia as the wife of Carl Pinschof, the Austrian consul. The opera school she founded at Albert Street presented an annual season at various city theatres from 1898 onwards. Rehearsals were held in the ballroom and gardens of the Pinschofs' Italianate mansion, Studley Hall, in Kew. Wiedermann's friendship

THE VOICE

Dr A. E. Floyd, Australian organist and broadcaster, said of Melba: 'Of course, I never heard her in the middle of her great operatic career. I first heard her here in Melbourne a little over 40 years ago, I think, when she was getting on over seventy. And I remember that when she began to sing I said to myself "Is this the great world-famous Melba?" And then I gradually realised that she had switched over from the coloratura arias with which she'd made a great name in her heyday in Europe – she realised that she had to treat her voice with consideration – she'd switched over to atmospheric French songs, which gave her unique opportunities of using the best part of her voice. And it had an indescribable quality. I think the nearest to a true description that I've ever read is in that rather disagreeable book written by a man who was at an earlier stage a protégé of hers but who later wrote a rather disagreeable novel.... But he does in the course of the book give a description of a party in a big house in London, Melba present, and someone persuaded her to sing. Perhaps her hostess. "And", says Beverley Nichols, "she stood up, and there came on the air that voice like a disembodied spirit, like a little boy's voice that seemed to come –" I don't know whether *he* says this or whether it's what *I* say in a very deliberate effort to tell the truth as I see it – "seemed to come from everywhere and nowhere. There it was in the air – poised, and perfect" '.[1]

1. Thompson, *op. cit.*, pp. 16–17

with Lady Loch, the cultured wife of the Governor, made involvement in her circle socially desirable and the promotion of her school a duty readily accepted by an upper middle class still trying to shed the bumptious image of the colonial *nouveau riche*. The school produced a long line of distinguished singers among them Kate Samuels (Madame Benda), Florence Towl, Evelyn Scotney, Florence Fawaz (Florence Austral) and the Pinschof daughters, Carmen, Elizabeth and Louise.

Wiedermann's social position, her musical influence and even her career as a singer gave her the rank of rival in Melba's eyes. Here in her own home town was a second great soprano forced off the stage by matrimonial circumstance rather than war, as in Melba's case, and with a reputation still very much alive. In 1881 she had been a member of the first German opera company to give a London season under the baton of Hans Richter. She had appeared frequently with Hans von Bülow, had sung before Queen Victoria and Edward and had been reigning diva at the Vienna State Opera for ten years. When Melba stepped into her vacated shoes at Albert Street, Wiedermann had already set up a new school on campus using the hall which bore Melba's name. Wiedermann resigned from Albert Street on 2 March 1915 just as a letter campaign in the press got into full swing, arguing for and against German music and alien teachers gaining a foothold at the university. Within academia there were moves to hold an official debate on the lack of university policy on the employment of aliens and a tabled demand to Council by Marshall-Hall's long-term enemy, the Warden of Trinity College, the Reverend Dr Alexander Leeper, that unnaturalised citizens of an enemy country employed by the university should be expelled. The debate was postponed in the finish, but not before the reporting of it had managed to stir up a good deal of ill feeling against the university conservatorium.

Meantime an announcement appeared in every paper in town:

> Madame Melba wishes it to be made known that for the remainder of her stay in this State she will take a personal interest in every student of singing at the Albert St Conservatorium of Music, which is under the direction of Mr Fritz Hart. She has intimated her intention of attending at the institution once a fortnight for this purpose.[6]

What Melba was offering was individual tuition and only that. She took a very decided stance on this. In 1909 she wrote:

> My views on the value of individual training are well known and carry with them a consequent opposition to class tuition. It is impossible for a singing student to give out her best as one of a group directed by a supervision which must in its very essence partake of the perfunctory. The singers who have succeeded after class training have been those whose personality and endowments

have made them independent of circumstances. Reliance on choir or chorus singing as a helpful factor in the early period of vocal study I hold to be a most unwise course, as an unplaced voice may easily be permanently injured by its free employment in any such body.[7]

When Melba gave her first 'class' at the Albert Street conservatorium on 12 April 1915 it was far from the kind of mindless mass exercise she so detested. It was more a matter of individual instruction before one's peers, as an eyewitness observed:

Melba herself sat at the piano, and heard twenty or so who came before her sing scales and exercises, and to each one she gave personal advice and direction.

Throughout the two hours during which Melba taught she continually emphasised the necessity of relaxation of the throat muscles, and she concluded the morning's work by singing two songs to the staff of the Conservatorium and the students.[8]

By May she was teaching on a weekly basis. Thirty years later Vida Sutton and Winifred Tregear, who were among her earliest students, wrote:

For many days beforehand an air of suppressed excitement pervaded the sombre old building – a sense of something about to happen – a feeling, that first of all infected the staff and then mysteriously spread to the humblest of the students.

Then came the notice in large letters, pinned on the notice-board, to the effect that all students were to see Mrs Clark – the lady superintendent – with regard to certain uniform required to be worn for these great occasions. Many of us dreamed of new frocks, of shade and cut to impress even the most fastidious – and as to the ornaments we were going to wear! – well! they, too, would be irresistible!

Imagine our disgust when the patterns were dished out! – material – did you ever hear of it? – white cotton gabardine style – the working overall – buttoned down the front with turn-down collar – and sleeves to the wrist – and mark you – white cotton stockings and white canvas shoes with cotton laces. Strictly no jewellery – (wedding ring only!) – and the hair simply dressed (it was the day of long straight hair! – no perms, girls, to help nature.) Our badges were to be pinned just so! – on the left side – so far down the shoulder – all dresses to be the same length so many inches from the ground! Rebellion was rife in the ranks! – but common sense came to the rescue on second thoughts – and how wise were the 'powers that be' – in keeping us all the same! Can you see us then – simple and unadorned – lined up the length of the old grey stairs on either side of the red carpet, shivering with excitement,

MELBA'S ADVICE TO HER FIRST SINGING CLASS

On 12 April 1915 a reporter attended Melba's first singing class at the Albert Street conservatorium and recorded what she said.

'How many of you have seen a vocal chord? . . . I call them my two little bits of cotton, chiefly because cotton is so easy to break, and once you have to mend it there is always a knot which can never be remedied. The same thing applies to the vocal chords, and I would strongly advise you to leave any teacher who makes your throat tired. If it is tired at the end of your lesson, it is because these little bits of cotton are being strained. There is another thing you must guard against, that is the hard attack of the glottis. If you constantly hit hard at anything a sore place comes, and with the vocal chords this takes the form of a little corn, the hardening of which means the loss of a voice . . . Sometimes you'll hear a husky voice. This means that the chords are not straight, and there is a little hole between them . . . Again, you'll hear vocalists who can sing loud, but not piano; that is the beginning of the end . . . I would like all the pupils who come to my lessons to go to a throat specialist and ask him to show them and teach them about the vocal chords . . . Another thing which is absolutely necessary for an artist is health. No one can hope to have a career unless they are physically and mentally very strong. Musical intelligence, grip, determination and tenacity are also necessary. If a student wants to become great she must let nothing stand in her way of reaching the desired end . . . students cannot hope to become prima donnas unless they are willing to sacrifice everything to their art.'[1]

1. Clipping, Melba Memorial Conservatorium Diary 1915.

awaiting with scarcely concealed impatience the arrival of the great diva?

Then the bustle at the front door as her car drew up and Mr Hart went to greet her and escort her to the South Gallery, with us thronging to our places.

All thoughts of personal appearance faded, however, as the great teacher took charge and called on this or that girl to sing – and when the number was finished, how we all strained to hear her comments. [But those comments sometimes took an odd turn:]

On one occasion, when a student, nervous and on the verge of tears, was attempting a song in French, she became so exasperated she seized the poor wite [sic] by the shoulders and shook her and said: 'I wouldn't be taking this trouble with you if I didn't think you were worth it. Now, do it again.'[9]

There was more to the Melba involvement than these wartime lessons, however:

What of the social parties given at the Con. by her to the students! What of the excitement of the concerts and café chantants in aid of Red Cross – the concert parties taken to Lilydale to aid various charities – and above all the coveted invitations to Coombe Cottage?

On the occasion of her grand-daughter's christening when a choir of Con. students travelled by train to Lilydale, and on to Coldstream, where they dined at the local hotel with Dame Nellie herself as hostess.

Then again who remembers the Sunday trip, when Dame Nellie turned chef and clad in Russian boots, cook's apron and cap, she cooked sausages for us over an open fire in the field?

Then the concert in aid of the parish hall at Lilydale, when she herself counted (and commented on!) the proceeds (calling for help from the girls in the addition), at the back of the stage, while the concert still went on? Who could forget coming home by train that night – steam train to Croydon and change, which involved a wait; how we sang all the repertoire of the concert and choral class madrigals, part songs and 'what nots,' while Mr Hart conducted and the welkin rang with our singing and the local inhabitants got out of their beds to listen at 1 a.m.[10]

But the climax of what was thought of as 'these exciting days' was a series of charity concerts in the Melbourne Town Hall, concerts for which the public queued all night outside Allan's, waiting for the box office to open. The singing school was lined up on stage dressed in uniform every time, a highly conspicuous white advertisement. Melba's appreciation ran to dinner for the entire class after the performances. This exposure of her students was interpreted as pure vanity on Melba's part, but in fact was a way of pushing the individual hrough her membership of a defined elite. Melba wanted the public o be aware of her women singers as a body and to respect their pecial training. For that career benefit they needed to become known under her name and she took every opportunity to let their public know they were there.

Ultimately Melba's women students found themselves involved in he annual opera performances which were a part of the Albert Street conservatorium's tradition. Under Elise Wiedermann's direction to 1913 scenes from some thirty-three operas had been performed, including Marshall-Hall's *Alcestis* and *Romeo and Juliet* and Mona McBurney's *The Dalmation*. Melba was to continue the patronage of local opera but she limited her attention to the work of one composer – the director of the conservatorium, Fritz Hart.

Fritz Bennicke Hart was 42 years old when he met Melba. Born at Greenwich near London in 1873, he was to live in Australia for twenty-six years; but for all his entanglement in Australian cultural life he refused to be identified as either an Englishman or an Australian. What he claimed to be was a Celt; on his mother's side the proud descendant of Mallory's Cornish King Ban of Benwk and, more recently and prosaically, of the bassoon-playing owner of the Bicton Mills in St Martins. His father, a commercial traveller in the woollen trade, was a descendant of the 17th-century Irish peer Thomas Eyre, Lord Carbery.

As a child Hart was reared on Celtic folk tales and folk songs. In 1920 he met A.E. – the alias of George William Russell, poet laureate of the Celtic revival. He never recovered. Somehow he missed out on the politics, but like a true Celt he enjoyed the awfulness of exile, writing operas on fading Irish themes, quite a number of them under Melba's influence.

Eighteen of his twenty-two operas, 267 of the 514 listed songs (he destroyed several hundred more), and three of his four large choral works were composed in Melbourne for the use of the women of the school. Women were the dominating factor in Fritz's life; he could never resist an invitation. Except one in particular, if, in fact, it was ever made. It is *not* true that Melba bore Hart's bastard son as rumour had it; she was 54 years old when she met Fritz. Her friend, however that may be construed, he may have been, but the elective father of her child? No.

Vocal music and Melba aside, he also found time to write fifteen extended orchestral works, including one symphony, a number of chamber and solo instrumental works, unaccompanied choruses, part songs, transcriptions and arrangements, and a book of poems – published in 1913 as *Appassionata: Songs of Youth and Love.* He left hundreds of paintings and sketches of the Hawaiian Islands (where he died in 1949 after eighteen years as conductor of the Honolulu Orchestra) and no fewer than twenty-three unpublished novels.

LESSONS WITH MELBA

The following extracts come from the diary of Beryl Fanning, one of Melba's earliest vocal students in Australia. She took tuition in 1909 from Melba at the University of Melbourne Conservatorium before the diva adopted the Albert Street conservatorium as her teaching base in Melbourne.

'Monday. 27. 9. 09.

Madam Melba arrived punctually at 10.30 and after a few words from the Prof. and Mr Laver, the real work began. Instead of trying our voices separately we were obliged to sing slow exercises and isolated notes that was more trying than half a dozen songs. Madam was so kind and interested that I really was less nervous with her than any other teacher. She said I had a "a dear little voice", and was good enough to say she would teach me . . .

'September 29th.

This was our first real lesson, and I have never been so interested, or felt more keen – the days will never pass quickly enough between each lesson. As a little outward expression of the gratitude we feel towards Madame it has been arranged that a 3rd subscription shall be paid every lesson, towards a small bouquet to be given to her at the lesson. Madam was most painstaking and generous in her teaching. I sang Grieg's *Princess* and although she found much that was wrong she still was kind enough to say I sang "charmingly". She asked me to go and see her on Sunday and I gathered that she would be adorable enough to let me sing to her then. One cannot go on with a continuous stream of superlative thanks and it is very difficult to show that her extraordinarily generous offer is really appreciated! . . .

'October 3rd 1909.

It was with some little excitement that I went to the telephone this morning – wondering if Melba had forgotten that she had asked me to ring her up! It was she herself who answered – and directly I gave my name she asked me to come at about 5 o'clock – It was such a disgusting day as regards weather that only such a magnet as Melba could have drawn me out, but Dad gave me a hansom over and true to her word Madam was there to the minute and so kind in her manner that I lost what nervousness I had felt on first entering! We were alone together for some minutes, and she asked me a lot about my work and seemed interested in all I said. Miss Alkins [Atkins?] then came in – She is a girl from Tasmania whom Madam thinks a good deal of – and both she and I had a lesson that ought to do us a world of good. I attempted *Si mes [?] iers* and *Mattinata* and although my French was faulty to a degree, I think Madam was pleased with my general intelligence. I was there until 6.30 – and Madam was all more-than gracious. Somehow I seem to lose my extreme nervousness with her – and although she has never raved in any way about my voice, I feel that she finds it better on acquaintance – She is so compelling, so magnetic in her way of teaching, that her

At the age of 10 Hart became a chorister at Westminster Abbey under the direction of Sir Frank Bridge. In 1893 he entered the Royal College of Music where he formed what were to become lifelong friendships with Gustav Holst, William Hurlstone, Samuel Coleridge-Taylor and, later, with Ralph Vaughan Williams and John Ireland and, later still, with Percy Grainger and Peter Warlock.

Hart wrote the librettos for two early Holst operas and for two choral works of 1896–98. He was godfather to Holst's daughter Imogen, whose career as conductor and composer he followed eagerly from half a world away. He remained in correspondence and on visiting terms – there were several return trips 'home' – with some of the best minds working in composition in England, exchanging scores, information, opinions, swapping gossip and generally keeping abreast of developments, Melba acting as go-between on several occasions.

When J. C. Williamson found him in 1909 Hart had some thirteen years of theatrical experience behind him as an actor, as a composer of incidental music and as a musical director with Wilson Barett, of one of the Savoy opera companies, and a touring George Edwards company. Williamson offered him a four year contract to conduct a new comic opera company, playing everything 'post-*Floradora* and pre-*Maid of the Mountains*', as his son Basil has described it.

In late 1913 Hart and composer Alfred Hill founded the Australian Opera League whose first performance, given on the eve of the First World War at the Repertory Theatre, Sydney, included the première of Hart's first opera *Pierette*. Four other operas were presented at the Playhouse, Melbourne, with Melba's direct support, using the resources of the singing school: *Ruth and Naomi* (1917), *Malvolio* (1918), *Deirdre in Exile* (1926), and *The Woman who Laughed at Faery* (1929). Only seven of the twenty-two operas have been performed, though choral works fared somewhat better, mainly through ABC radio exposure when Hart won three of its composer competitions.

In 1924 the Royal College of Music rewarded all this industry by making Hart a Fellow. Melba, ever practical, did it another way. In January 1926 she wrote from Paris:

> I am sure you are glad to learn that The Method is well on its way and that Chappell is doing it. He has now taken the American rights too and we are receiving £500 advance royalties. You ought to receive £250 almost as soon as this letter. *I hope so,* and I am so glad for your sake and for Mary's sake too – and think we shall make a lot of money out of it. Chappell is delighted with it – *Hurrah!* I have called it *The Melba Method* and I have written you and Mary a letter thanking you, etc, – which I think you will both like.[11]

This book was, of course, the famous singing method, ghosted by Fritz and Mary Campbell. In effect it was a routine book of vocal exercises with a commonsense text on the relaxation methods then in general use, but Melba's name worked its usual magic and for a time it sold well. It made no claims to Garcia's kingdom but the derivation is obvious.

Hart later wrote of Melba as a perfectionist, a hard taskmaster and lovable friend 'whose hearty contempt for indifferent work kept her students constantly in fear of her'. Over the years he conducted for her concerts and operatic performances many times in Melbourne and found her 'extraordinarily easy' to accompany since her sense of rhythm was so precise that there was never any doubt of what she intended to do in ritardandos, accelerandos or even pauses. He found her often nervous before a performance but as soon as she went on stage her anxiety disappeared and she became cool and resourceful. Before her final *Bohème* in Melbourne on 27 September 1928 (her last appearance in opera) she showed all the signs of being about to turn and run, but Hart, who conducted, heard her 'calmly save the bacon of one of the singers who went utterly astray' only minutes later.

For fifteen years Hart and Melba continued the Wiedermann–Marshall-Hall tradition of presenting students in opera and in concert, but though Melba lent her name and her girls to these annual events it must be admitted that it was Hart and the staff of the singing school who did most of the work. Melba's restless travelling kept her working time at the conservatorium, and her appearances at its concertising, to a minimum, though her presence seems to have been felt at every turn.

The operas produced by the school during the Melba reign, all of them given at the Playhouse in St Kilda Road, included Purcell's *Dido and Aeneas* (1915, 1917 and 1924); Gluck's *Iphigenia in Aulis* (1916 and 1917), *Orpheus* (1918 and 1926), and *Iphigenia in Tauris* (1919); Hart's *Ruth and Naomi* (1917 in excerpt and 1929 complete), *Deirdre in Exile* (1926), *Malvolio* (1918 in excerpt), *The Woman who Laughed at Faery* (1929); Flotow's *Martha* (*circa* 1923); Beethoven's *Fidelio* (1927); Mozart's *Marriage of Figaro* (1920), *Il Seraglio* (1929) and *The Magic Flute* (1925). In the season immediately after Melba's death Hart's *St George and the Dragon* (1931) was produced, the last of the operas under her immediate influence.

But as well as this training through amateur performance, Melba also pushed her students into contact with professionals whenever possible. For a while after the 1911 opera tour she was telling the English and American press that the quality of young Australian voices was far above that she had experienced anywhere else. It was pure propaganda for the launching of singing careers for several of her girls, but her imported chorus master for that season, Signor Sacerdote, shared her high opinion, so there may have been something more to it than publicity. He told the press that the women of his chorus had

excitement is passed on to you – and one can but work for her. I *dont* suppose she ever intended to *train* our voices – but rather to give us hints, and to teach us special songs that may be used for the concert in December . . .

'Monday 4th.
Before going to Madam at 10.30, we singing students had a French lesson – but Melba arrived to the minute and was with us till close on half past one. I had not much chance of improving *Si mes vers* [sic] but it seemed to go rather better than the day before, and she gave me several little isolated words of praise – and said "Pretty note!" a couple of times. She asked me to bring *Una voce* for next lesson – It was afterwards that I had the pleasure of a drive in her lovely motor – for I acted as guide to the Tait's house where she was lunching. She was most natural and I was struck as I am at each meeting – with her good nature, her real kindliness and her ability. She spoke bitterly of the adverse criticism the papers gave of even this great kindness on her part – the teaching of us girls at the Con! "I do wish I could find a really high soprano – because those wretches say I am too jealous to teach any but contraltos" she said. I am really a good hearted woman and I felt then as if I could have fought the narrow minded creatures who attribute every action to the furtherance of "self" in the eyes of the world. Melba may be spoilt – be the pet of the public and the lion of the song world, but there is marvellous stuff in her, and a

generosity that is worthy of admiration . . .

'Monday Oct. 11th 1909.

Today, instead of the whole class attending en masse, we were divided into two groups – our places drawn in lots – and went in in turns. I was in the second batch, and Madam gave me a most interesting lesson – She praised *Si mes vers* [sic] and *Una voce* – although she altered a great deal of the ornamentations, is to be studied as soon as she can find her own edition. Her cadenzas are much fuller and more advanced – and when I hazarded a doubt as to my ability she said she was sure I could do it . . .

'Monday 18th Oct. 1909.

The lesson was rather more nervous work than usual, as Mrs Barrett and Mother swelled the numbers of listeners! But Madame herself is always so delightfully confidence-inspiring that she is capable of getting out ones "very best" – I don't think mine was a very good "best" this morning, as it was my first lesson on *Le roi d'Ys* [third opera by Lalo] and I scarcely sang two words uncorrected. I always feel so very eager to do well – and if I could not show her how I really wanted to do all she advised – but she is a very understanding person, much as I admire and appreciate her – never inspires me with fear! . . .

'Monday 24th October 1909.

Le Roi d'Ys went better today – Madame said I had made great progress. We had a long lesson of three hours and as I was almost the last, I felt very tired, when it came

the enthusiasm, the love of music, the brains and the voices . . . I would wish for nothing better . . . Yes, they are better, I think, than the chorus of Italy. The voices are the same but the enthusiasm is more. In Italy the chorus is composed of old women, women without intelligence, women without enthusiasm, save for the money. Here the singers are of good family, they love the work. Of course they have not the experience of the choruses in other parts of the world, but that would be a fault easily remedied if they had grand opera here more frequently . . . My only regret is that, having seen this chorus grow to something nearly perfect, it should have to be disbanded.[12]

That first opera chorus assembled by Melba had a few extras, women not associated with the school, professionals and teachers known to her, but the second Melba–JCW company of 1924 was drawn almost exclusively from Albert Street. By 1928 and the third company the chorus was being taken over by experienced professionals. That year Melba moved Hart's *Deirdre in Exile* out of the decent obscurity of the Playhouse for a one night stand at Her Majesty's in tandem with *I Pagliacci* on 22 June with John Brownlee as Conchubor, Lilian Crisp as Deirdre, Lilian Stott as Mrs Larcombe/Lavarcham, and Hart's son Basil as the doctor. Fritz conducted. It was the best Melba could do for Fritz; the Melbourne public remained resolutely uninterested in Australian compositions, let alone opera. Hart could get a hearing for orchestral work once he inherited the Melbourne Symphony Orchestra in 1927 after the death of Alberto Zelman jun., but that was all.

At the end of 1915 war concerts took Melba to America and Canada. She left California on 5 March 1916, en route for home via New Zealand, intending to stay until October and return to North America for opera engagements in November. David Mitchell's death occurred while she was still at sea and left her curiously exposed emotionally. As was her custom under such stress she buried herself in work. As she left Spencer Street station clad in deepest black, sympathisers crowded towards her. She drew Fritz Hart aside: 'Half past ten on Monday', she snapped. And at 10.30 a.m. that day she resumed classes, at her side a new American protégé brought back from Honolulu. The press reported the remark, the arrival of the new girl and the fact that Mitchell left the equivalent of $200 000 to each of his children; only Melba had the use of her capital. Melba refused to comment on any of it. Three months later, at the first students' concert she directed after her return, she was still wearing an elegant version of mourning – black tulle over silk and a circlet of diamonds with a black osprey in her hair – and upstaged the début of her prize pupil, Gertrude Johnson, who was later to found the National Theatre movement and lay the foundations for the Australian Opera.

...ba had a passionate interest in cars. She had a chauffeur ...probably also drove herself. *(Performing Arts Museum)*

Left to right: Fritz Hart, director of Melba's Conservatorium, Melba, her son George Armstrong and George's second wife Evie, *circa* 1924. *(Herald & Weekly Times)*

...ide Coombe Cottage: the drawing-room, the ante-room and ...the medallion) the stables tower, which is inscribed 'East, ...st, Home's Best'. *(Performing Arts Museum)*

Melba *(far right)* arrives in Melbourne with her protégés Stella Power and Beryl Fanning. John Lemmone is on the left of the observation platform. *(Sonia McKillop)*

Melba holding her granddaughter Pamela Armstrong (later Lady Vestey) who was christened at Coombe Cottage in November 1918. *(Melba Memorial Conservatorium)*

Sir John Longstaff's 1923 portrait of Melba with the lights of Sydney in the background. The figure was modelled by Longstaff's housekeeper. *(The Age)*

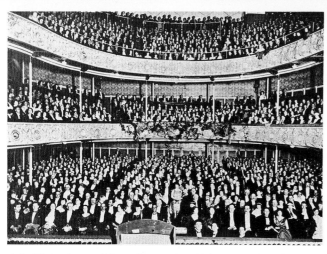

A flashlight picture of the audience at Her Majesty's, Sydney, for the 1924 Melba–JCW season's performance of *La Bohème*. (*Sonia McKillop*)

Above: Melba's farewell to opera in her home town at His Majesty's Theatre, 13 October 1924. The backspread reads: 'Australia's Greatest Daughter, Our Melba'. (*Herald & Weekly Times*)

Left: Queueing for Melba's Covent Garden farewell in 1926. (*La Trobe Library*)

Melba arriving in England by ship in March 1919. (*Performing Arts Museum*)

Programme for the Melbourne end of the 1928 J. C. Williamson–Melba opera season. (*Melba Memorial Conservatorium*)

A programme sent by Melba to Mary Campbell at the Albert Street Conservatorium. (*Melba Memorial Conservatorium*)

In August Melba announced that she was offering a two-year competitive scholarship to the school. There was a flood of applications and in October it was awarded to Doris Leech. During the examining process Melba was distressed to discover that many of the candidates had false teeth and warned 'Such a handicap will prevent the girl becoming a good singer. The plate gives a false resonance to the voice. There is not the same interference if the teeth have been screwed on. This fact ought to be impressed upon every dentist.'[13] Unfortunately, Australians of that generation and the next have been afflicted with bad teeth; but false teeth or not they have continued to gravitate to the opera stage, two baritones among them to my certain knowledge coping with the situation by removing their plates when they sang. Their Australian accents were blamed for the awful diction that resulted, but otherwise no one seemed to mind.

Melba kept up her award for the rest of her life, sometimes adding exhibitions or secondary prizes, but by and large it remained a prestigious scholarship which gave a female singer two years' free tuition at Albert Street, not just lessons in the singing school.

During her first absence from the conservatorium in late 1915 Melba wrote to a director still anxious about being swallowed up by the university conservatorium:

Darling Fritz Hart, Please do not *worry* about anything. We can afford to go on in our little way and be perfectly independent. If only the war would end all would be well. I cannot write any more for I *have fever* ... I sang last night at Springfield with tonsilitis and 102 degrees of fever. Give them all my best love and blessings. The same message to my dear lieutenants and to you.[14]

At the time Fritz's nervousness did not seem justified. A year later she saw the seriousness of Melbourne gossip that challenged the authority of anyone standing in for her. This time she sent Hart a notice to be printed in the prospectus and used in advertisements:

I leave all my Pupils at the Albert Street Conservatorium in the hands of my Lieutenants, in whom I have absolute confidence; and I wish it to be recognised that the vocal tuition they receive is completely in accordance with my own methods, Nellie Melba.[15]

This endorsement went into every subsequent prospectus.

A long stream of letters, brief, light and usually undated, fluttered from the diva to Fritz and her students, written on trains and ships, from hotel rooms and backstage dressing-rooms. In them her concern is genuine, her interest practical and sustained. Through them she kept watch on the daily affairs of the little institution that was to be her only true, if now neglected, memorial:

Dear Fritz Hart, I am a proud woman this morning because I

to my turn. As I had a lift down town in her lovely car I got my lunch sooner than I might have done ...

'Thursday 28.10.09.
All the pupils had a delightful lesson this morning, Madam was specially kind – and as I had gone to Fairlie House before going on to the Con she took me in in her taxi. Mrs Purchase was with us and Lady Carmichael and Miss Tallot [?] came to hear the lessons for about an hour. I had the most satisfying lesson as yet! *Mattinata* was sung through uncorrected and I was almost wondering if it was so bad that she was waiting till the end to heap contumely on my head – When she told me it "was very good" and I knew by her smile that she really liked it ...

'Monday 1st 1909.
It was very disappointing to find that my voice had suddenly disappeared when I started to have a lesson this morning! Madam was sweet about it and said it was the going out at night and so much I had to retire ignominiously and wait till another day! ...

'Tuesday Nov. 9th.
I got on all right today and had a lesson in the *Chant Venetian* which is a divine little thing she used to sing so much the first time she was out here! ...

'Nov. 16th 1909.
It was rather alarming to find Sugden [the *Argus* critic] was to be present at the class today! Madam was in a delightful humour – it was the day following her

successful charity-concert and she seemed in the best of spirits. I had to open the performances with the Chant *Le Roi d'Ys*. She said the former was good – but I always funk the last cadence in *Le Roi d'Ys*. She was most amusing and most kind – said "The only excuse for singing ballads is to sing them well". I can't bear to think what it will be like when all these lessons are over!"[1]

1. Diary of Beryl Fanning, MS 9902, La Trobe Library, State Library of Victoria. Reproduced by courtesy of Mrs Sonia Mackillop, Beryl Fanning's daughter.

consider the performance of last night [Hart's *Ruth and Naomi*] *could be* given at any theatre in any part of the English speaking world with success. The fresh voices and the staging were delightful and I feel sure everyone in the little theatre enjoyed it, but no one enjoyed it more than I did. I congratulate you, the staff and the pupils on the excellent work done and I am amply repaid for anything I have done to help the dear pupils... I am most anxious to hear the rest of your opera. The music is *very fine* of the act you did.[16]

Dear Fritz Hart, I am delighted to hear Mr Harold Browning is joining our Conservatorium for I have heard all about his singing. I tried to go to his recital but I could not manage it. Please tell him that I hope to see him on my return to Melbourne and perhaps he will allow me to hear him give a lesson. Is he teaching Mr Geddes? Such a pretty voice. First concert a great success. I sang *Blackbird*, but badly. Better tomorrow I hope.[17]

Dear Fritz, Please ask *all* the girls to learn *Over There, Australia Will Be There* and *Tipperary*. Thanks so much for help. It [a wartime concert] MUST go with a *great* swing. Nothing but popular things. Please ask Mr Steele to play the organ, it will be great fun having the organ for these songs. I think Dorothy Murdoch might sing *Abide With Me* to the organ.[18]

Dear Fritz Hart, We are jogging along in my private car which is a great experience for Stella [Stella Power, an Albert Street protégé on tour with her]. I am more than pleased with her. She has developed wonderfully and is singing better and better. She often gets double encores at my concerts. Were you not pleased about the Schwab scholarship? I may be returning to Australia for a few months in August so please, I want to give a Greek opera in my garden and use the bathing pool [possibly Gluck's *Iphigenia* I or II or *Orfeo*]. It will be great fun to do this about November or December. It will be quite easy to arrange about the lighting and we ought to have it when it is full moon. Miss Campbell [Hart's assistant] will have a great deal to tell you. [She had escorted Stella Power to Melba from Australia.] I think she enjoyed it but will be glad to get back to her pupils ... We *really must* begin to make the pupils understand who have been at the Conservatorium for more than three years, that they must leave and make room for new ones. I shall be sorry to lose them, of course, but they must fight their own battles and work up their own interpretations now or they *never will*. I shall be glad to give them hints occasionally – another thing I will *not teach* any girl who leaves the Con when I leave. This is *unpardonable* and very rude, so do not allow any absconder to return before I do. Be careful about this.[19]

Dear Fritz, I am wondering how you are getting on with the opera. There is a clever young man here [in Adelaide] who does wonderful scenery. Would you like me to ask him over to help or have you everything? I return on Wednesday. I shall call in at the Con. after 11. I would like a rehearsal for the kindergarten concert [possibly 8 October 1918 for the Free Kindergarten Union of Victoria] on Friday morning at 10 o'clock. I do hope the seats are going well. Adelaide is very slow but I think the concert will be a success. I like the sub leader in *The Age*. Did you write it? [Hart was a contributor, usually as a critic not a staff writer, for this daily.] If only we could get some enthusiasm and intelligence with *some* *one*. It is all so heart breaking. Why don't you do a Mozart before my two Mozart arias to create an atmosphere. I am singing *Porgi d'amour* and *Voi che sapete*, [and] a group of French songs with piano.

It *must* be a big success – so don't think of opera rehearsals till this is over. My love to you all.[20]

Dear Fritz Hart, *Trials* and *tribulations*. Orchestra hopeless! £160 for charity matinee, singing two scenes of opera with piano and organ. Obliged to steal cherub from his commandment (?) etc. etc. etc. What a country! I fly away on 29th November and I wonder if I shall ever *return*. *Heart breaking* and yet I love the Conservatorium and everybody in it – especially *you*.

We opened the sale of tickets at 9 and all were sold at 11 – guinea seats for my matinee on Thursday. . . .

Dear Fritz Hart, I am so very sorry to hear your little son has had an accident and sincerely hope that now all danger is passed. I too had an accident – and I don't know why I was not killed. I enclose two articles which I hope you will read to the pupils. I was doing the vision scene [*Faust*] and when the time came the light would not light. The man on the roof pulled the wrong rope and the whole of the scenery and apparatus fell on me. Of course I was unconscious and it was difficult to find me I was so covered with debris of all sorts. However the doctors decided there were no bones broken. (The train is so rough I can hardly write) so still dazed and feeling very sick I decided to save the performance and sing (there were 17,000 dollars in the house) so don't you think I am plucky. If my head had been three inches further forward, my neck would have been broken – instead of my neck the spinning wheel was smashed to pieces and my left leg from thigh to the toes very bruised and lacerated. Also my left arm, left breast and my back slightly strained. It was a horrible experience. I have had to go on with my performances always in *great* pain, which makes me very sick. Fancy singing *Faust* three times a week and travelling the rest of the time sometimes not arriving until 4 in the afternoon and

THE MYTH

Mrs Donna Shinn Russell's husband, Henry, was impresario at Covent Garden in 1903 and from 1909 to 1914 he was manager of the Boston Opera Company. As a young man in London Melba supplied him with his first singing pupils. In 1924 he was also artistic director of the Melba Grand Opera Company. Mrs Russell writes: '. . . We were house guests at Coombe Cottage . . . I could not forget how badly Dame Nellie had treated a friend of mine, a promising young American girl she had brought out to Italy to study with Maestro M. and then abandoned after a few months. The girl was forced to work as a servant to pay for her tuition, and I used to wonder how small Dame Nellie must have felt when my friend finally reached stardom. Oh yes, her reputation for stinginess was well known'.

Over tea in the garden at Coombe Cottage Melba talked of this reputation for meanness. She happened to use the story of the American as an example of her financial tactics with protégés, not knowing that Mrs Russell was a friend of the girl's.

'Was she referring to my friend? Was I to learn after all these years why Dame Nellie had treated her so outrageously? I was all ears.

'"My protégé had a glorious voice, but she lacked character", continued my hostess. "She was unstable, spoiled, conceited and lazy. The Maestro had been teaching her at my expense for some time but realised that with her temperament there was little hope for her ultimate success; he suggested that I pretend to withdraw my support for a while. I was very upset. What would her admirers in America think of me for my action? She had left home in a blaze of glory and extravagant publicity. Now, no doubt, she would write to her family and call me every name in the devil's book, but in spite of how badly I felt, I agreed with the Maestro that something had to be done. Though I was to continue paying for her lessons, she must believe I had given her up as a poor risk. Maestro M. would then offer to teach her gratis, provided she would help his wife with the housework and the care of their six grandchildren. (Their mother, his daughter, had died in childbirth the year before.) . . . Six months later the Maestro refused to accept any more money from me for her tuition; she was earning her way. Many months later I arranged for her to gain experience in several small opera houses in Italy.''

' ''. . . why didn't you (later) tell her about your arrangement with the Maestro?'' I asked.

' ''Tell her? The memory of one's hardships is the sweetest part of victory. I couldn't deprive her of that!''

'. . . As we walked through the long grass she turned to me and remarked with a chuckle, ''It is said that the reason I gather mushrooms on my estate is because I'm so stingy. Did you know, my dear, that I am supposed to be the meanest woman in the world?''.'[1]

1. *Opera News*, New York, 1 November 1964.

singing in the evening. *And* there are some people who say a singer's life is such an easy one. Ye Gods![22]

Dear Fritz Hart, I was very touched to receive the cable from the staff and students of the Conservatorium. First of all I must tell you that I met your sister at Vancouver and heard her sing. She has taste but the voice is badly posed and I advised her to go and study at our conservatorium and then I think she could make money singing and teaching. At present they are trying to run a chicken ranch which seems a hopeless proposition . . . I am sure you will be sorry to hear that I caught cold in the train coming from Vancouver and have been *very ill* since. I have already missed two performances of *Faust* so you can imagine how unhappy I am. However I am beginning to get better. *I think* and hope to sing in a day or two. I shall be going hard until March and I haven't the slightest idea when I shall be returning. *This is entre nous.*[23]

[On *Elaine*, having sent Hart twelve copies of the opera, possibly intending an Australian performance.] There are some lovely bits in it – the Ballads can be sung with 6 contraltos and 6 sopranos giving the reply to the solo – very pretty. The last act could be sung and acted. This is my favourite act – where Elaine is dying.[24]

I have had a wonderful season and am a very proud and happy woman. It was perhaps the greatest season of my whole career – London, Covent Garden Theatre mean so much to me and I did not realise how much I missed them both until I returned. I shall have a very interesting winter. I first open my autumn season at the Albert Hall where I have already given three *packed* concerts on Sept. 28th, then go through the provinces until the middle of November. I then sing at the Centenary of Gounod at the Grand Opera Paris in December – then I sing at the Théâtre de la Monnaie Brussels in January and then Monte Carlo in March. It is good to come back to all my old loves and to know they must have me – am I blowing my trumpet!!!! . . . I find we sing *well* in Australia and in England the singing is *very bad*. William Boosey is very anxious to engage my pupils here in London.[25]

. . . perhaps I can sympathise with you more than anyone [on Hart's father's death] because when my beloved Daddy was taken from me, *my heart broke, I lost my all.*[26]

Dear Fritz Hart, It was hard (*very*) to say goodbye to you and all those dear pupils of mine because you have all become *very dear to me* and I am already looking forward to the time when I shall be with you again. The little serenades both at the concert and at the station were charming and I am sending you all my warmest thanks for the kind thought and also because I know it was done *con amore*: for I am conceited enough to *know* you all love me just a little tiny bit.[27]

Dear Fritz Hart, This is to say au revoir to you all. It may be a long time before I see you again, but I know things will go on just as though I were there and I leave everything in your very able hands with the greatest confidence. I heard ten voices yesterday. Three I have asked to go to you – two of their voices have been torn to pieces by Goosens. *It is wicked.*

Poor John Lemmone is very ill, a slight stroke which is unthinkable and unbearable for his friends who love him. I handed him a cheque for £2120 – not bad in a week.[28]

'A long time before I see you again' – so it was. Melba did not return until 1921. The little notice recording her faith in her lieutenants in her absence remained in the prospectus but Melba herself acted only by the remote control of the letters. Over the years the pattern was repeated – sudden visitations, long absences. There was no long-term contact even in the retirement years. The day-to-day teaching was done by a staff that remained publicly only a grey background to her but which remained faithful to her methods. A few of those teachers were there at her insistence – Haigh Jackson, one of her touring associates and a Royal Academy of Music graduate, was one. He was a pupil of Jean de Reszke, Chaliapin, Felix Mottl and Sabbatini and had appeared at Covent Garden and the Met. and was at one time a member of the Carl Rosa Company. And there was Francis Harford, formerly on the staff of Manchester College and known as a soloist with the Royal Choral Society, the Bach Festivals in Queen's Hall and at the Joachim, Halle and Handel Society concerts. But the majority were local women with local experience, chosen by Hart solely for their ability to teach. They had to have Melba's approval before being appointed but Hart's judgement and hers generally ran together. Between 1915 and 1931 the teaching staff included Mary Campbell, Constance Browne, Anne Williams, Ruby Gray, Alice Rees-Vogrich, Aimee Elvins, Cecil Outtrim, Guido Cacciali, Ivor Boustead, the composer Mona McBurney who taught Italian in 1920, Jessie Mc-Michael, Harold and Mrs Browning, Jean Center, Lillian Stott, Ethel Ross, Rita Coonan, Vera Crellin, H. Scriven and W. G. Donald.

In her will Melba left £8000 to establish a bequest scholarship 'in the hope that another Melba may arise'. Before the Second World War it was the country's most valuable scholarship for singing. The brief to search for another Melba was taken seriously. Even in war time elimination contests were held as far apart as Western Australia, Queensland and New Zealand and the finalists brought to Melbourne where they sang for the final round dressed in white to honour their patron. Hinemoa Rosieur, a New Zealander, was the first winner in 1937. She was killed in 1940 in an air raid in London. The second,

THEY SAY

John Lemmone: 'What remains as the most wonderful and touching thing about Dame Nellie was her series of concerts for the people . . . In 1921 we had been giving a series of concerts [all] over Australia, and Melba was receiving letters from people all over the country who could not afford to pay guineas, but who wanted to hear her. "What can we do, John?" asked Melba. "We must do something. I think we had better take the Exhibition Building in Melbourne and give concerts for the people."

'I reminded her . . . that this could not be done, as a few years ago when we had given [concerts] there the public had been greatly disappointed. Out of an audience of 14,000 people only about 2000 were able to see and hear Melba. The hall, which was not at all suitable for concert work, had wings branching off the main hall. A stage had been built in the centre underneath the dome, but only the people around her could hear to advantage.

' "The Town Hall has a seating capacity of 2200. Multiply that by five and that gives us 11,000 people." I proposed we arrange the best program we could – one that people would pay a guinea for, engage a good symphony orchestra and charge a universal price of five shillings for admission, every seat to be reserved – and repeat the program at each succeeding concert.

'This was done. It was the month of January. For the convenience of patrons the box plan was opened at 7 a.m. and the whole five concerts were booked out by nine o'clock, while outside the booking offices was a crowd of 10,000 disappointed people who were unable to get seats'

Mr Lemmone got in touch with Melba and arranged for a further series of five concerts. This time the box office opened at 11 p.m. to allow people to book who had come prepared to spend the night waiting for the doors to open. In a few hours these concerts were fully booked, and there was yet another crowd of some 10,000 left disappointed, and a third series was arranged to cope with the demand for seats.

Still the people were not satisfied. There were numerous country people who could not come long distances in the evening who wanted to hear Melba, so a special afternoon concert was arranged commencing at 2 p.m. and finishing at 4 p.m. This was crowded. Among the audience were two old-timers, one 86 and the other 91 years of age, and they waited behind to see Melba. Mr Lemmone presented them, and after expressing their joy at hearing and meeting Melba, the older of the two said the last great singer she had heard was Jenny Lind.'[1]

1. John Lemmone, 'Reminiscences of Nellie Melba' interview by Alma Simpson in *Musical Courier*, 11 April 1931.

Jean Loue, went on to become a concert singer in America. The third Sybil Wiley (1940), won further scholarships to the Juilliard School in New York. But it was the fourth holder of the bequest, soprano Elsie Morrison (1943), whose career at Covent Garden finally justified Melba's posthumous search.

Still, there was one singer Melba personally promoted as her heir, Stella Power, billed by her teacher as the Little Melba, a title with unfortunate connotations that proved to be all too true. The voice was as smooth as Melba's but it was small, and though she had a successful solo début in Melbourne late in July 1917 after a class début on 2? November 1916 under J. and N. Tait's management, not even Melba's influence could place her securely on the operatic stage.

Late in 1917 Melba cabled for Stella and one of her teachers at Albert Street, Mary Campbell, to join her as the associate artist for that year's war-relief concert tour in Chicago, Portland, Seattle, Philadelphia, Brooklyn and in a series given on the west coast. Stella wrote home to Mary Campbell, who had returned to the conservatorium after delivering her charge:

> You can see by paper that we are great style with our Private Car, we are having a lovely time, three concerts are over, thank god and they were a great success, each time the houses have been packed and hundreds turned away . . . Last night we sang at Camp Lewis to 20,000 soldiers . . . Of course it is useless to tell you about Madame's reception, perfectly marvellous and she is that to me, I just adore her . . . We arrived at Portland at 10.30pm and were met by a man who wanted to know if we were the theatrical party and Madame was mad, she gave it to him, it was too funny for words . . . went for a long walk with Madame, Frank and De Bourg and in the middle of the walk we went to a picture show to see Douglas Fairbanks . . . Madame . . . is taking me to supper . . after the concert (I am frightened Auntie) and I haven't got you to say it to now so I say it to Madame and she slaps me. [29]

In June Stella left for Australia. In December she married William O'Rourke at St Patrick's Cathedral with her patron present and a guard of honour formed by members of the singing school. Melba's wedding present was a travelling case with silver fittings, but for all the public blessings she was uneasy about her protégé's future. At the reception she drew the groom aside and told him, 'Stella isn't going to give up her singing. Get her to London as soon as you can'.

By the time Stella reached London Melba had arranged an audition for her at the Albert Hall. The girl began to sing to Melba's accompaniment. Suddenly she stopped playing. 'Are you having a baby?' she demanded. Stella answered, 'Yes'. Melba stormed off acrosss the stage, calling for Lionel Powell, the entrepreneur. When he appeared she shouted, 'The bloody little fool is going to have a bloody baby'.

Stella went on to make her European début in a cloud of matriarchal anger. The critics were lukewarm. Melba kept on pushing her in concerts wherever she could but the operatic career she had hoped for never eventuated, though as a platform singer Stella had a modest success that continued into the 1950s.

There were other protégés – the Americans Elizabeth Parkina and Elena Danieli and the Australian Gertrude Johnson, who had some success at Covent Garden, but another Melba did not appear. Why anyone, let alone Melba herself, should expect it remains a mystery considering the rarity of such voices. Joan Sutherland's emergence in another generation of Australians is just as much a mystery and can hardly be traced to Melba's influence, though the attempt has been made.

Thorold Waters wrote of this urge of Melba's:

Never in the history of great singers has there been one who permitted herself to be so needlessly interested – if only fleetingly – in so many lesser singers from her own and other lands . . . The expectation of so many that the successor to Adelina Patti would be able to push them forward became pathetic. The wonder was that she lent a temporary hand in one after another of these cases. A woman of her exalted place had nothing to gain by it; in some ways, it was inevitable that she should lose, for of a truth it led to a deal of misunderstanding, some of it very wilful, among her fellow-Australians as to the efforts Melba should or should not have made for them.[30]

What Waters and others have failed to understand is that Melba was concerned for more than the one lesser singer – she was a teacher intent on moulding a generation and in this she was very successful.

THEY SAY

'Perhaps her kindest action was her offer to sing at [the] Melbourne auditorium with violinist Zimbalist whose season was failing owing to his following on a long train of visiting virtuosi. The announcement packed the building, and the resultant show was gloriously entertaining, if not particularly artistic. Melba sang to Zimbalist's playing, and he fiddled to her playing. Then they both sang 'Home sweet home' while she pounded the ivories. Finally he kissed her hand and she kissed him on the forehead, while the crowd yelled its approval. Subsequent audiences continued to fall off, however, though the Dame resolutely attended and spurred the fiddler on with her Bravos'.[1]

1. *Bulletin*, 4 March 1931.

Chapter 11

FAREWELL AND MORE FAREWELLS

The success of the 1911 Melba–J. C. Williamson season had long since made Melba certain that a second, even a third season could be just as effective artistically and financially. War put an end to such ambitions but in 1924 and again in 1928 the old partnership was revived to everyone's satisfaction.

The 1924 season began on 29 March with a gala *La Bohème*, Melba as Mimi and Nino Piccaluga as Rodolfo. Eighteen operas were offered *Aida, Otello, Rigoletto, Il Trovatore, La Bohème, Tosca, Madame Butterfly, Carmen, The Barber of Seville, Lucia di Lammermoor, Tales of Hoffmann, Faust, Samson and Delilah, Cavalleria Rusticana, I Pagliacci, Sonnambula, Don Pasquale* and *Andrea Chenier*.

Apart from Melba the sopranos were Toti dal Monte, Lina Scavizzi, Augusta Concato and Aurora Rettore. The mezzos were Aga Lahoska, Phyllis Archibald and Carmen Tornari. The tenors were Dino Borgioli, Nino Piccaluga, Antonio Marques, Alfred O'Shea, Luigi Cilla and Luigi Paradi. The baritones were Apollo Granforte, Alfred Maguenet, Luigi Ceresol, Edmondo Grandini and Antonio Laffi. The basses were Gustave Huberdeau, Umberto di Lelio, Gaetano Azzolini, Alexis Obolensky and Oreste Carozzi. There were some Australians in the minor roles – Stella Power, Violet Concanen, Vera Bedford, Doris McInnes, Rita Miller, Vida Sutton, Rupert Swallow, Rosa Pinkerton, Ruby Dixson and Gordon Peart – most of them from the Melba stable at Albert Street. The conductors were Franco Paolantonio, Arnoldo Schiavoni, Frank St Leger and Piero Crespi, but though the women of the chorus were also Australians the men were Italian imports, a matter that caused mutterings of anti-Australianism in the press.

It was not a cast Melba chose personally. She had gone to Italy with Nevin Tait and John Lemmone in 1923 to select it but was rushed back to London for urgent intestinal surgery before anything was decided. The attendances for the twelve-week Melbourne season totalled 211 200 and the take for the first three nights was a record £6000. Melba had been unsure of the public responding as quickly as was necessary for the Sydney and Melbourne seasons to show a profit and had resorted to the 'beat up' story technique that had been a staple of her American press relationships.

THEY SAY

Wilfrid Thomas, on his first meeting with Melba: 'She advanced towards me and she said, "What's your name?", you see, and I said, "Wilfrid Thomas". I was terrified. And she said, "How old are you?" I said, "Twenty-one, Madam, please". And she said, "My God! I wish I were". Then she said, "All right, sing".[1]

1. K. S. Inglis, *This is the ABC*, p. 165.

Someone phoned the *Sun* in Melbourne with the news that the house in Toorak in which Melba was staying had been burgled. The thief took a bathmat, towels, two bottles of champagne, two of whisky and two of beer – a total of £5 worth. The next day Melba denied all knowledge of the matter but the little news item had been enough to get tongues wagging. Melba was in that day's news – mission accomplished. Later there was a mysterious madman who invaded dal Monte's dressing room to propose marriage, but by then the queues at the box office were lengthening and the story faded rapidly.

When it came time to catch the Sydney express ahead of the company, Claude Kingston, the publicist for Williamson's, was sent along with Melba to cope with the expected barrage of reporters at the station. When Melba read Kingston's press hand-out some miles from Sydney she tore it up in front of him, saying, 'You have a lot to learn. *I'll* speak to them'. Within hours Sydney was flaunting posters proclaiming, 'Melba bitten by fleas on train'. There were hot denials from railways commissioners and an inspection in two states, but she had made her point – Melba was in town and everyone knew her season was about to start.

The two-city season was laconically dubbed 'Melba's Wopera'. Anticipating her Mimi, *Truth* said: 'We heard the old wonder do the part thirteen years ago, with McCormack as Rodolfo. If she does it only half as well today, she will be worth hearing' – which proved to be the case. She sang several times in *Bohème*, *Otello* and *Faust*, ending with her first farewell – to the Australian opera stage – on 13 October.

Not all the publicity that came Melba's way that season was as harmless as the burglar, madman and fleas stories, however. When Henry Russell, artistic adviser for Williamson's, tried to discredit the rival comic opera company that threatened to draw off some of the Melba–JCW audiences by saying publicly that its chorus girls were too scantily clad and showed too much bare leg, he brought on the kind of press attention that not even Melba welcomed. He compounded the offence by denouncing Australian talent at a Rotary luncheon, this time as a matter of self-defence over hiring an Italian male chorus and not an Australian one. Melba once described Russell as 'a clever, dangerous man, and a Jew . . . but I can keep him in order'. Unfortunately she couldn't. Hugh J. Ward, in charge of JCW's operations in Sydney, was so exasperated by Russell's ham-fistedness that during an unrelated court case, when Russell's reputation accidentally entered the proceedings, he called him 'a liar and a serious one at that'.

While all of this was going on Melba was engaged in her own personal publicity campaign – the memoirs expected of retiring divas, a kind of literary equivalent of the farewell appearances, intended to put a rustle in the singer's bank account for the long silences ahead. Melba was following custom rather than looking for cash, though the

MELBA IN POLITICS

'Madame Nellie Melba, noted singer, has entered politics in Great Britain and as soon as she recovers from an illness, it is reported, she will announce her candidacy for a seat in the House of Commons.'[1]

1. Toledo *Blade*, 2 June 1923, Melba file, New York Public Library.

THE MYTH

'I should love to sing in China, should love, even, to climb to the top of some remote mountain in Tibet and sing psalms with the Grand Lama.

'The nearest approach I have ever made to singing songs in Tibet was I imagine when . . . I visited India (on my way home from Australia) and sang a long trill in the Taj Mahal. It was in some ways the most uncanny sensation I have ever experienced. The moonlight, the warm, scented darkness, the soft radiance of marble, and then — my voice echoing out in a trill which never seemed to stop. It went on, long after I had finished, until it seemed that all round my head were circling flocks of clamourous birds'.[1]

1. Melba, *Melodies and Memories*, p. 220.

returns from publication rights were considerable. She wanted to help yet another protégé, but this time her judgement was sadly astray.

In 1923 Melba met English journalist and popular writer Beverley Nichols. He became her constant companion in the period before she left for the 1924 Melba–JCW season in Australia. She soon found she missed his company and sent for him, keeping him by her at Coombe and introducing him everywhere, an urbane, witty, handsome boy of twenty-three. Tongues wagged as usual but Nichols' interests, he implied, did not include the kind of personal service it was presumed he was providing. Nichols' real aim in letting himself be led about in this fashion was to persuade Melba to have him ghost her autobiography. This she did. *Melodies and Memories* was first published in 1925 and was reissued in 1980.

Forty years after he dashed off her memoirs, Nichols wrote that Melba was so intent on appearing in a good light that all the guts and humour had to be deleted:

Everybody had to go down as charming and delicious, whatever her true opinion of them might be. I felt that this was carrying the golden-hearted pose to extremes; nevertheless, I stuck to it manfully . . . she had curious ideas of what might interest the public. When I asked her to give me a few frank words about Tetrazzini, whom she detested and despised, she waved her hands and said: 'Say she was a charming artist! a *delicious* artist!' I pointed out that only yesterday Melba had said that she looked like a cook and faked all her top notes. 'I can't *possibly* say things like that. I must be *generous*'. . . . And so it went on.[1]

Nichols got his own back after Melba's death when his novel *Evensong* was published, a recognisable portrait of his patron in old age. In Australia, where the memoirs were written while Nichols was a guest at Coombe during the 1924 opera season, there was a good deal of outrage at his rough handling of a local heroine, though the rest of the world seems to have been merely amused by this elegant if spiteful misrepresentation. Its author wound up admitting that he had once said to Melba: 'I should like to write a book about the sort of woman you might have been if you had not been you'. She replied, 'Go ahead. Everybody will say it is me, but I don't care a damn'. So the novel about a great but faded diva giving one last farewell performance after another went onto the shelves.

Melba cooled to Nichols only late in the piece. She told friends she was disappointed that he had chosen to align himself with what she saw as a school of cynical young writers. Nichols sold the serial rights of the memoirs to *Liberty* magazine in America and negotiated book rights in New York and London, receiving one half of the fees. The profits were enough to enable him to buy a house and a car, to hire a butler and to embark on a career as a popular writer. When he met Melba he was a young reporter on the *Daily Mail* who had come to England to get 'the woman's angle' on a famous English murder case. When they parted he was independently wealthy. In 1949 Nichols wrote of the Melba exercise:

> Melba, I decided, must write her autobiography, or rather must permit me to write it for her. Her brain was a treasurehouse of the sort of material for which editors, as Fleet St had taught me, were prepared to pay through the nose. Hers was still a great name in England and America; the gossipy autobiography was at its highest peak of popularity; all I had to do was to take down these stories as she told them at the dinner-table, string them together, sprinkle them with an appropriate coating of sugar – for it was essential, if we were to obtain really large figures for the serial rights, that the central figure should be presented, not only with a golden voice but also with a golden heart – and then, take them into the market to seek the highest bidder.[2]

When the autobiography appeared Melba had decided that the time had come for her to retire. For her official Australian farewell in opera she gave *La Bohème* at a charity night for limbless and tubercular ex-soldiers in His Majesty's Theatre, Melbourne. With the boxes at £100 each it was hardly surprising that Melba raised £18 000 from the event. Radio 3LO broadcast the performance by landline for the inauguration of the new service. Joan Lindsay, reporting for the *Herald*, wrote:

> Few cared how she sang, although if there is a time limit to the fresh glory of even the greatest of voices, there is none to the unrivalled stage and musical artistry which is Melba's. But the honor which was paid last night, first in a breathless quiet and later in an ascending and tumultuous clamor, was paid perhaps more to the very rare personal character than to the glorious voice.[3]

In a theatre hung with gum leaves, before a background of globes flashing out 'Australia's Greatest Daughter, Our Melba', and wearing a cape of gilded laurel leaves presented by the cast, Melba bowed herself out under a storm of flowers and streamers, cheering and cooees from a tearful audience. Next day the press was full of telegrams from notables all over the world wishing her well in her retirement. But, of course, it was not the end.

The post-war years were full of tours – farewell tours after 1924 – and though the pace was not quite as frantic as it had once been, it was still taxing. By 1926 Melba was ready to say her farewells to Covent Garden and on 8 June she sang from its stage for the last time. London society, royals and all, turned out for the night. She gave the second act of *Roméo et Juliette* with Charles Hackett as Roméo and Jane Bourguignon as the nurse, and conducted by Percy Pitt; the

MELBA'S PORTRAIT

'Melba believed in herself. One day we were having tea in her trophy-strewn sitting-room at the Empress Club, and upon an easel was a recently painted portrait of the diva – a solid, elderly woman looking from the canvas with rather supercilious disdain. Judgment was invited upon it. We – a parson, a young *protégée*, the journalist who should always be last and least in any company – acquitted ourselves of our delicate task as well as we could. But our hostess pooh-poohed our attempted appreciations. She was not interested in the painter's art. She was interested in herself. "I should never have been Melba if I'd looked like that", was her comment.'[1]

1. H. E. Wortham quoted in Colson, *op.cit.*, p. 220.

opening of the last act of *Otello* with Bourguignon as Emilia, and conducted by Vincenze Bellezza; and the third and fourth acts of *La Bohème* with Aurora Rettore as Musetta, Browning Mummery as Rodolfo, John Brownlee (in his Covent Garden début) as Marcello, Frederic Collier as Schaunard, and Edouard Cotreuil as Colline, with Bellezza again conducting. Most of the performance, including Melba's farewell speech, was, unknown to Melba, recorded by His Master's Voice.

Brownlee was Melba's choice. She had met him in 1922 when he was still an accountant and singing was a sideline. She heard him in a Melbourne Philharmonic Society performance of *Messiah* and went backstage afterwards to invite him to visit her at Albert Street, which he did. She advised him to give up figures for singing. He was so excited at the end of the interview that he grasped one of Melba's hands between both of his, almost crushing it. She was wearing a large ring which cut into her fingers under the pressure making her start back in pain. She slapped Brownlee's hands away. As he wrote: 'My action reflected a lack of composure, and composure was important to Melba'. When he arrived in London a year later she took Brownlee to Dinh Gilly, at one time a baritone at the Met. during Gatti-Casazza's regime, for vocal training. For a time the protégé lost touch with his patron but one night in Paris when he was singing at the second-rate Trianon-Lyrique in Gounod's *Mireille*, Melba was in the audience. She liked what she heard and summoned him to sing duets next day at Bemberg's apartment in the Rue Victor Hugo, where she was staying. Brownlee wrote:

> She was sixty-seven [in fact sixty-five] and she sang beautifully. Later she took me along to some parties where we performed duets together. Fantastic parties! Looking back now, I almost feel they never happened. I remember the soirées in the house of Boni de Castellane, when the large place was lit by hundreds of candles. Women wearing exquisite gowns and wonderful jewels and men in full evening dress walked between rows of liveried footmen. The powerful and the rich and the famous of the whole of Europe were there, but Melba was always the center of attraction, the undisputed queen of these parties. There was something electrifying about her mere presence. She was more than the greatest prima donna of her time. She was a dynamic personality that attracted people magically wherever she went.[4]

Then, out of the blue, Melba asked if he'd sing at her farewell and did he know the role of Marcello in *Bohème*? He'd never heard the opera but said yes and learned the part in a week, rehearsing in Melba's rooms with Maurice Renaud as tutor and with Renaud's costumes. Brownlee thought that much of the audience for the Covent Garden farewell had come with dire forebodings that they were to witness an embarrassing fiasco. There was a lot of open talk of being sorry for the old lady whose marble bust stood, decked with flowers, at the head of the foyer staircase; but for all that, Wechsberg wrote:

The auditorium was a sea of gowns and tiaras and uniforms and decorations and white shirtfronts. The atmosphere was charged almost beyond endurance. [But] Melba's ordeal became Melba's triumph. She confounded her staunchest admirers. She sang so beautifully that the years seemed to recede as in a fairy tale, and there stood again the great prima donna of a quarter of a century ago. The voice had almost a youthful charm and freshness. The heavenly legato was still there, and the wonderful technique. She was a miracle. The people who had come out of a sense of duty were as in a trance. Then they went wild with excitement. After the last act of *La Bohème*, the curtain came down and the stagehands quickly arranged all the flowers that Melba had received. When the curtain went up, she stood in front of a six-feet-high sea of flowers. In all my life at the opera I've never heard another ovation that had such overtones of love, affection and adoration. Only the supposedly cold English can bestow such a tribute upon an artist whom they worship.[5]

In less ecstatic tones the London *Telegraph* reported:

It were stupid to say that time has not had an effect. It certainly has; but even so, if a little of its old mellowness is gone, no singer, not even the youngest of the day, is steadier in tone, or hits the notes, as it were, more precisely or accurately. For Dame Melba, the excessive *vibrato* and and *tremolo* so commonly found today is not, and never was characteristic. The art is still there as shown in the extraordinarily touching singing of the *Salce!* and the *Ave Maria* from *Otello* . . . a colossal night of music and a glorious exhibition of the noble art of singing as singing should be.[6]

Millions heard the selections from *Bohème* and the farewell speech on radio and were as moved as Melba herself was by her farewell words. At the end she broke down and wept, as did many in the audience. But it was not the first time she had been heard on British radio. As far back as June 1920 she had featured in England's first broadcast concert and in July of that year one of her concerts was broadcast from England by wireless-telephone to Sweden, Spain, France, Germany, Holland, Scotland and Ireland, and throughout England itself.

Melba's official farewell London concert took place at the Royal Albert Hall on 25 June 1926, with Sir Henry Wood conducting and John Brownlee, Lionel Tertis (viola) and Harold Craxton (piano) as the associates. Melba sang 'Addio' from *Bohème*, the 'Ave Maria' from *Otello*, 'L'amero' from Mozart's *Il Ré Pastore*, 'Clair de lune' by Szulc,

THEY SAY

Tommy Cochran, the friend of her last years, wrote: 'And Melba could be terribly sentimental . . . wherever she travelled she always carried some tapestries, ornaments and family photographs so that her rooms always gave an impression of home: a private personal look; the Melba touch.

'She always carried with her a little silver kettle. Fastnidge, her maid and dresser for many years, said of this: "Melba loved to hear her kettle singing. Even when she did not want any tea she would ask me to put the kettle on. She loved to hear the water boiling, and the cheery whistling noise of the steam . . . " Melba's [kettle] was willed to her grand-daughter with an injunction that she should always cherish it . . .

'Melba's attention to detail in opera was one characteristic. When singing Desdemona she always brought her own bed linen for the death scene; the covering of the bed was old original velvet from Venice, and the tapestry on the *prie dieu* where she sang her ageless *Ave Maria* was some matchless brocade that she had found in Italy. Her dressing room was always neat and tidy; everything was hung up, nothing was left lying about'.[1]

1. Tommy Cochran, 'Around the World in Eighty Years', pp. 255–6.

'Chanson Indoue' by Rimsky-Korsakoff, and 'Serencole' by Richard Strauss. The encores were 'Voi che sapete', 'Comin' through the rye', Tosti's 'Goodbye' and 'Home sweet home'.

She sang again at a charity performance in aid of the Sadler's Wells Theatre Fund at the Old Vic on 7 December 1926, giving the last act of *Otello* and the last two acts of *La Bohème*. After the Australian tour that followed she sang in what was indeed her last public performance in England on 5 October 1929 at the Brighton Hippo-drome, again for charity – the Sussex Eye Hospital. But there was still one semi-public appearance to go – at a charity concert at the Hyde Park Hotel in May 1930, according to Wechsberg. Her com-panion of the time, Tommy Cochran, says she appeared a month later at the Park Lane Hotel in Piccadilly, in aid of the Children's Adoption Association, wearing a Natier-designed platform gown of blue voile under a chinchilla stole, a long Cartier diamond necklace glittering as she breathed. She left for Australia again a few weeks later and was seen off by John Brownlee and his wife: 'Melba had always been casual about departures', he records.

> She was going away so much. It was bye-bye, see-you-soon, the smile and wave of the hand. But that day she broke down and cried as the boat train pulled out. She knew in her heart that she would never come back.[7]

Between 1922 and 1928 Australian pianist Lindley Evans was Melba's accompanist for tours of England and Australia. He remembers her practising assiduously for these concerts, a daily ritual of scales and vocalises as well as work on the repertoire, no matter how well worn. He found her to be nervous before a concert even then, but then she lost all trace of it once on stage. In her last years she began to explore music that her audiences were reluctant to accept from her, often keeping it a strictly private practice – Debussy, Chausson, Duparc, Richard Strauss, Rachmaninov, Fourdrain and others.

During the First World War Melba had formed a special friendship with a shipping clerk from Dalgety's, Tommy Cochran, described by one columnist as her aide-de-camp. For the rest of her life Cochran was her confidante and sometime companion. In his memoirs, 'Round the World in 80 Years', he speaks of her as a simple, warm-hearted, lonely woman, grateful for her gifts as a singer but searching for appreciation of herself as a person beyond the voice. And it is true that in the letters she wrote to him the public Melba disappears and the woman Cochran knew emerges. Sarah Bernhardt's death figures melodramatically in the ghosted memoirs, for example, but Melba's real feelings were kept for Cochran:

> Sarah is gone and I am sad – the passing of one of the greatest women the world has ever known. I saw her a month ago – it is

too sad – we both realized it was the great farewell and she clung to me as though she felt I could help her – She said 'you have always the golden voice and me, I will die.' Poor Sarah.

Tommy dear I am not well and I wonder if I am cracking up (between us) I don't much care if I do go, I don't feel I have much left to live for – what a tragedy life is. I had to have another septic tooth out yesterday and another has yet to come out and I who have always been so proud of my teeth . . . The income tax people threatened to writ me. I gave them 500 pounds some time ago to keep them quiet. Today I was forced to give them a cheque for £3462/17/8. It is killing me and taking all the spunk out of me – I can't go on.[8]

I give my first concert at the Albert Hall on May 2nd next Sunday. It is such a sight to see 12,000 people all for poor little me – I feel so small. I am not [to] sing at Covent Garden. I dislike Beecham and his methods. I shall only sing if the King commands me. I love *London* and England all the same. I am returning to Australia next year about the end of February so don't you dare to leave before then. Must have my court jester otherwise I should die of ennui. I am so slim and have such a supple figure and complexion like a two year old – so you may fall in love.[9]

Dear Tommy, I am so ill and am going into a Nursing Home on Wednesday. You can imagine how depressed I am – something internal: but this is of course quite 'entre nous.' Would you like to come up with Evie and me tomorrow and spend the night, and take me to the hospital?[10]

The Evie in this last letter was George's second wife, Evie Doyle, whom he married in 1913. She was a mezzo soprano of some talent and sometimes appeared with Melba in her war-relief concerts. When Evie's first child died shortly after birth, Melba was devastated:

I can't write to you because I am too heart broken, such a beautiful baby boy weighing 9lb 2 oz – fair with big blue eyes – and what happened. *No one knows* – he cried and he cooed – God! what a tragedy, if you could see Evie's heart broken eyes you would cry like a baby. They are worrying me and if I don't get away I shall have a nervous breakdown . . . I am heart broken and don't care what happens to me.[11]

At times her own illnesses brought out a streak of irony: 'I shall meet you at Scotts tomorrow – but I must be at the Conservatorium

THE MYTH: RECEIVED WISDOM

Sir Thomas Beecham, in *A mingled chime*: 'I am inclined to think that she was wanting in a genuine spiritual refinement which deprived the music of some virtue essential to our pleasure; and perhaps it was for this reason that in the maturer culture of the Continent she had comparatively little success, her popularity being confined to England and those other Anglo-Saxon communities where the subtler and rarer sides of vocal talent are less valued.'[1]

1. Quoted in Melba, *op. cit.*, p.x.

THEY SAY

at 2.30 as Their Excellencies are going – I am very ill and the doctor thinks *gall stone. Such is life*.[12]

Occasionally she was irritable and censorious:

I am still stunned and cannot understand and don't know what to do for the best – only wait and pray I suppose. I fortunately have Susan Birth with me who is so helpful and such a darling. I did my cure at Evrain les Baines [*sic*]. I am now here for some sea bathing and sun baths. The beaches here are dreadful and I hate the way they go about *naked*.[13]

But in spite of encroaching age and illness she was determined not to let it get the better of her, summoning Cochran whenever she needed distraction: 'Shall we continue our diet – same place same time – and shall we continue jaunting and perhaps to South Yarra. Rather depresses'; and, 'Come at one to Scotts and gobble quickly a fish with me. I just feel I want to see you – and *that is all*. What fun. N.'.

On 2 March 1927 Melba gave what was advertised as a 'Home-Coming Concert, the First Concert of the Farewell Tour!' at the Auditorium, Melbourne. Lindley Evans was her accompanist and solo pianist, John Lemmone her flautist, and the bass, Stuart Robertson, was the associate. The Melbourne Symphony Orchestra under the joint conductorship of Alberto Zelman jun. and Fritz Hart was to supply the backing and separate orchestral items, but Zelman had been ill for some time and Fritz took over. Zelman died the following day.

A month later, on 9 and 13 April, Melba gave two concerts in the Sydney Town Hall. For the first of these she sang 'Porgi amor', 'Voi che sapete', with an encore of the 'Aubade' from *Le Roi d'Ys*, then the Prayer Scene from *Otello* with three encores – 'Home sweet home', 'Comin' through the rye' and 'Swing low sweet chariot'. She ended with Szulc's 'Claire de lune', Richard Strauss' 'Serenade', in English (and according to a witness, very fast), and 'Waters of Minnetonka'. For the second concert it was 'Addio' from *Bohème*, encored with 'Voi che sapete', then the Prayer Scene from *Otello* encored with 'Swing low sweet chariot', 'Se saran rose' and 'Annie Laurie'. Finally she gave 'Le temps des lilas', Rimsky-Korsakoff's 'Chanson Indoue', Richard Strauss' 'Serenade' (repeated), and, to her own accompaniment, 'Home sweet home'.

In May she sang the National Anthem and 'Land of hope and glory' at the opening of the new Parliament House in Canberra, then toured New South Wales, Queensland, Victoria and South Australia by car, trailing Evans, Lemmone and Robertson in her wake. It was a joyous, back-country affair of bad roads and worse pianos in draughty, dingy halls but warm, homespun farming people. She raised money for anyone who wanted it, from the Red Cross to the Shire of Lilydale, when it needed new lavatories for the local park. But this last tour

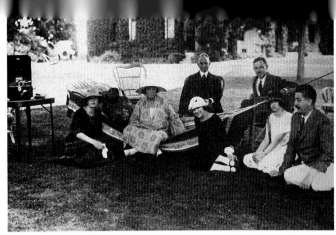

...lba, in the white decorated hat (*left*), promoting Australian ...ports with Lady Kyne, wife of the Australian High ...mmissioner (*centre*), in London in the 1920s. *(Performing ...ts Museum)*

Melba with visitors at Coombe Cottage in the late 1920s. John Lemmone is seated behind at her left. *(Mitchell Library)*

...elba and Fritz Hart with women from her Albert Street ...onservatorium in January 1927. *(Herald & Weekly Times)*

Melba being 'adored' by Beverley Nichols, ghostwriter of her 1925 autobiography. *Left to right:* Mrs W. J. Cowell, Nichols, Melba and Lady Bridges. *(The Age)*

Above: Melba the chef at a chop picnic for her conservatorium students at Coombe, November 1927. *(Melba Memorial Conservatorium)*

Left: Melba sings the National Anthem for the opening of Federal Parliament in Canberra on 9 May 1927. *(La Trobe Library)*

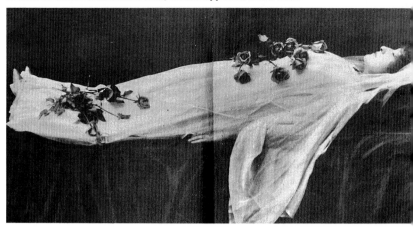

Left: A portrait of Melba at Coombe Cottage, 1931, by Spencer Shier. *(La Trobe Library)*

Below: Melba had herself photographed as the dead Juliette with the proviso that the print was not to be released until she died, when it appeared world-wide.

Left centre: Melba with her godchild Isobel Brownlee and her aunt, outside Notre Dame d'Auteuil after the child's christening on 20 September 1930.

Crowds line Collins Street, Melbourne, for the start of the funeral procession on its way to Lilydale cemetery. *(Herald & Weekly Times)*

Left: The grave in Lilydale cemetery. Mimi's words, 'Addio senza rancore', are cut into the step. *(Performing Arts Museum)*

was made primarily for the benefit of her old friend, John Lemmone, as a tribute to him for his sterling service in her cause. In any case, as she told her flautist, 'I must sing or I will die'. Twice these last concerts were broadcast, once from Brisbane in 1927 and once, a year later, from Healesville in Victoria when she sang for a Soldier's War Memorial Fund.

On 12 May 1928 the third and last Melba–Williamson opera season was launched in Melbourne, but Melba was not billed as one of the singers to appear. The top line names of 1924 were re-engaged – Toti dal Monte, Lina Scavizzi, Aranghi Lombardi, Fernando Antori, Apollo Granforte, Angelo Minghetti, John Brownlee, Browning Mummery and Elena Danieli – for the thirty-one operas given: *Adriana Lecouvreur, Aida, Andrea Chénier, The Barber of Seville, La Bohème, Madame Butterfly, Carmen, Cavalleria Rusticana, The Daughter of the Regiment, Don Pasquale, Faust, Fedora, Gianni Schicchi, Lodoletta, Lohengrin, The Love of Three Kings, Lucia di Lammermoor, Manon Lescaut, I Pagliacci, Rigoletto, Soeur Angelica, Il Tabarro, The Tales of Hoffmann, Tannhäuser, Thaïs, Tosca, La Traviata, Il Trovatore, Turandot, The Valkyries* and, on 22 June, in tandem with *I Pagliacci*, Fritz Hart's *Deirdre in Exile*.

But the season's profits were not all that the Tait brothers, acting as JCW, had hoped. For one thing Melba's share of the proceeds ran at £3000 a week, and the conductor and director, Gaetano Bavagnoli, insisted on a standard that required heavy expenses for extra rehearsals. On top of that it was decided to run both Italian and German works in the same season, which made extra Wagnerian voices necessary. The Taits maintained that the season was run for the sake of Australian music and not for huge profits, but the press and the public were not inclined to agree with the brothers.

Melba gave her final opera performances (as distinct from official farewells) as afterthoughts to, not as part of, the 1928 seasons in Melbourne and Sydney. In Sydney she was heard on 7 August in acts 2, 3 and 4 of *La Bohème* with Danieli, Mummery, Brownlee and Fernando Antori; Gaetano Bavagnoli conducted. It was followed by the Prayer Scene from *Otello*. At the Saturday matinée of 11 August she sang a complete *La Bohème*, according to a member of the audience, 'with most of the high notes missing'. In Melbourne at the matinée of 27 September she gave the third and fourth acts of *La Bohème* and the same *Otello* excerpt as at Covent Garden in 1926: 'with the difference that her voice cracked on the final phrase of the *Otello Ave Maria*'.

Immediately after this matinée she and the company left for Adelaide, where on Tuesday 2 December 1928 she was to sing one last *La Bohème*. She was due to leave Australia with her protégé Elena Danieli on 6 November; Melba intended Danieli to be promoted in a concert tour of England, then to appear at Covent Garden. By

There's Peche Melba and
  ham, and chicken and
  jelly;
In fact, everything's there
  excepting Dame Nellie.

There's a butcher's horse on
  Toorak Road
That gallops like mad with a
  double load,
And never, I wean, had a
  butcher's cart
Borne such a freight of chops
  and Art.

For Desdemona and
  Marguerite
Reclined at ease on the
  butcher's meat;
But the butcher drove for
  Dame Nellie's sake
And never he drove with so
  much at steak.

There's a clatter of hoofs at
  Stonnington door
And the guests all stare; and
  an aide says 'Lor!'
While his Lordship gasps,
  'Do I wake or dream?'
If it isn't the meat, then it's
  La Boheme!

Though he might well doubt
  for 'twas past belief
That a guest should come
  with the veal and beef,
Till the driver spoke, 'If y'
  please, y'r Honner;
Will you take your order, one
  Prima Donner;
And a finer one you couldn't
  wish.'
And His Ex cried, 'Right! Hi!
  bring a dish!'[1]

1. Cochran, *op.cit.*, pp. 243–5.

THE VOICE

John Amadio, Australian expatriate flautist and one of Melba's obbligatists, said, 'I shall never forget her voice. Of course she was miraculously controlled. The one outstanding quality she had was the steadiness of her voice. If you hear any of her old recordings put on now, even with the imperfect recording of her day, you'll notice the wonderful pure steadiness – like Caruso!'[1]

Sir Bernard Heinze, Australian conductor and Ormond Professor of Music at the University of Melbourne during Melba's last years in Melbourne, wrote: 'A young fresh beautiful voice. Full of lustre, full of beauty, clear and pure. And that was one of the most extraordinary things about her voice, I think more than anything else, the absolute purity of it. There was no visible effort to the naked eye. There was of course a physical effort of her own, but it created no disturbance to her physical being. The sort of thing that one sees so frequently in other artists, you know, the flushing of the face or the filling of the throat – nothing of that sort with her. The thing flowed freely and with the greatest possible beauty. It was helped of course by the fact that she was a woman of extremely good constitution. She was a powerful woman but not fat. She was well built and a big woman but it was all good strong earnest being'.[2]

1. Thompson, *op.cit*, p. 16.
2. *Ibid*.

January 1929 Melba hoped to be in Paris where 'private interests' were to discuss plans for a Melba Conservatorium as a training ground for young instrumentalists as well as singers. The project was to be under Melba's direction, but she was determined not to agree to the proposals unless a hostel was added, as she said, 'to see that students are correctly fed and encouraged to guard their physical as well as their mental development. There are many pitfalls in Paris'. But she announced that she would not return to Australia for two years and it would seem her long-range plans did indeed include this school.

Melba said farewell from perhaps too many stages, but in spite of the derogatory phrase that entered the Australian vernacular – 'more farewells than Nellie Melba', it is debatable whether she held the record for the field. The holder still seems to be Adelina Patti. In any case the phrase has been coined out of popular ignorance of a common practice. An earlier tradition permitted a great performer to declare a final farewell in the places where a reputation was made. The profits were the equivalent of a pension. The more famous the performer, the more places there were to exact the toll. Some of them overstepped the mark, at which point the audiences stayed away. That never happened to Melba.

The farewell speeches were far less common – notably at Covent Garden, when a farewell letter in her own hand was reproduced in the programme; but for Australians her real farewell had been made on 13 October 1924 when, from the stage of His Majesty's she proclaimed:

I have done my best ... I have tried to keep faith with my art. For all that Australia has done for me, for all the beauty that she has shown me, for all the love she has offered, I wish to say, thank you from the bottom of my heart ... I never was prouder than I am tonight to be an Australian woman.[14]

The same day every paper in town carried her final letter to the Australian public. On Coombe Cottage letterhead paper and monogrammed with her initials, it read:

I have to say today a very difficult word – 'Farewell' – but it helps me to know that the word contains a heartfelt wish for welfare. To my fellow Australians I wish all good, happy to [have] known myself the object of their sympathetic affection, proud to feel that my voice has been raised not only in song, but to make the big world outside through me, understand something of the spirit of my beloved country. Nellie Melba.[15]

The voice and the woman lingered, fading, until 1931 when legend took over. Today all that remains is that legend, a diffused teaching heritage, and the discs she made in the early days of recording. But where the recordings were once considered irritatingly imperfect and a travesty of the voice by a generation impatient with a new technology, they are now being heard with retuned perception.

Melba made her first recordings for her father – some sources say in London, others in Australia – as early as 1902. Some time later she approved of test pressings made by the Gramophone Company from the March 1904 sessions recorded in the drawing-room of her London home in Great Cumberland Place.

There were already a bevy of great voices available on phonograph recordings, ranging from Caruso to Calvé, Chaliapin to Santley, but Melba had distrusted the medium until Landon Ronald, then a Gramophone Company employee, persuaded her to make trials. She allowed the 1904 London tests to be pressed and sold commercially only when a royalty on each copy sold was agreed to; she would not settle for the customary fixed fee for each recording session. Her contract stipulated that she was to receive a shilling more than was paid the year before for the Tamagno recordings which sold for a pound; in other words she sold at a guinea a disc. Melba and Patti were the two great voices that had eluded the Gramophone Company. With Melba enlisted Patti gave in and in 1905 provided the late vintage sound that spurred Melba into trying new methods as techniques improved and to re-record items in order to preserve on disc something less worn and unrepresentative than the aged Patti had managed.

Between March 1904 and December 1926 Melba made what are now referred to as the London and the American recordings, though her one Parisian recording is included in reissues of the London items. In 1907 she began recording for the Victor Company. She was 42 years old when the first London sessions were taken and 65 years old at the time of the last takes – a mid to late vintage picking, most of it transmitted via techniques of the acoustic pre-electric period of recording (1877–1925) when phonograph cylinders and gramophone discs were made by mechanical means.

Thomas Alva Edison's 1877 invention had been turned to commercial use for the transcription of court proceedings and office dictation by Chichester A. Bell (a cousin of Alexander Graham Bell's) and Charles Sumner Tainter. They founded the American Gramophone Company in 1887 to turn out dictating machines using wax cylinders. That same year the first disc gramophone was patented by Emile Berliner, a Washington inventor who used a lateral-cut groove on a greased zinc disc.

Edison, alerted to new possibilities, improved his machines and marketed them. In 1888 Gianni Bettina, a wealthy Italian married to New York socialite Daisy Abbott, bought one and began to record his friends from the Met. He persuaded Melba to sing for him but so far the takes have not surfaced.

In March 1900 Lionel Mapleson, librarian of the Met., bought an

THEY SAY

'In the 1920s Australia's Madame Melba was occupying a large Adams place in Mayfair – furnished with good solid Chippendale in place of the gold stuffed divans and second-rate Louis Seize she had previously admired – Melba was in her early sixties, her hair dyed a soft black, her jewels had been fashionably reset, and her Covent Garden farewell performance was behind her. But her voice was still of miraculous beauty. She agreed to sing into an audiometer, a device invented for photographing sound. Her auditors asked her to sing middle E, then she sang a scale rather grumpily. She sang to A flat. She was flickering her fingers restlessly and staring at the machine as if it were a hostile audience. Then Melba sang a trill. A few days later, after recording the voices of several other celebrated sopranos, the auditors returned with the graph-like photographs. The results were astonishing and conclusive. All the other singers' trills had strayed all over the film, varying in line and shape. But Melba's trill might have been drawn by a geometrician. It was uniform, parallel and flawless.

'Melba's reaction was typical. She observed that science was a wonderful thing. She also expressed the hope that her perfect trill might be reproduced across three columns of the *Daily Mail* accompanied by the inferior trills of her rivals. "That would show them", she said.'[1]

1. Dame Nellie Melba's trill, unsigned typescript, MS 1123, State Library of New South Wales.

NEVILLE CARDUS SUMS UP

'Melba was in the late forties when I first heard her sing, but her voice was still a remarkable instrument, with only a few worn places in the highest reaches of her two-and-a-half octave span. In her most brilliant *fioritura* every note was as clear as a bell, and as individual as a star; she tossed off a high B flat with the ease of a great tennis-player lobbing a ball over the net. It is doubtful whether there ever has been a woman singer whose vocalism was so easefully controlled. It seemed just as natural with her as talking. To this day, the connoisseurs talk about the beauty of Melba's long shake at her exit after "Caro nome" in *Rigoletto*.

'In 1894, Bernard Shaw, . . . writing of Melba's performance of Juliette, expressed the following, for him, ecstatic opinion: "You never realize how wide the gap between the ordinary singer who simply avoids the fault of singing obviously out of tune and the singer who sings really and truly in tune, except when Melba is singing".

'Melba's perfect command of intonation remained with her to the end; I heard her at her last performance in opera at Covent Garden, when she was sixty-three years of age, and in Mimi's death scene in *Bohème* every note was of such perfect pitch that you could almost see the printed music. It was certainly extraordinary vocalism to come from the throat of a character supposedly about to give up the ghost . . .

'And this brings me to Melba's very serious limitations as an artist. Never

Edison wax-cylinder recording device for use in the prompt box during actual stage performances of opera. On 28 January 1901 he recorded Melba in the second part of the Queen's air from *Les Huguenots*, which she sang in French. In 1937 the cylinder was re-discovered and transferred to a 78 r.p.m. disc as part of the historic Mapleson transferrals, which included some 120 other recordings. Singers who had known Melba – Geraldine Farrar and Emma Eames among them – declared that the Mapleson recording had the true sparkling sound of Melba in spite of the wheeze and thump of the machinery used. There was common agreement that the commercial recordings were poor by comparison, with the possible exception of the 1904 operatic recordings. At the moment the authenticity of the Mapleson–Melba cylinder is under discussion precisely because of its perfection but it remains in the discographies, even if it bears a question mark.

By 1901 the American Victor Company, an associate of the English Gramophone and Typewriter Company, had cornered the American disc market. Edison continued with the cylinder techinque. At the time there was a continual exchange of matrices between aligned companies, making the most important issues available on both sides of the Atlantic. In 1903 the Columbia Company in America began to compete for artists. In Europe the pioneer Zonophone Company was bought out by the Gramophone Company, but the French Pathé Company remained intact. In Italy the Fonotipia Company and its French and German associates, the Odean group, recorded exclusively from the vast pool of Italian and German opera houses, until the English and American firms began to send teams to record in the field. But the results of the acoustic methods used universally suffered severe restrictions of dynamics and of frequency range, though the human voice usually came off better than instruments. Electrical recording, begun in the mid 1920s, expanded the dynamic and frequency range and permitted larger groups to be satisfactorily re-corded. What had been primarily a singer's market now became swamped by orchestral sound, though it was hamstrung by the five-minute limit per side of a 78 disc. Some of Melba's final recording sessions used this method.

Melba had nine recording sessions in London, the first a distinct failure as far as she was concerned. Melba had the unapproved matrices returned to her to dispose of personally. Whether she in fact destroyed them is not known. When the remakes were finally thought good enough they were released in July 1904 under Melba's special lilac label; they were sold out in days. The second session, her first at a studio – then called a laboratory, took place at 21 City Road on 20 October 1904, the press in attendance to provide some very gushy ink about it all the next day. Kubelik was the obbligatist in the Bach–Gounod 'Ave Maria'. The other sessions were on 4 September 1905, in July 1906, May 1910, May 1913, on 12 May 1921, 8 June

1926 (using the electrical process on stage at Covent Garden during her farewell – it includes parts of *La Bohème* and her farewell speech), 17 December 1926 (at Small Queen's Hall, ten days after the charity farewell at the Old Vic), and the Paris recording, probably of 9 May 1908.

The best of the recordings, American or English, are thought to convey much of the voice accurately, but unfortunately Victor used a recording diaphragm that, though successful with male voices, distorted the middle register of sopranos, giving them a 'tinny' sound. The later Melba recordings suffer from this. The best of the London recordings, however, demonstrate that she had, in fact, a mellow middle register. Original copies, unmodified by modern adjustment techniques, were hard to listen to, often with ugly recording, blasting on high notes, the tone cold and dull as the singer was distanced from the recording horn. This was especially true of the Melba sound and accounts for at least some of the lack of emotion often attributed to her.

In the idiosyncratic phrasing (possibly learned from the composer) of the first session's Mad Scene from *Hamlet*, the famous 'Caro nome' with its spectacular trills (sometimes decried as matronly and laboured, but to my mind the optimum of bel canto control), and the alien, perhaps antique, style used for the Mad Scene from *Lucia*, the essential Melba is very obviously with us still, though to 'hear' her requires great concentration in order to block out the flak of recording over-sound and the emissions of the machinery. What is creamed off, strained out, and coloured over in the process is equally essential to our understanding but since it is simply not there we must 'hear' it in and supply it ourselves. Not an easy task.

The 7 July 1906 recordings are thought of as her best; those of 12 May 1921 as the worst; yet the farewell recording, the voice of an old woman, is limpid and warm if unsupported by the breathing. The melodramatic tones of the speech that ended the night are, though it is hard to believe, genuine.

The entire series was reissued on five records by EMI as RLS719 under the title *Nellie Melba: The London Recordings 1904–1926*. The American Victor recordings have been reissued as *Melba: The American Recordings 1907–1916,* on five records as RCS (Australia) Ltd VLR50365, issued to mark the 50th anniversary of the ABC.

The American series began on 3 March 1907 at the height of the Manhattan affair. Melba was 46 years old, with over forty titles already on records. She returned to Victor in 1909, 1910, 1913 and finally in 1916. The 24 March 1907 takes included the 'O soave fanciulla' with Caruso. The 1 January 1909 session features Melba as her own accompanist and on 26 August 1910 she appeared for the only time on disc as Lemmone's accompanist. The first two Victor sessions are from their 'fail-safe' period when the singer was kept too far back from the horn in order to prevent hooting. The result is a very dimmed Melba.

once did her singing move me in an imaginative way; it was flawless vocalism pure and simple; but never in my experience did it enter the deeper world of music. She always reminded me of the phrase of Berlioz about "performers on the larynx". Whatever she was singing, it was always Melba, the incomparable vocalist. I am assured by experienced opera-goers that even when she attempted the part of Elsa in *Lohengrin* she remained on much the same plane as when she was singing Violetta in Verdi's *Traviata*. She is not remembered by any performance in music that bites into life; her best work was done in the operas of Gounod, Rossini, and in early Verdi. It is true that she made a brave effort to express the more searching pathos as Verdi's Desdemona in *Otello*; but even here her voice was too pellucid to assume the shadows of ill-starred humanity.

'Still, an artist has a right to specialize in a certain school of art, one that is suitable for his or her particular gifts, and on the whole Melba was wise to recognize her aesthetic limitations. She was once foolish enough to attempt the part of Brünnhilde in New York, with the result that she so wrecked her voice that she could not sing at all for several months. If it can be said that she had a defect in technique, it was in the general texture of her highest register. Although she could execute isolated top notes marvellously, she could not control them in dramatic phrases. And her acting was always rather static, artificial, not to say wooden in her movements and gestures. She really belonged to the *prima-donna* period of opera, the period in which performance was regarded as all-important in itself, and not primarily as a means to the expression of poetic experience.

'The Wagnerian reaction in the nineties against opera as a vocalist's holiday was, no doubt, carried too far; and as a consequence the art of singing lost a good deal of classic ease and purity. So long as Melba was able to sing at all, she constantly reminded us of the traditions. In recent years, the greatest opera singers have demonstrated to us that it is possible to combine with really musical singing, a dramatic energy and style. Nobody in his senses would try to belittle Melba. My only intention in this article is to point out what she could do supremely well, and in what direction she was not adequately equipped.

'Melba did incalculable service for music in Australia. In fact, she placed Australia musically on the map. It can be said, to use the phrase of our own period, that she sang before all the crowned heads of Europe, and that at a time when the majority of people in Europe did not even know where Australia was. . . . In her own country, she left behind her a lasting influence and example; and, though it is said that she had a hard side to her nature, there are many artists both in this country and on the other side of the world, who would willingly admit their indebtedness to her.'[1]

1. Neville Cardus, *Music for Pleasure*, pp. 69–71.

The discography information supplied by the National Film and Sound Archive of Australia lists 187 Melba recorded items in all, which amounts to a separate career in an area in which everything musical and economic was new. Melba began her recording life at a time when she was committed to the established life of the opera house and the concert platform – all very predictable. For her this was high adventure, something of a gamble, but as it turned out, one that paid off handsomely.

The Melba vocal legacy is embedded in these 187 recorded items; the money they made has long since been absorbed into the lives of the beneficiaries of her will. She left £181 000 – not the fortune she was supposed to have possessed. It was said at the time that she lost heavily over German and Austrian investments during the First World War and later in Australia, but it seems more likely that she gradually divested herself of taxable assets as she listened to predictions of rising death duties. The only money left for music was the £8000 for the Melba Scholarship. In all the time that she had been teaching she had not accepted a penny from her students.

The teaching school survived her death, its effects still invisibly present in the voices and the teaching methods of her students and their students (including Gertrude Johnson whose National Theatre provided the training for the first generation of singers of the Australian Opera), a chain that links back to Marchesi, Garcia and beyond. It is nebulous but pervasive, an Australian claim to an illustrious musical ancestry. Yet Melba herself was part of that chain, taking out of the country the cumulative effect of travelling opera troupes (whose members were trained by the Garcias and others), of colonial alertness to opportunity, and of the growing wealth of the not quite so new country. She brought back personal and national glory. The nation was proud of her.

The legend is probably the true Melba legacy, a matter of inspiration as well as pride. Australian pioneer women dragged pianos half-way across the world to give their children the culture they were leaving behind. They went into debt for these sacred objects later, determined to better their family life through what they believed were the civilising influences of music. They founded and sustained choral societies, sang and played and taught, using the music teacher's pittance to keep souls afloat and children fed, and the sociability of the choirs and concerts to find husbands and friends. It was the women of Australia who took Melba to heart, a lesson on how to use a woman's artistic skills to the best possible social and financial advantage, yes, but to the highest cultural advantage as well. Melba remains their special property, a downright, forthright Aussie who put their country on the map and gave them a sense of pride in themselves as cultivated women, a unique voice singing the triumphant praises of the land and the people she loved, for all they said of her – the Voice of Australia.

APPENDICES

MELBA'S OPERATIC REPERTOIRE

Composer	Opera	Role
Bemberg	Elaine	Elaine
Berlioz	La Damnation de Faust	Marguerite
Bizet	Carmen	Micaëla
Delibes	Lakmé	Lakmé
Donizetti	Lucia di Lammermoor	Lucia
Goring Thomas	Esmeralda	Esmeralda
Gounod	Faust	Marguerite
	Roméo et Juliette	Juliette
Leoncavallo	I Pagliacci	Nedda
Mascagni	I Rantzau	
Massenet	Le Cid	L'Infanta
	Manon	Manon
Meyerbeer	Les Huguenots	Marguerite de Valois
Puccini	La Bohème	Mimi
Rossini	The Barber of Seville	Rosina
	Semiramide	Semiramide
Saint-Saëns	Hélène	Hélène
Thomas	Hamlet	Ophelia
Verdi	Aida	Aida
	Otello	Desdemona
	Rigoletto	Gilda
	La Traviata	Violetta
	La Travatore	Leonora
Wagner	Lohengrin	Elsa
	Siegfried	Brünnhilde
	Tannhäuser	Elisabeth

Melba also sang in one act of *Le Nozze di Figaro* at a Brussels gala performance and sang (in a private performance) the 'Forest bird' from *Siegfried*. She learned, but apparently never performed, the roles of Tosca, Mireille, Martha (in Flotow's opera) and Senta in *The Flying Dutchman*.

WHAT MELBA SANG AT THE MET.

(From: William H. Seltsam, *Metropolitan Opera Annals*.)

1893	December	4	Lucia di Lammermoor	Lucia
		6	Hamlet	Ophelia
		11	I Pagliacci	Nedda
		22	I Pagliacci	Nedda
		29	Rigoletto	Gilda
1894	January	12	Semiramide	title role
		14	concert	'Air du Rossignol' ('Penserioso'), Handel; Tosti's 'Goodbye'
		19	Roméo et Juliette	Juliette
		21	concert	Mad Scene, *Lucia di Lammermoor*; Waltz, *Roméo et Juliette*
		29	Tannhäuser	Elizabeth

	February	6	Lohengrin	Elsa
		10	Roméo et Juliette	Juliette
	Undated concert between 14 and 16 February			Gala. Act 4, *Rigoletto* and Act 2, *Hamlet*
		18	concert	'Sweet bird' ('Penserioso'), Handel; Duet (unspecified), Handel; 'Se saran rose', Arditi
		23	Faust	Marguerite
		25	concert	'Ballatella', *Pagliacci*; 'Caro nome', *Rigoletto*

1894 supplementary season

	April	16	Faust	Marguerite
		20	Semiramide	title role
		22	concert	'Sweet bird'; 'Bel raggio', *Semiramide*

	26 *Lucia di Lammermoor*	Lucia
Undated concert		Gala.
		Mad Scene,
		Hamlet
1894–95 season		
November	19 *Roméo et Juliette*	Juliette
	26 *Carmen*	Micaëla
	28 *Lucia di Lammermoor*	Lucia
	29 *Carmen*	Micaëla
December	1 *Faust*	Marguerite
	7 *Rigoletto*	Gilda
	9 concert	
	12 *Faust*	Marguerite
	15 *Lucia di Lammermoor*	Lucia
	17 *Elaine* (US première)	title role
	19 *Roméo et Juliette*	Juliette
	22 *Lohengrin*	Elsa
	26 *Les Huguenots*	the Queen
	28 *Faust*	Marguerite
	29 *Rigoletto*	Gilda
1895 January	5 *Elaine*	title role
	12 *Les Huguenots*	the Queen
	14 *Lucia di Lammermoor*	Lucia
	19 *Rigoletto*	Gilda
	21 *Les Huguenots*	the Queen
	25 *Semiramide*	title role
	26 *Rigoletto*	Gilda
February	5 *Les Huguenots*	the Queen
	9 *Roméo et Juliette*	Juliette
	10 concert	
	15 *Les Huguenots*	the Queen
	16 *Faust*	Marguerite
Post season		
April	16 *Les Huguenots*	the Queen
	20 *Lucia di Lammermoor*	Lucia
	27 *Faust*	Marguerite
	30 concert	Gala. Mad
		Scene, *Lucia*
		di Lammermoor
1895-96 season		
December	27 *Roméo et Juliette*	Juliette
	30 *Faust*	Marguerite
1896 January	1 *Lucia di Lammermoor*	Lucia
	4 *Rigoletto*	Gilda
	5 concert	Mad Scene,
		Lucia di
		Lammermoor
	8 *Les Huguenots*	the Queen
	10 *Faust*	Marguerite
	13 *Les Huguenots*	the Queen
	17 *Carmen*	Micaëla
	18 *Faust*	Marguerite
	20 *Roméo et Juliette*	Juliette
	25 *Lucia di Lammermoor*	Lucia
	27 *Manon*	title role

February	3 *Carmen* (afternon)	Micaëla
	3 *Manon* (at night)	title role
	7 *Lucia di Lammermoor*	Lucia
	8 *Les Huguenots*	the Queen
	12 *Les Huguenots*	the Queen
	14 *Faust*	Marguerite
Post season		
April	17 *Lucia di Lammermoor*	Lucia
	20 *Carmen*	Micaëla
	22 *Faust*	Marguerite
	24 testimonial for	Mad Scene,
	Abbey and Grau	*Lucia di*
		Lammermoor
		and Act 4,
		Faust
1896-97 season		
November	16 *Faust*	Marguerite
	21 *Faust*	Marguerite
	23 *Roméo et Juliette*	Juliette
December	2 *Roméo et Juliette*	Juliette
	6 concert	'Sevillana',
		Don César de
		Bazan,
		Massenet; 'Se
		saran rose',
		Arditi
	9 *Faust*	Marguerite
	12 *Roméo et Juliette*	Juliette
	16 *Lucia di Lammermoor*	Lucia
	18 *Les Huguenots*	the Queen
	21 *La Traviata*	Violetta
	26 *Lucia di Lammermoor*	Lucia
	30 *Siegfried*	Brünnhilde
1897 January	16 *Roméo et Juliette*	Juliette
1898-99 season		
December	2 *Roméo et Juliette*	Juliette
	12 *Roméo et Juliette*	Juliette
	24 *Faust* (matinée)	Marguerite
1899 January	11 *Faust*	Marguerite
1899–1900 season		Not present
1900–1901 season		
1900 December	18 *Roméo et Juliette*	Juliette
	22 *Roméo et Juliette*	Juliette
	(matinée)	
	26 *La Bohème*	Mimi
	29 *La Bohème*	Mimi
1901 January	4 *Faust*	Marguerite
	11 *La Bohème*	Mimi
	16 *Le Cid*	the Infanta
	19 *Le Cid*	the Infanta
	28 *Les Huguenots*	the Queen
	30 *Roméo et Juliette*	Juliette
February	9 *Rigoletto*	Gilda
	18 *Lucia di Lammermoor*	Lucia

24 concert	'Nymphs et Sylvains', Bemberg; Mad Scene, *Lucia di Lammermoor*; Quartet, *Rigoletto*		

		18	*La Bohème*	Mimi
		22	*Rigoletto*	Gilda
	April	29	concert	Mad Scene, *Lucia di Lammermoor*

Not present for subsequent seasons until 1904-05

March	2	not stated		
	9	*Roméo et Juliette*	Juliette	
	11	*Les Huguenots*	the Queen	
	16	*La Traviata*	Violetta	

1904 December 16 *La Bohème*   Mimi

Not present for subsequent seasons until 1910–11

1910 November 24 *Rigoletto*   Gilda

            29 *La Traviata*   Violetta

No appearances after this date

WHAT MELBA SANG AT THE MANHATTAN

(From John Frederick Cone, *Oscar Hammerstein's Manhattan Opera Company*.)

At the Manhattan Opera in New York
1906-07 season

1907 January	2	*La Traviata*	Violetta
	11	*Rigoletto*	Gilda
	19	*La Traviata* (matinée)	Violetta
	28	*Lucia di Lammermoor*	Lucia
	31	*Rigoletto*	Gilda
February	8	*Faust*	Marguerite
	14	*Rigoletto*	Gilda
	16	*Lucia di Lammermoor* (matinée)	Lucia
	23	*La Traviata* (matinée)	Violetta
	25	*Rigoletto*	Gilda
March	1	*La Bohème*	Mimi

	6	*La Bohème*	Mimi
	11	*La Bohème*	Mimi
	20	*Rigoletto*	Gilda
	25	*La Bohème*	Mimi

1908-09 season

1908 December	14	*La Bohème*	Mimi
	19	*La Bohème*	Mimi
	23	*La Bohème*	Mimi
	25	*Otello*	Desdemona
1909 January	2	*Otello*	Desdemona
	4	*Otello*	Desdemona
	11	*Rigoletto*	Gilda

Manhattan Opera Co. appearances at the Philadelphia Opera House

1908 December	17	*La Bohème*	Mimi
	29	*La Bohème*	Mimi
1909 January	1	*Traviata* (matinée)	Violetta

MELBA'S APPEARANCES AT COVENT GARDEN

* = role shared
RIO = Royal Italian Opera
ROS = Royal Opera Season
GOS = Grand Opera Syndicate

Year	Season	Operas; no. of performances by Melba
1888	RIO (spring-summer)	*Lucia di Lammermoor* 2 *Rigoletto* 1
1889	RIO	*Rigoletto* 2 *Roméo et Juliette* 7
1890	RIO (Harris)	*Esmeralda* 3 *Hamlet* 1 *Lucia di Lammermoor* 3
		Rigoletto 3 *Roméo et Juliette* 5
1891	RIO (Harris)	*Carmen** 7 *Lohengrin** 9 *Lucia di Lammermoor* 2 *Rigoletto** 5 *Roméo et Juliette** 8
1892	RIO (summer) (Harris)	*Elaine* 5 *Faust** 5 *Lohengrin** 5 *Roméo et Juliette** 3 *Aida* 2 *Faust** 6 *Lohengrin* 4 *Otello* 2 *Rigoletto* 1

1893	ROS (summer) (Harris)	Faust* 6
		Lohengrin* 6
		I Pagliacci 9
		I Rantzau 1
		Rigoletto 1
		Roméo et Juliette 7
1894	ROS (summer) (Harris)	Elaine 2
		Faust* 7
		Lohengrin* 4
		Lucia di Lammermoor 1
		I Pagliacci* 9 (from Royal Opera House archives only — not Rosenthal)
		Rigoletto 3
		Roméo et Juliette 7
1895	ROS (summer) (Harris)	Carmen* 6
		Faust* 6
		Les Huguenots 1
		Lucia di Lammermoor 2
		Rigoletto 3
		Roméo et Juliette 6
1896	ROS (summer) (Harris)	Faust* 6
		Les Huguenots 1
		Lucia di Lammermoor 2
		Manon 2
		Rigoletto 1
		Roméo et Juliette* 8
1897	ROS (summer) (GOS)	Faust* 7
		Roméo et Juliette* 6
1898	ROS (summer) (GOS)	Il Barbiere di Siviglia 1
		Roméo et Juliette* 4
		La Traviata 1
1899	ROS (summer)	La Bohème 4
		Faust* 8
		Lucia di Lammermoor 2
		Roméo et Juliette* 5
1900	ROS (summer) (GOS)	Il Barbiere di Siviglia 1
		La Bohème 3
		Faust* 8
		Lucia di Lammermoor 2
		Roméo et Juliette 5
1901	ROS (summer) (GOS)	La Bohème 4
		Faust* 8
		Roméo et Juliette* 5
1902	ROS (summer) (GOS)	La Bohème 4
		Faust* 5
		Rigoletto 5
		Roméo et Juliette* 7
		La Traviata 2
1903	ROS (summer) (GOS)	La Bohème 4
		Faust* 8
		Rigoletto* 5
		Roméo et Juliette* 6
1904	ROS (summer) (GOS)	La Bohème 6
		Faust* 6

			Hélène 2
			Rigoletto 6
			Roméo et Juliette* 2
			La Traviata 3
1905	ROS (summer) (GOS)		La Bohème* 6
			Faust* 7
			La Traviata 1
	Autumn opera season (Rendle)		La Bohème 6
			Faust 2
			Rigoletto* 5
1906	ROS (summer) (GOS)		La Bohème* 9
			Faust* 4
			Rigoletto* 4
			La Traviata 2
			La Bohème 7
			Faust* 6
			Rigoletto* 4
			La Traviata* 3
1907	ROS (summer) (GOS)		La Bohème* 9
			Lucia di Lammermoor* 3
			Rigoletto* 4
			La Traviata* 5
1908	ROS (summer) (GOS)		La Bohème 5
			Otello 5
			Rigoletto* 5
			La Traviata* 7
1909	Absent		
1910	ROS (summer) (GOS)		La Bohème 6
			Otello 1
			La Traviata* 7
1911	ROS (summer) (GOS)		La Bohème* 5
			Faust 2
			Roméo et Juliette 4
1912	Absent		
1913	ROS (summer)		La Bohème* 7
			Faust 2
			Rigoletto 1
			Roméo et Juliette 2
			La Traviata 2
1914	ROS (summer) (GOS)		La Bohème* 6
			Otello* 4
			Rigoletto 2
1915-18	Covent Garden closed during World War I		
1919	(Beecham and GOS)		La Bohème* 10
			Faust* 6
			Roméo et Juliette 3
1920-21	Absent		
1922-23	Winter season		La Bohème
1923	British National Opera season		La Bohème* 5
			Faust* 3
1924-25	Absent		
1926			Melba's farewell, 8 June, in La Bohème

Compiled from Royal Opera House archives and Rosenthal, *Two Centuries of Opera at Covent Garden.*

THE PROVINCIAL TOUR OF GREAT BRITAIN WITH JAN KUBELIK 1912–13

1912
October 5 London
7 Nottingham
10 Liverpool
12 Manchester
14 Edinburgh
15 Glasgow
17 Belfast
18 Dublin
21 Newcastle
23 Middleborough
24 Doncaster
28 Hull
29 Huddersfield
31 Preston
November 2 Reading
4 Hanley
6 Lancaster
8 Halifax

11 Birmingham
16 Southport
20 Cardiff
23 Bournemouth
27 Portsmouth
29 Brighton
December 6 Bradford
1913
January 16 Norwich
18 Derby
20 Leamington
22 Chester
25 Cheltenham
27 Bristol
30 Plymouth
February 1 Torquay
4 Bedford
8 Eastbourne
11 Northampton

15 Oxford
19 Cambridge
(Between April and July Melba
appeared at Covent Garden.)
May 2 Guildford
4 London
June 1 Melba's Jubilee
concert, Royal
Albert Hall, London
14 Tunbridge Wells
August 12 Bournemouth
14 Margate
16 Colwyn Bay
19 Douglas, Isle of Man
21 Douglas, Isle of Man
24 Blackpool
26 Harrogate
29 Llandudno
31 New Brighton

THE AMERICAN–CANADIAN TOUR WITH JAN KUBELIK OF 1913–14

1913
September 29 Montreal
October 7 Toronto
9 Cincinnati
12 Chicago
14 Buffalo
16 Syracuse
19 Boston
(Melba only)
21 New York
(Melba only)
23 Philadelphia
(Melba only)
25 Altoona (Kubelik only)
26 Cleveland
28 Rochester
30 Montreal
November 2 New York
4 Wheeling
6 Pittsburg
8 Toledo
11 Toronto
13 Detroit
14 Port Huron
16 Chicago
18 St Louis
(? Missing)
22 Kansas City
24 St Paul
25 Duluth
28 Spokane
December 1 Seattle

4 Portland
7 San Francisco
9 Los Angeles
11 San Diego
14 San Francisco
27 San Francisco
31 Oakland
1914
January 2 Los Angeles
7 Denver
9 Des Moines
12 Omaha
14 Minneapolis
15 La Crosse
(Kubelik only)
16 Madison
(Melba only)
19 Peoria
21 Milwaukee
22 Green Bay
25 Chicago
27 Colombus
30 Nashville
February 2 New Orleans
4 New Orleans
6 Memphis
9 Chattanooga
10 Macon (Kubelik only)
11 Atlanta (Melba only)
13 Raleigh
14 Richmond
19 Baltimore

21 Trenton
22 Washington
(Kubelik only)
24 Philadelphia
March 1 New York
3 Hartford (Melba only)
11 London, Ontario
(Kubelik only)

The tour was officially billed to end on 5 March 1914 in Springfield, Massachusetts, after which Melba was to join the Boston Opera Company. Kubelik continued with separate engagements for concerts.

Melba's programmes were selected from the Mad Scene (*Lucia*), 'Depuis le jour' (*Louise*), 'Addio' (*Bohème*), 'Chanson triste' by Duparc, 'Phidyle' (Duparc), 'Ave Maria' (Bach-Gounod) with Kubelik, Debussy's 'Romance' and 'Mandoline', 'Ave Maria' (*Otello*), 'Lo! Here the gentle lark', 'Voi che sapete' (*Figaro*), 'Se saran rose' (Arditi), the Mad Scene (*Hamlet*), 'Magdalen at Michael's Gate' (Liza Lehmann), *Il Rè Pastore* (Mozart) with Kubelik, 'L'allegro ed il pensieroso' (Handel). For an encore she chose between 'Comin' through the rye', 'John Anderson My Jo' and Tosti's 'Goodbye'.

DISCOGRAPHY

Compiled by William Hogarth. Reproduced from *The Record Collector*, March 1982. Updated by T. Radic, 1986.

EXPLANATORY NOTES

Layout is the usual – discography number, matrix number and title: underneath the single, then double face, numbers of the recording company, followed by those of the partner company–Gram. Co./Victor, or Victor/Gram. Co. as applicable. The IRCC/AGS numbers at the end of this line are of pressings from original masters.

Where 'Unpublished' appears instead of an original catalogue number this means the title was not released by the company in its normal pattern of trading. The masters were on file, however, and white label 'special pressings' were obtained of most of them when the company was still providing this service, as was done also for the reissues of the IRCC and American Gramophone Society. A blank in the sequence indicates a missing matrix.

Eventually everything available to the Gramophone Company was transferred to five long-play discs and issued as a boxed set RLS 719. All that is missing is the recently discovered 25 cm 'Jean' (No. 106) and another take of 'Ave Maria', presumably 1904. It could be discography No. 33, a test pressing of which exists in the USA. It is unusual in having no label at all, nor any of the expected inscriptions such as the usual 'Melba' or matrix number on the completely blank centre. RCA/Victor has transferred holdings to VRL5 0365 as a boxed set with notes by William R. Moran. No details are available of the Bettini cylinder issues Melba is known to have made before 1900, nor of the putative 1903 ('for private purposes only') series, all masters of which were destroyed at her request.

The 1904 series included a recording of Annie Laurie, according to the late Carl Russell, of Melbourne, derived from reliable information provided by the Mitchell family.

Re discography Nos. 62 and 120, the situation has been confused by the Gramophone Company allotting No. 62 the catalogue number 053108 and No. 120 the number 2-053029, but later re-allotting No. 120 the catalogue number 053108. When single-sided issues were deleted in 1924 the subsequent doubled-sided issue on DB 346 proved to be No. 62, this time with the number 2-053029. The two versions can be distinguished one from the other by virtue of the presence or otherwise of the 'Follie, follie' sung just before the 'Sempre libera'.

Many of the later DB and Archive VB pressings were made from mechanical dubbings, that is remastered stampers made by Hayes using acoustical methods. For example No. 67 on DM 117, 81 and 93 as coupled on DB 702, 95 on DB and VB, 99 on DM 118, etc.

Item No. 130: label for DB 366 shows 053211, but the inner safety groove used by Victor to distinguish post-1909 re-recordings would confirm that the stamper used came from 2-053022.

London, March/1904

1. 1(3)   Mattinata (Tosti)
   03015   95022 (matrix has Roman iii above it)

2. 2   Nymphes et sylvains (Bemberg)
   03016   95023   IRCC 123

3. 3

4. 4

5. 5

6. 6   TRAVIATA: A fors'e lui, Follie, Sempre libera (Verdi) (Because the label would have covered part of the music the Follie-Sempre libera was milled out and covered so as only to issue the Andante part)
   03017   95014

7. 7(7-B?)   Comin' thro' the rye (Trad)
   03018 (unpublished)

8. 8

9. 9   Se saran rose (Arditi)
   03019   95019

10. 10

11. 11

12. 12   LUCIA DI LAMMERMOOR: Mad Scene—Cadenza (Donizetti) (Flute obbl. Gaubert)
    03020   95013

13. 13

14. 14

15. 15–1   IL PENSIEROSO: Sweet bird (Handel) Incomplete, speaking at the end by Melba. Unpublished.

16. 15–2   IL PENSIEROSO: Sweet bird, with Cadenza (Handel)
    03021   95016

17. 16–3(?)   Goodbye (Tosti) two verses only
    03022   95012

18. 17

19. 18
20. 19
21. 20   HAMLET: Mad scene, part 1 (Thomas) (orch)
    03023   95020   IRCC 47
22. 21   HAMLET: Mad scene, part 2 (Thomas) (orch)
    03024   95021   IRCC 47
23. 22–3   RIGOLETTO: Caro nome (Verdi) (orch)
    03025   95018   IRCC 2
24. 23–2   TRAVIATA: Sempre libera (without Follie)
    (Verdi) (r)
    03026   95015
25. 24
26. 25–3   Three Green Bonnets (d'Hardelot)
    03027   95017   IRCC 181
27. 26–1   NOZZE DI FIGARO: Porgi amor (Mozart)
    03028   95024HMV   VB 40 is a dubbing
    IRCC2
28. 27–1   Si mes vers (Hahn)
    30029   95024
29. 28–1   LA BOHEME: Addio (Puccini)
    03030   Unpublished

London, 20 October 1904

30. 6149   Chant Venetien (Bemberg)
    Unpublished
31. 6150–2   Chant Venetien (Bemberg) Composer at piano
    3575   94002
32. 6151–2   Les Anges pleurent (Bemberg) Composer at
    piano
    3576   94001   IRCC 54
33. 400c   Ave Maria (?)
    Unpublished
34. 401c–2   Ave Maria (Gounod) Violin obbl. Kubelik
    03033
35. 402c–2   La Serenata (Tosti)
    03034
36. 403c
37. 404c–2   ROMEO ET JULIETTE: Valse (Gounod)
    03035 DB 367
38. 405c–2   Chant Hindou (Bemberg) Composer at piano
    03036
39. 406c–2   LA BOHEME: Addio (Puccini)
    03037

London, 4 September 1905, this group of six all 25 cm

40. 7200   God Save the King (Trad) Band of Coldstream
    Guards, conducted Rogan
    3625
41. 7201½   Auld Lang Syne (Trad) with vocal trio—
    Gwladys Roberts, Ernest Pike and Peter Daw-
    son and Band
    3615   94004
42. 7202½   Come back to Erin (Claribel), with Band acc.
    3616   94003   IRCC 150
43. 7203   Old folks at home (Foster) with Band and Trio
    as above
    3617 DA 337   94005
44. 7204   Goodnight (Sir A. Scott-Gatty), Trio as above,
    with pf. acc.
    3618   94006
45. 7205   Away on a hill there runs a stream (Landon
    Ronald) Composer at piano
    3619 DA 337   94007

London, 5 September 1905

46. 520c   Sur le lac (Bemberg) Composer at piano
    03046   95028   IRCC 123
47. 521c   Lo, here the gentle lark (Bishop) Flute by
    Fransella
    03047 DB 347   95027
48. 522c   FAUST: Jewel song (Gounod)
    03048
49. 523c   Home sweet home (Bishop)
    03049   95026
50. 524c   Goodbye (Tosti) (three verses)
    03050

London, 7 July 1906

51. 689c   Ave Maria (Gounod) Cello obbl. W. H.
    Squire
    30369
52. 690c   ELAINE: L'amour est pur, with female
    chorus. Composer at pf.
    Unpublished   IRCC 17
53. 691c   Pastorale (Bizet)
    03070   IRCC 35
54. 692c   LA BOHEME: Racconto di Mimi (Puccini)
    This version is cut but ends with a few lines
    of recit.
    03071
55. 693c   LE ROI D'YS: Aubade (Lalo)
    03072   HMV VB 13 is a dubbing

For series 1 to 55, piano accompanist was Landon Ronald
except where shown otherwise.

London, 11 July 1907

56. 8473b   White sea mist (Ronald)
    Unpublished

New York & Camden, 24–30 March 1907, all with
orch. except where shown otherwise.

57. C4281–2   LA BOHEME: Racconto di Mimi (Puccini)
    88074   053106
58. C4282–2   TOSCA: Vissi d'arte (Puccini)
    88075   053115
59. C4283–2   RIGOLETTO: Caro nome (Verdi)
    88078 6213B,   053110 DB 346
60. C4326–1   LA BOHEME: O saove fanciulla, with
    CARUSO (Puccini)
    85200   054129 (takes 2, 3, 4 unpublished)
61. C4330   FAUST: Jewel song (Gounod)
    88066   033029
62. C4339–2   TRAVIATA: Ah, fors'e lui (Follie) Sempre
    libera (Verdi)
    88064   053108, 2–053029, DB 346 (see
    footnotes on this and Serial 120)
63. C4340   Goodbye (Tosti)
    88065   03091
64. C4341   LA BOHEME: Addio (Puccini)
    88072   053111
65. C4342–2   La Serenata (Tosti) Harp by Ada Sassoli
    88079 6221A, 053114 DB 349
66. C4347–2   Per valli, per Boschi, with Charles Gilibert,
    bar. (Bemberg)
    89011   054128 DM 117

67. C4348–1 Un ange est venu, with Gilibert, bar.
89012   034014.
DM 117 was a dubbing of this item.

68. C4349–2 LUCIA DI LAMMERMOOR: Mad scene,
Cadenza only, flute obbl. by North
88071   053112

69. C4350 Lo here the gentle lark (Bishop) Flute by
North
88073   03090

70. 4351 ?

71. C4352 Si mes vers (Hahn) Harp by Ada Sassoli
88080   033026 DB 361

72. C4353 NOZZE DI FIGARO: Voi che sapete
(Mozart)
88067   053113 (reduced orch.
introduction)

73. C4354–2 HAMLET: Mad scene, Part one (Thomas)
88069   033028 DB 710 AGS B7

74. C4355–3 HAMLET, Mad scene, Part two (Thomas)
88070   033027 DB 710 AGS B7

75. C4356 Se saran rose (Arditi)
88076   053109

76. C4357 ROMEO ET JULIETTE: Valse (Gounod)
Unpublished

77. C4358 IL PENSIEROSO: Sweet Bird (incl. Cadenza)
(Handel)
88068   03089   Flute obbl. by North

78. C4359 Ave Maria (Gounod)
Unpublished

79. C4360 Mattinata (Tosti) pf. acc. by Melba
88077   053107

80. C4361 RIGOLETTO: Tutte le feste, duet with
Campanari, bar. (Verdi)
Unpublished

Paris, circa 9 May 1908
81. 602j LA BOHEME: On m'appelle Mimi (Puccini)
033062, DB 702 was a dubbing of this title

New York, 1 January 1909
82. C6697 En sourdine (Debussy) Melba at piano?
03376 allocated but unpubl. IRCC 35

83. C6698 Down in the forest (Ronald) Melba acc. at
piano
03130 allocated but unpub. AGS B67,
IRCC 52

84. C6699 White Sea Mist (Ronald) Melba acc. at piano
03134 allocated by unpub. AGS B53,
IRCC 52

85. C6700 D'une Prison (Hahn) Melba at piano?
88151   033077 allocated but unpub.
Gram. Co.

86. C6701–2 Believe Me If All Those Endearing Young
Charms (Moore) Melba at piano?
88156   03131 & 03694, DB 357

87. C6702

88. C6703

89. C6704 OTELLO: Salce, salce (Verdi)
88148   053211

90. C6705 OTELLO: Ave Maria (Verdi)
88149   053212

91. C6707 O lovely night (Ronald)
88157, 88182; 03133, both this & 132
issued on 88182

92. C6707 Ye Banks and Braes (Trad) Melba at piano?
88190, 6218B; 03132 & 03696, DB 362

London, 11 and 19 May 1910
93. 4183f TOSCA: Vissi d'arte (Puccini)
2–053020, DB 702

94. 4184f DON CESAR DE BAZAN: Sevillana
(Massenet)
unpublished

95. 4185f LOHENGRIN: Elsa's Dream (Wagner) (It.)
2–053019; DB366 & VB 53 are both
dubbings

96. 4186f TOSCA: Vissi d'arte (Puccini)
unpublished

97. 4187f TRAVIATA: Duet with John McCormack
(ten.)
Unpublished, master destroyed

98. 4188f FAUST: Final trio with McCormack and
Mario Sammarco (Gounod)
Unpublished

99. 4189f RIGOLETTO: Quartet, with Edna Thornton,
McCormack and Mario Sammarco (Verdi)
2–054025, DM 118, IRX 1007

100. 4190f FAUST: Final trio with McCormack and
Mario Sammarco (Gounod)
Unpublished originally, later on IRX 1006,
Victor Heritage 15–1019B and IRCC 7B

101. 4191f

102. 4192f

103. 4193f Bid me discourse (Bishop)
03188, DB 347

104. 4194f The sounds of earth (Ronald), composer at
piano
Unpublished

105. 4195f HAMLET, Part of Mad scene used as
distance test (Thomas)
Unpublished

106. 11689e Jean (Burleigh) acc. pf.
Unpublished

107. 4206f DON CESAR DE BAZAN: Sevillana
(Massenet)
Unpublished

108. 4207f DON CESAR DE BAZAN: Sevillana
(Massenet)
Unpublished

109. 4208f LE CID: Pleurez, mes yeux (Massenet)
2–033020, DB 711

110. 4209f Soir Paien (Hue)
Unpublished

111. 4210f Spring (Henschel)
Unpublished, matrix destroyed

112. 4211f O for the wings of a dove (Mendelssohn)
Unpublished, matrix destroyed

113. 4212f–2 O for the wings of a dove (Mendelssohn)
03199, DB 351

114. 4213f Spring (Henschel)
03328   IRCC 181

115. 4214f Pur dicesti (Lotti)
Unpublished

Camden, USA 3–7 November 1910

116. C4281–   LA BOHEME: Racconto di Mimi (Puccini)
    1 & 2   88074, 6210A; 2–05325, DB 356

117. C4282–2 TOSCA: Vissi d'arte (Puccini)
                88075, 6220A, 2–053024

118. C4337   NOZZE DI FIGARO: Voi che sapete
                Unpublished

119. C4338–2 FAUST: Jewel song (Gounod)
                88066, 6215A; 2–033022, DB 361

120. C4339   TRAVIATA: Ah fors'e lui-Follie-Sempre
                libera (Verdi)
                88064   2-053029 – see note re this & No.
                62

121. C4340–3 Goodbye (Tosti)
                88065, 6222A; 03206, DB 358

122. C4341–2 LA BOHEME: Addio (Puccini)
                88072, 6210B; 2–053028, DB 356

123. C4349–2 LUCIA DI LAMMERMOOR: Mad scene,
                Cadenza only (Donizetti) Flute obbl.
                Lemmone
                88071, 6219B; 2–053026, DB 364

124. C4350–   Lo here the gentle lark (Bishop) Flute
    2 & 3   Lemmone
                88073 take 3, 6214A; 03203 take 2, DB
                348

125. C4353   NOZZE DI FIGARO: Voi che sapete
                (Mozart)
                88067, 6219B; 2–053027, DB 367

Camden, USA, 24 & 25 August 1910

126. C4356–2 Se saran rose (Arditi)
                88076, 6220B; 2–053023, DB 349

127. C4358–2 IL PENSIEROSO: Sweet bird (Handel) Flute
                Lemmone
                88068, 6214B; 03089, DB 350

128. C6702

129. C6703

130. C6704–1 OTELLO: Salce, salce (Verdi)
                88148, 6211A; 2–053022, DB 366 – shows
                053211 on label

131. C6705–4 OTELLO: Ave Maria (Verdi)
                88149, 6211B; 2–053021, DM 118

132. C6706–2 O lovely night (Ronald)
                88182, 6222B; 03204, DB 350 AGS B67

133. C9370–2 DON CESAR DE BAZAN: Sevillana
                (Massenet)
                88252, 6216B; 2–033023, DB711, also on
                Vic. 88662

134. C9371–2 HAMLET: Mad scene (condensed version)
                (Thomas)
                88251, 6215B; 2–033024, DB 364

135. C9352   LE ROI D'YS: Aubade (Lalo) or. W. Rogers
    –1,–2   88250, 2–033025, DB 354

136. C9373   STABAT MATER: Inflammatus (Rossini)
                Unpublished

137. C9374   Bid me discourse (Bishop)
                Unpublished

138. C9375–2 By the Brook (Wetzger), flute solo by John
                Lemmone with piano accompaniment by
                Melba
                70023, 55111B; 09151, D 477

London, May 1913

139. Y 16572e Chanson triste (Duparc) Lapierre at piano?
                7-3304, DA 334

140. Z 7321f   Ave Maria (Gounod)
                Matrix destroyed

141. Z 7322f–3 IL RE PASTORE: L'amero saro costante
                (Mozart)
                2–053083, DK 112. Violin obbl. by
                Kubelik

142. Z 7323f   Ave Maria (Gounod) violin by Kubelik,
                organ by Roper
                03333

143. Z 7324f

144. Z 7325f   Le Temps des Lilas (Chausson)
                2–033037   IRCC7

Camden, USA 2–4 October 1913

145. C13896   IL RE PASTORE: L'amero saro costante
                (Mozart)
                89074, 2–033044 – (Unpublished?), vl.
                Kubelik

146. C13897–2 Ave Maria (Gounod) violin obbl. Kubelik
                89073,   03333, DK 112, HMV labels
                incorrectly show with organ accompaniment

147. C13898–2 Magdalen at Michael's Gate (Liza
                Lehmann)
                88452,   03370, DB 709

148. C13899–2 Romance; Mandoline (Debussy)
                88456,   2–033042, DB 709

149. C13800–2 LOUISE: Depuis le jour (Charpentier)
                88477, 6216A; 2–033076, DB 354

150. 13901   Phydile (Duparc)
                Unpublished

151. C13902   Le Temps des Lilas (Chausson)
                Unpublished

152. C13903   LOUISE: Depuis le jour (Charpentier)
                Unpublished

153. C13904–2 Old folks at home (Foster)
                88454, 6217B; 03362, DB 348

154. C13905–2 John Anderson my Jo (White)
                88455,   03371, DB 363

155. 13906   Chanson triste (Duparc)
                Unpublished

156. C13907   Comin' thro' the rye (Trad)
                88449, 6218A; 03369, DB 362

157. C13908–1 Les anges pleurent; Chant Venetien
                (Bemberg)
                88457,   2–033043 – allocated but
                unpublished

158. C13909   Vocal lesson Number One, Melba at the
                piano.
                Unpublished

Camden, USA, 12 January 1916

159. C17001   Annie Laurie (Scott)
    –1 & 2   88551, 6217A; 03523, DB 357

160. C17002–2 Songs my mother taught me (Dvorak)
                (Orch)
                88485,   03695, DB 363

161. C17003   Annie Laurie (Scott)
                Unpublished

162. C17004–1 Songs my mother taught me (Dvorak)
88553 – allocated but unpublished.
Released as a 17cm private pressing,
33r.p.m. for the Stanford Archive of
Recorded Sound, StARS 1000B, F.St.Leger
at pf.

London, 12 May 1921
163. Cc147–2 SADKO: Chanson Hindoue (Rimsky-
Korsakov)
03759, DB 358
164. Cc148 Away on a hill – Down in the forest
(Ronald)
Unpublished. Composer at the piano.
165. Bb149 By the waters of Minnetonka (Lieurance)
2–3568, DA334
166. Bb150 Annie Laurie (Scott)
Unpublished
167. Cc151–1 Home sweet home (Bishop)
03049, DB351

**Royal Opera House, Covent Garden, London, 8 June
1926.** Live recordings of Melba's Farewell Performance, with
(a) Browning Mummery, (b) John Brownlee, (c) Frederick
Collier, (d) Edouard Cotreuil, (e) Aurora Rettore. Conductor
was Vincenzo Bellezza.
168. CR 417 OTELLO: Salce, salce (Verdi)
(2–053263), DB 1500
169. CR 418 OTELLO: Salce, Part 2 (Verdi)
Unpublished
170. CR 419 OTELLO: Ave Maria (Verdi)
Unpublished
171. CR 411 LA BOHEME: C'e Rodolfo with (b)
(Puccini)
Unpublished
172. CR 412 LA BOHEME: Addio (Puccini)
(2–053264), DB 493 & DB 1500
173. CR 413 LA BOHEME: Addio dolce svegliare, with
(a), (b) & (e) (Puccini)
Unpublished
174. CR 414 LA BOHEME: Entrata di Mimi, with (a),
(b), (c), (d) and (e) (Puccini)
Unpublished
175. CR 415 LA BOHEME: Sono andati, with (a)
(Puccini)
Unpublished
176. CR 416 LA BOHEME: Morte di Mimi, with (a),
(b), (c), (d) and (e) (Puccini)
Unpublished
177. CR 421 Melba's Farewell Speech
(01182), DB 943

Queen's Hall (Small Hall) London, 17 December 1926.
These four titles with piano accompaniment by Harold
Craxton.
178. Cc9550–1 TRAVIATA: Dite alla giovine, duet with
John Brownlee, bar. (Verdi)
(2–054171), DB 987, VB 64
179. Cc9551– Un ange est venu, duet with John
1A Brownlee, bar. (Bemberg)
(2–034041), DB987, VB 64

180. Cc9552–2 Clair de lune (Szulc)
(2–033115), DB 989; 6733A
181. Cc9553– Swing low, sweet chariot (arr. Burleigh)
1A (03894), DB 989; 6733B

**Metropolitan Opera House, New York, January–March
1901.** The following titles are from the Mapleson (Librarian
of the opera house at the time) collection of cylinder
recordings made during actual performances. Much recent
research has been done on these and it may be that other
Melba titles will emerge. Some of the tracks below, all
including Melba, were issued on two long-play discs (with
many other artists' tracks from the same collection) by the
International Record Collectors' Club, USA, except No. 187
which originally appeared as a single-sided 78 r.p.m. shellac
pressing, in 1938 as IRCC 5002. (Some time ago Dr John
Stratton, Canada, concluded that this excerpt was by Suzanne
Adams and not Melba, Ed).

182.	LE CID: Alleluia (Massenet)	16 Jan. 1901	IRCC L7004
183.	LE CID: Concertato, Act 1, with Breval, Jean & Ed. de Reszke, Plancon & Sizes.	19 Jan. 1901	
184.	LUCIA DI LAMMERMOOR: Verrano o te, with Saleza, ten. (Donizetti)	2 Mar. 1901	
185.	FAUST: Jewel song, first part only.	28 Mar. 1901	IRCC L7004
186.	FAUST: Final trio, w. Saleza and Ed. de Reszke (Gounod)	4 Mar. 1901	Item on L7004 features Calvé, etc.
187.	LES HUGUENOTS: A ce mot tout s'anime (both verses of cabaletta)	11 Mar. 1901	IRCC 5002, last verse only on IRCC 3034B and L7006
188.	TRAVIATA: Un di felice (2nd part only) with A. Dippel, ten.	16 Mar. 1901	L7006
189.	LUCIA DI LAMMERMOOR: Spargi d'amaro pianto (Donizetti)	18 Mar. 1901	L7004
190.	ROMEO ET JULIETTE: Valse (Gounod)	Date not known	

The following unconfirmed titles are supposed to have been
made:
A. LUCIA DI LAMMERMOORE: Verrano a te, with
Charles Dalmmores, ten., probably in USA 1907.
B. LA BOHEME: Mimi e ver, with Sammarco, probably
London 1910.
C. PAGLIACCI: E allor perche di. with Sammarco, probably
London 1910.
D. SAMSON: Let the bright seraphim (Handel), probably
London 1910.

If the reader is interested in an even more detailed
discography I suggest William R. Moran's lists and notes in
Nellie Melba: A Contemporary Review (Greenwood Press,
Westport, Connecticut, 1985).

NOTES

1. ADDIO SENZA RANCORE

1. Obituary section of William Beaumont Morris Melba Tribute Book, MS 8626, a book compiled without titles of newspapers being present but with spasmodic dating. La Trobe Library, Melbourne.
2. *Ibid.* 25 February 1931. No newspaper title present.
3. Maie Casey, *Melba Re-visited*, p. 22
4. Anonymous source. Taped interview with author, 22 August 1984. Not to be released for twenty years on donor's request.
5. Morris, *loc. cit.*
6. Joseph Wechsberg, *Red Plush and Black Velvet*, p. 6.
7. Nellie Melba, *Melodies and Memories*, p. 12.
8. Beverley Nichols, *Evensong*, pp. 32–3.
9. Melba, *op.cit.*, p.1.

2. HELEN PORTER MITCHELL

1. Melba, *op. cit.*, p. 3
2. *Ibid.*
3. Leon Caron. The cantata *Victoria*, words by J. W. Meaden. First performed 1 October 1880. (Published vocal score, London, Novello Ewer, n.d.) Grainger Museum, University of Melbourne. The Melbourne firm of Allans is given as the co-publisher.
4. Melba, *op. cit.*, p. 1.
5. Agnes G. Murphy, *Melba: A Biography*, p. 2.
6. *The Globe Song Folio*.
7. W. A. Carne, *A Century of Harmony*, p. 85.
8. M. O. Reid, *The Ladies Came to Stay*, p. 2.
9. Barbara Mackenzie and Findlay Mackenzie, *Singers of Australia*, p. 113.
10. *Ibid.*
11. *Sydney Morning Herald*. Clipping 1927 quoted in Mackenzie and Mackenzie, *op. cit.*, p. 37.
12. Reid, *op. cit.*, pp. 90–91. Some confusion of dates has occurred here. Melba spoke on 14 November, but Wilson's letter is given as 4 November. The text of Reid gives him as present at the speech but his letter below it says he was not.
13. *Sydney Gazette* 1827 quoted by Eric Irvin in article, 'Australia's First Public Concerts' in *Studies in Music No. 5*, pp. 77–86.
14. Melba, *op. cit.*, p. 4.

3. MRS ARMSTRONG

1. Graeme Davison, *Marvellous Melbourne*, p. 12.
2. Davison, *op. cit.*, p. 209, quoting the Rev. Charles Strong. *Church-going and a Sermon* (Melbourne, 1880), p. 24.
3. *Ibid.*, quoting Ada Cambridge, *Thirty Years in Australia* (London, 1903), p. 185.
4. *Ibid.*, quoting H. G. Turner, 'Personal Memorabilia' (MSS, La Trobe Library, n.d.).
5. Thorold Waters, *Much Besides Music*, pp. 110–11.
6. *Ibid.*
7. *Ibid.*, p. 112.
8. *Ibid.*, p. 65.
9. Melba, *op. cit.*, p. 7.
10. Waters, *op. cit.*, pp. 110–19.
11. *Ibid.*, pp. 114–15. Alice Elmblad (or Emblad), a Melbourne-born pianist, had returned to Australia with her husband, a Swedish singer, whom she married while studying abroad.
12. *Con Amore*, No. 13, 1946. Melba Memorial Conservatorium Archives.
13. Melba, *op. cit.*, p. 10.
14. Waters, *op. cit.*, p. 115.
15. Letter, 16 August 1885. Performing Arts Museum, Melbourne.
16. Letter, Melba to Arthur Hilliger, 31 August 1885, from Doonside. Mitchell Library, AM 82.2.
17. Letter, Melba to Hilliger, 10 September 1885, from Doonside. *Loc. cit.*
18. Letter, Melba to Hilliger, 21 September 1885, from Doonside. *Loc. cit.*
19. Letter, Ann Fraser Mitchell to Hilliger, 1 October 1885. *Loc. cit.*
20. Letter, Ann Fraser Mitchell to Hilliger, 31 July 1885. *Loc. cit.*
21. Melba., *op. cit.*, p. 8.
22. *Ibid.*

4. MARCHESI'S MELBA

1. Letter, Melba to Rudolph Himmer c/o Allan's Melbourne, 13 May 1886, from 89 Sloane Street, London. MS 1496, National Library of Australia.
2. Letter, Melba to Pietro Cecchi, 27 June 1886, from Burley House, Belgrave, Leicester. Waters, *op. cit.*, pp. 116–17.

3. Melba, *op. cit.*, p. 17.
4. *Ibid.*, p. 18.
5. Melba, *op. cit.*, p. 28.
6. Robert Harborough Sherard, *Twenty Years in Paris*, p. 345.
7. Murphy, *op. cit.*, p. 29.
8. *Ibid.*, pp. 29–30.
9. Percy Colson, *Melba: An Unconventional Biography*, p. 31.

5. A RIGHT ROYAL AFFAIR

1. *Royal Opera Covent Garden Jubilee Souvenir Programme 1908.* Note by Henry Trevor. (Dover Street Studios, London, 1908.) Melba Memorial Conservatorium archives.
2. Melba, *op. cit.*, p. 35.
3. Ibid.
4. Harold Rosenthal, *Two Centuries of Opera at Covent Garden*, p. 227.
5. Murphy, *op. cit.*, p. 43.
6. Muriel Campbell, 'Victorian Women in Music' in *The Centenary Gift Book* (eds Frances Fraser and Nettie Palmer), p.88.
7. Roger Covell, *Australia's Music: Themes of a New Society*, p. 106.
8. Murphy, *op. cit.*, p. 44.
9. *Ibid.*, p. 45.
10. Melba, *op. cit.*, p. 37.
11. *Ibid.*, p. 47.
12. *Ibid.*, p. 22
13. *Ibid.*, p. 41
14. Colson, *op. cit.*, p. 56.
15. Murphy, *op. cit.*, p. 52.
16. *Le Ménestral*, 15 December 1889.
17. *Ibid.*
18. *L'Art Musical*, 15 December 1889.
19. *L'Evénement*, 2 November 1891.
20. *Ibid.*
21. Sherard, *op. cit.*, p. 346.
22. *L'Evénement*, 2 November 1891.
23. Casey, *op. cit.*, p. 29.

6. A TOAST TO MELBA

1. *Sunday Australian*, 11 April 1971.
2. Wechsberg, *op. cit.*, pp. 196–8.
3. *Ibid.*
4. *Ibid.*
5. Hetherington, *op. cit.*, quoting from Henry Russell, *The Passing Show*, p. 97.
6. Colson, *op. cit.*, pp. 26–7.
7. Peter Dawson, *Fifty Years of Song*, p. 190.
8. Rosenthal, *op. cit.,* p. 250.

9. Murphy, *op. cit.*, p. 84.
10. Melba, *op. cit.*, pp. 83–4.
11. Murphy, *op. cit.*, p. 93.
12. John Thompson, *On Lips of Living Men*, p. 23.
13. Colson, *op. cit.*, pp. 133–4.
14. *Ibid.*
15. Murphy, *op. cit.*, p. 125.
16. Melba, *op. cit.*, p. 110.

7. HOME SWEET HOME

1. Melba, *op. cit.*, p. 115.
2. Murphy, *op. cit.*, p. 143.
3. Interview with James Graham, grandson of Covent Garden stage-hand Albert Timsen. 3 May 1985.
4. Murphy, *op. cit.*, p. 182.
5. Melba, *op. cit.*, p. 138.
6. Murphy, *op. cit.*, pp. 198–200.
7. Hetherington, *op. cit.*, pp. 119–20.
8. *Ibid.*, quoting Cyril Pearl, *Wild Men of Sydney.*
9. *Ibid.*, pp.121–2.

8. MANHATTAN VERSUS METROPOLITAN

1. Melba, *op. cit.*, p. 175.
2. *Ibid.*, p. 226.
3. *St Louis Star*, 15 November 1908.
4. *Telegraph* (London), 1905.
5. Rosenthal *op. cit.*, p. 309.
6. *New York Herald*, 19 August 1906.
7. *The World* (New York), 6 May 1906.
8. *Ibid.*
9. *Ibid.*
10. Melba, *op. cit.*, p. 172.
11. *Ibid.*, p. 170.
12. Melba, *op. cit.*, p. 172.
13. *The Sun* (New York), 2 March 1907.
14. Murphy, *op. cit.*, pp. 269–70.
15. *Ibid.*, p. 267.
16. Winifred Ponder, *Clara Butt: Her Life Story*, p. 137.
17. Murphy, *op. cit.*, pp. 284–5.
18. *Ibid.*, pp. 290–91.
19. *The Philadelphia Inquirer*, 10 January 1909.

9. SINGING 'EM MUCK

1. Melba, *op. cit.*, p. 179.
2. *Ibid.*, p. 182.
3. Letter, John Grainger to Percy Grainger, 5 September 1911. Grainger Museum.
4. *The World Wide Magazine*, pp. 78–83, 1910 n.d. Melba File, New York Public Library.

5. *Argus*, 31 January 1911.
6. Clipping n.d. at 19 October 1911. Melba Memorial Conservatorium Diary, 1911.
7. Clipping n.d. at December 1911. *Ibid.*
8. *Chicago Tribune*, 8 June 1913.
9. Hetherington, *op. cit.*, p. 177.
10. Adelaide Lubbock, *People in Glass Houses: Growing Up at Government House*, p. 64.
11. Clipping, 14 August 1917, Melba Memorial Conservatorium Diary, 1917.
12. Percy Grainger, MS: 'The Aldridge–Grainger–Ström Saga'. Grainger Museum.
13. *Musical Courier*, 11 January 1917, quoting *Free Lance*, 1 December 1916. New Zealand.
14. Clipping n.d., 1918 context. Melba File, New York Public Library.
15. Letter, Melba to Fritz Hart, 28 November 1917. Performing Arts Museum, Melbourne.
16. Letter (n.d.), Melba to Fritz Hart, 17 October. From Des Moines. *Loc. cit.*
17. Hetherington, *op. cit.*, p. 176.
18. *Ibid.*, p. 190.
19. *Melbourne Triad*, 28 August 1919.

10. MELBA'S GIRLS

1. Melba *op. cit.*, p. 215.
2. Rosenthal, *op. cit.*, p. 399.
3. Thérèse Radic, *G.W.L. Marshall-Hall: Portrait of a Lost Crusader*, p. 17.
4. Clipping at 8 March 1909. Melba Memorial Conservatorium Diary 1909.
5. *Argus*, 24 November 1909.
6. Clipping n.d. at 24 March 1915. Melba Memorial Conservatorium Diary 1915.
7. *The Lone Hand*, 1 January 1909.
8. *Australian Musical News*, 1 May 1915.
9. *Con Amore: the Melba Memorial Conservatorium Magazine*, Jubilee Year Issue, 1945. No. 12. Under the heading 'Those were the days'.
10. *Ibid.*
11. Letter, Melba to Fritz Hart, 13 January 1926, postdated. Performing Arts Museum, Melbourne.
12. Clipping n.d. at 13 December 1911. Melba Memorial Conservatorium Diary 1911.
13. *Musical America*, 23 December 1916.
14. Letter, Melba to Fritz Hart, 14 November 1915, postdated. Performing Arts Museum, Melbourne.
15. Melbourne Conservatorium of Music Prospectus 1917, Melba Memorial Conservatorium Archives.
16. Letter, Melba to Fritz Hart, n.d. *circa* July 1917. From Coombe Cottage. Performing Arts Museum, Melbourne.
17. Letter, Melba to Hart, n.d. from Edgecliff, Sydney. *Loc. cit.*
18. Letter, Melba to Hart, n.d. no designation. *Loc. cit.*
19. Letter, Melba to Hart, 12 March (no year given). *Loc. cit.*
20. Letter, Melba to Hart, 27 September (no year given). From Government House, Adelaide. Envelope with inscription 'Invest in 7th War Loan'. *Loc. cit.*
21. Letter, Melba to Hart, n.d. From Double Bay, Sydney. *Loc. cit.*
22. Letter, Melba to Hart, 1 November *circa* 1918. En route, Pullman car. *Loc. cit.*
23. Letter, Melba to Hart, 17 October *circa* 1918. *Loc. cit.*
24. Letter, Melba to Hart, *circa* 1919. From La Turbie, Alpes Maritimes. MS 2809, National Library of Australia.
25. *Ibid.*
26. Letter, Melba to Hart. Letter 8. Photostat. MS 2809, *loc. cit.*
27. Letter, Melba to Hart, 8 August (no year given). Performing Arts Museum, Melbourne.
28. Letter, Melba to Hart, 21 January 1919. *Loc. cit.*
29. Letter, Stella Power to Mary Campbell, 13 March 1918. Melba Memorial Conservatorium Diary 1918 insert.
30. Waters, *op. cit.*, p. 13.

11. FAREWELL AND MORE FAREWELLS

1. Beverley Nichols, *A Voice There Breathed* and *Evensong*, quoted in William R. Moran, *Nellie Melba; A Contemporary Review*, pp. 215–16.
2. Nichols quoted in Moran, *Melba: The American Recordings 1907–1916*. RCA reissue with ABC. 1982. Notes accompanying the discs.
3. *Herald*, 14 October 1924.
4. Wechsberg, *op. cit.*, pp. 364–5.
5. *Ibid.*, p. 367.
6. Rosenthal, *op. cit.*, p. 445.
7. Wechsberg, *op. cit.*, p. 370.
8. Letter, Melba to Tommy Cochran, n.d. Inscribed 'Easter Sunday'. Performing Arts Museum, Melbourne.
9. Letter, Melba to Cochran, 25 April (no year given). *Loc. cit.*
10. Letter, Melba to Cochran, 10 October 1921. *Loc. cit.*
11. Letter, Melba to Cochran, n.d. *Loc. cit.*
12. Letter, Melba to Cochran, n.d. *Loc. cit.*
13. Letter, Melba to Cochran, n.d. *Loc. cit.*
14. *Argus*, 14 October 1924.
15. *Argus*, 13 October 1924.

BIBLIOGRAPHY
Published sources

Armstrong, William. *The Romantic World of Music*. (E. P. Dutton, New York, 1922.)

Australian Dictionary of Biography. Vols. 5, 6, and 7. Bede Nairn, Geoffrey Serle and Russel Ward (eds). (Melbourne University Press, 1974, 1976, and 1986 respectively.)

Baily, Leslie. *Scrapbook 1900–14*. (Muller, London, 1957.)

Barrymore, Freda. 'The Great Melba' in *Sydney Morning Herald*, 14 April 1964.

Beecham, Thomas. *A Mingled Chime*. (Hutchinson, London, 1944.)

Black, J. Anderson, Madge Garland and Frances Kennett. *A History of Fashion*. (Orbis, London, 1982.)

Braddon, Russell. *Joan Sutherland*. (Collins, Sydney, 1962.)

Briggs, John. *Requiem for a Yellow Brick Brewery: A History of the Metropolitan Opera*. (Little, Brown, Boston, 1969.)

Brockway, Wallace and Herbert Weinstock. *The World of Opera*. (Methuen, London, 1963.)

Brookes, Mabel. *Crowded Galleries*. (Heinemann, London, 1956.)

Brownlee, John. 'Melba and I' in New York *Saturday Review*, 25 December 1954.

———. *Memoir of Melba*. New York Public Library Melba file.

Building Societies Gazette. 1888.

Burgess, Henry. *My Musical Pilgrimage: An Unconventional Survey of Music and Musicians*. (Simpkin, Marshall, Hamilton, Kent, London, 1911.)

Calvé, Emma. *My Life*. (D. Appleton, New York, 1922.)

Cambridge, Ada. *Thirty Years in Australia*. (London, 1903. No publisher given.)

Campbell, Muriel. 'Victorian women in music' in *The Centenary Gift Book*. Frances Fraser and Nettie Palmer (eds), for the Women's Centenary Council, Melbourne. (Robertson and Mullens, Melbourne 1934.)

Cane, Anthony. In notes accompanying album VRL50365, RCA (Australia) with the Australian Broadcasting Company, 1982, entitled *Melba: The American Recordings 1907–1916*.

Cardus, Neville. *Music for Pleasure*. (Angus and Robertson, Sydney, 1942.)

Carne, W.A. *A Century of Harmony*. (Royal Melbourne Philharmonic Society, Melbourne, 1954.)

Casey, Maie. *Melba Re-visited*. Essay in limited edition. (Melbourne, 1975.)

Clark, C.M.H. *A History of Australia*, Vol. 4. (Melbourne University Press, 1978.)

Clarke, Hamilton. 'Two Years Music in Australia – A Personal Narrative by one of the Survivors' in *Argus,* 17 March 1894, reprinted from a lecture delivered before the Royal College of Organists, London.

Clisson, Eugène. 'Le Divorce de Mme Melba' in *L' Evénement* 2 November 1891. (Paris.)

Colson, Percy. *I Hope They Won't Mind.* (Eveleign Nash and Grayson, London, 1930.)

_____ . *Melba: An Unconventional Biography.* (Grayson and Grayson, London, 1932.)

Con Amore: The Melba Conservatorium Magazine. Melba Memorial Conservatorium archives. 1941, 1945, 1946.

Cone, John Frederick. *Oscar Hammerstein's Manhattan Opera Company.* (University of Oklahoma Press, Norman, 1966.)

Covell, Roger. *Australia's Music: Themes of a New Society.* (Sun Books, Melbourne, 1967.)

Dane, Clemence. *London has a Garden.* (Michael Joseph, London, 1964.)

Danieli, Elena. 'What Melba Did To Help Me' in *Music and Musicians,* London, May 1961.

Davis, Ronald L. *Opera in Chicago.* (Appleton-Century, New York, 1966.)

Davison, Graeme. *Marvellous Melbourne.* (Melbourne University Press, 1979.)

Dawson, Peter. *Fifty Years of Song.* (Hutchinson, London, 1951.)

Dicker, Ian G. *JCW: A Short Biography of James Cassius Williamson.* (The Elizabeth Tudor Press, Sydney, 1974.)

Eames, Emma. *Some Memories and Reflections.* (D. Appleton, New York, 1927.)

Eaton, Quaintance. *The Boston Opera Company.* (Appleton-Century, New York, 1905.)

_____ . *The Miracle of the Met: An Informal History of the Met. Opera 1883–1967.* (Meredith Press, New York, 1968.)

_____ . *Opera Caravan: Adventures of the Met. on Tour 1883–1956.* (Farrar, Straus and Cudahy, New York, 1957.)

Escoffier, G.A. *A Guide to Modern Cookery.* (Heinemann, London, 1907.)

Eulass, Elizabeth. 'Melba's Debut Fifty Years Ago' in *Opera News,* Vol. 8, No. 6. 29 November 1943. New York.

Evans, Lindley. *Hello Mr Melody Man.* (Angus & Robertson, Australia, 1983.)

Exhibition: *My Name is Melba,* catalogue, Performing Arts Museum, Melbourne, 1982.

Fairweather, Ian. *Your Friend Alberto Zelman.* (Zelman Memorial Symphony Orchestra, Melbourne, 1984.)

Fitzpatrick, Kathleen. *PLC Melbourne — The First Century 1875–1975.* Pamphlet. (PLC, Melbourne, 1975.)

Foster, Roland. *Come Listen to My Song.* (Collins, Sydney, 1949.)

Garden, Mary (with Louis Biancolli). *Mary Garden's Story.* (Simon and Schuster, New York, 1951.)

Gattey, Charles Neilson. *Queens of Song.* (Barrie and Jenkins, London, 1979.)

Gill, G. Hermon. ' "The Vics": An Historical Record' in *The Gallery on Eastern Hill.* C.B. Christensen (ed.). (Victorian Artists' Society, Melbourne, 1970.)

The Globe Song Folio. (Bayley and Ferguson, Glasgow and London, 1901.)

Goossens, Eugene. *Overture and Beginners: A Musical Autobiography.* (Methuen, London, 1951.)

Greenwood, Gordon (ed.) *Australia: A Social and Political History.* (Angus and Robertson, Sydney, 1955.)

Grout, Donald Jay. *A Short History of Opera* (2nd ed.). (Columbia University Press, New York, 1965.)

Haddon, J. Cuthbert. 'Melba' in *Modern Musicians.* (Peter Davies, London, 1913.)

Harris, Max. *The Unknown Great Australian and Other Psychobiographical Portraits.* (Sun Books, Melbourne, 1983.)

Hart, Fritz. 'Some Memories of Dame Nellie Melba' in *Con Amore: The Melba Conservatorium Magazine.* No. 1. Christmas 1934. Melba Memorial Conservatorium archives.

Hetherington, John. *Melba.* (F.W. Cheshire, Melbourne, 1967.)

Hibberd, Jack. *A Toast to Melba.* Stage play in *Three Popular Plays* by Jack Hibberd. (Outback Press, Melbourne, 1976.)

Hogarth, William. 'The Discography of Nellie Melba' in *The Record Collector,* March 1982.

Holmes, Paul. (ed.) notes to album RLS 719, EMI *Nellie Melba: The London Recordings 1904–26.*

Hurst, P.G. *The Age of Jean de Reszke: Forty Years of Opera 1874–1914.* (Christopher Johnson, London, 1958.)

Hutton, Geoffrey. *Melba.* Monograph. (Oxford University Press, Melbourne, 1962.)

Inglis, K.S. *This is the ABC: The Australian Broadcasting Commission 1932–1983.* (Melbourne University Press, 1983.)

Irvin, Eric. 'Australia's First Public Concerts' in *Studies in Music* No. 5. (University of Western Australia Press, 1971.)

Jackson, Stanley. *Caruso.* (W.H. Allen, London 1972.)

Keily, Henry. 'The Tendency of Popular Taste in Music and How to Elevate it' in *The Victorian Review,* 1 March 1880.

Kingston, Claude. *It Doesn't Seem a Day Too Much.* (Rigby, Adelaide, 1971.)

Klein, Hermann. *Great Women-Singers of My Time.* (George Routledge and Sons, London, 1931.)

_____ . *The Golden Age of Opera.* (George Routledge and Sons, London, 1933.)

_____ . 'Melba: An Appreciation' in *The Musical Times,* London, 1 April 1931.

_____ . *Musicians and Mummers.* (Cassell, London, 1925.)

_____ . *Thirty Years of Musical Life in London 1870–1900.* (William Heinemann, London, 1903.)

_____ . *Unmusical New York: A Brief Criticism of Triumphs, Failures and Abuses.* (John Lane, London and New York, 1910.)

Knox, T.A. *The Boy Travellers in Australia.* (New York, 1889.)

Kobbé, Gustav. *The Complete Opera Book.* (G.P. Putnam's Sons, London, 1922.)

Kolodin, Irving. *The Story of the Metropolitan Opera. 1883–1950: A Candid History.* (Alfred A. Knopf, New York, 1953.)

_____ . *The Metropolitan Opera 1883–1939.* (Oxford University Press, 1940.)

Koroleticz-Wayda, Janina. *My Memoirs.* (National Ossolineum Institute, Wrollaw (Breslau), 1958.)

Landely, A. 'Theatre National de l'Opéra: Lucie de Lammermoor' in *L' Art musical,* 15 December 1889, Paris.

Lang, Paul Henry. *Music in Western Civilization* (J.M. Dent and Sons, U.S.A. 1941, London 1942.)

Lawrence, Marjorie. *Interrupted Melody*. (Falcon Press, London, 1952.)

Lawton, Mary. *The Last of the Titans*. (Macmillan, New York, 1940.)

Ledbetter, Gordon T. *The Great Irish Tenor (John McCormack)*. (Charles Scribner's Sons, New York, 1977.)

Legge, Robin H. 'Melba' in *Saturday Review*. London, 28 February 1931.

Leiser, Clara. *Jean de Reszke and the Great Days of Opera.* (London, 1933.)

Lemmone, John. 'The Merry, Merry Pipes of Pan' in the *Herald,* Melbourne, 7 June 1924.

Le Massena, C.E. *Galli-Curci's Life of Song*. (Paebar, New York, 1945.)

Lindsay, Joan. *Time Without Clocks*. (F.W. Cheshire, Melbourne, 1962.)

Love, Harold. *The Golden Age of Australian Opera*. (Currency, Sydney, 1981.)

————. 'W.S. Lyster's 1861–68 Opera Company: Seasons and Repertoire' in *Australasian Drama Studies* Vol. 2. October 1983.

Lubbock, Adelaide. *People in Glass Houses: Growing up at Government House*. (Thomas Nelson, Melbourne, 1977.)

McCormack, John (as told to Pierre V.R. Key). *John McCormack: His Own Life Story*. (Small, Maynard, Boston, 1918.)

McKay, Claude. *This Is the Life: An Autobiography of a Newspaperman*. (Angus and Robertson, Sydney, 1961.)

Mackenzie, Barbara, and Findlay Mackenzie. *Singers of Australia*. (Lansdowne Press, Melbourne, 1967.)

Magnus, Philip. *King Edward the Seventh*. (John Murray, London, 1964.)

Maine, Basil. 'Melba' in the *Spectator,* London, 28 February, 1931.

Marchesi, Blanche. *A Singer's Pilgrimage*. (Grant Richards, London, 1923.)

Marchesi, Mathilde. *Marchesi and Music: Passages from the Life of a Famous Singing Teacher*. (Harper and Brothers, New York, 1897.)

Marshall, Ian. 'The Melody Lingers On' in the *Sunday Mail,* 9 April 1972.

Matthews, Enid N. *Colonial Organs and Organ Builders* (Melbourne University Press, 1969.)

Melba, Nellie. 'Dame Nellie Melba: Her Methods Explained – Valuable Help for Singers' in the Adelaide *Advertiser,* 6 articles run during April 1922. The first was incorporated in Melba's teaching manual *The Melba Method.*

————. 'The gift of song' in *Century Magazine,* New York, June 1907.

————. 'Grand Opera' in *Lippincott's Monthly Magazine,* Philadelphia, April 1895.

————. *The Melba Method* (Chappell, London and Sydney, 1926.)

————. *Melodies and Memories.*(First published 1925; reissued 1980, Nelson, Melbourne.)

————. 'Music as a Profession: Some Personal Advice' in *Lone Hand,* Sydney 1 February 1909.

————. 'Where is Happiness? Is It In Fame?' in the *Herald,* Melbourne, 10 September 1927.

Moncrieff, Gladys. 'Sneezes, Songs and Melba' in *Woman's Day,* Melbourne, 23 January 1950.

Moore, Edward C. *Forty Years of Opera in Chicago*. (Horace Liveright, New York, 1930.)

Moore, Grace, *You're Only Human Once*. (Invincible Press, Melbourne, 1944.)

Moran, William R. 'The Musical Triumphs of Nellie Melba' in *Melba: The American Recordings, 1907–1916*. Notes accompanying RCA Record Album VRL-0365. (RCA (Australia) and ABC, Sydney, 1982.)

Morena, H. 'Lucie de Lammermoor à l' Opéra' in *Le Ménestral,* 15 December 1889. Paris.

Morton, Frederic. *The Rothschilds.* (Secker and Warburg, London, 1962.)

Murdoch, William. 'Melba: 1861–1931 in *Monthly Musical Record,* 1 April 1931, London.

Murphy, Agnes G. *Melba: A Biography.* (Doubleday, Page, New York, 1909.)

Nash, William P. 'Melba' in *Margin* No. 13, 1984. Monash University.

Newton, Ivor. 'I Knew Melba' in *The Listener,* 29 September 1938. London.

―――. *At the Piano: Ivor Newton: The World of an Accompanist.* (Hamish Hamilton, London, 1966.)

Nichols, Beverley. *All I Could Never Be.* (Jonathan Cape, London, 1949.)

―――. *Are They the Same at Home?* (Jonathan Cape, London, 1927.)

―――. *A Voice There Breathed* and *Evensong* quoted in *Nellie Melba: A Contemporary Review* by William Moran. (Greenwood Press, Westport, Connecticut, 1985.)

―――. *Evensong.* (Jonathan Cape, London, 1932.)

―――. *Father Figure.* (William Heinemann, London, 1972.)

―――. *The Sweet and the Twenties.* (Weidenfeld and Nicolson, London, 1958.)

―――. *25; Being a Young Man's Candid Recollections of His Elders and Betters.* (Jonathan Cape, London, 1926.)

Noel, Edouard, and Edmond Stoullig. *Les Annales du Théâtre de la Musique.* (Bibliothèque Charpentier, Paris, 1890.)

Norton, John. 'Concerning Her Champagne Capers, Breaches of Public Faith, Outrages Against Good Manners, and Insults to Australian Citizens' in *Truth,* Sydney, 28 March 1903.

Noseda, Aldo. 'Mme Melba's début: La Scala' in *Corriere della sera,* 17 March 1893.

Noskowski, L. de. Articles in the *Australasian:* 'Melba's Surrender', 2 August 1924, and 'Melba's Early Success', 14 June and 21 June 1924.

Orchard, W. Arundel. *Music in Australia.* (Georgian House, Melbourne, 1952.)

Parkinson, Violet C.E. 'Madame Elise Wiedermann and the Opera School' in *Con Amore: The Melba Conservatorium Magazine* No. 12. Jubilee Issue, 1945.

Peake, George. *Historical Souvenir.* Pamphlet. (Melbourne, 1913.)

Pearl, Cyril. *Wild Men of Sydney.* (W. H. Allen, London, 1958.)

Perkin, H. *Melbourne Illustrated and Victoria Described.* (Melbourne, 1880.)

Ponder, Winifred. *Clara Butt: Her Life Story.* (Harrap, London, 1928.)

Pougin, Arthur. 'Opera: Hamlet. Début de Mme Melba' in *Le Ménestral,* 12 May 1889.

Pritchard, Katharine Susannah. *Child of the Storm.* (Angus and Robertson, Sydney, 1963.)

Radic, Thérèse. *Bernard Heinze* (Macmillan, Melbourne, 1986.)

―――. *G.W.L. Marshall-Hall: Portrait of a Lost Crusader.* (University of Western Australia, 1982.) Monograph 5.

―――. 'Australian Women in Music' in *LIP* 1978–9 (Carlton Feminist Co-operative, Melbourne.)

―――. 'Music of the Centennial International Exhibition' in *Australia 1888,* Bulletin No. 7. April 1981.

_____ . 'Nellie Melba: The Voice of Australia' in *Double Time*. Marilyn Lake and Farley Kelly (eds). (Penguin, Melbourne, 1985.)

Rankin, David. *The History of the Music of St Francis' Church 1839–1979*. (Society of Jesus, Australia, 1979.)

Rees, Leslie. *The Making of Australian Drama*. (Angus and Robertson, Australia, 1973.)

Reid, M.O. *The Ladies Came to Stay*. (Melbourne, *circa* 1960 u.d.)

Ronald, Landon. 'About Melba' in *Chamber's Journal*, London, 22 April 1922.

_____ . 'More About Melba' in *Chamber's Journal*, London, 29 April 1922.

_____ . *Myself and Others: Written Lest I Forget*. (Samson Low, Marston, London, *circa* 1931. u.d.)

_____ . *Variations on a Personal Theme*. (Hodder and Stoughton, London, 1922.)

Rosenthal, Harold and John Warrack. *Concise Oxford Dictionary of Opera*. (OUP, London, 1924.)

Rosenthal, Harold. *Two Centuries of Opera at Covent Garden*. (Putnam, London, 1958.)

Russell, Donna Shinn. 'The Meanest Woman in the World' in *Opera News*, New York, 1 November 1964.

Russell, Frank A. 'Melba Looks Back' in the *Herald*, Melbourne, 13 October 1924.

Russell, Henry. *The Passing Show*. (Thornton Butterworth, London, 1926.)

Sadie, Stanley (ed.) *The New Grove Dictionary of Music and Musicians* (Macmillan, London, 1980.)

Saint, Andrew, B.A. Young, Mary Clarke, Clement Crisp and Harold Rosenthal, *A History of the Royal Opera House Covent Garden, 1732–1982*. (Royal Opera House Publications, London, 1982.)

Sales, Jules. *Théâtre Royal de la Monnaie, 1856–1970*. (Nivelles: Editions Havaux, 1971.)

Saunders, E. *The Age of Worth, Couturier to the Empress Eugénie*. (Longman, London, 1954.)

Scott, Ernest. *A History of the University of Melbourne*. (MUP with OUP, 1936.)

Selby, Isaac. *The Memorial History of Victoria*. (Old Pioneers' Memorial Fund, Melbourne, 1924.)

Seltsam, William H. *Metropolitan Opera Annals*. (The H. W. Wilson Company in association with the Metropolitan Opera Guild, New York, 1947.)

Shaw, Bernard. *London Music in 1888–89 as heard by Corno di Bassetto*. (Constable, London, 1937.)

_____ . *Music in London 1890–94* (criticism contributed week by week to *The World*, 3 vols.) (Constable, London, 1931.)

Shawe-Taylor, Desmond. *Covent Garden*. (Max Parish, London, 1948.)

Sheean, Vincent. *The Amazing Oscar Hammerstein*. (Weidenfeld and Nicolson, London, 1956.)

Sherard, Robert Harborough. *Twenty Years in Paris*. (Hutchinson, London, 1905.)

Sherman, Paul. *Melba*. Stage play in *Contemporary Australian Plays: 6*. (University of Queensland Press, St Lucia, Queensland, 1976.)

Simpson, Alma. 'Reminiscences of Nellie Melba', interview with John Lemmone in *Musical Courier*, 11 April 1931.

Skill, Marjorie. *Sweet Nell of Old Sydney*. (Urania Publishing, Sydney, 1974.)

Slonimsky, Nicolas. (Reviser). *Baker's Biographical Dictionary of Musicians*. (Schirmer, New York, 1958.)

Standing, Percy Cross. 'Madame Melba' in the *Strand*, London, January 1899.

Summers, Joseph. *Personal Reminiscences 1865–1910*. (Perth, 1910.)

Szigeti, Joseph. *With Strings attached: Reminiscences and Reflections*. (Alfred A. Knopf, New York, 1947.)

Tait, Viola. *A Family of Brothers*. (Heinemann, Melbourne, 1971.)

Le Temps. Interview with Charles Armstrong from the Dalxiel agency. 19 November 1891. Paris.

Tetrazzini, Luisa. *My Life of Song*. (Cassell, London, 1921.)

Thompson, John. *On Lips of Living Men*. (Lansdowne Press, Melbourne, 1962.)

Trevor, Henry. *Royal Opera Covent Garden Jubilee Souvenir Programme 1908* (Dover Street Studios, London, 1908.)

The Vagabond. 'Lilydale and District' in *Illustrated Australian News*, Melbourne, 1 February 1894.

Vaughan, Constance. 'Melba, Dictator of Song, Suffered No Rivals', interview with Blanche Marchesi in *Sunday Referee* London, 19 January 1936.

Uncredited article: 'Melba on Life After Death' in the *Herald*, Melbourne, 26 October 1925.

_____ . 'Melba's Indictment: "Our Musical Reputation a Myth"' in the *Herald*, Melbourne, 5 September 1927.

_____ . Report of Charles Armstrong's reaction to the royal affair in *Le Temps*, Paris, 19 November 1891.

_____ . Signor Pietro Cecchi in *Table Talk*, Melbourne, 6 December 1889.

_____ . 'Sunset? The Pathetic Fading of Melba' in *Truth*, Sydney, 10 April 1927.

Véron, Pierre. 'Opera: Début de Mme Melba' in *Le Charivari*, Paris, 10 May 1889.

Victorian Tourist Guide. (Melbourne, 1885.)

Victorian Year Book 1973. Centenary edition. (Commonwealth Bureau of Statistics, Victorian Office, 1973.)

Walsh, T.J. *Monte Carlo Opera 1879–1909*. (Gill and Macmillan, Dublin, 1975.)

Waters, Thorold. *Much Besides Music*. (Georgian House, Melbourne, 1951.)

Wayner, Robert. *What Did They Sing at the Met.?* (Wayner Publications, New York, 1981.)

Wechsberg, Joseph. *Red Plush and Black Velvet*. (Weidenfeld and Nicolson, London, 1962.)

West, John. *Theatre in Australia*. (Cassell, Australia, 1978.)

Whitehill, Clarence. 'Famous Protégé Tells of Melba' u.d. clipping in New York Public Library Melba file.

Wood, Henry. *My Life of Music*. (Victor Gollancz, London, 1938.)

Yarwood, Doreen. *The Encyclopaedia of World Costume*. (B.T. Batsford, London, 1978.)

Manuscripts

Australian Dictionary of Biography article files, Australian National University, Canberra.

Baron Podhragy Collection, MS 2647, National Library of Australia.

Bridges, Doreen. 'The Role of Universities in the Development of Music Education in Australia 1885–1970'. Unpublished PhD thesis, University of Sydney.

Brookes Collection MS 1924, National Library of Australia, Canberra.

Carrington, R.N. Typescript u.d. of article for *Age,* AM82 Mitchell Library, Sydney.

Cochran, Tommy. Typescript 'Round the World in 80 Years' u.d. Performing Arts Museum, Melbourne.

Fanning, Beryl. Diary 1909. MS 9902 La Trobe Library, Melbourne.

Grainger, Percy. MS. 'The Aldridge–Grainger–Ström Saga'. Grainger Museum.

Gunning, H.W.J. Typescript of evidence from residents of Mackay whose parents knew the Melba period. MS 1123 Mitchell Library, Sydney.

Hart Collection MS 9528 La Trobe Library, Melbourne.

Heinze Collection, MS 9824 La Trobe Library, Melbourne.

Hince Collection MS 1691, National Library of Australia, Canberra.

La Trobe Library biographical files.

Melba, Nellie. Family data. MS 1123 Mitchell Library, Sydney.

Melba, Nellie. Receipts from Covent Garden. MS 1370 National Library of Australia.

Melba Collection, Performing Arts Museum, Melbourne.

Melba Memorial Conservatorium Melba Archives. Melbourne.

Metropolitan Liedertafel artists' lists, annual reports, programmes, minutes. Royal Victorian Liedertafel Library, Grainger Museum, University of Melbourne.

Morris, William Beaumont. Melba Tribute Book. MS 8626 La Trobe Library, Melbourne.

New York Public Library Melba file.

Noskowski lists. Australian Opera Library, Sydney.

Radic, Thérèse. 'Aspects of Organised Amateur Music in Melbourne 1836–1890'. Unpublished MMus thesis. 1969. University of Melbourne.
_____ . 'Some Historical Aspects of Musical Associations in Melbourne 1888–1915'. Unpublished PhD thesis 1978. University of Melbourne.

Ross, David Ian. 'Singing and Society: Melbourne 1836–1861'. Unpublished MMus thesis 1982. University of Melbourne.

Royal Opera House Archives Opera Performance lists. Covent Garden, London.

Turner, H.G. Personal Memorabilia. u.d. MS La Trobe Library, Melbourne.

INDEX